Presented to:

Samanth McAleer

By:

Karen Thomas
~ Grace Point

Date:

9-11-2022

Sam,
May the Lord
use this devotion to
grow you into a God's own
woman after
heart~

Love +
prayers
Karen

THE QUIET PLACE

Daily Devotional Readings

THE QUIET PLACE

Daily Devotional Readings

Nancy DeMoss Wolgemuth

MOODY PUBLISHERS
CHICAGO

All Scripture quotations, unless otherwise indicated, are taken from *The Holy Bible, English Standard Version.* Copyright © 2000, 2001 by Crossway Bibles, a division of Good News Publishers. Used by permission. All rights reserved.

Scripture quotations marked NASB are taken from the *New American Standard Bible*®, Copyright © 1960, 1962, 1963, 1968, 1971, 1972, 1973, 1975, 1977, 1995 by The Lockman Foundation. Used by permission. (www.Lockman.org)

Scripture quotations marked NKJV are taken from the *New King James Version.* Copyright © 1982 by Thomas Nelson, Inc. Used by permission. All rights reserved.

Scripture quotations marked NIV are taken from the Holy Bible, New International Version®, NIV®. Copyright © 1973, 1978, 1984, 2011 by Biblica, Inc.™ Used by permission of Zondervan. All rights reserved worldwide. www.zondervan.com

Scripture quotations marked KJV are taken from the King James Version.

Scripture quotations marked HCSB are taken from the *Holman Christian Standard Bible*®, Copyright © 1999, 2000, 2002, 2003 by Holman Bible Publishers. Used by permission. Holman Christian Standard Bible®, Holman CSB®, and HCSB® are federally registered trademarks of Holman Bible Publishers.

Emphasis in Scripture is the author's.

Content in this book has been edited and adapted from the writing and teaching ministry of Nancy DeMoss Wolgemuth.

Library of Congress Cataloging-in-Publication Data

DeMoss, Nancy Leigh.
  The quiet place / Nancy Leigh DeMoss with Lawrence Kimbrough.
     p. cm.
  Includes indexes.
  Soft Touch ISBN 978-0-8024-0506-7 / International ISBN: 978-0-8024-5846-9
  1. Devotional calendars. I. Title.
  BV4811.D45 2012
  242'.2--dc23

2012006260

Interior Design: Julia Ryan / www.DesignByJulia.com
Cover Design and Illustration: Maralynn Rochat
Author photo: Nathan Bollinger

We hope you enjoy this book from Moody Publishers. Our goal is to provide high-quality, thought-provoking books and products that connect truth to your real needs and challenges. For more information on other books and products written and produced from a biblical perspective, go to www.moodypublishers.com or write to:

Moody Publishers
820 N. LaSalle Boulevard
Chicago, IL 60610

7 9 10 8

Printed in the United States of America

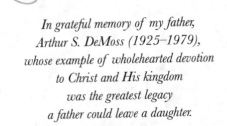

In grateful memory of my father,
Arthur S. DeMoss (1925–1979),
whose example of wholehearted devotion
to Christ and His kingdom
was the greatest legacy
a father could leave a daughter.

His practice of beginning each day with the Lord,
in the Word and on his knees,
made a profound and enduring mark on my life.
This collection is the fruit of his life,
and his fingerprints are unmistakable throughout.

As you meet Christ each day in a "quiet place,"
may your life bear the imprint of His likeness.
And may the example of our devotion
inspire those who follow behind us
to seek Him with their whole heart.

Come to the Quiet Place

IT'S NOT EASY TO FIND A QUIET PLACE THESE DAYS. Every parent with little ones (or teens or grandkids) knows what I'm talking about. So do students. And those working in the marketplace. And anyone who shops at retail outlets or eats out in restaurants. (I'd like a nickel for every time I've asked a server: "Any chance you could turn down the music a bit so we can talk?") For that matter, it can be hard to find a quiet place in our own homes —even for those of us who live alone.

From environmental clatter over which we have no control, to clamor of our own making and choosing, we are subjected (or subject ourselves) to phones chirping and buzzing, pagers beeping, email reminders chiming, music blaring, appliances ding-donging, Skype *whoosh*-ing, people chattering, horns honking, video games, well, what noise *don't* they make?!—even "white noise" masking other noises in many of our workplaces. And beyond all that, there's the inner racket that often reverberates in our heads and hearts —perhaps the hardest realm of all to find a quiet place.

Truth be told, in many cases, we find it difficult to live without our noise. Certainly one of the curses of our age is that we can't bear to be alone, to be still, to be *quiet*.

I am currently in my fiftieth year of walking with the Lord. One of the greatest delights of those years has been the joy of communing with Him, hearing Him speak through His Word, by His Spirit. At the same time, one of my greatest, perennial struggles has been the temptation to let other sounds and voices crowd out His voice . . . not getting still enough, long enough, to hear His voice; trying in vain to cultivate intimacy with the Savior while on the run and in the midst of incessant hullabaloo and activity.

Far too often, far too many of us—myself included—opt for checking Facebook over meditating on His Book, playing Words with Friends over savoring the Word of our dearest Friend.

Even with an endless array of games, toys, and electronic gadgets, we are easily bored. Given a momentary lull in the action, we can't resist picking up our smartphones; texting, IM'ing, or calling a friend; checking email, blogs, Facebook, or Twitter; playing computer games, listening to music, turning on the TV, watching YouTube clips, or clicking on news, weather, and sports apps.

And here's what's so sad: Despite the proliferation of devices to fill the empty spaces of our lives and hearts, pervasive poverty of soul is epidemic, even among those of us who claim to be followers of the Prince of Peace.

It is my hope that this volume will help you cultivate a quiet heart and find fresh springs of blessing in the presence of the Lord.

Over the years, the devotional writings of the likes of our Puritan forebears (*The Valley of Vision*), Charles Spurgeon (*Chequebook of the Bank of Faith*, *Morning by Morning*, *Evening by Evening*), Oswald Chambers (*My Utmost for His Highest*), Mrs. Charles E. Cowman (*Streams in the Desert*), Elisabeth Elliot, and John Piper, along with numerous lesser known authors, have served to help collect my distracted heart and to whet my appetite for Christ and His Word.

It is my hope that this volume will help you cultivate a quiet heart and find fresh springs of blessing in the presence of the Lord.

I would hasten to remind you that, however useful such a resource may be, it can in no way substitute for getting into the Word itself. Think of this book, or any other devotional book, as merely an appetizer, a "pre-taste" of the meal to come. These readings are not intended to supplant your need for God's Word, but simply to create hunger, stimulate your appetite, and tune your senses and heart to long for more of Him. One sure way to be spiritually scrawny is to attempt to subsist on short devotional readings that were intended only to send you to His Book for the "real meal."

In order to get the most out of these readings—and more importantly, the "main course" of Scripture reading and meditation—look for a quiet place, away from unnecessary distractions. Your quiet place may be indoors or out; it may be lovely or plain, perhaps nothing more than a small closet. When you get to that place, hard as it might be, impossible as it may seem, I would encourage you to turn off your electronic devices—better yet, leave them in another room! Ask God to give you a quiet heart; pray with the psalmist: *"I will hear what God the LORD will speak . . ."* (Ps. 85:8 NKJV). Then, with an open Bible, listen for the still, small voice of your Shepherd. And when He speaks, be quick to say, "Yes, Lord. I have heard, and I will follow."

Nancy DeMoss Wolgemuth
September 2012

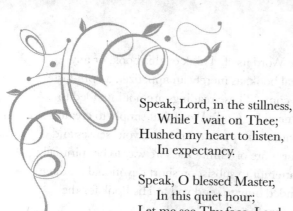

Speak, Lord, in the stillness,
    While I wait on Thee;
Hushed my heart to listen,
    In expectancy.

Speak, O blessed Master,
    In this quiet hour;
Let me see Thy face, Lord,
    Feel Thy touch of power.

For the words Thou speakest,
    They are life indeed;
Living bread from heaven,
    Now my spirit feed!

All to Thee is yielded,
    I am not my own;
Blissful, glad surrender,
    I am Thine alone.

Speak, Thy servant heareth,
    Be not silent, Lord;
Waits my soul upon Thee
    For the quickening word.

Fill me with the knowledge
    Of Thy glorious will;
All Thine own good pleasure
    In Thy child fulfill.

Like a watered garden,
    Full of fragrance rare,
Lingering in Thy presence,
    Let my life appear.

Emily May Grimes (1868–1927)

First Thing

And rising very early in the morning, while it was still dark, he departed and went out to a desolate place, and there he prayed.—Mark 1:35

 JESUS HAD BEEN UP LATE THE NIGHT BEFORE, concluding a long, intense day of ministry. People were clamoring for His attention; desperate needs pressed in on Him endlessly, as word spread of His supernatural power over demons and disease. Yet at the break of day, our Savior was found in a quiet place, away from the crowds, seeking and enjoying fellowship with His heavenly Father. This was not something He "had" to do—it was His supreme delight.

By comparison, many believers I've known approach their "quiet time" with a sense of obligation; they dutifully go through the routine but have little sense of actually meeting with God. Others struggle with consistency; they've failed so many times, they're tempted to give up—or already have. Still others have no personal devotional life at all, and have no idea what they are missing.

And then there are those few whose lives evidence the sweet, rich fruit of meeting with God on a consistent basis. The fragrance of their lives makes me long to know Him in a deeper way.

You see, more than a duty of the Christian life, a daily devotional habit is an incredible opportunity to know the God of the universe. Amazingly, He has issued to you and me an invitation to draw near to Him, to walk humbly and confidently into the Holy of Holies, to enter into a growing love relationship with Him.

Jesus said, "If anyone thirsts, let him come to me and drink" (John 7:37). This devotional collection is for thirsty souls. It is an invitation to come to *Him*. So come and drink deeply. Let Him quench your thirst, day after day. And then watch as rivers of living water flow out through you to quench the thirst of those around you.

 Do you think of a daily devotional life as a duty or a delight? Ask God to make you thirsty—to increase your desire to enjoy daily communion with the Lover of your soul.

One Thing

*One thing have I asked of the L*ORD*, that will I seek after.*—Psalm 27:4

 HOW WOULD YOU FINISH THIS VERSE FROM PSALM 27? If you had to boil down the greatest desire and longing of your heart to just "one thing," how would you summarize it? If only a single sentence could be spoken of you at the end of your life, what would you want it to be?

Our response to these questions offers an explanation for much of what we do—our choices, our priorities, our use of time, the way we spend our money, the way we respond to pressure, whom or what we love. So it's worth thinking about. Our "one thing" matters.

King David landed on the following answer: If I could only ask the Lord for one thing, it would be this—"that I may dwell in the house of the Lord all the days of my life, to gaze upon the beauty of the Lord and to inquire in his temple." His number-one priority was to *live* in the presence of the Lord, so that he could *look* on His splendor and glory and *learn* the heart and ways of the Almighty.

And, no, David didn't do it perfectly. He blew it in some of the most crucial relationships of his life. But because the Lord had placed this passion in his heart, his Lover-God would not let him go. With a confronting, convicting, cleansing love, God continued to pursue and restore him.

One might have wondered at points, *Why does God bother with a guy like David?* The same reason He bothers with any of us— because He is a Lover in pursuit of relationship. And because His love for unlovable sinners puts His amazing grace on display. Even when we fail to live the "one thing" we most desire, we can be assured our God will keep working—stripping us of lesser loves, drawing us to Himself—till He becomes our sole consuming desire.

 Try writing out your "one thing" response, and put it in a place where you can be reminded of it throughout the year ahead.

Untold Riches

. . . that according to the riches of his glory he may
grant you to be strengthened with power through
his Spirit in your inner being.—Ephesians 3:16

DEEP INSIDE THE EARTH ARE VAST RICHES still waiting to be found. Some experts estimate that six billion dollars' worth of sunken treasure lies undiscovered, scattered across the darkened ocean depths of the globe. The world's deepest gold mine, located near Johannesburg, South Africa, extends two full miles into the earth, having produced more than a hundred million ounces of pure gold—three thousand tons—since it first began operations. The Driefontein mine employs nearly 17,000 people working in shifts that span all day every day, gathering gold from the earth.

And still there's more—this one mine is expected to produce at least a million ounces a year, for the next twenty years.

Yet God's riches go deeper still.

The Bible talks about the "riches of his kindness and forbearance and patience" (Rom. 2:4), the "riches of his glory" (9:23), and the "riches of his grace, which he lavished upon us, in all wisdom and insight" (Eph. 1:7–8). Yet unlike the riches on the ocean's floor, which could all be collected if someone knew how to reach them—unlike the riches of a gold mine, which are eventually extracted until no more can be found—the gold in God's mine will never be emptied. It is limitless. Inexhaustible.

God will never experience economic collapse or uncertainty. Instead, the Scripture promises that He will "supply every need of yours according to his riches in glory in Christ Jesus" (Phil. 4:19). His ever-available provision will never strain or drain the budget of the Most High. Rather, He will continue pouring into your life from His fathomless resources. Whatever your need, whatever the deficit, the riches of God are always more than what's required.

What are some needs you are experiencing at this time?
What are some of the "riches" He has promised to supply
to meet your need?

His Smile

*The LORD make his face to shine upon you
and be gracious to you; the LORD lift up his
countenance upon you and give you peace.*—Numbers 6:25–26

 WHEN GOD'S FACE SHINES UPON HIS PEOPLE, it means He takes pleasure in them. I think of a high school athlete who's been sitting on the bench for most of three seasons, but finally, in the last quarter of the last game of his senior year, he gets into the game and scores a basket. Where does he immediately look? He looks to his coach, to his teammates, to his dad in the stands. He wants to see that smile. He wants to know they are pleased.

Often in life we must deal with the frowns of those whose acceptance we crave. You may have experienced rejection from one or both of your parents. Perhaps your spouse is cold, inattentive, and distant. Or maybe your boss constantly belittles you in front of others. You long to be looked upon with favor and grace.

When Jesus came to earth, He put a human face to God. Jesus was God smiling upon His people, becoming flesh so we could *see* the blessing and love of the Father. "In the light of a king's face there is life, and his favor is like the clouds that bring the spring rain" (Prov. 16:15).

Yes, we know we're dealing with One who can see right through us, before whom all things are "naked and exposed" (Heb. 4:13). But because Christ bore our sin on the cross, taking the full brunt of God's frown and the rejection we deserved, the *terror* of His face has become for us the *favor* of His face. And with the smile of God, we can survive the frowns and rejection of life.

 What does it mean to you today to know that God smiles upon you and looks upon you with favor and grace?

A Great Big Thank-You

*And whatever you do, in word or deed, do everything
in word or deed, do everything
in the name of the Lord Jesus, giving thanks to
God the Father through him.*—Colossians 3:17

 WHERE DOES GRATITUDE RANK on your list of Christian virtues? In an arsenal that's supposed to include things like mountain-moving faith, radical obedience, patient long-suffering, and second-mile self-denial, *gratitude* can feel like an optional add-on. Nice if you can get it, but not all that critical to making life run the way it should.

And yet this issue of gratitude is far more significant than its lightweight reputation would suggest. What appears at first to be merely an accessory—an accent piece—is in reality a much weightier, much more powerful, much more necessary component to your Christian life.

Try, for example, to sustain persevering faith—without gratitude—and your faith will eventually forget the whole point of its faithfulness, hardening into a practice of religion that's hollow and ineffective.

Try being a person who exudes and exhibits Christian love—without gratitude—and over time your love will crash hard on the sharp rocks of disappointment and disillusionment.

Try being a person who sacrificially gives of yourself—without the offering being accompanied by gratitude—and you'll find every ounce of joy drained dry by a martyr complex.

True gratitude is not an incidental ingredient. Nor is it a stand-alone product, something that never actually intersects with real life, safely denying reality out on its own little happy island somewhere. No, gratitude has a big job to do in us and our hearts. It is one of the chief ways that God infuses joy and resilience into the daily struggle of life.

 Where do you most notice a lack of gratitude in your life as you go about your day? What tends to fill the spaces in your heart left vacant by its absence?

Healing Climate

*Gracious words are like a honeycomb, sweetness to the soul
and health to the body.*—Proverbs 16:24

IF YOU LOOK UP THE WORD *HEALING* IN A THESAURUS, you
will likely find words like *therapeutic, medicinal, curing.*
What a blessing it is to experience physical healing
from sickness, to feel yourself getting stronger, able to
function freely and normally again. An even greater
blessing, however, is when God uses you as an instrument of
spiritual healing in the lives of others.

"A gentle tongue is a tree of life," Scripture tells us (Prov.
15:4). It can refresh the weary. It can provide support for the
anxious. It can minister grace to young and old alike. It can
even defuse tense situations, preventing misunderstandings from
progressing into bitter conflict.

When the men of Ephraim hurried to meet Gideon, furious
that he hadn't included them in his historic assault on Midian,
thereby making them feel left out of the victory, his humble
response put an end to the discord. "'What have I done now
in comparison to you? Is not the gleaning of the grapes of
Ephraim better than the grape harvest of Abiezer?' . . . Their
anger against him subsided when he said this" (Judges 8:2–3).

We, too, can create a calm, healing climate in our homes,
churches, and workplaces by the way we respond to those around
us, even when they're not acting as they should. Soft, gentle
words minister grace, strength, and encouragement—words
like, "I love you," "I'm praying for you," "I'm sorry I treated
you that way," "Would you please forgive me?" "I appreciate
you so much."

May God keep watch over our lips, using them to heal,
rebuild, and restore.

*Who needs to hear something from you that would help restore
emotional or spiritual health? Write a note, make a call, go out of
your way to be an instrument of healing in someone's life today.*

Called by His Name

You are to be holy to Me, for I the LORD am holy,
and I have set you apart from the peoples
to be Mine.—Leviticus 20:26 NASB

 IN THE OLD TESTAMENT, Israel was set apart by God to be a "holy nation" (Ex. 19:6). This didn't mean their *conduct* was always holy or that they were inherently more upright than anyone else. God called them "holy" because He had set them apart from other nations—a distinction and privilege that came with an obligation to live holy lives.

But not only were they set apart *by* God; they were set apart *for* God. The biblical concept of holiness carries with it a sense of belonging to God, much as a mother might claim, "These children are mine."

I remember first discovering as a child something of what it means to be set apart for and by God. My parents established for us what they felt to be wise practices and limitations for our family. At times we would complain, "But everyone else . . . !" Their response was often along these lines: "But you don't belong to 'everyone else.' You belong to God!" They convinced us there was something special about being set apart for God rather than being squeezed into the world's mold.

Being set apart for God is not a punishment. It is not an attempt on God's part to deprive us or condemn us to a cheerless, joyless lifestyle. It is a privilege—a call to belong, to be cherished, to enter into an intimate love relationship with God Himself; to fit into His grand, eternal plan for this universe; to experience the exquisite joys and purposes for which we were created; to be freed from all that destroys our true happiness.

 What difference would it make if you were more conscious of being set apart by God, for God? Thank the Lord for the privilege of belonging to Him, and ask Him to make your life reflect that high calling today.

A Thousand Things

Can you find out the deep things of God? Can you find out the limit of the Almighty? It is higher than heaven. . . .—Job 11:7

 YEARS AGO, I HEARD PASTOR JOHN PIPER make a statement that resonated deeply in my heart. I've shared it countless times since: *"In every situation and circumstance of your life, God is always doing a thousand different things that you cannot see and you do not know."*

Just in case you flew by that sentence too quickly, go back and read it again. Let the eternal perspective of this statement become permanently etched into your thinking.

I repeated this line recently while talking with a mom whose daughter has chosen a prodigal lifestyle. Looking back at me through tears, even as her face showed visible signs of hope and relief, she said, "I need that quote hanging in my home where I can look at it all the time." It's a truth we *all* need hanging in our hearts.

Regardless of what crisis or complexity may be threatening to engulf your life, *God is at work.* You may not see it, but you need to know it's true. And He's not just doing one or two or a few things in that situation. He is doing *a thousand* or more things.

Although at times He may allow us to see some of His purposes, enabling us to say, "Oh, that makes sense," the vast majority of what He is doing is behind the scenes, providentially obscured from our finite view.

You will never be able to fully fathom what God is doing in your life. You cannot possibly see the end or the outcome of each situation. *Not yet* anyway. But you can be sure that He knows what He is doing. He is God and He is working—purposefully, skillfully, lovingly. And one day when you look back on your journey from heaven's perspective, you will see His hand in all those inexplicable circumstances, and you will say with wonder and worship: "You have done all things well!" Count on it.

 How might your attitude toward a knotty problem be different if you were convinced He was carefully overseeing every step and detail along the way and doing countless things to glorify Himself through that situation?

The Ministry of Encouragement

*For I have derived much joy and comfort from your love,
my brother, because the hearts of the saints have been
refreshed through you.*—Philemon 7

 AT THE TURN OF THE TWENTIETH CENTURY, the
Boer republics were waging war in South Africa
with the armies of the British Empire. During
one protracted siege in the city of Ladysmith,
a woeful citizen began wandering the streets,
certain that doom was imminent, speaking demoralizing words
to the soldiers. He never fired a shot for the enemy, but his
discouragement was ultimately deemed a chargeable offense.
When brought before a court-martial judge, he was found guilty
and sentenced to a year's imprisonment.

Discouraging others, it seemed, was against the law.

Most of us would probably be a little nervous if
discouragement were actually declared illegal. But I do believe
one of the most needed ministries in the church today is the
ministry of encouragement. Even the apostle Paul frequently
made reference to other people who had helped him in his
ministry; he treasured their friendship and support. They were a
"comfort" to him (Col. 4:11), translated from the Greek *paregoria,*
from which we get our word "paregoric," a medicine that soothes
an upset stomach. Encouragers soothe and comfort our hearts,
giving us new hope, energy, and confidence. We all want to be on
the receiving end of encouragement. But we need to be on the
giving end, as well. Thirtysome times in the New Testament, we
read of things we are to do for "one another." Be kind to one
another. Love one another. Among them is the exhortation to
"encourage one another" (Heb. 3:13 NASB). When we represent
the "God of endurance and encouragement" in this way (Rom.
15:5), we actually become a channel of His grace to others.

 *Who has refreshed your heart with their love and encouragement?
How could God use you today to refresh the hearts of His people?*

The God Who Pursues

"Return, faithless Israel," declares the LORD.
"I will not look on you in anger, for I am merciful.
. . . I will not be angry forever."—Jeremiah 3:12

GOD HAD TOLD HIS PEOPLE through the prophet Jeremiah that He remembered what it was like in the early days of their relationship—"the devotion of your youth, your love as a bride" (Jer. 2:2). He remembered the sweet, simple, pure-hearted affection the children of Israel had once felt and demonstrated toward Him. Perhaps He was thinking back to those days when they sang His praise at the Red Sea, or when they stood at the foot of Mount Sinai, saying, "All that the LORD has spoken, we will do" (Ex. 19:8).

But something had changed. His people had forsaken Him. More than merely forgetting Him, they had turned their backs on Him to follow other lovers, becoming "treacherous" and "unfaithful." So in Jeremiah 3, God makes His case against His bride. He is heartbroken by their appalling infidelity. He uses the graphic language of harlots and whores to describe the depths of their wantonness, things we don't even like to say in polite company. He speaks as a jilted, betrayed lover.

Yet He never ceases to be a lover—a reconciling, redeeming God who relentlessly pursues His wayward bride, pleading with His people to come back, in spite of how gravely they have forsaken Him, forgotten Him, and followed after other suitors.

This is the gospel—the good news—the gospel for *saved* people, the gospel we need preached to us every day of our lives, reminding us how God continues to seek us and woo us back to Himself. He wants a restored relationship. He pleads with us to return and when we do, He promises to extend mercy and heal our faithlessness.

Is there anything that has drawn your heart away from the devotion and love you once had for Christ? Do you need to return to Him? Remember—as badly as you want your fellowship back, He wants it more.

Pray for Us

*You also must help us by prayer, so that many will
give thanks on our behalf for the blessing granted to us
through the prayers of many.*—2 Corinthians 1:11

I DON'T THINK WE CAN EVEN BEGIN TO FATHOM the effect of
our prayers on the lives of others, nor of the effect
of their prayers on us. Actually, I believe much of my
life is the product of prayer, and of a praying great-
grandmother in particular.

I never met "Yaya," my father's Greek immigrant grandmother. She lived in upstate New York with her two sons, two
daughters-in-law (who were also sisters), and four grandsons
(one of whom was my dad), all in the same house.

My dad's cousin Ted shared a bedroom with Yaya when he
was a little boy. I've heard him tell of nights when she would be
on her knees, praying in her native tongue as he went to sleep,
praying for her family, including the salvation of my dad who
chose a rebellious, destructive path until the Lord captured his
heart in his midtwenties. On some mornings, Ted told us, he
would awaken to find Yaya *still* on her knees, having prayed
through the night.

Yaya didn't live to see my dad converted to Christ; she
never knew any of her great-grandchildren, most of whom are
walking with the Lord today and raising godly families of their
own. Her prayers planted seeds that are still producing fruit
today for God's glory.

Perhaps you know what it is to cry yourself to sleep at night,
concerned about a child or grandchild, a hurting relative, a
prodigal. You may feel as if you have nowhere else to turn but
to prayer. *Then pray.* When you are at your wit's end, not sure
what to do, pray. And *keep* praying. Because someone needs you.
In fact, many of us are counting on you to "help us by prayer."
In the end, perhaps for generations to come, "many will give
thanks . . . for the blessing granted through [your] prayers."

*Take time right now to pray for one or two people who are
most on your heart. God is working. Don't stop praying!*

The Battle after the Battle

Abram said to the king of Sodom . . . "I would not take a thread or a sandal strap or anything that is yours, lest you should say, 'I have made Abram rich.'"—Genesis 14:22–23

 ABRAM HAD JUST FOUGHT AND WON an impressive victory against a massive military alliance from the east, in the process, rescuing his nephew Lot, who had been taken as a prisoner of war. This was a public battle, a supernatural outcome, a God thing.

But when Abram returned home, he was faced with a second battle—a private battle. We can all relate to those moments in the afterglow of a significant victory, when we are vulnerable, depleted, and tired and when it is easy to forfeit much of what we have gained.

Returning home victorious from the major battle, Abram was met by two kings. Melchizedek, the *king-priest of Salem*— thought by some to be a preincarnate appearance of Christ Himself—fed Abram with bread and wine, blessed him in the name of God Most High, and led him to worship. The *king of Sodom*, on the other hand, while appealing for the return of any captives taken in battle, bargained with Abram by encouraging him to "take the goods for yourself" (Gen. 14:21). *You deserve it! Indulge yourself in the rewards of your labor.*

Abram could have justified accepting the pagan king's offer in a hundred ways—some of the same ways we often do after exhausting our energies, especially after a major season of hard work and effort. But he had sought his refreshment first in the fellowship and presence of the Lord, and as a result was able to resist the temptation to seek relief in fleshly pursuits or temporal rewards.

We are sure to lose the "battle after the battle" if we do not quickly receive the provision, rest, and replenishment of soul that Christ, our King of Salem (peace), offers.

 When you finally unwind from a period of great exertion or responsibility, what kinds of temptations are you most likely to be vulnerable to? How could you better prepare for the "battle after the battle"?

Heart Health

"I will give you a new heart, and a new spirit I will put within you. And I will remove the heart of stone from your flesh and will give you a heart of flesh."—Ezekiel 36:26

 OVER AND OVER AGAIN, Jesus looked the most religious men of His day in the eye and confronted them concerning their obsession with putting on a good appearance and an impressive performance, while their hearts were empty and corrupt.

It didn't matter if they tithed everything they owned, down to the herbs; or if they washed their hands every time they ate and could quote the Law from beginning to end; or if they scrupulously observed every feast day, fast day, and Sabbath day; or even if everyone else respected them as devout believers. If their hearts weren't right, *they* weren't right. And if ours aren't right, neither are we.

The medical profession stresses the importance of regular checkups. Anyone with a family history of heart disease is encouraged to get his or her cholesterol tested. We don't assume that just because we look fine outwardly, we have nothing to worry about. If our heart is not functioning properly or we have a blockage in our arteries, we want to know about it so we can do whatever is necessary to deal with the situation.

Should we be any less concerned about our *spiritual* heart condition—especially when we realize we all have a family history of "heart disease"? We need to regularly ask the Lord to diagnose conditions we may be unable to see in ourselves. For the good news of the gospel is that the Great Physician has made available a cure for our deceived, diseased hearts. Jesus came to do radical heart surgery—to give us a *new* heart; to cleanse and transform us from the inside out.

 How long has it been since you took time to let the Lord give you a spiritual heart checkup? Has His Spirit identified any heart issues you need to allow Him to address?

Bottom Line

I am not ashamed, for I know whom I have believed,
and I am convinced that he is able to guard until that
Day what has been entrusted to me.—2 Timothy 1:12

ONE OF THE CHALLENGES of complete surrender to Christ is that we have no way of knowing all of what that surrender might entail down the road. Some of us might be more inclined to yield our lives to Him if He would hand us a contract with all the details filled in. We'd like to know what to expect: "What will this cost me? Where will God expect me to go? What will He ask me to do?" We want to see all the fine print so we can read it over, think about it, and then decide whether to sign our name.

But that's not God's way. He says instead, "Here's a blank piece of paper. I want you to sign your name on the bottom line, hand it back to Me, and let Me fill in the details." Why? Because He is God; because He has bought us; because He is trustworthy; because He loves us; because we exist for His glory, and not for our own pleasure.

Signing that blank paper is risky . . . *if* God isn't real, if He cannot deliver, or if He is ultimately proven a liar. But the reality is that we have nothing to lose by signing the blank contract. Oh, we may lose some things that certain people consider valuable or essential. But in the eternal scheme of things, we cannot lose, because He is completely trustworthy.

If we will let Him, God will fill in the details of our lives with His incomparable wisdom and sovereign plan, written in the indelible ink of His covenant faithfulness and love.

Have you ever "signed your name on the bottom line," fully surrendering your life to God without expecting Him first to fill in the details? Does that seem scary to you? What truths can help you make that kind of surrender and live it out day by day?

Yours for Life

His divine power has granted to us all things that pertain to life and godliness, through the knowledge of him who called us to his own glory and excellence.—2 Peter 1:3

 WHEN I HEAR THAT WORD "GRANTED," I think of someone who receives a scholarship to help lower the cost of his college education. It's a gift. He doesn't have to pay it back. Or I think of a researcher applying to a foundation for funding on a potential project. If the request is approved, he is issued a grant to be used in the pursuit of that program or endeavor. And though the foundation will want to know how the money is used, they do not consider their investment a loan. It's a gift—a grant.

God has "granted" magnificent gifts to us, His redeemed people, by virtue of "His divine power." He possesses the full ability and resources to do this. And unlike a college scholarship or charitable grant, which might not be enough to cover the entirety of a person's need, God's gracious gift has already provided us "all things" that are necessary for pursuing a godly life, for worshiping Him well and applying His Word.

We now have *all* we need for salvation, *all* we need for sanctification, *all* we need for every step, every season, every struggle and strain of life.

You say you need the power to be more patient and disciplined? *You have it.* You need the desire to be more caring and thoughtful? *You have it.* You need the resources and enablement to keep you from being overcome by fear, discouragement, and doubt? *You have it.* These have all been "granted" to you so that "you may become [a partaker] of the divine nature" (2 Peter 1:4).

 How would you approach your day differently if you really believed that God had already granted you all you need to overcome yourself and your sin? Thank Him for His divine power and grace!

Table Talk

When he had given thanks, he broke it, and said,
"This is my body which is for you. Do this in
remembrance of me."—1 Corinthians 11:24

 IT IS ONE OF THE HOLIEST MOMENTS any of us spend in the average week, month, or year—when we come to the table of the Lord to partake of the symbols of His body and His blood. One by one the elements rest in our hand, reminding us that our very lives hang in the balance of what these items represent. The sins of the past week—perhaps even the past few hours—parade into our thoughts. Things that seemed so justified, so compelling, so valid to us at the time now seem in this holy setting utterly foolish. Shameful. *What were we thinking?*

But at some point in this process of repentance, with the weight of our fallenness resting heavily and horribly all around us, hope reawakens in our soul. We are *not* impossibly saddled to these sins forever. In fact, they have already been forgiven! Jesus' grand statement—*"It is finished"* (John 19:30)—applies to us as well. By virtue of His death and resurrection, we are free from the guilt, the weight, the penalty of our sin. *Thank You, Lord!*

It is this very moment—this "thank-you" moment—that sums up the whole objective of what we are doing here. The word *eucharist* (the more liturgical term for what many of us call Communion or the Lord's Supper) comes from the Greek word *eucharistia,* meaning "the giving of thanks." So when we partake of Communion, we are engaged in gratitude. Gratitude to God. Gratitude for the gospel. From guilt, through grace, to gratitude . . . all celebrated as we meet together at His table.

 Even on this ordinary day, perhaps far from the
Communion table, celebrate the glorious freedom
from your sins with a knee-bending prayer of gratitude.

Meeting Point

Moses used to take the tent and pitch it outside the camp, far off from the camp, and he called it the tent of meeting. . . . When Moses entered the tent . . . the LORD would speak with [him].—Exodus 33:7, 9

 THE GOLDEN CALF INCIDENT at the foot of Mount Sinai had created a major chasm in the relationship between God and His people. Moses' job had just gotten that much harder. And yet even with the separation caused by sin, even with the need to trek "outside the camp, far off" from his own tent, even with the incredible strains on his life as CEO of a nation, he frequently stopped what he was doing and ventured into God's presence.

You don't get the impression that Moses was multitasking while in the tent of meeting. "The pillar of cloud would descend and stand at the entrance of the tent, and the LORD would speak with Moses" (Ex. 33:9). I picture him on tiptoe, or on the edge of his seat. Or perhaps he stood erect and motionless, in complete awe and stillness. Maybe he lay prostrate before the Lord. I don't know.

But I know when he entered that tent of meeting, he was not just checking something off his to-do list: "Had my devotions today." He came to those moments expecting and experiencing a meeting with God.

We can talk all we want about our relationship with Christ and how much He means to us. But like the Israelites who stood at the doors of their tents and watched Moses coming and going from the tent of meeting (verse 10), others will see what we truly value.

To be transformed by the presence of God, we must not be satisfied with mere head knowledge of God, or with keeping Him at the periphery of our lives. We must be intentional about stepping away from the hubbub of our daily lives, to commune with Him, listen to Him, and cultivate an intimate relationship with Him.

 How often do you linger in the presence of the Lord, without being distracted by tasks on your "to-do" list, email, social networking, and so on? When can you set aside time to meet with Him in the next twenty-four hours?

Sacrifice of Praise

And he said, "Naked I came from my mother's womb, and naked shall I return. The LORD gave, and the LORD has taken away; blessed be the name of the LORD."—Job 1:21

NO UNDERSTANDING OF GRATITUDE CAN BE complete without realizing something further—*what it costs*—and how it can both survive and thrive in the midst of pain, loss, and adversity.

I think of my longtime colleague Charles Archer whose life was rocked one summer with the staggering news that his wife of thirty-eight years had been afflicted with ALS—Lou Gehrig's Disease. All too quickly Joann's strength and capabilities ebbed away from her. She lost her ability to speak, to feed herself, to lift herself into or out of bed.

After thirty-one months of deteriorating health and strength, the Lord finally delivered her from the prison her body had become, and took her home to heaven (accompanied by His angels, of course)!

Throughout their difficult ordeal, Charles regularly sent out emails, updating friends and coworkers on Joann's condition. In spite of so little positive news to report, I was struck by the way he often signed his name at the bottom: *"Thankfully, Charles."* His confidence in the goodness and wisdom of God—in giving and taking his precious wife—enabled him to bless the Lord and express gratitude when faced with circumstances that could have driven him to bitterness and despair.

No, the days don't always get easier. The nights can drag on until utter exhaustion finally pulls you under for a few hours' sleep. But those who say no to resentment and yes to gratitude, even in the face of excruciating pain, incomprehensible loss, and ongoing adversity, are the ones who do more than merely survive. They stand against the tide of memories, threats, loss, and sadness, and answer back.

With gratitude.

What circumstance are you facing where the natural response would be something other than gratitude? What do you know about the heart and ways of God that could enable you to bless Him in the midst of your trial?

All We Need

The LORD appeared to Abram and said to him, "I am God Almighty; walk before me and be blameless, that I may make my covenant between me and you, and may multiply you greatly."—Genesis 17:1–2

 THE NAME *EL* IS A SHORT FORM OF THE NAME OF GOD —*Elohim*—the name that speaks of His power, omnipotence, strength, and might. It tells us that God is able to do anything He wants to do.

But He is not only *El*; He is also *El Shaddai*— translated "God Almighty" in Genesis 17:1. *Shaddai* is a tender, compassionate word that many scholars believe is derived from the Hebrew word for "breast." It brings to mind a nursing mother drawing her infant close to her and supplying the child with all that he needs.

In this passage God reassured Abram that He still intended to provide him with offspring. But Abram was ninety-nine years old at the time! Romans 4:19 tells us his body was "as good as dead." It had been a full twenty-four years since God had first made this incredible promise to him, and now its fulfillment seemed more utterly impossible than ever. But rather than despair in his own weakness and insufficiency, Abram rested his faith in the nature of the One who had promised: El Shaddai.

El Shaddai is the all-mighty One who supplies, nourishes, and satisfies His people. When an infant grows fretful and disturbed, expressing a need for nourishment, his mother can pull him to her breast and quiet the needy child until he is rested and satisfied.

What a picture of the way God wants us to live with Him— God Almighty, our All-Sufficient One. He delights for us to be at a place where we are helpless to meet our own need and must rely wholly on El Shaddai.

He wants us in a position where we recognize how desperately we need Him, where we discover that He alone can—and will— supply our needs.

 Rest in this truth today, no matter your feelings or circumstances. Know that He will fulfill His promises, that El Shaddai will fully supply your every need.

Overcome or Overcoming?

*"I have said these things to you, that in me you may have peace.
In the world you will have tribulation. But take heart;
I have overcome the world."*—John 16:33

IT'S A FACT OF LIFE: as long as we live in this fallen world, trials, pain, and wounds are unavoidable. Our experiences will differ from others' in details and degree. But all of us will suffer harm of some kind, likely many times along the way. We will all encounter situations that provide fertile ground for resentment and unforgiveness to take root and bloom in our hearts.

But here's another fact of life that may not be so obvious: The outcome of our lives is not determined by what happens to us or how others treat us but by how we *respond* to those "hard things."

We will be affected, of course, by these painful circumstances that are a part of the fabric of our lives. But horrendous as they may be, those things do not have the power to control the outcome of who we are. They do not possess the authority to declare us *victims*.

Now this may not sound like good news, because it seems to place the burden of responsibility back on us, leaving us no one to blame for our issues. But I assure you that embracing this truth is vital in your spiritual journey.

When we as God's children realize that His grace is sufficient for every situation, at that point we are no longer victims. We are free to rise above and move on beyond whatever may have been done to us, to release those who have wronged us, and to become instruments of grace, reconciliation, and redemption in the lives of other hurting people—even in the lives of our offenders.

Yes, we can be free, if we choose to be.

*Counsel your heart with this truth: I do not have to be a victim
or a prisoner to circumstances or people that have hurt me.
By God's grace, I can walk in peace, wholeness, and joy, even
in the midst of the tribulations of this world.*

Fiery Speech

The tongue is a small member, yet it boasts of great things.
How great a forest is set ablaze by such a small fire!—James 3:5

 ONE HOT AUGUST DAY in the Black Hills of South Dakota, a middle-aged woman stopped by the side of the road to light a cigarette. Tossing the still-burning match onto the ground, she saw it catch fire in the nearby underbrush. Instinctively, she sped away. By the time the resulting blaze was contained—now known among area residents and environmentalists as the Jasper Fire—it had burned 83,000 acres of woodland, destroying timber valued at more than 40 million dollars. She was eventually convicted on both state and federal charges and sentenced to more than thirty years in prison.

It's easy to hear this story and think, *How dare someone leave a burning match in a dry forest?* Yet how often do we throw out our spoken words with similar carelessness? Like this irresponsible smoker, we may just walk away after saying things that deeply wound others, not caring to look back at the enormous damage we have caused.

Too often I talk without thinking, especially when I'm under pressure or perhaps being unguarded with family, close friends, or colleagues. I fail to consider how my words are going to be received, even when I have no intention of hurting others. I can speak thoughtless, impatient words that wound rather than heal, words that tear down rather than build up.

Yet while our words are able to inflict great damage, leaving behind a charred forest to be restored, the Scripture tells us that "a gentle tongue is a tree of life" (Prov. 15:4), the beginning of something strong and enduring.

May our words be under the control of His Spirit, giving grace, blessing, and hope to those around us.

 Ask God to guard your heart and your tongue today and to make you conscious of the impact of your words on those around you.

Switching the Price Tags

What is man that you are mindful of him, and the son of man
that you care for him? Yet you have made him a little lower than
the heavenly beings and crowned him with glory and honor.
—Psalm 8:4–5

 PART OF THE TWISTED THINKING of the fallen human condition is a tendency to switch the price tags on God's creation—to devalue human life while elevating the importance of other created things. We can sometimes be more concerned about the condition of our pets and our flower beds, for example, than about the people with whom God has chosen to populate our lives. For while each of these individual specimens of His creation is certainly important to Him—important enough that He feeds the "birds of the air" and adorns the "lilies of the field" (Matt. 6:26, 28)— His uncommon care for mankind goes beyond all other loves.

Even in the act of creation itself, we see God *speaking* many things into existence—trees, plants, animals, fish, the moon, sun, and stars. But when creating human life, it was as though He rolled up His sleeves and got His hands involved, forming man "from the dust of the ground" (Gen. 2:7), then fashioning woman from a rib taken out of the man's side (verses 21–22).

This is why we are not surprised when we later see the tender, caring heart of Jesus reaching out to the poor, the weak, the oppressed and disenfranchised—dirtying His hands over people many would consider of far less value than the other "things" in their lives.

We know from observing our God in Scripture that every life is precious to Him, to be treated with great care, affection, and compassion. May our affections and actions be shaped by the priorities that matter most to Him.

 Has your love for others grown cold in comparison
to other interests and concerns? Ask God to adjust
your values to reflect His.

Song of the Redeemed

They offered great sacrifices that day and rejoiced, for God had made them rejoice with great joy . . . and the joy of Jerusalem was heard far away.—Nehemiah 12:43

 SOME BIBLE COMMENTATORS BELIEVE that before Lucifer exalted himself against God and was cast out of heaven, he may have had a major role in leading its music and worship: "The workmanship of your timbrels and pipes was prepared for you on the day you were created" (Ezek. 28:13 NKJV).

One thing we know for sure about him: as a fallen creature, he certainly understands the power of music as a means of praise. He knows how much God loves to hear the musical praises of His creatures. He knows the power of praise to exalt God and to deliver us from earthly, selfish preoccupations. So he strives to keep us from singing.

On a couple of occasions, I have had the privilege of participating in the weekly Tuesday evening prayer meeting at the Brooklyn Tabernacle in New York City. One of the things that particularly touched me in those services was the congregational singing—so earnest, uninhibited, and heartfelt.

And no wonder. Many of these men and women have come to Christ out of backgrounds of drug addiction, alcoholism, violent crime, and sexual promiscuity. They know what it means to be enslaved by sin, to be without hope, without Christ. They know what they are singing about. And they sing like they mean it. Because they do.

Discouragement, fear, anxiety, depression, grief—in many cases these will flee as we sing to the Lord. How often I have seen Him lift the dark clouds hanging over my spirit as I sing to Him, even with quavering voice and emotions—and then quickening my heart and displacing the darkness with the sunlight of His peace and grace.

 Regardless of where life finds you, sing to the Lord.
Go ahead, do it—right now! Let Him lift your spirit
and overcome Satan's attempts to pull you down.

Fresh Oil

My speech and my preaching were not with persuasive words of human wisdom, but in demonstration of the Spirit and of power.—1 Corinthians 2:4 NASB

WHEN PEOPLE ASK HOW THEY CAN PRAY FOR ME, my most common answer is this: "Pray for 'fresh oil'—that God will grant the anointing of His Spirit on my life and ministry." That is perhaps the prayer I pray most frequently for myself, for I know that I am helpless, powerless, and useless apart from the energizing, enabling work of His Spirit.

Oil in the Scripture is often used as a symbol of the Holy Spirit. Old Testament prophets, priests, and kings were anointed with oil, signifying that they had been set apart and empowered for ministry. The Bible tells us that when Samuel anointed a young shepherd boy as king of Israel, "the Spirit of the LORD came mightily upon David from that day forward" (1 Sam. 16:13 NASB).

The apostle Paul recognized the importance of the Spirit's anointing in his ministry: "Our gospel came to you not only in word, but also in power and in the Holy Spirit and with full conviction" (1 Thess. 1:5).

This divine enabling of the Spirit is not reserved for some select few saints. Every New Testament believer has been "anointed" by God, who has "given us his Spirit" (2 Cor. 1:21–22).

Whether you are a small group or worship team leader in your church, a parent of toddlers or teens, or are serving God in some other capacity, you undoubtedly know what it is to feel weak, inadequate to accomplish what He has given you to do. That is a good place to be! Pray for an outpouring of grace and the fresh supply of His Spirit. Ask Him to enable you to serve Him in a way that is unexplainable apart from His supernatural hand and power. And by faith, believe Him to grant the anointing you desire and need.

What will likely be the result of our lives and ministries if we remain satisfied with business as usual, with simply doing the best we can do?

Snow Clothes

*She is not afraid of snow for her household, for all
her household are clothed in scarlet.*—Proverbs 31:21

 WINTERS IN ISRAEL ARE GENERALLY FAIRLY MILD, but the temperatures can drop and in some parts of the country it may occasionally even snow—not often but it does happen, which makes this statement from Proverbs 31 even more revealing and instructive. Here is a woman who is not caught off-guard even by a crisis that is uncommon and unexpected because she has thought ahead, anticipated what would be required, and made the necessary preparations for her family's needs to be met.

In other words, she is *proactive*, not reactive. She makes the kinds of choices today that enable her to face the future without fear, worry, or panic.

Interestingly, the word "scarlet," describing the clothes she provides for her household, could actually be translated "double thickness." Some of the oldest Bible translations say "double garments," which speaks to the added protection from the cold. But perhaps "scarlet" has continued to be the most common translation because it reflects the fact that scarlet dye was rare in the ancient Mideast and clothes colored with the dye were of the highest quality, more expensive, harder to come by.

This woman illustrates the importance of anticipating and making adequate preparation for the needs of those God has entrusted to our care, whether family members or others whom we serve and for whom we bear responsibility in some way.

And as we consider their temporal, physical needs, how much more concerned ought we to be about their eternal, spiritual needs? By filling their minds with the Word of God, teaching them how to think biblically about the circumstances of life, and pointing them to Christ and His gospel, we know they will be prepared for whatever the future may hold—both in time and eternity.

 *How can you best prepare yourself and those you love for
whatever may lie ahead—in this life and the next?*

Fixer-Upper

He saw that there was no man, and wondered
that there was no one to intercede.—Isaiah 59:16

 MANY OF US ARE BORN "FIXERS." Our natural tendency is to take matters into our own hands, to fret and worry, to demand solutions, to feel responsible for changing the people around us—coworkers, spouses, children, friends, pastors—anyone who's doing things differently than the way we'd prefer they do them.

Yet in the process, we often bypass the most effective means of making a difference in their lives. A little plaque in my study provides a frequent and much-needed reminder: "Have you prayed about it?" Unfortunately, I too often ignore this simple question until I've exhausted all my other ideas and bombarded people with my "suggestions" for how they can improve.

Sometimes I imagine God sitting in heaven, watching us frantically trying to manage everyone else's lives and solve their problems. I can almost hear Him saying, "Do you really want to take care of this yourself? Then go ahead. Oh, you want *Me* to handle it instead? Well, that's better. Now sit back and let *Me* show you what I can do!"

I'm convinced if you and I would spend a fraction of the time praying for others that we spend worrying about them, talking about them, and trying to fix them to our own liking, we would see a lot more positive results.

Why not enter God's presence today, praying, "Lord, I can't meet this person's need or change their way of thinking. I can't solve this problem or fix things for them. But I know that nothing is too difficult for You. Please show me how to be the person they need me to be. Draw them to Yourself, even as You draw me closer too."

 Why are we so slow to believe what God can do?
Who do you need to be praying for today?

For What It's Worth

*As you come to him, a living stone rejected by men but in the
sight of God chosen and precious, you yourselves like living stones
are being built up as a spiritual house.*—1 Peter 2:4–5

 I'VE MET A LOT OF PEOPLE who are desperately seeking
affirmation, driven to gain the approval of others. It's
as if they are trying to balance the scales against all the
negative input they have received in life. But in many
cases, no amount of positive strokes can outweigh the
heap of hurtful expressions that have led them to believe they
are worthless. They could get a hundred compliments about
how nice they look or what good work they do, but let one
person offer a criticism, and they are devastated. Why? Because
they are letting others determine their worth.

Jesus knew what it was to be "rejected by men"—the
very ones He had created for Himself, those He loved and for
whom He laid down His life. But their opinion was not what
determined His value. What determined His worth was that in
God's sight He was "chosen and precious." And when it comes
down to it, that's the only opinion that really matters!

It's conceivable that someone who did not recognize or
appreciate fine art could toss a masterpiece into the trash.
But would that make the painting any less valuable? Not for
a moment. Its true worth would be seen when an art collector
spotted the painting and said, "That's a priceless piece. I'm
willing to pay any amount to acquire it."

When God sent His only Son to earth to bear your sin and
mine on the cross, He put a price tag on us, declaring the value
of our soul to be greater than the value of the whole world. So
whose opinion are you going to accept? His . . . or theirs?

*Have you allowed the words and opinions of others to determine
your value? What difference would it make if you were to truly
accept the worth God places on your life?*

To Prayer

Out of the depths I cry to you, O LORD!
O Lord, hear my voice! Let your ears be
attentive to the voice of my pleas for mercy!
—Psalm 130:1–2

 I HAVE COME TO BELIEVE that one of the greatest reasons we don't pray more than we do is this: *we're not desperate.* We are not really conscious of our need for God. As Puritan pastor William Gurnall wrote, "The hungry man needs no help to teach him how to beg."

In comparison to that of many people, my life has been relatively trouble-free. Most days, humanly speaking, I could convince myself that I can operate on my own efforts and resources, quite apart from His grace and intervention.

I have a dear friend, however, whose third child was born with multiple birth defects, including the hardship of having no esophagus. For years her son remained in critical condition, in and out of hospitals, undergoing life-threatening surgeries, requiring a breathing apparatus every night, prone to choking, and frequently unable to breathe. Do you think anyone had to tell that mother to pray for her son? You couldn't *keep* her from praying.

She was desperate. She knew her son's only hope of survival was for God to intervene and spare his life. And she knew the only way she could get through all those long days and even longer, sleepless nights was for God to pour His grace into her life, to grant her supernatural strength and enabling.

Though my natural instinct is to wish for a life free from pain, trouble, and adversity, I am learning to welcome anything that makes me conscious of my need for Him. If prayer is birthed out of desperation, then anything that makes me desperate for God is a blessing.

 When was the last time you were truly desperate for God? How might you maintain that level of thirst and dependence on God, even when your need isn't quite so obvious?

Freed to Serve

"You yourselves know how I lived among you . . . serving the Lord with all humility and with tears and with trials."—Acts 20:18–19

 WHETHER WE REALIZE IT OR NOT, each of us is involved in ministry. It may be Bible teaching or other forms of what people typically think of as "ministry." But being a parent, a marriage partner, a friend, a neighbor is no less "ministry." Our lives are filled with ongoing opportunities for "serving the Lord" by serving others.

The word for "serving," as Paul used it in reflecting on his ministry among the Ephesians in Acts 20, could be literally translated "slaving." He understood that what looked like serving others was actually "slaving" Jesus, being His bond servant, toiling for Him in ways that produced the fringe benefit of bearing fruit in others' lives. Serving Christ was his true, primary compulsion for ministry.

When we recognize that we are slaves of Jesus, we are freed to serve as He Himself served, regardless of whether we receive reward or recognition, payment or accolades. "We are unworthy servants; we have only done what was our duty" (Luke 17:10)— joyfully, willingly, lovingly. Glad to serve. To serve *Him*.

To our modern ears, the thought of being a "slave" of Christ may seem demeaning. But in reality, it's the only way we can sustain the ability to be of any use to others over time, whether family members, those we're discipling and mentoring, or others in our sphere of influence. If we are serving anyone or anything other than Christ, we simply will not have the staying power to endure the inevitable seasons of opposition, rejection, and adversity.

Only by serving *Him*—"slaving" *Him*—will we be able to do with strength, dignity, and joy what God has called us to do in serving others.

 Have you noticed your motivation or energy dwindling when pouring yourself out for others? Remember that it is the Lord you are serving; draw upon His grace to continue serving, even through tears and trials.

Get It Together

No one has ever seen God; if we love one another,
God abides in us and his love is perfected in us.—1 John 4:12

EBENEZER BAPTIST CHURCH in Saskatoon, Saskatchewan, was the epicenter of a revival that swept much of Canada and portions of the United States in the early 1970s. During the initial days of this movement, two brothers were marvelously reconciled who had not spoken to each other for two years—even though they attended the same church! God broke through their hardness and pride one evening, and they fell sobbing into each other's arms. The church was amazed at the drastic change in the two men, and God greatly used their testimony to spread and deepen the work of revival.

Right relationships—especially within the family of God—are among our most powerful means of communicating the gospel. "For he himself is our peace, who has made us both one and has broken down in his flesh the dividing wall of hostility" (Eph. 2:14). Through the cross of Christ, those who were once separated from God can now draw near to Him. And through that same cross, the "dividing wall of hostility" that so easily rises between us and others has been broken down as well, making it possible for us to be reconciled, to live at peace together as those who were once estranged humble themselves before Him.

Revival and reconciliation are inseparable. When believers cannot get along with one another, when we fail to resolve conflicts biblically, we actually discredit the gospel. But when God's people are reconciled to each other, we demonstrate the power of the cross and make it believable to others. Who in your life could be the next testimony to His reconciling work as you ask for His grace to break through in that relationship?

If you have done all you think you can do to heal a damaged relationship, don't hesitate to ask God for a miracle. Keep praying. Keep loving. To the extent it is possible, keep pursuing reconciliation. God desires it as much or more than you do!

At a Loss for Love

*If I have prophetic powers, and understand all mysteries
and all knowledge, and if I have all faith, so as to remove
mountains, but have not love, I am nothing.*—1 Corinthians 13:2

YOU COULD SAY IT THIS WAY: though I keep a spotless house, and though I'm faithful in church attendance, and though I work in the nursery one Sunday a month, and though I lead a small group Bible study, and though I homeschool my children—if I do it without love, I am *nothing*.

If I take care of my sister's kids while she's recovering from surgery, and if I make enormous sacrifices for my family, but I do it from a sense of obligation or a desire to impress—rather than being motivated by love—it's worth *nothing*.

If I stay married to the same person for fifty years, but don't have God's love for my mate, and if I bring my aging parents to live in my home and care for them throughout their older years, without doing it out of a heart of love—what does it profit? *Nothing*.

And though I share my faith with others, and though I read my Bible and memorize Scripture, and though I give generously to the poor and the missionaries, and though I volunteer in local community efforts—yet I have not love—it's all less than *nothing*.

Most of us make sacrifices of one sort or another to do what we do. We give of our time, our energy, our abilities, our resources. Many of these sacrifices go unappreciated and unrecognized. But genuine love means giving of ourselves to meet the needs of others without expecting anything in return. Love is not only the act; it is the heart behind the act.

Where do you most often find yourself giving and serving for some motivation other than genuine love? Ask God to make love for Him and others the spring from which your service overflows.

High and Low

"But the tax collector, standing far off, would not even
lift up his eyes to heaven, but beat his breast, saying,
'God, be merciful to me, a sinner!'"—Luke 18:13

OVER THE YEARS, I have come to realize that the higher up we find ourselves in terms of power, influence, and wealth—in other words, the more people look up to us—the more vulnerable we become to pride and self-deceit, and the more prone we are to be blind to our spiritual needs and deficiencies.

Once we have a position of influence, we have a reputation to maintain. We have more to lose by getting honest about our real spiritual condition—what would others think?! For those of us who have walked with the Lord for many years and are respected by others, the subtle encroachment of pride may be more dangerous than any other kind of failure, more likely to render us useless to God and others.

Our pride causes us to be more conscious of the sins and failures of others than our own. But could it be that God is more offended by our proud, unteachable spirits—despite appearing so respectable and spiritual—than by adulterers or drunkards who make no pretense of being godly? The sobering reality is that proud, unbroken Christians have done far more damage to the church than sinners outside the church could ever hope to inflict.

In focusing on the needs and failures of those we consider less spiritual than ourselves, and in working so hard to protect our image, we miss the heart and the gospel of Christ. The message of repentance is not just for prodigals and profligates; it is no less needed by elder brothers (Luke 15:25–30) and Pharisees. Yet the good news is this: the grace of God is always available to those who lay down their pride and offer God the sacrifice He most desires—a broken, contrite heart.

How long has it been since you found yourself crying out to God for mercy, as the tax collector did? Ask God to deepen your awareness of His holiness and your sinfulness, that you might be cast on His grace.

Wholly Living

*Speak to all the congregation of the people of Israel, and say to them,
"You shall be holy, for I the LORD your God am holy."*—Leviticus 19:2

 IF YOU'VE EVER TRIED WADING through the book of
Leviticus, you may have wondered, *Why did God give so
many detailed instructions about cleansing and ceremonial purity?
Why so many explicit directions about sacrifices?*

He did it as an object lesson to the children of
Israel—and to us. He wants us to understand that He is holy,
and that holiness is not an option for those who belong to Him.
He wants us to know that He is concerned with every detail and
dimension of our lives. He wants us to grasp both the blessings
of holiness and the consequences of unholiness.

The book of Leviticus reminds us that holiness is serious.
And it is comprehensive.

And, contrary to what some believe, that doesn't change
by the time we reach the New Testament. As Jesus instructed
His disciples—and us—"You therefore must be perfect as your
heavenly Father is perfect" (Matt. 5:48). Everyone. In everything.

So holiness is not merely for a few select, pious saints who sit
around all day with nothing else to do but to "be holy." Holiness is
for moms who battle a sense of uselessness and discouragement,
tempted to escape into self-pity and romance novels. It's for
students constantly bombarded by pressure to conform to
the world and indulge in its decadence. It's for lonely widows,
divorceés, and singles struggling to stay sexually abstinent. It's for
husbands and wives wrestling with bitterness toward a difficult
mate. It's for men tempted to cheat on their expense reports or
abdicate their spiritual leadership in the home.

"Everyone who names the name of the Lord" (2 Tim. 2:19)
is called to live a holy life. Not just in the Old Testament but
even more so now, under the new covenant of grace—grace that
enables the holiness God requires.

*What light does Christ's sacrificial death as the
Lamb of God shine on your sin? How does it motivate
and enable you to live a holy life?*

Listen and Learn

Give instruction to a wise man, and he will be still wiser; teach a righteous man, and he will increase in learning.—Proverbs 9:9

HOW OFTEN DO YOU HEAR SOMEONE SAY: "I was wrong"? How often do those words come out of *your* mouth?

I remember receiving an email from a radio listener who wrote, "God has been working through my boss and others around me to show me how prejudiced, critical, impatient, and stubborn I am." That's a person who has a teachable spirit, who instead of responding defensively to criticism says, "If all these people are telling me this, maybe they're right."

Do you solicit and welcome counsel from others? Do you have people around you who will speak truth to you? Are you easy to correct? Do you have a teachable spirit?

Most of us have a tendency to buck against others' perceived intrusions and opinions. We may not actually *say* we don't need their advice, but in our hearts, do we prefer they wouldn't offer it? Do we typically assume we are right and our critics are wrong? The Bible has a word to describe people who respond like this: "The way of a *fool* is right in his own eyes, but a wise man listens to advice" (Prov. 12:15).

You can learn the hard way through painful, personal experience, or you can learn from others' experiences. One is the way of the "scoffer," who "hates" the thought of being instructed. The other is the way of the "wise man," who grows to "love" those who are willing to challenge him, point out his blind spots, and protect him with godly correction and counsel (9:8). Wise people discover that those who care enough to risk what we may think of them in order to tell us what we need to hear are our truest friends.

Have people been trying to make you aware of issues that need attention in your life? Have you humbly asked the Lord to show you if there is any truth to what they have said and what He wants to teach you through their input?

Life on the Altar

Send out your light and your truth; let them lead me; let them bring me to your holy hill and to your dwelling! Then I will go to the altar of God, to God my exceeding joy.—Psalm 43:3–4

 PERHAPS THE MOST APPROPRIATE SYMBOL of Abraham's life is an altar. On four distinct occasions, at different stages in his pilgrimage, he responded to God by building an altar. First at Shechem (Gen. 12:7), then between Bethel and Ai (12:8), then at Hebron (13:18), Abraham erected altars—silent symbols of surrender and faith.

Then, on a mountain named Moriah, he built yet another altar (22:9), where at God's unmistakable yet incomprehensible direction, Abraham placed his own son. It was the ultimate demonstration of surrender, a relinquishing of all he held dear.

In an act not unlike a resurrection, God spared Abraham's son. The test had been passed. God knew that when Abraham laid his precious, long-promised son on the altar and prepared to plunge the knife into his heart, Abraham himself was on the altar. All that he was and all that he had were God's.

Each of those earlier altars had been preparing him for this moment when he would be called upon to make a supreme sacrifice. With each act of surrender, Abraham had been establishing in his heart the trustworthiness of God and His promises.

The same is true of us. Each "small" step of surrender that we take confirms again that God is worthy of our trust, and each act of surrender prepares us to trust Him with even bigger surrenders that may be required down the road. In being willing to be consumed on the altar, even in "small" ways, we increasingly give our whole lives to the One for whom the altar is built—the One who on an altar called Calvary "did not spare his own Son, but gave him up for us all" (Rom. 8:32).

 Is God calling you to "erect an altar" and surrender something today? How might a surrender you make today deepen your trust in Him and lead you to a more fully consecrated life?

Heavenly Sunlight

Oh that you would rend the heavens and come down,
that the mountains might quake at your presence!—Isaiah 64:1

 I WAS SITTING IN A CONDO overlooking Lake Michigan, the gracious gift of a friend who had invited me to stay there as I worked on a message for an upcoming conference. On this particular day, the sky was unusually dark and dreary, with rain falling steadily throughout the day, making the mood even more dismal.

Then shortly before dusk, the rain subsided. A shaft of sunlight in the western sky began to burn through the heavy, low-lying clouds, glimmering on the surface of the water. Over the next few minutes, I watched as the sun burst through the dark clouds in a glorious display of light. Even though much of the early evening sky remained dark and foreboding, the window opened by the sun's rays painted a picture for me of what I believe God wants to do in our day.

Spiritually speaking, the weather outside is dark and dreary—with signs of even more rain in the forecast. There are many days when it is difficult to see evidence of God's presence in our land, even in our own lives. But beyond the ominous clouds, beyond the darkness, God's rule and reign are as sure as the morning. Conditions may seem hard, cold, and steely gray at the moment, but the One who made the heavens and the earth lives forever. And He will have the final word.

As I sat there that evening and watched the setting sun dominate the forbidding clouds, I found myself praying, "O Lord, may Your glory and the light of Your presence shine through my life and through Your people and dispel the darkness of our land." With all my heart, I believe God desires and is able to do just that!

 Ask God to break through the darkness of your day (or of your life) and shine through with the glory of His presence.

A Word for All Seasons

*I will meditate on your precepts and fix my eyes
on your ways. I will delight in your statutes;
I will not forget your word.*—Psalm 119:15–16

 PSALM 22 WAS WRITTEN a thousand years before the crucifixion of Christ, hundreds of years before the practice was even invented by the Persians. Yet in this messianic psalm, we see an amazingly detailed, accurate description of the sufferings that Christ endured on the cross, as well as a prophetic anticipation of words He spoke while dying.

Verse 1: "My God, my God, why have you forsaken me?" Verse 31: "He has done it"— similar to His triumphant cry, "It is finished" (John 19:30). From start to finish, this psalm of David foretells the supreme moment in the life of the Son of David: the redemption of sinful man through the sacrifice of the sinless, unblemished Lamb of God.

It appears, then, that Jesus was actually meditating on this psalm while hanging on the cross. He may, in fact, have recited the entire passage from beginning to end in His mind. After all, answering life with Scripture seemed to be His pattern. We know He quoted Scripture when He was tempted in the wilderness, when He was responding to questions from His opponents, when He was teaching His disciples. Why not when He was suffering for the sins of His lost and dying people?

What a vivid reminder to us of the importance of Scripture memory and meditation, particularly for times of extreme crisis and suffering. As we fill our hearts with His Word, preserving its truths in our minds, when we find ourselves in the midst of painful realities, His Word will be there to minister the comfort and perspective of His far greater, eternal realities.

 When faced with difficult or painful situations, do your thoughts go quickly to His Word? How can you be intentional today about meditating on His Word?

Against Him

*Against you, you only, have I sinned and done what is
evil in your sight, so that you may be justified in your
words and blameless in your judgment.*—Psalm 51:4

 IF YOU GREW UP IN THE CHURCH AS I DID, you probably
learned early on that the essence of sin is breaking God's
law. The primary Hebrew word for "sin" in the Old
Testament means "to miss the mark." Other words that
are used to describe sin indicate man's failure to measure
up to a divine standard or expectation.

This legal or judicial definition of sin is certainly important
and helpful. In recent years, however, I've been struck by the
realization that sin is not merely an objective "missing of
the mark," a lack of conformity to an impersonal standard.
Sin is also intensely personal; it contains profound relational
implications. What makes sin—*all* sin—so heinous and grievous
is that it is against God. Yes, sin harms others, and yes, there are
consequences for those who sin. But above all, sin violates God's
holy character. It is *against Him.*

After having risen to a measure of trust and respectability
in Egypt, Joseph refused to fall prey to the advances of his boss's
wife. He recognized that if he yielded, he would not merely be
wronging the woman and her husband; he would not just be
violating his own conscience and tarnishing his own reputation.
He was restrained by this compelling logic: "How then can I do
this great wickedness and sin *against God?*" (Gen. 39:9).

You and I will never experience appropriate grief and
brokenness over our sin until we see how deeply we grieve
the heart of God when we choose to ignore His life-giving
instruction.

 *Ask God to help you put a "face" on your sin, to help you
understand the extreme cost of forsaking fellowship with
Him in order to pursue your own pleasures.*

Deeper Still

*The eternal God is your dwelling place, and underneath
are the everlasting arms.*—Deuteronomy 33:27

 ON JANUARY 23, 1960, a U.S. Navy lieutenant and a Swiss scientist took a deep-diving, submersible vessel known as a bathyscaphe down to the deepest spot on earth—the Marianas Trench, a chasm in the Pacific near the island of Guam. Seven miles straight down beneath the ocean's surface—a massive, record-setting feat. It took them nearly five hours, but they were finally able to locate the bottom of the ocean floor. It was an amazing feat. They could go no deeper.

This is not the case, however, with the depths of God. Five hours, five years, five lifetimes would not be enough to plumb the depths of His riches, wisdom, and knowledge. He is inexhaustible, limitless, immeasurable.

Though we can never reach the bottom of God's unfathomable ways, we do know what it's like to reach the bottom of our own strength. Perhaps you've been there—perhaps you *are* there—down where life drags the floor of all human abilities, where everything feels helpless and impossible to handle. This is where many people give up and call it quits, or slink away into a pit of bitterness, or turn their frustrations on those nearest them—*anything* to cope with life at the bottom.

Yet deeper than your own limitations and problems is the bedrock of God's faithfulness, power, and knowledge. His unseen, sovereign, eternal purposes are underneath it all, holding everything together—including you. Your problems may be deeper than ever. Your issues and challenges may never before have reached such depths as you're experiencing now. But no matter how low they've taken you, there is always something—always Someone—who is deeper still.

 How have you seen that God's ability to sustain and support you is deeper than the problems that threaten to sink you? Who could you encourage with this truth and your personal testimony of His faithfulness?

The Model Father

"And I will be a father to you, and you shall be sons and daughters to me," says the Lord Almighty.—2 Corinthians 6:18

OUR VIEW OF GOD is often greatly influenced by our fathers, either positively or negatively. I am blessed and deeply grateful to have had a loving, faithful, involved dad. This has made it easier for me to trust my heavenly Father and receive His love throughout my life.

Many people, however, have had just the opposite experience. Your father may have been distant, absent, harsh, abusive, or unable to express love. If so, the idea of God being your "Father" may make you cringe. If you have been wounded by a father, you may find it extremely difficult to trust God. You may feel fear, disappointment, or even anger toward Him.

But you must believe me when I tell you that God is unlike any man you have ever known. The wisest, kindest earthly father is but a pale reflection of our heavenly One. The God of the Bible is infinitely more wonderful, pure, and loving than even the most wonderful dad. He is tender. He is compassionate. He is merciful.

This doesn't mean He gives us everything we want. (No wise father would.) It doesn't mean we always understand His decisions. (He is far too great for that.) It doesn't mean He never allows us to suffer pain. At times, in fact, He actually *inflicts* pain and hardship upon us to correct and teach us. But that's because He loves us and knows what is best for us.

Regardless of how you feel or what you think, the fact remains that He is a good Father who dearly loves His children—a Father who, if you are truly His child, can be trusted with your life.

How has your relationship with your earthly father colored the way you feel about relating to your heavenly Father? How does the Scripture renew your thinking about the Father heart of God?

Heaven Rules

He does as he pleases with the powers of heaven and the peoples
of the earth. No one can hold back his hand or say to him:
"What have you done?"—Daniel 4:35 NIV

HENRY DRUMMOND, a nineteenth-century evangelist and science lecturer, once wrote about a children's book called *The Chance World*, in which nothing was predictable from one day to the next. The sun might come up in the morning, or it might not. Just because a person jumped up in the air and came back down to earth today didn't mean the same thing would happen tomorrow. In other words, no one was in charge. Anything could happen. That's because without the stability of a sovereign ruler and designer, the result would not be more freedom but more chaos.

Most of us are too independently minded to naturally embrace the idea of a sovereign God—One who rules over everything He has created, maintaining the absolute right to order His world and to determine our purpose according to a wise, magnificent master design.

We may be able to accept this concept in regard to the *good* things that happen in our lives, but what about the hard things, the inexplicable things, those things for which we cannot see any reason or answers?

The good news is that this is not a "chance world." This is my Father's world! The whole counsel of Scripture leaves us with one inescapable conclusion: *heaven rules.*

So when everything in your world seems to be giving way and spinning out of control, the fact on which you can stay your heart, mind, and emotions is the reality that God is sovereign, that He is on the throne, and that He has established not only the laws of nature but the duration and outcome of your days.

What are you facing today that you cannot understand and
are struggling to endure? He will receive glory—and you will
experience peace—as you trust His sovereign reign over this
world, including every circumstance in your life.

Is It Enough?

And my God will supply every need of yours according to his riches in glory in Christ Jesus.—Philippians 4:19

MANY OF OUR FEARS about relinquishing total control of our lives to God fall into four broad categories. Over the next several days, we're going to take a look at each of these areas—both the questions they raise and the answers God provides for us in His Word. The first fear is one of *provision*: "Will I have what I need?"

What if I lose my job? Can we afford to have more children? How will we pay for their education? What if God asks us to give more money than we can spare? What if the economy goes under? What if my spouse gets sick or dies? What if God calls us into vocational ministry? Will we have enough to get by?

God knew we would naturally be concerned about these things, yet His Word frequently exhorts us not to worry about how our future needs will be met. Rather, Scripture says, "Seek first the kingdom of God and his righteousness, and all these things will be added to you" (Matt. 6:33). We can "be content with what [we] have, for he has said, 'I will never leave you nor forsake you'" (Heb. 13:5).

Trusting God in matters of practical provision is no small matter. If we are unwilling to do so, we can expect to be plagued by such things as greed, cheating, worry, covetousness, lack of generosity, and all the unsettledness that comes from centering our lives around money.

His Word, however, provides us a sure basis for anxiety-free living by promising that He will "supply every need" (though not necessarily every *want*). Rather than fretting, striving, or manipulating, we can simply stand on His promises and confidently ask Him to provide.

Do you find yourself being worried or fretful about provision for your material needs? What do these kinds of responses say to those around you about the trustworthiness of God and His promises?

My Pleasure

They feast on the abundance of your house, and you give them drink from the river of your delights.—Psalm 36:8

 A SECOND FEAR that makes many people hesitant to wholly surrender themselves to God is that of losing *pleasure*: "Will I be happy?"

Will I be able to do the things I enjoy? What if He wants me to give up my career, or sports, or my favorite hobby, or my best friend, or the foods I really like? Would He make me stay in this unhappy marriage? Will I be fulfilled if I obey Him?

It's true that pain is unavoidable in this fallen world and that suffering is an instrument God uses to mold and sanctify those He loves. But it's also true that God created us to experience intense pleasure and joy. In fact, one of the sacred "duties" of God's people is to "rejoice before the LORD your God in everything you do" (Deut. 12:18 HCSB).

The problem is that we are prone to seek pleasure in things and people that cannot ultimately satisfy the deep longings in our hearts. For our hearts can never be truly satisfied with less than Him. The unsurrendered heart pursues paltry pleasures, compared with the pure, infinite pleasures God wants to give us: "the path of life," the "fullness of joy," the "pleasures forevermore" that flow from His loving and generous "right hand" (Ps. 16:11).

If we are unwilling to trust God with our happiness and well-being, if we insist on the pursuit of temporal pleasures, we may eventually become dominated and obsessed by alluring yet destructive desires such as overeating, drinking, sexual promiscuity, pornography, irresponsibility, living beyond our means.

But if we put our confidence in the joy that Christ alone offers, He will lift us beyond our circumstances and provide us with a deeply satisfying foretaste of heaven's eternal pleasures, even in the midst of sorrow, suffering, and struggle.

 How have you seen the shallowness of earth's temporal pleasures? How have you experienced the pleasures found in knowing and walking with God?

On Guard

In peace I will both lie down and sleep; for you alone,
O LORD, make me dwell in safety.—Psalm 4:8

 FEAR IN RELATION TO *PROTECTION* may cause you to be reluctant to fully trust God: "Will I be safe? Will He take care of those I love?"

What if my child is born with a mental or physical disability? What if I have an accident and am injured for life? What if I get cancer? What if someone breaks into our house? Might God choose to take my mate or my children? If my child goes to the mission field, will he be safe? Will she be protected?

Our God describes Himself as a "refuge," a "fortress," a "shelter," One who will "deliver" us from the harms and threats that swirl around us (Ps. 91:1–3). He doesn't promise that we will never face danger, but He does promise that those who trust Him will find protective cover "under his wings" (verse 4).

Those who refuse, however, to entrust their safety to Him, who demand human assurance of protection and security, will be subject to fearfulness, worry, and mistrust of others; they may also experience an unwillingness to be vulnerable, a fear of intimacy, a tendency toward hatred, prejudice, and paranoid thinking.

Yet God affirms that not only can He defend us and those we love, He can also keep us free from fear, no matter what comes our way. With trust in His promises, there is nothing we need to dread, including "the terror of the night, nor the arrow that flies by day, nor the pestilence that stalks in darkness, nor the destruction that wastes at noonday" (verses 5–6).

Our strong, loving Protector is able to defeat every foe. He may keep us *from* the battle or He may keep us *in* the battle. But we can be sure that those who entrust themselves to His care will never regret doing so.

 Some may feel that a self-protective mindset is necessary and healthy—their way of keeping safe. But what has worry ended up costing you that faith could alleviate?

Never Alone

*Whom have I in heaven but you? And there is
nothing on earth that I desire besides you.*—Psalm 73:25

 ONE FINAL FEAR that can threaten our complete surrender to God—in addition to concerns about *provision*, *pleasure*, and *protection*—is the fear of how it might threaten our *personal relationships*: "Will my relational needs be met?"

What if the Lord wants me to stay single all my life? How can I live without sex or romance? What if my mate leaves me? What if God doesn't give us children? How do I handle the rejection of my parents? What if my best friend moves away? What if people snub our family and me because of our commitment to biblical standards?

It's true that God may lead us into solitude for a season. But His Word reveals that an intimate relationship with Him forms the true basis for the richest of human relationships. Having "fellowship . . . with the Father and with his Son Jesus Christ" makes it possible to enjoy authentic "fellowship with one another" (1 John 1:3, 7).

If we do not value God as our primary relationship, we will always live in fear of losing human relationships, setting ourselves up for being possessive, controlling, manipulative, and jealous, perhaps compromising toward adultery and even subject to taking (or giving) abuse.

Throughout the Scripture, whenever one of His children was fearful to step out alone without human support, God's simple response was, *I will be with you*. The implication was, *I am enough. If you have Me, you have everything you need*. The man or woman who trusts His promises can never truly be alone. "My flesh and my heart may fail," they admit, "but God is the strength of my heart and my portion forever" (Ps. 73:26).

 If today finds you feeling lonely, rejected, or misunderstood, take your needy heart to Him in prayer and praise. You will find in Him a faithful and true Friend.

True Blessing

*It is good for me that I was afflicted, that I might learn
your statutes. The law of your mouth is better to me than
thousands of gold and silver pieces.*—Psalm 119:71–72

 GOD'S IDEA OF BLESSING and our idea of blessing
are not always the same. We think blessing means
having what we want, when we want it, having all
our desires satisfied without the intrusion of pain,
problems, and pressures. But God always has the
long-term view in mind. He brings situations and circumstances
into our lives that may not *seem* like blessings, and yet they
ultimately result in our good and our joy.

The richest blessings are spiritual and internal. True
blessing includes having the Holy Spirit at work in our lives,
being adopted into the family of God, enjoying the assurance of
receiving every spiritual blessing in Christ, having been chosen
from eternity past to belong to Him.

True blessing means receiving what God has given, being
enabled by His Spirit to live with a clear conscience, experiencing
real contentment because He has promised us everything we
need for our present peace and happiness.

Now that's blessing.

And because of what God knows about who we are, He
understands that we often only learn to embrace Him and His
blessings when we are stripped of other temporal blessings. Our
hearts more easily become detached from earth and attached
to heaven when we are deprived of the things we may want but
don't ultimately need.

True blessing is not the absence of hard things but Christ's
presence in the midst of hard places—the grace to dwell with
difficulty and still know that He is bestowing upon us the greatest
of all blessings: *the gift of Himself.*

For that is all we really need.

 *Do you sometimes measure and define God's blessing in temporal
rather than eternal terms? How has He tested your dependence on
Him by exposing your dependence on these lesser things?*

Clothes Selection

And the Lord God made for Adam and for his wife
garments of skins and clothed them.—Genesis 3:21

 As the tempter had promised, when Adam and Eve ate the forbidden fruit, their eyes were opened; but what they saw was not pleasant. They learned that they were naked; for the first time, they experienced shame and guilt.

In a desire to cover their nakedness, they hastily "sewed fig leaves together and made themselves loincloths" (Gen. 3:7). They tried to come up with a remedy for their guilt on their own, fashioning "aprons" (KJV) to provide at least some measure of covering.

Realizing that the fig leaves were inadequate to cover their shame, they "hid themselves from the presence of the Lord" (verse 8). But, in an amazing display of mercy and grace, God did not leave them hiding in fear and shame; He came to them, reached out to them.

"Who told you that you were naked?" God asked. "Have you eaten of the tree of which I commanded you not to eat?" (verse 11). Adam and Eve's primary concern was their nakedness; God's primary concern was that they had disobeyed His direction and that their relationship with Him had been broken.

When He finally came to the clothing issue, the Hebrew text suggests that He covered not just their private parts but their bodies, making clothes for them, as many commentators believe, from animals sacrificed for that purpose. And so, we have a foreshadowing of the gospel, in which Christ, the blameless Lamb of God, was sacrificed to cover and atone for our sin.

Adam and Eve's attempt to dress themselves pictures man's efforts to cover sin with self-made righteousness. In God's provision of clothing, we see the necessity of having a righteousness that can only come from God, and we are reminded that this gracious provision requires the slaying of an innocent substitute and that it is fully sufficient to clothe our sinful souls.

 What are you trusting to deal with your sin and shame?
A righteousness of your own making? Or that provided by
God through the sacrificial death of Christ?

Foretaste of Home

And the effect of righteousness will be peace, and the result of
righteousness, quietness and trust forever. My people will
abide in a peaceful habitation, in secure dwellings, and in
quiet resting places.—Isaiah 32:17–18

 WILLARD WIGAN IS A BRITISH SCULPTOR who carves miniature works of art from single grains of sand or individual granules of sugar, often setting his masterpieces in the eye of a needle or on the head of a pin. Using such tools as paintbrushes made from a human eyelash, he painstakingly fashions complex designs that cannot even be seen unless viewed through a microscope.

His amazing craftsmanship is a remarkable reminder that little things can make a stunning impact—little things like *your home.* Your home may seem tiny and insignificant in the grand scheme. And yet it can make a loud statement about the gospel you believe and the God you serve.

Your home matters. Whether you're married or single, whether it's a palatial mansion or a prison cell, whether you live on one side of a dorm room or in a double-wide trailer—God can transform any place you live into a "miniature masterpiece" that points people to His amazing artistry.

God, you see, is the ultimate Homemaker. If you are His child, He is right now preparing "a place" for you to live forever with Him (John 14:2). In the meantime, our homes here on earth can provide a foretaste of that heavenly Home. He wants your home and mine to reflect His heart and grace. To be a place where the reality and presence of Christ are felt. A place where His Word is honored. A place where the atmosphere is one of authentic love, kindness, and truth. A place where both those who live there and those who visit encounter Him.

 What does your home communicate? How well does it express
the hospitable, gracious heart of God? Ask God for His enabling
grace as you seek to put Him on display through your home.

A Promising Alternative

*As far as the east is from the west, so far has He
removed our transgressions from us.*—Psalm 103:12 NASB

 AS MUCH AS ANYTHING ELSE we could say about forgiveness, this truth captures it well: *forgiveness is a promise*—a promise never to bring up that sin against that person again. Not to God, not to the person who committed it, not to anyone else. It is a deliberate decision to deal with another's sin by doing away with it, pushing the "delete" button, and wiping it off your slate.

Sometimes a woman will say to me, "I've forgiven my husband" or "I've forgiven so-and-so," and then begin listing all the hurtful things that person has done. While I applaud her for recognizing her need to forgive, her own words reveal that she hasn't truly, fully forgiven—because forgiveness is a promise.

It's a promise God made to us.

What we did to Him was real. What we continue to do against Him is real. But by the atoning blood of His Son, God has chosen not to remember our offenses. He has "cast all [our] sins behind [His] back" (Isa. 38:17)—not because we deserve it or have gone through all the right steps to become forgivable but because forgiveness is at the heart of the gospel, a promise from God that we can take into all eternity.

We of all people should appreciate the joy that flows from forgiveness. We know what a treasure it is to be purely and perfectly forgiven. And when we extend to others the forgiveness that Christ extended to us on the cross, we reflect His mercy and grace to a world that desperately needs to be forgiven as well.

 Could making the promise to forgive someone who has wronged you even come close to costing you what Christ's promise has cost Him? How does His forgiveness both inform and inspire your forgiveness of others?

Getting the Picture

Beloved, we are God's children now, and what we will be has not yet appeared; but we know that when he appears we shall be like him, because we shall see him as he is.—1 John 3:2

I ENJOY WORKING JIGSAW PUZZLES. When I first open the box, however, it's hard to believe there's actually a picture contained in all those oddly shaped pieces. So I keep looking at the picture on the box, which shows me what the puzzle is supposed to look like when it's finished. Without that picture, I'd be lost.

As we look at the jumbled pieces of our lives, sometimes it's hard to fathom that they could ever form anything attractive. But God has given us a picture that shows what we will look like when He has finished His sanctifying, transforming work in us. *It's a picture of Jesus*—His relationship with His Father, His relationship with others, His values and priorities, His words and character.

In Christ we see a perfect reflection of our holy God, for "he is the radiance and the glory of God and the exact imprint of his nature" (Heb. 1:3).

Of course, no amount of striving or self-effort can make us holy. Only Christ can do that. But He is the pattern for our lives. Jesus is holiness with a face. That's why we need to keep looking at His picture throughout the assembly process, turning our eyes upon Him, being constantly reminded what the finished product is supposed to look like. Only then will we desire Him more fully—His beauty, His righteousness—instead of the sparkling enticements this world has to offer.

In time we will look like the picture on the box. We will be transformed into His likeness.

What aspects of Christ do you see that you most desire to characterize your life? What might God be doing right now to shape you into His likeness?

Full-Grown Sin

Then desire when it has conceived gives birth to sin, and sin when it is fully grown brings forth death.—James 1:15

SIN IS PLEASURABLE—no doubt about it. If that weren't the case, why would we find it so tempting? However, we need to remind ourselves that those pleasures are "fleeting" (Heb. 11:25) and that in the long run, whatever perceived benefits we may derive from sin can never outweigh its ultimate cost.

I have a friend who keeps in his billfold a list of the consequences of sin—things such as: *sin steals joy* (Ps. 51:12); *sin removes confidence* (1 John 3:19–21); *sin breaks God's heart* (Eph. 4:30); *sin opens the door to other sins* (Isa. 30:1). He has a dozen or more of these on his list. All terrible things. Whenever he is tempted to disobey God in some matter, my friend pulls out this list and reads it, then asks himself, "Is this a price I really want to pay? Is this a price I can afford?"

Sometimes the consequences of our sin are not seen until months or years down the road; sometimes they don't show up until the next generation. But make no mistake: *sin has consequences*. The day of reckoning will come. And when it does, every child of God will wish with all his heart that he had chosen the pathway of obedience.

We cannot persist in foolishly thinking that we have somehow managed to get away with our sin. Rather, we must recognize that one of God's purposes in delaying sin's consequences is to give us time to repent.

After years of toying with sin and enjoying its "pleasures," King Solomon finally came to this conviction: "Though a sinner does evil a hundred times and prolongs his life, yet I know that it will be well with those who fear God. . . . For God will bring every deed into judgment, with every secret thing, whether good or evil" (Eccl. 8:12; 12:14).

Think of a temptation to sin that you frequently face. Rehearse the consequences listed above, and ask yourself, "Is this a price I really want to pay?" Remember that whatever momentary delight or relief sin may offer, it is never worth the cost.

If Only

*Mary said, "Behold, I am the servant of the Lord;
let it be to me according to your word."*—Luke 1:38

I HAVE COME TO BELIEVE that we can manage to acquire just about anything that we're determined to have. If we want to be married badly enough, we can find someone who will marry us. If an unhappy spouse wants to get out of marriage badly enough, he or she can get out. If we want a newer model car or a college education, we can take out a loan.

But we need to be reminded of how dangerous it is to insist that God give us our own will. In fact, one of my fears is that God will give me everything I want! The history of the Israelites is a vivid reminder that when God gives us what we demand, we may also get "leanness" of soul to go along with it (Ps. 106:15 NKJV).

Over the years, I have grown to realize that contentment is a choice. True joy is not the result of having everything I want, but of gratefully receiving exactly what God has given me. The enemy has robbed many of us of our joy by getting us to live in that foolish realm of "if only."

"If only I had a husband." "If only I *didn't* have a husband!" "If only we had children." "If only we didn't have so many children." "If only I had a different job." "If only I lived in a different place." "If only I could own a home." "If only our winters weren't so long. . . ."

The fact is, if we are not content with what we have, we will never be content with what we think we want. The key to joyous living is to embrace the will of God and to receive with gratitude the gifts He chooses to give us in each season of life.

*Can you identify any areas of discontent that may have been
robbing you of the ability to fully enjoy what God has given you?*

The Compatible Christ

"Behold, I am laying in Zion a stone of stumbling, and a rock of offense; and whoever believes in him will not be put to shame."—Romans 9:33

IN MANY OF OUR CHURCHES, it seems we're knocking ourselves out trying to be "relevant" so we can attract more attention and bigger crowds. We don't want to appear too different or extreme, for fear of turning off unbelievers or being perceived as out of step with the culture. We've accommodated to the world rather than calling the world to accommodate to Christ.

But when will we realize that the world is not impressed with a religious version of itself? Our greatest effectiveness is not to be found in being like everyone else around us but in being distinct, in being like Jesus!

We have more varied means of reaching people with our message—Christian concerts, conferences, strategies, media events, books, radio/TV broadcasts, blogs, and podcasts—than any generation in history. Could it be that the absence of true revival and of deep, lasting impact on outsiders is not from a shortage of creativity or cutting-edge methodologies, but from the lack of irrefutable evidence of His presence among us?

One ministry leader said to me in the middle of a prayer gathering, "Lots of people are praying and repenting, but so few are changing their lifestyle." The truth is, if we're not changing our lifestyle, we're not repenting. And if we're not repenting, then all our singing, praising, praying, and producing are useless—perhaps *worse* than useless—because all the noise and activity may deceive us into thinking we're okay the way we are without the transforming power of the gospel. And the world around us will continue to be disinterested in what we have to offer.

Our distinctiveness *is* our message. Our changed lives *are* our testimony. What makes Christ irresistible to others is His uniqueness, not how compatible we can make Him to the culture.

What wrong motives could taint our efforts to appear attractive to outsiders? How can a proper view of Christ and confidence in His Word embolden us to pursue holiness and maintain a distinctive witness in the world?

Praying God's Will

He who searches hearts knows what is the mind of the Spirit,
because the Spirit intercedes for the saints according to the
will of God.—Romans 8:27

 WE ALL KNOW THAT WE ARE TO PRAY "according to the will of God." But how can we know His will? There are many matters on which His specific plan and desire may be difficult to ascertain. But we can be sure of one thing: *the Word of God is the will of God.* When we pray His Word back to Him, we are praying according to His will.

I have some dear friends, for example, whose marriage is in deep trouble. I often feel at a loss as to how to pray for them. But I know I can pray confidently when I pray according to God's will, as He has revealed it in His Word.

I know, for instance, that God's will for this husband is to love his wife in the same selfless, sacrificial way as Jesus loves His church (Eph. 5:25). I know that God's will for this wife is to reverence her husband, regardless of his faults and failures, and to submit to his leadership in the home (verses 22–23). I know God's will is that they would walk in love (verse 2), in oneness (Col. 3:14), and in truth (3 John 3). So I can pray these and other passages for them, calling upon God to fulfill His will in their lives.

The same holds true when it comes to our own needs. When we lay hold of His will as He has expressed it in His Word, we can pray with great boldness and confidence, knowing that God not only hears us but that "we have the requests that we have asked of him" (1 John 5:14–15).

 As you read and meditate on God's Word today, ask Him to show you how to pray according to His will in relation to your own situation or that of others who may be on your heart.

Oppressing or Blessing?

"You shall not wrong one another, but you shall fear your God, for I am the LORD your God."—Leviticus 25:17

YOU HEAR A LOT OF PEOPLE IN OUR CULTURE TODAY, even within the church, talking about how they've been wronged and victimized, wounded and sinned against. And this is all sadly true in many cases. But the fact is, not only have you and I been wrongfully treated and oppressed by others, we have also been oppressors ourselves. All of us.

We have done it with our tongues—belittling others, cutting them down, saying things to hurt them. We have done it with gossip—spreading unkind, often untrue words about other people. Even in silence, we have done it with our attitudes— just a look of the eyes or an overall demeanor that expresses the harshness of our feelings toward another person, our insensitivity to their needs.

And here's why that is such a serious matter: When we sin against each other, we sin against God. When we sin against another member of the body of Christ, we sin against Christ Himself.

In recognizing and repenting of this evil in our own hearts, we find motivation to change as we learn to fear the Lord, living in the constant, conscious awareness that God is here. He sees. He knows how you're talking to that person. He knows how you're treating your three-year-old. He knows how you talk to (or about) that mother-in-law or boss or roommate who's hurt you.

We cease being oppressors and adding to the pain in others' lives when we understand that God Himself is aware of and concerned about the way we treat those around us. By not wanting to offend Him, we will find ourselves blessing rather than oppressing those around us.

Have you been treating someone in your life in a way that does not reflect reverence and respect for God? First ask God's forgiveness; then humble yourself and seek forgiveness from the one you have wronged.

Everyday Blessings

Blessed be the LORD, who daily loads us with benefits,
the God of our salvation.—Psalm 68:19 NKJV

CHARLES SPURGEON ONCE SAID, "Let us daily praise God for common mercies—common as we frequently call them, and yet so priceless that when deprived of them we are ready to perish."

Truly, if we take those "common mercies" for granted, if we think life just shows up with these gifts already in place, if we deceive ourselves into believing that everyday household items come from the grocery store rather than from a gracious God, we walk right past countless reasons for worship without even knowing it.

Things like toothpaste and bath soap. Hot water and dishwashing detergent. Air-conditioning and houseplants. Sunsets and sunglasses. Ink pens and notepaper. Wildlife and wildflowers. Paved roads and car insurance. Autumn leaves and attic space. Blue skies, blankets, and birthday cards. Fresh fruit, flashlights, and family photos. Sticky notes and popcorn. Measuring cups and beautiful music. Books and bookcases. Warm clothes and clean sheets.

These aren't just nice to have. They're among the "every" good and perfect gifts "coming down from the Father of lights" (James 1:17). They're included in the biblical appeal for "giving thanks always and for everything to God the Father" (Eph. 5:20).

People who draw a blank when asked what they're thankful for—after running through the fairly automatic litany of faith and family and good health—can never be those who draw nearest to God, not when He has given us so many ways to answer this simple question. But those who remember to thank Him for everything from pliers and pruners to paper plates are people who know what "everything" is all about.

And why shouldn't that person be you?

As you look around you today, more consciously aware than usual, perhaps, of the multiplied ways that God both cares and provides for you, give Him uncommon thanks for these "common mercies."

Dead to Rights

Though he was in the form of God . . . [he] made himself nothing, taking the form of a servant, being born in the likeness of men.
—Philippians 2:6–7

 "YOU DESERVE IT." You hear this message in advertisements for everything from chocolates and clothing to day spas and vacation packages. Parents argue for their children's teams at ball games. Siblings fight over their turf at home. Road-enraged drivers shout and point, sometimes running the objects of their wrath off the highway. (It's happened to me.)

It's so ingrained in our thinking—this entitlement mindset, this demanding of rights—that we don't always stop to see how completely contrary it is to the Spirit of Christ.

I remember hearing a radio message by Warren Wiersbe, catching me on one of those mornings when my heart was uptight and irritated, insisting on my rights and my way. Pierced with conviction from his appeal to come down off our thrones, as Christ did, and see ourselves as servants, I wrote the following entry in my journal:

> I have been thinking and acting as a sovereign whose will and way are to prevail or "off with your head." Everybody bow down to "Queen Nancy" and make me happy. When I feel my "rights" and expectations have been violated or unfulfilled, I become petulant, peevish, and impossible to please. Forgive me, Lord. You came with a towel on bended knee to serve Your creatures. So also You have called me to love and serve my fellow servants.

By looking again to Christ, we see the heart of the gospel—that He humbled Himself, took on the form of a servant, and laid down His life for us.

Do others, by looking at us, see an example of self-serving, rights-claiming pride, or do they see a clear portrait of the humble, servant-hearted Christ?

 In what practical ways could you pick up a "towel" today and serve others as Christ has served you?

Find Us Faithful

We will not hide them from their children, but tell to the coming generation the glorious deeds of the LORD, and his might, and the wonders that he has done.—Psalm 78:4

ONE OF THE GREATEST HEARTACHES of my adult life has been to watch so many young adults who have grown up in our Christian homes and churches, who demonstrate so little interest in spiritual matters, or worse yet, claim to be Christians while living in ways clearly contrary to His Word. We have to ask ourselves what's causing this lack of passion to follow hard after Christ.

What's happening—or *not* happening?

Yes, each individual is responsible for his own choices. But I think we in their parents' generation have to ask if we bear any responsibility for these trends. Every generation of believers is charged with passing on a godly heritage to the next. We are responsible for the seeds we sow, and we must live with the harvest that results. We cannot plant seeds of halfhearted, undisciplined, worldly lives, and then hope for "crop failure" in the next generation.

Our enemy is determined to claim the children of God's people for his purposes. His agenda is furthered when we fail to be intentional about pursuing Christ ourselves or about urging our children to do the same.

That is not to suggest that the children of faithful parents will always choose to follow Christ, or that all unfaithful children are the product of unfaithful parents. We know that is not the case in Scripture or in our own experience. It is to say that the next generation is taking its cues from us, as to what really matters and what they will choose (or not choose) to live for.

Oh for a generation of parents who purpose to live out the truth before their children, and to train and nurture their children in God's ways, trusting Him to capture their hearts by His grace, that they might not drop the baton of faith but pass it on intact to their children.

Whether you have children of your own or not, what are you doing to pass on to the next generation the message of God's character and ways and of His redeeming grace and love?

Emotion Overload

Teach me to do your will, for you are my God!
Let your good Spirit lead me on level ground!—Psalm 143:10

GOD MADE US TO BE EMOTIONAL CREATURES. Imagine not being able to feel joy and ecstasy, or even pain and sorrow. Feelings and emotions are gifts from the Lord. Yet too often we find our lives dictated and driven by what I call "rogue emotions"—thoughts and feelings we know are out of order, but just can't seem to get under control. We feel irritated, or angry, or stressed, or frustrated. And even when we know what we should do or how we should react, these runaway feelings tell us otherwise.

But the fact is—by God's grace—we *can* bring these emotions under the control of His Spirit. We *can* clear our minds and receive the power to discipline our flesh, even when we're really wanting to stay angry or resentful.

I have discovered two vital keys to ruling over rather than being ruled by our emotions. *First, the Word.* The times when my emotions are the most out of line are generally times when I haven't been faithfully meditating on Scripture, bringing "every thought captive to obey Christ" (2 Cor. 10:5). God's truth, illuminated and applied by the Spirit, has the ability to stabilize us, tempering and leveling our emotions, giving us the perspective and authority we need to tell these feelings of ours who's boss.

Second, His people. When we're feeling upset and out of sorts, we may be tempted to withdraw and isolate ourselves. We don't want to be exposed. We want to nurse our emotions. But it's important in those times to let others into our hearts. We don't need to run from those who can help reorient us, nor from those who, as we minister to their needs, enable our own hearts to be renewed.

Stay grounded. Stay connected.

You may not always feel like staying connected to God's Word and His people. Ask God to give you grace to do what is right, based on faith, and to bring your feelings under the control of His Spirit.

Till We Weep

Let them come quickly and wail over us till our eyes overflow with tears and water streams from our eyelids.—Jeremiah 9:18 NIV

 Sin's toll is evident everywhere around us. Crazed gunmen enter schools and shopping malls and commit random murders. Multiplied millions of children are shuttled back and forth between two parents who have broken their marriage vows; in many cases they are also violated at the hands of stepfamily members. Complete strangers meet by way of the Internet and proceed to abandon their marriages and families. Young people—even in Christian homes—embrace a partying lifestyle and become entangled with sinful strongholds from which they spend the rest of their lives trying to break free.

And how do we respond to these calamities? We blink. We change the channel. We check last night's ball scores. We check out emotionally, ultimately becoming numb and indifferent to the barrage of such realities.

The prophets of old remind us that there is a time to mourn, to grieve over what is happening in our world, our homes, and even our churches. And there is ample cause for weeping, when we consider the in-your-face rebellion and immorality of our day, the worldliness of many congregations, as well as our own "respectable" sins of entitlement, self-sufficiency, unforgiveness, prayerlessness, and lack of compassion.

I realize, of course, that tears are not something we can manufacture. But when we get in the presence of God—when we wait there long enough to hear His heart and His Spirit—He will shatter our complacency, turning our easy laughter into mourning and our joy into heaviness over the havoc sin has wreaked in our world (James 4:9).

Yes, comfort and joy are part of our inheritance in Christ—gifts from the Father, the fullness of which we will experience for all eternity in His presence. But first comes the mourning. Where, O Lord, are the mourners?

 Even as you enjoy God's good and gracious gifts, ask Him to stir and break your heart with the things that grieve His heart.

Pain Reliever

"His master was angry, and delivered him to the torturers until he should pay all that was due to him."—Matthew 18:34 NKJV

 MEDICAL RESEARCH has consistently shown that people who harbor pent-up emotions such as anger, bitterness, and inner hostility will often manifest these issues in their physical bodies. Such individuals frequently show a propensity for high blood pressure, impaired immune function, muscle spasms, hormonal changes, memory loss, even an increased risk of heart attack. Interestingly, both the words *anger* and *angina* share the same Greek root.

Please hear me. I'm not saying for a moment that every ache or pain is caused by bitterness or unforgiveness. I don't want to make anyone who suffers from organically rooted diseases to feel condemned, or to suggest that you shouldn't pursue medical treatment for physical ailments. But I'm convinced that more often than we realize, some of the chronic mental, emotional, and even physical disorders that people struggle with are rooted in anger we're unwilling to release. God never intended our bodies to hold up under the weight of unresolved conflict.

In the parable of the unforgiving servant in Matthew 18, Jesus linked a refusal to forgive with God turning us over to "torturers" ("tormentors" [KJV]; "jailers" [ESV]). When I find myself dealing with persistent, unexplainable physical symptoms, I think it's important to at least *ask* the Lord if there's anything He's trying to get my attention about, any residual anger or bitterness that might be taking a toll on my body.

Being a forgiving person will not guarantee a pain-free life. But I can't help wondering how much pain we might be spared (and how much money we could save on doctors' and therapists' bills) if we refused to let bitterness take root in our hearts.

 Is there any unresolved issue in your heart that could be having an adverse effect on you—physically, mentally, emotionally?

Number One

*One of the scribes came up and heard them disputing
with one another, and seeing that [Jesus] answered them well,
asked him, "Which commandment is the most important
of all?"*—Mark 12:28

JESUS ANSWERED THIS MAN'S QUESTION with a command
from Scripture that every Jew would have quoted every
morning and every evening—one so familiar that they
could have mouthed the words along with Him as He
spoke them aloud: "Hear, O Israel: The Lord our God,
the Lord is one. And you shall love the Lord your God with all
your heart and with all your soul and with all your mind and
with all your strength" (Mark 12:29–30).

Most of us are familiar with these words, as well. And we
know that if we love Him, everything else He's told us to do will
flow naturally from that source. Love for God will result in the
forsaking of all idols and in genuine love for others. "Love is the
fulfilling of the law" (Rom. 13:10).

But we also know that our love for God is far less wholehearted than it should be, less intense than we wish it were—not
usually because of a complete blowout or breakdown but rather
from slow, undetected leaks.

We don't have it within us to manufacture deep, authentic
love for God. But, as with human relationships, we can remove
impediments to intimacy, and we can put in place practical
measures that help cultivate an ever-deepening love.

Do you really want to love God more? I know I do. And if
you are His child, you do as well. Then let us stop ignoring Him
for days at a time. Let us surround ourselves with people whose
influence on us will deepen our love for Him. Let us set apart
time to be alone with Him. And let us, by His grace, *receive* from
Him the love He wants us to return to Him.

*What are some things that are competing for your love,
wanting the place in your life reserved for God alone?
Name them. Purpose to remove them. He is worth it!*

How?

We know that for those who love God, all things work together for good, for those who are called according to his purpose.—Romans 8:28

HOW CAN THIS BE TRUE? How can something as evil and threatening as what you (or someone you love) may be facing today ever be redeemed or result in anything of value?

The answer, at least in part, lies in the next verse—it's the fact that "those whom he foreknew he also predestined to be conformed to the image of his Son" (verse 29). If you're a child of God, the ordeal you're undergoing—however wrong, unfair, or heartless—will be used in His providence and His skillful hands to take you deeper into His heart, to a place of greater dependence and trust, a place where you are more perfectly refined into the likeness of Christ.

Somewhere truly good.

Think again of the cross and its implications for those who suffer the vilest consequences of life in a fallen world. Here is undoubtedly the most heinous wrong ever committed in the universe. Who would ever have planned Calvary? Who could have seen one good thing coming from such an atrocity? Only the God who had masterminded the whole story and could see ahead to resurrection.

And He is the same One who has measured the scope of your pain and injustice, who closely monitors the depth, length, and height of every trial you endure, and who will not allow into your life a single circumstance that will thwart or derail His eternal, loving plan for you.

If even the scourge of the cross could not stop Him from completing the plan He had for His Son, how could any difficulty in your life overcome His desire and ability to complete the plan He has for you?

 For everything in your life today that seems bad or worse, there is a God who makes "everything beautiful in its time" (Eccl. 3:11). Trust Him.

Take a Bow

"I lay down my life that I may take it up again. No one takes it from me, but I lay it down of my own accord."—John 10:17–18

 JOHN'S ACCOUNT OF THE CRUCIFIXION provides a significant detail that is not included in the other Gospels. We are told that after Jesus drank the vinegar, "he bowed his head and gave up his spirit" (John 19:30). He didn't just slump over. In that final moment of His life, He performed one last, powerful, volitional act. He chose the pathway of surrender, so you and I could inherit eternal life.

He bowed His head.

And just as Christ's surrender took Him to a cross, so ours will take us to the cross as well. Every time we purposefully "bow our head" in surrender to the will of God, our flesh is crucified and Christ is exalted as Lord.

Every time our flesh wants to watch that raunchy program. Every time we want to lash out in anger. Every time we want to pass along a critical report about someone. Every time we are tempted to complain about our circumstances. Every time we rise up against an authority we consider unreasonable. Every time we want to hurt someone who's wounded us. Every time we want to say something that makes us look good. Every time we want to indulge in sexual fantasies. Every time we want to eat to excess. Every time we want to hoard our financial resources out of fear. Every time we want to shade the truth to protect our reputation . . .

Every time we bow our heads in acceptance of and surrender to the will of God, we embrace the cross. We manifest to the world the heart of Christ, who bowed His head to the will of the Father.

 How would "bowing your head" make a difference in the way you approach the rest of this day? What might it mean giving up or letting go?

Into the Light

"Nothing is covered up that will not be revealed,
or hidden that will not be made known."—Luke 12:2

I WAS ONCE IN A GROUP where everyone was asked to share something about themselves that no one else in the group knew. I shared that I used to play the cello in high school. Very true. Something no one else knew.

Of course, we only disclosed things about ourselves that we didn't mind everyone else knowing. We all had parts of our story that we weren't about to reveal in that circle.

Can you think of something in your past or current life that you'd just as soon others not know? Perhaps it's a child who has chosen a deviant or destructive lifestyle. Perhaps a personal struggle with sin, or a devastating financial situation. What's the area of your life that you want to keep walled off so no one ever sees?

True, there are appropriate times and settings for sharing some of these things. These are not topics for casual conversation. But I'm reminded of the woman at the well who wanted to keep her sordid past (and present) walled off from Jesus. In order to receive the "living water" Jesus wanted to give her (John 4:10), she had to be willing for Him to know everything.

If you're longing for Christ to satisfy your thirsty soul, you too must be willing to step into the light and open up that hidden place in your heart.

As we humble ourselves before God and, as needed, before others, we will receive an infusion of His restoring, healing, enabling grace. He will not only redeem those broken places of our lives but will speak through us into the lives of others, revealing a Savior who can transform their lives as well.

Is there anything you need to bring into the light? Start by telling the Lord. Then ask Him if there is another person you need to share with—to obtain a clear conscience, to break the bondage of the secrecy, or to encourage someone else who may need to let down the walls.

Have You Become Messala?

"Blessed are the peacemakers, for they shall be called sons of God."—Matthew 5:9

"IT'S AS THOUGH YOU HAD BECOME MESSALA."

If you've seen the classic movie *Ben-Hur*, you remember those stinging words from Esther, childhood sweetheart of Judah Ben-Hur, after hearing his drive for revenge toward his once inseparable friend Messala who had betrayed him to the Romans. Wrongfully accused of assaulting a Roman centurion, Judah had seen his family's home and possessions confiscated. His mother and sister had been imprisoned in an underground cell where they both contracted leprosy. He himself had been lashed as a galley slave in the belly of a Roman warship before escaping and eventually returning to his ruined home.

As it happened, that very day, Esther had been deeply touched by the teaching of a man named Jesus on a nearby hillside. She pleaded with Judah to choose a different way—Jesus' way—of responding to his anger and hatred. When he scoffed at her appeal to make the radical choice to forgive and love his enemy, she responded tearfully, "It was Judah Ben-Hur I loved! What has become of him? You seem to be now the very thing you set out to destroy. . . . *It's as though you had become Messala.*"

Let that sink in for a moment. If you have long struggled to forgive an offense committed against you, is it possible you're unwittingly becoming like the one who hurt you?

God wants you, instead, to become like His Son—to be filled with *His* Spirit, displaying His attitudes and characteristics, expressing the merciful heart of your heavenly Father.

Unforgiveness will turn you into a different person, someone you never intended to be, displaying the spirit, attitudes, and characteristics you detest in others. Only through forgiveness can you become the person He created and redeemed you to be.

Why give someone else the power to make you a person you don't want to be? Will you continue to allow your heart and reactions to be defined by what they did?

The High Cost of Complaining

We must not put Christ to the test, as some of them did and were destroyed by serpents, nor grumble, as some of them did and were destroyed by the Destroyer.—1 Corinthians 10:9–10

ACCORDING TO THE FIRST CHAPTER OF NUMBERS, more than 600,000 men above the age of twenty departed from Egypt during the exodus. Add to that the number of wives among them, and we can easily estimate that at least a million adults were on hand to witness deliverance from Egyptian bondage. Some forty years later, however, a new census (Num. 26) revealed that of the original Hebrews, only a few survived the wilderness years to enter the Promised Land.

Three, in fact.

And something about what happened to all the others—accounting for an average of *seventy funerals a day* during their forty long years of wandering—is supposed to be an "example" to us, "written down for our instruction" (1 Cor. 10:11) so we do not repeat their mistakes.

Some of their sins were quite glaring and obvious: idolatry, sexual immorality, an incessant craving for evil. But in addition to these heinous iniquities was one other sin pattern worth noting—and no less deadly: grumbling and complaining.

Yes, one of the evils that "destroyed" the children of Israel and kept an entire generation from the Promised Land was the scourge of discontentment—wanting something God had not given, even though He had given them so much: freedom, deliverance, one demonstration after another of His presence and power.

Paul insisted that we should take note of this, in order to keep the same disease from infecting our own hearts with its deadly properties. For God has promised to provide us "a way of escape" (verse 13) if we will trust Him to deliver us from our whining ways.

 Has discontentment wormed its way into your thoughts, words, and habitual responses to life? What has it already started to "destroy" in you?

Slope Intercept

In the path of righteousness is life, and in its pathway there is no death.—Proverbs 12:28

IT'S SURPRISING HOW EASILY INGRATITUDE can worm its way into our habit patterns. But actually it shouldn't be a surprise to us at all, because ingratitude is the taproot out of which grows a host of other sins. If we do not put the axe to that root, we provide Satan with a wide, vacant lot on which to set up his little shop of horrors in our hearts.

Do you think I might be overstating the case a bit? Well, when you think of the first chapter of Romans, what comes to mind? You may remember how Paul talks about the "wrath of God" being revealed "against all ungodliness and unrighteousness of men" (verse 18). These examples include "all manner" of things, such as "murder, strife, deceit, maliciousness" (verse 29), as well as a horde of other sins, including homosexual perversion and its acceptance and approval in our culture—just about every awful thing you can imagine.

But what is the beginning point for this vast array of vile activities? What starts people and civilizations down this path toward ever more serious sin? The answer is found in verse 21: "For although they knew God, they did not honor him as God *or give thanks to him.*" This seemingly insignificant, innocuous matter of ingratitude turns out to be the fountainhead for the numerous other evils Paul lists in this chapter.

There's really no end to what can grow from the root of ingratitude. When we give in to whining, murmuring, and complaining, we embark on a destructive slide that can take us to depths we never could have imagined ourselves going. Truly, ingratitude is our first step away from God.

Can you identify how some recurring sin in your life is connected to a lack of gratitude? How could a thankful heart help you overcome that particular sin?

Victory Cry

*"I dwell in the high and holy place, and also with him who is
of a contrite and lowly spirit, to revive the spirit of the lowly,
and to revive the heart of the contrite."*—Isaiah 57:15

 WHEN I SPEAK ON THE SUBJECT OF BROKENNESS, I
often ask at the close, "How many of you know
there is some step of brokenness God wants
you to take, but there's a battle going on inside,
and your pride is keeping you from taking that
step?" Invariably, many hands go up all across the room.

At that point, I tell them the same thing I want to tell you
today: *The battle inside will stop the moment you wave the white flag
of surrender and say, "Yes, Lord."* By the same token, the longer
you delay, the harder you resist, the more difficult it will be to
humble yourself and obey God.

Is there a battle going on in your heart? Is pride or fear
keeping you from doing something you know God wants you to
do? Perhaps there is a secret sin you need to bring into the light
and confess; maybe there is an estranged family member you
need to reach out to . . . or something He is prompting you to
give away . . . or a struggle He wants you to share with another
believer, for accountability and prayer . . .

Whatever it is—please, don't delay another day. If you want
a revived heart and relationship with God, run head-on into
whatever your pride is telling you not to do (*what will others think?*).
Humble yourself, step out by faith, and obey God! As you take
that first step, pride will be crushed and He will give you grace
to take the next step.

You can't imagine the joy that awaits you on the other side
of true brokenness—the power of His resurrection life that will
be released through your death to self, the wholeness that will
be born out of your brokenness. Best of all, Christ will be seen,
magnified, loved, and worshiped by others.

 *Have you been "negotiating" with God over a needed step of
humility and brokenness? His Spirit is not tugging to hurt you
but to help and heal you.*

Swimming Upstream

"For whoever would save his life will lose it, but whoever loses his life for my sake will find it."—Matthew 16:25

 AMY CARMICHAEL WENT TO INDIA as a twenty-eight-year-old single woman in 1895. What she discovered there were countless children and young women—even infants—who had been taken captive and sold into the custody of the Hindu religious fathers, raised to be temple prostitutes. Her heart broke at what she saw.

And so she stayed. For fifty-five years. Without a furlough. One life at a time, she and her little band of coworkers rescued children from the temples in which they were held. It was dangerous, difficult work. She had to withstand religious and cultural views that were entrenched in centuries of tradition and superstition. But she saw a need. She heard His calling. And she continued on against the flow.

When I think of her sacrificial life, I'm reminded of salmon swimming upstream to deposit the eggs that contain their young. The journey can leave them bloodied and beaten by the rocks and other obstacles they face along the way. But they are determined to give birth, to give life. Then, once their mission is accomplished, they die.

You wonder, *Who would choose that path?* But what a picture of the heart of Christ—swimming upstream, against the tide, being beaten and bloodied on His way to giving spiritual life, even at the cost of His own physical life.

Like Amy Carmichael, we as His followers have been given the task of rescuing those who have been taken captive by the enemy. It can be dangerous, difficult work. An uphill battle. An upstream swim.

But is Christ not worth it? And are those souls He died to redeem not worth it? A life poured out on behalf of others is costly; but whatever sacrifices we may make in this life will surely be turned to great gain in the next.

 Where do you see the darkness consuming people's hearts and lives around you? Begin praying about how you can reach out to those He has placed in your path.

To Tell the Truth

Having put away falsehood, let each one of you speak the truth with his neighbor, for we are members of one another.—Ephesians 4:25

 I HAVE NOT ALWAYS BEEN A TRUTH-SPEAKER. As a young woman wanting to make a good impression on others, I would sometimes "exaggerate" the truth (read, I lied). In fact, over time, this became a pattern in my life—one I felt helpless to overcome.

I can still remember sitting in a church service many years ago, miserable under the heavy hand of the Spirit's conviction. I had lied on a number of weekly reports that I had turned in to my college music department, and I knew if I wanted to be right with God, I had to go back and make it right.

At the same time, I was also prompted to share this stronghold with two mature believers, and to ask them to pray for me. It was one of the hardest things I ever had to do. But to my joy and amazement, as soon as I was willing to humble myself before God and others, the stranglehold of deception in my life was broken, and I was set free.

Though it often seems that people who lie succeed, Proverbs says that "a false witness will not go unpunished, and he who breathes out lies will not escape" (19:5). Further, those who deceive will not last, but the effect of true words will be enduring (12:19).

Because of my desire to be completely truthful in my communication, I made the following commitment all those years ago: (1) to speak the truth to every person, in every situation, regardless of the cost, and (2) anytime I failed to speak the truth, to go back and make it right. At times over the years, I've had to confess being untruthful, both privately and publicly. But as a result, I've experienced the freedom and joy of having a clear conscience before God and others, and speaking truthfully has become a passion and deeply engrained pattern in my life, for which I praise God!

 Have you resolved in your heart to speak the truth to every person, in every situation? That is one way our lives can point people to Christ who is the Truth.

Singing in the Shadow

*And when they had sung a hymn, they went out to
the Mount of Olives.*—Matthew 26:30

 WE KNOW FROM HEBREW TRADITION that Psalms
113–118 (known as the *Hallel*) were traditionally
sung at national Jewish feasts, such as the
Passover. Read those few pages again yourself,
and you won't have to look hard to spot the
resounding theme of triumph, praise, and deliverance. "Not to
us, O LORD, not to us, but to your name give glory" (115:1). "For
you have delivered my soul from death, my eyes from tears, my
feet from stumbling" (116:8). "Oh give thanks to the LORD, for
he is good" (118:29).

But imagine now you're not singing these psalms in
celebration of God's dramatic rescue, watching a rehydrated
Red Sea still foaming before your disbelieving eyes. Imagine
instead you're singing these psalms where Jesus likely was singing
them—in the dim light of the upper room, mere moments from
your violent capture and arrest, mere hours from trial, torture,
and death.

To be able to sing a hymn of praise in that moment—
that's serenity. That's "blessed assurance." That's realizing your
Father is wise and good and that He can be implicitly trusted.
It's refusing to factor your own feelings into your faith decisions.
It's valuing His great redemptive plan above your own comfort
and safety. And it's choosing to recognize traces of life, hope,
glory, and joy in the same situations where most can see only
fear, doubt, anxiety, and self-pity.

But that's what His suffering love has earned us the right
to experience. Because of Christ's sacrifice, the same song that
brightened the shadow of the cross can cast its calming light
into the room where you're sitting today. His heart at rest can be
music to your weary, worried soul.

 *What kinds of circumstances are likely to trigger stress
and drive away your serenity? What are the first signs that
reveal you've crossed over the line into fear and panic?*

Spoken in Silence

Like a lamb that is led to the slaughter, and like a sheep that before its shearers is silent, so he opened not his mouth.—Isaiah 53:7

 OF ALL THE THINGS WE LEARN FROM WHAT JESUS SAID throughout His earthly ministry, we learn one of our greatest lessons from what He *didn't* say. Standing mocked and bloodied before His accusers, holding more than enough evidence to refute every unjust charge leveled against Him, Jesus' self-defense throughout each of His trials was marked most notably by His extraordinary silence.

Yes, silence—a response that stands in such stark contrast to our typical reactions, we are wise to sit back and wonder why we are so un-Christlike in the way we often react when threatened, challenged, or called to account for our actions.

I am convinced Jesus' silence was not motivated by mere stoicism, a stiff upper lip. Nor was He sullen and angry, depressed and hopeless. I believe the silence we "hear" from Jesus comes from His sense of absolute, composed surrender to the Father's will—a strength we, too, can maintain amid our own unfair trials and circumstances.

Like Jesus, we would not be so prone to fire back at those who misunderstand or malign us if we had confidence that God was still on His throne and that nothing and no one can thwart His eternal purposes. We would not raise an accusing finger toward the Father if we had already taken our concerns to Him and had chosen a settled confidence in His will and His plans.

There are, of course, times when it is appropriate (and Christlike) to speak up in the face of injustice and opposition. But when you're secure in who you are, in whose you are, and in His wisdom, goodness, and love, you don't have to talk so much. You can let your own silence reflect the heart and spirit of Jesus.

 Are you facing a situation where your natural inclination is to defend yourself verbally or to make a harsh or hasty retort? Ask the Holy Spirit to rein in your heart and your tongue. And remember that sometimes silence is more powerful than words.

Blessing for Cursing

*Bless those who persecute you; bless and
do not curse them.*—Romans 12:14

ABDUCTED BY A PHILIPPINE TERRORIST GROUP,
missionary Gracia Burnham and her husband,
Martin, endured more than a year of torture,
deprivation, and abuse in the wilds of a tropical
jungle. She was eventually freed in a rescue
operation by the national military. Martin, however, was killed
in the resulting firefight.

As you can imagine, the thought of extending grace and
blessing to their captors, in light of her memories and her
irredeemable loss, was a daunting challenge for Gracia.

Gracia remembers one of those men in particular, a young
man who was always sullen, cranky, and argumentative. They
never knew what might set him off or what he was capable of
doing. But one day they discovered that he suffered from severe
headaches (which were perhaps partly to blame for his touchy
reflexes). So Martin began offering him pain relievers from
their small stash of medicines and crude provisions. "From that
moment on," she recalled, "my husband was his friend."

Such a simple act. A caring observer. An aspirin. Yet going
there required that Martin get past a million reasons for not just
being unconcerned about this man but secretly wishing he could
give all his captors a serious headache!

Now on this side of their horrendous ordeal, Gracia looks
back and says, "To this day, I have a warm spot in my heart for
that young man because of what Martin did for him."

God can give you a complete change of heart toward those
who have caused you irreparable damage. But you must take
seriously—and literally—what God expects, which includes
something that may sound unthinkable and is only possible by
His grace: *blessing your offenders.*

 *Is there a positive, proactive step of blessing you could
take today toward someone who has greatly wronged you?*

The Word of Forgiveness

Jesus said, "Father, forgive them, for they know not what they do."—Luke 23:34

 FOLLOWING YESTERDAY'S READING, I want to take you back to the place where the concept of blessing an offender was modeled in the most powerful, sacrificial way possible. The Lord Jesus, following a horribly unjust trial and the rigors of extreme torture, hangs naked from a wooden cross, suffering in unspeakable pain, on display before a noisy, jeering crowd.

And in this unimaginably excruciating condition—enduring a punishment so severe that Roman soldiers were known to cut out the tongues of their victims to quiet their loud cursings—Jesus utters His first words from the cross. Not a cry of hatred and vindictiveness but rather . . .

A prayer.

Centuries earlier, the prophet Isaiah had said the Messiah would bear the "sin of many" and make "intercession for the transgressors" (Isa. 53:12). And here in Jesus' prayer, we detect no anger or bitterness, no appeals for His own rescue. In the face of heinous rejection, injustice, and abuse, we hear words that are even more powerful than human cruelty.

A prayer of forgiveness.

That prayer was for the Roman soldiers who laughingly tormented Him. It was for Pilate and Herod, whose coldness and cowardice had sentenced Him here. It was for the wild mob crying out, "Crucify Him!" It was for His closest disciples—nowhere to be found, for the most part, in these final hours of His earthly life.

And it was for you. And me. The only thing keeping us from experiencing the storm of God's righteous wrath is the fact that Jesus covered us with the shield of His grace on that awful day, that glorious day, when He prayed through pain made even more biting because of our treacherous sin, "Father, forgive them." And we are forgiven.

 Have you ever realized your part in nailing Christ to the cross? Have you experienced the forgiveness He died to purchase? It can be yours, by His amazing grace.

The Word of Assurance

And he said to him, "Truly, I say to you, today you will be with me in Paradise."—Luke 23:43

 ROBBERS. PLURAL. The day our Lord was nailed on a cross to die between two thieves, the Bible says *both* of them "reviled him in the same way" (Matt. 27:44), letting their anguish and pain spill out in blasphemy toward the so-called "Son of God."

And then—something unexplainable happened. One of them suddenly rebuked the other (Luke 23:40–41). He had heard enough. His heart had changed. He saw his own sins for what they were and this Man next to him for who He was. He had been given the ability, even in that brief window of time as he faced his imminent death, to repent of his many failures and to issue a desperate cry of faith: "Jesus, remember me when you come into your kingdom" (verse 42).

In this account, we see how grace works. We see the wonder of the gospel on display. For thieves and criminals. For doctors and lawyers. For you and me. We did not choose God; He chose us. And for that reason—and no other—we can face death with this confidence: "Today you will be with me in Paradise."

If you worry about what will happen to you when you die, this word gives assurance that your eternal destiny is not determined by the life you have lived or the sins you have committed but is based on simple trust in Christ and His grace. If you are unsure about whether a loved one will spend eternity with the Lord, this word gives hope that mercy may be sought and granted even in the final moments of life.

Jesus had told His disciples that He would come to take them home with Him, "that where I am you may be also" (John 14:3). And now this promise even included a dying thief without a single good deed to his name. Heaven is the gift of God for all who believe and receive Christ's death on the cross.

 Do you have friends and loved ones who continue to reject Christ's forgiveness? Ask for opportunities to share the great gospel story with them.

The Word of Devotion

When Jesus saw his mother and the apostle John standing nearby, he said to his mother, "Woman, behold your son!" Then he said to the disciple, "Behold, your mother!" And from that hour the disciple took her to his own home.—John 19:26–27

THE SUPREME PURPOSE OF JESUS' DEATH, we know, was to save our souls, to spare us from the wrath of God that we deserved for our sin. And yet in His third statement from the cross, we see that Jesus died to provide more than our eternal salvation; He died to redeem everything about this broken, dysfunctional world. Not only does He meet our spiritual needs; He tends to our physical, emotional, and relational needs as well.

We have a Savior who cares—One who cared that His mother was provided for, One who still cares today that our relational and practical needs are met in Him and through His people.

Life takes us through stages and seasons where present sources of provision and comfort are removed from us. History suggests that by the time Jesus was crucified, Mary was already a widow following the earlier death of Joseph. She was now being separated from her beloved Son who would have been expected to assume responsibility for her needs.

And yet as He was preparing to leave this earth, Christ made provision for her care and covering, not, as might have been expected, through other blood relatives, but through a bloodline of faith that was even stronger and more enduring.

You may be concerned about how your needs will be met as you age, about whether your money will hold out, whether your children will be there to help you. You can be assured that through Christ, your needs will be fully met. Through His people, you will never lack for true "family."

As you look around, what needs might Christ want to meet through you—particularly for other believers in need of "family" connections?

The Word of Dereliction

About the ninth hour, Jesus cried out with a loud voice,
"Eli, Eli, lema sabachthani?" that is, "My God, my God,
why have you forsaken me?"—Matthew 27:46

 THE FIRST THREE STATEMENTS OF CHRIST from the cross, which we've been revisiting these last few days, each occurred in the morning, during the early part of His daylong ordeal. At noon, pitch-black darkness fell over the earth. For the next three hours, He went through the most painful, difficult part of His redeeming work—not only suffering at the hands of men but now being subjected to the hand of God.

Some have suggested that Jesus was not really forsaken by God—that He just *felt* forsaken by God. But the Scripture indicates that Jesus *was* forsaken by His Father, that He *had* to be forsaken, cut off from God, to redeem us from our sins. The intimacy He had always enjoyed with His Father was broken. He experienced all the consequences, the full measure of judgment, that we deserved for our sin.

We know that "it was the will of the LORD to crush him" (Isa. 53:10) and that "he made him to be sin who knew no sin" (2 Cor. 5:21). When Jesus cried out "My God, my God, why have you forsaken me?" the Father was actively, intentionally, directly involved in imputing our sin to His Son and executing our judgment on Christ.

And yet even at this extreme height of holy anguish, Jesus' cry of distress was not a cry of distrust. The Father's face had been eclipsed—yes—but Jesus knew He was still there, through the darkened distance, not only carrying Him through this torment but finding satisfaction in a job well done by His beloved Son.

You may be at a low point in your life. At times, you may feel abandoned by God or others. But if you have trusted Christ as your sin-bearer, you will never be truly forsaken—because your Savior was forsaken for you.

 If not you, there's likely someone in your life today who's dragging rock bottom. Tell them of a Savior who's been there and back.

The Word of Agony

After this, Jesus, knowing that all was now finished,
said (to fulfill the Scripture), "I thirst."—John 19:28

 GOD DOESN'T GET THIRSTY. For our Lord and Savior to utter these words from the cross can only mean that He was indeed fully man, as well as fully God. Yet while this admission of physical craving does speak to His humanity, it also reveals something even deeper and more awe-inspiring: His reverence for the Word of God.

Jesus had already fulfilled multiple prophecies and predictions concerning His life and death. More were yet to come, of course, until *all* was fulfilled. But even this relatively incidental one—a statement expressing His thirst—was on His mind as He neared the end of this climactic moment.

"My throat is parched," the psalmist David had spoken in messianic prophecy (Ps. 69:3). "For my thirst they gave me sour wine to drink" (verse 21). "My strength is dried up like a potsherd, and my tongue sticks to my jaws" (22:15).

Jesus knew these Scriptures. He was familiar with them. He had likely been meditating on them, even while battling the intense demands on His body, the struggle for each breath, each painful gasp. And so intent was He on completely fulfilling the Word of God concerning His death, that He did not overlook even this one minor detail.

What if you knew that your own suffering was an opportunity to honor God's Word? When He says to cast "all your anxieties on him, because he cares for you" (1 Peter 5:7), are you careful to handle life's pressures in this way so others can see the Scripture fulfilled? When He says to "give thanks in all circumstances" (1 Thess. 5:18), do you realize that doing so says to those around you that you believe and honor God's Word?

 As you read Scripture in the coming days, consider whether your life is confirming or discrediting His Word.

The Word of Triumph

When Jesus had received the sour wine,
he said, "It is finished."—John 19:30

 DEPENDING ON HOW A PERSON READS THE inflection in Jesus' voice, this cry from the cross could be interpreted a number of ways. They could hear Him saying, "Whew! It is finished"—relieved this whole nightmare is over. Or, yes, "It is finished," but the long ordeal has left Him shattered and undone. Or it could even be taken as an admission of defeat, conquered by a stronger foe.

But this wasn't the moan of a vanquished warrior or a spent sufferer. This was the shout of a victor announcing that the battle was over and His earthly mission was complete. When Jesus "cried out again with a loud voice and yielded up his spirit" (Matt. 27:50), He was declaring this a moment of triumph. It was a cry of jubilation!

So what was finished? For one, the prophecies about His birth, life, ministry, and atoning sacrifice had been fulfilled. Further, everything He had been sent to do was accomplished. The storm of God's wrath had been poured out on Him, and now the eternal plan of redemption was totally complete. All the types and shadows of the old covenant had found their fulfillment in Christ. The battle against sin and Satan had been fought and won. As had been promised in the garden of Eden, in exchange for a bruised heel, the Lord Jesus had bruised the serpent's head (Gen. 3:15). And now our Savior triumphantly declared the final victory: *"It is finished."*

All that's left now for those redeemed by the Savior's blood is to celebrate the canceling of the "record of debt that stood against us"—our monstrous slate of sin that He has "set aside, nailing it to the cross" (Col. 2:14). His cry of victory is now ours, as final today as when it first resounded atop Calvary. We, too, are free, for "it is finished!"

 "There is therefore now no condemnation for those who are in Christ Jesus" (Rom. 8:1). Meditate on what this means for you today.

The Word of Confidence

Then Jesus, calling out with a loud voice, said,
"Father, into your hands I commit my spirit!"
And having said this he breathed his last.—Luke 23:46

 THESE LAST SIX DAYS, we have pondered Christ's six hours on the cross; as we come to the end of His suffering, my mind goes back to a scene in Gethsemane the night before. Jesus is there with His heavy-eyed disciples who are fighting to stay awake while He faces His anguish alone. Returning to awaken them a third time, Jesus says to them, "See, the hour is at hand, and the Son of Man is betrayed into the hands of sinners" (Matt. 26:45).

"Into the hands of sinners . . ."

How remarkable that our Lord, maker of heaven and earth, would willingly allow Himself to fall into the proud, contemptible hands of His own creation—to be tortured, persecuted, reviled, and ultimately executed. Yet here, with His final breath, He makes it clear that He has not died a martyr's death at the hands of men. His life—like ours—is in the "hands" of God.

We so often find ourselves chafing against second causes—those people, circumstances, and events that seem to be wrecking our lives, making things so difficult and unbearable for us. But ultimately, we are not in the hands of other people and their sinful designs. We are not in the hands of chance or circumstance. As children of God, saved by His perfect sacrifice, our lives are in the safe care and keeping of our heavenly Father, and no one is able to "snatch" us from those hands (John 10:28).

Find rest in this assurance today. Find hope in the midst of opposition, confusion, and despair. There is life in these hands. Eternal life. Even in death.

 Jesus died as He lived, fully trusting His Father.
Consider that your final hours, too, will reveal where
you have truly placed your confidence.

Carried by Angels

"The poor man died and was carried by the angels to Abraham's side."—Luke 16:22

ANGELS APPEAR MORE OFTEN IN SCRIPTURE than you might think; they perform many wonderful roles in our lives as "ministering spirits sent out [by God] to serve for the sake of those who are to inherit salvation" (Heb. 1:14).

One of their most comforting responsibilities toward us takes me back to my early twenties when I was leading a summer day camp for elementary school children. We had taken the day off to celebrate Independence Day, and several of our camp counselors decided to spend the day hiking in the Blue Ridge Mountains. I'll never forget receiving the call letting me know that one of those college students—a young woman—had slipped on the path and tragically had fallen 150 feet or more to her death.

You can imagine our anguish, not only at this heartrending loss but also in trying to explain to the children the next day why Miss Vicki wouldn't be there anymore. The Lord brought to mind this passage in Luke's gospel where Jesus spoke of angels carrying a man to heaven when he died. I shared with the children that when it looked to us like Miss Vicki had slipped and fallen on that hiking trail, what we couldn't see was that God had sent His angels to go get Miss Vicki and carry her to Jesus.

What may sound like wishful thinking for young children's imaginations is actually a sweet reality for every true believer in Christ, as we face our own deaths as well as those of our loved ones and friends. When you find yourself frightened by such thoughts and uncertainties, know that none of God's children must walk unaccompanied into the next life. His powerful angels, after faithfully serving, protecting, and ministering to us on earth, will escort us into the presence of God to live with Him forever.

Thank God for the ministry of His angels in your life as a believer—in unseen ways during your days on earth, all the way to your final journey to His presence.

Whatever He Says

"My Father, if it be possible, let this cup pass from me; nevertheless, not as I will, but as you will."—Matthew 26:39

 ONE OF THE SWEET BY-PRODUCTS of spending time alone with God in His Word and prayer is that our lives are brought into submission to God and His will. Yes, *submission.*

Now I'll be the first to admit that the "S" word is not one of the most popular in our free-spirited era. The idea of submitting to the control or will of another is utterly contrary to our sinful human nature.

When we became children of God, however, we received a new nature, one that recognizes God's right to rule over us. Yet even though our *spirit* now wants to obey Him, our *flesh* (our natural inclination) wars against our spirit and still wants to have its own way.

As a result, there are times when we resent, resist, or run from what God has brought into our lives. We view difficult, annoying people and circumstances as a problem, resenting the pressure they place upon us. In so doing, we end up pushing against God Himself, resisting His sovereign choices and purposes for our lives.

But when we place ourselves under the ministry and microscope of His Word, our resistance is exposed. We see the wise hand of God that is acting for our good. We realize the folly of trying to "box" with God.

Whether the problem is earth-shattering or a mere blip on the radar screen, the real issue often comes down to this: "Do I trust that God is wise and good? And will I submit to His hand and purposes in my life?"

 Is there an issue (big or small) in your life where your flesh is resisting the will of God? As you meet with Him, ask Him to bring you to a place of wholehearted submission and trust, until you can say, "Yes, Lord! Not as I will, but as You will."

Washed in His Word

I have stored up your word in my heart,
that I might not sin against you.—Psalm 119:11

 GOD HAS PROVIDED MANY DIFFERENT "means of grace" to help us in the process of becoming "holy, [as he is] holy" (1 Peter 1:16)—activities and provisions that put us in a place where we can receive and experience His sanctifying, transforming grace in our lives. Over the next several days, I want to highlight six of these "means of grace" that have been particularly significant in my own walk with God.

The first is *the Word of God*. His Word has the power not only to protect us from sin but also to purify us when we do sin. As I read Scripture, I often pray that the Lord will wash me with His Word (Eph. 5:26), that He will use it to purify my mind, my desires, and my will.

In addition to its cleansing properties, the Word also has the power to renew our minds, transform us into the image of Christ, and infuse us with Christian graces. When Paul said farewell to the leaders of the church in Ephesus, he commended them "to God and to the *word of his grace*, which is able to build you up and to give you the inheritance among all those who are sanctified" (Acts 20:32).

The Word of God is a vital means of grace in every believer's life. None of us can withstand the assault of temptation and the encroachment of the world apart from a steady intake of the Word of God. Nor can we feed on a diet of worldly pursuits and unholy entertainment, then expect to develop or maintain a pure heart. But reading, studying, memorizing, and meditating on Scripture will help guard your heart from sin and stimulate your growth in grace.

Mark it down—your progress in holiness will never exceed your relationship with the holy Word of God.

 How would you describe your relationship with the Word?
What are some practical ways to make it a more consistent
influence in your life?

Cover or Confess?

Whoever conceals his transgressions will not prosper, but he who confesses and forsakes them will obtain mercy.—Proverbs 28:13

 WE CANNOT SIN AGAINST GOD AND JUST MOVE ON as if nothing's happened, without our spiritual growth being stymied. We cannot prosper spiritually until we humbly acknowledge our sin before God and, where necessary, to others. This is why *confession* is such an important means of grace in our lives.

David knew from painful experience what it was like to live under the weight of unconfessed sin: "When I kept silent [about my sin], my bones wasted away through my groaning all day long. For day and night your hand was heavy upon me; my strength was dried up as by the heat of summer" (Ps. 32:3–4). Not until he was willing to step into the light and uncover his sin did David experience the joy of being forgiven and clean once again.

Surely you know what it feels like to be weighed down under the heavy load of a guilty conscience, with all its physical, emotional, mental, and spiritual consequences—I certainly do. Like David, you can be freed from that burden—every last, draining ounce of it—through confessing your sin to God.

Because of Christ's sacrifice on the cross for our sin, God is willing to cover with His mercy every sin that we are willing to uncover. But He will ultimately expose every sin that we are unwilling to bring into the light.

What a wonderful provision God has made for us to apply the cleansing blood of Jesus to our defiled consciences, and to receive mercy as we humble ourselves and confess our sin—to God, as well as to those we have sinned against and to others who may be part of His restorative process in our lives: "Confess your sins to one another," His Word says, "and pray for one another, that you may be healed" (James 5:16) . . . that you may experience grace.

 Take the opportunity right now to bring any unconfessed sins into the light—to exchange the lead weight of guilt for the liberating freedom of a clear conscience.

The Table of the Lord

As often as you eat this bread and drink the cup,
you proclaim the Lord's death until he comes.
—1 Corinthians 11:26

 A THIRD MEANS OF GRACE IN A BELIEVER'S LIFE is the vital, sacred practice of Communion—the Lord's Supper. Participating in this time of corporate remembrance and proclamation of Christ's death provides a regularly scheduled opportunity—not to mention a powerful incentive—for self-examination. Scripture warns us, "Let a person examine himself" before partaking of the elements (1 Cor. 11:28), making sure our consciences are clear before God and others, judging ourselves so we will not come under the chastening hand of God.

I remember arriving at church one Sunday morning and noticing that we would be celebrating Communion during the service. No sooner had I taken my seat than the Lord brought to mind a situation that had taken place months earlier involving one of the senior members of our church. I had handled a particular issue in a way that I sensed could have wounded the spirit of this older man. And though we'd never discussed it between us, I had felt awkward around him ever since.

As we began to sing in preparation for taking Communion, I slipped out of my seat, crossed over to the other side of the sanctuary where he was sitting, and knelt by his side. I knew before I could freely partake, I needed to clear my conscience with this brother, expressing my sorrow to him over what I had done, as well as my desire to be right with him.

Communion offers us a sacred moment to see ourselves as we really are, then receive Christ's boundless mercy that covers every sin. Experience it as an instrument of grace.

 Let Him do His cleansing, restoring work as you come before Him in humility and honesty today. And consider how you might experience a greater measure of grace as you remember Christ in your observance of the Lord's Supper in the future.

Sound in Body

Exhort one another every day, as long as it is called "today," that none of you may be hardened by the deceitfulness of sin.—Hebrews 3:13

 As CHRISTIANS, we have not been left alone to deal with our sin. God has graciously put us within a group of believers who are called to look out for one another and to stand together against the enemies that would threaten our spiritual strength and stamina. This family—the body of Christ—is another wonderful provision, a vital means of grace, that God has given to help us in our pursuit of holiness.

This is why it is so essential for every believer to be in a committed relationship with a Christ-centered local church. Because while each of us is accountable to God for our personal holiness, He never intended that we should wage our battle single-handedly.

Is this an admission that we are weak and vulnerable? Yes, it is. I *am* weak. So are you. And the prideful independence that keeps us from taking off our mask and getting real before others is the same pride that inevitably causes us to fall into sin. Humbling ourselves by letting others into our lives and allowing them to help us and hold us accountable will release the sanctifying, transforming grace of God in our hearts. We need this kind of help from others; they need it from us, as well.

And not just on Sundays. For as the above verse from Hebrews 3 suggests, it takes less than twenty-four hours for our hearts—for any of us—to become hardened or deceived by sin. None of us can afford to be without the consistent, day-in, day-out accountability of our brothers and sisters in Christ.

 You and I need the support of our Christian family every day of the week, if we are to make it spiritually. How could you tap into this necessary resource in the next twenty-four hours?

Redemptive Measures

You are to deliver this man to Satan for the destruction of the flesh, so that his spirit may be saved in the day of the Lord.—1 Corinthians 5:5

 FOR THE LAST SEVERAL DAYS, we've been focusing on some of the different "means of grace" God has placed in our lives to keep us pursuing holiness. We've seen the sanctifying role of His Word, confession of sin, participation in the Lord's Supper, and daily engagement with other believers as part of the church, the body of Christ.

One important aspect of our relationship with His body may seem harsh or intrusive to some, but it is actually a preemptive, purifying blessing. I'm talking about the practice of church discipline—removing unrepentant, so-called believers from the fellowship and spiritual protection of the church. When a believer refuses to deal with his sin privately, it eventually becomes a public matter that requires the involvement and intervention of others in the body.

I recall attending a church that was exercising the final stages of discipline with two members of their congregation. As the situation was being addressed from the pulpit, I was reminded again of the seriousness and the consequences of sin—*all* sin, *my* sin. As the church grieved the hardened, unrepentant hearts of two of its members, I remember being filled with a fresh, healthy fear of the Lord, as well as a renewed longing for Him to guard my heart and keep it responsive and repentant.

The fact that so few churches practice the biblical process of church discipline (as described in 1 Cor. 5, Matt. 18, and elsewhere) has allowed every form of habitual sin, immorality, and ungodliness to flourish in the church. As distasteful as church discipline sounds and as painful as it can be to watch, we need this means of grace—for our own sakes, for the sake of fallen believers, for the purity of the whole body, and for the glory of God.

 How could the thought of corporate discipline and public exposure be a blessing and a means of grace to the body? To those living in flagrant disregard of God's Word? To you?

No Pain, No Gain

Before I was afflicted I went astray,
but now I keep your word.—Psalm 119:67

 NO ONE WANTS TO SIGN UP for the school of suffering. But suffering can be a powerful instrument of spiritual growth—another, highly effective means of grace. In fact, it's fair to say that the pathway to holiness always involves suffering of one kind or another. No exceptions or shortcuts.

When our lives are all roses with no thorns, all sun with no clouds, we tend to become spiritually complacent and careless, neglecting serious self-examination and confession. But affliction has a gritty, almost inescapable quality that strips away the stubborn deposits of selfishness and worldliness that can build up over the course of everyday life.

Suffering happens for different reasons. Sometimes it is God's *chastening* response to our sin, as He disciplines us "for our good, that we may share his holiness" (Heb. 12:10). It may also come in the form of *pruning*, cutting away unnecessary or unproductive twigs and branches from our lives so that we may "bear more fruit" for His glory and the fulfillment of our purpose in life (John 15:2). Often our suffering is simply the unavoidable pain associated with living in a fallen world that awaits "with eager longing" our final deliverance from the curse of sin (Rom. 8:19).

Regardless of its cause—and despite its discomfort—affliction remains a gracious gift from the hand of God, who loves and disciplines us in order to purge us from our sin and sanctify our hearts. As the apostle Peter exhorts, "Since therefore Christ suffered in the flesh, arm yourselves with the same way of thinking, for *whoever has suffered in the flesh has ceased from sin*" (1 Peter 4:1). And that is worth every "means of grace." Even this one.

 What have you learned from adversity that you might not have learned in any other way? Thank God for the fruit He has brought about in your life through suffering.

Watch Out

See to it that no one takes you captive by philosophy and empty deceit, according to human tradition, according to the elemental spirits of the world, and not according to Christ.—Colossians 2:8

YOU'VE PROBABLY HEARD THE STORY from Greek mythology of the Trojan horse—the deceptive gift that ended up being filled with Greek soldiers who emerged unexpectedly to capture the city of Troy. That account now has an application in the world of technology. A "Trojan horse" is a computer program that appears to be harmless and legitimate but, when opened, begins deleting files and destroying information. What appears to be a safe, useful tool can end up crashing your whole system.

Deception. Danger. The infection of a healthy unit that was once whole and functional. This threat applies to more than computer software; it is one of the consistent warnings of the New Testament, as seen in the many letters from the apostles to the early churches under their care. They understood that the potential for believers' hearts and minds to be compromised by doctrinal and spiritual error was not only great but extremely insidious. Sneaky, sinister, and often imperceptible to most.

The same is true today. Spiritual "infection" in a believer or in the church can come through traditions, through friends, through the continual drip of a secular world system that constantly presents to us "a different gospel" (Gal. 1:6). Satan doesn't care how he deceives you—appealing to your emotions, your intellect, your awe of the impressive—as long as in the end you don't *believe* the truth, don't *act* on the truth, and don't *spread* the truth to others.

So be alert. Stay discerning. Be teachable. Get grounded in God's Word. Stay close to Christ. Keep on your guard. Don't think it couldn't happen to you.

Can you think of any examples of doctrinal or spiritual error that many find appealing today? How can you not only guard against spiritual deception yourself but protect your children and others from its influence?

Above and Beyond

"But I say to you who hear, Love your enemies,
do good to those who hate you, bless those who curse you,
pray for those who abuse you."—Luke 6:27–28

MANY PEOPLE CONSIDER THE PROCESS of forgiveness complete once they've identified the people who have wounded them and have declared to their own satisfaction that they have forgiven them of their sin, that they've released them from their debt. But I believe the Scripture leads us to do something further, as Jesus clearly instructs us in Luke 6—something deeper, something even more healing and courageous.

As you think about those who have hurt or offended you, ask yourself if you have actively done good to them, expressed love to them, prayed for them—blessed them.

Or would it be more honest to say, even after considering yourself forgiving toward them, that you have *withheld* love from them, resented them, and stayed angry at them? Have you been bad-mouthing your ex-mate to your children, for example? Have you put up walls toward that annoying neighbor or that coworker who ridicules you for your beliefs? Have you given negative reports about that person who painted you in a bad light to your friends? Have you subtly retaliated against the in-law or sibling who has made your life difficult? Have you chosen the silent treatment toward your spouse, disengaging emotionally rather than pressing through to restored oneness?

To be sure, there are certain circumstances where it would not be wise or appropriate to reach out to or establish a relationship with an offender. But the business of forgiveness is not complete until you've let God fashion His love in your heart toward those who have sinned against you, until you have been willing to show them the grace He has extended to you through Christ.

How have you responded toward the person or the people you need to forgive? Ask God to show you how you could step out in faith and bless them for Christ's sake, as He has blessed you.

Suitable for Framing

Ascribe to the LORD, O families of the peoples,
ascribe to the LORD glory and strength!—Psalm 96:7

 MY REFRIGERATOR SERVES AS A BACKDROP for photos of my friends and their families. Mounted in acrylic frames with magnets on the back, at times, the pictures have covered almost every square inch of available space. Out of curiosity I once counted them up and found nearly ninety families represented, boasting a total of some three hundred children (not to mention scores of grandchildren).

On occasion, I sit back to survey the "big picture." Nearly all the faces in these photos are smiling. Yet behind some of the near-perfect poses, I know there is more to these families. Some carry a burden in relation to the critical physical or spiritual condition of a family member. Some are in the process of relocating geographically or transitioning into a new stage of life. Some are enduring circumstances that are deeply painful or unpleasant.

Yet as I ponder the scene before me, I am struck afresh with the wonder and significance of *family*—for better or worse. If things aren't well at home, every other area of life is affected. God uses the gift and, at times, the vise of family relationships to shine a light on who we really are, to humble us, to teach, mold, and change us, to deepen our capacity for relationship with Him, and to fit us and others in our family for our ultimate Home.

As you consider *your* family and *your* home, remember that with every act of service, every encouraging word you speak, every sacrifice you make, you are laying a foundation, building a memorial that will outlive you. Most importantly, you are building a habitat for His presence, a place where He is worshiped and loved and through which His glory can be displayed.

 Regardless of how things may appear in photos,
no family is "picture perfect." How could you be
an instrument of grace in your home today?

Life on the Battlefield

For we do not wrestle against flesh and blood, but against the authorities, against the cosmic powers over this present darkness, against the spiritual forces of evil in the heavenly places.—Ephesians 6:12

 THE FIRST TIME WE HEAR OF THE AMALEKITES in any detail in Scripture, they are on the attack against Israel (Ex. 17:8)—unprovoked, soon after the Israelite deliverance from Egypt. This altercation would be only the first in a long series of ongoing skirmishes that would continue off and on until Esther's day, when the last of the Amalekite descendants were finally destroyed in Persia.

First Corinthians 10, in speaking of various Old Testament happenings, reminds us that "these things took place as examples for us" (verse 6). The cruel, ruthless attacks of the Amalekites on Israel are a picture (a type) of the spiritual adversity we face today. These ancient nomadic enemies of God's people are representative of the evil forces (the world, the flesh, and the devil) that continue to oppose us—often unprovoked, unannounced, and unrelenting.

I'm sure you can attest to this. You're going along, minding your own business, doing what you think God wants you to do, trying to be an obedient follower of Christ, when here comes this thought that opposes God's will and authority. Here comes an obstacle in your path. Here comes a person to discourage and deflate you. At this point, many suffer unnecessary defeat simply by being surprised that such an occurrence would happen to them.

You may have heard it said that "the Christian life is not a playground; it's a battleground." Yes, we have every reason to be confident that "he who is in [us] is greater than he who is in the world" (1 John 4:4), but that does not spare us from having to engage in the battle. Victory is ours, but immunity is not.

 How can the expectation of enemy attack help prepare you to deal with it and be victorious in the battle?

Try Praying for a Change

*And he told them a parable to the effect that they ought
always to pray and not lose heart.*—Luke 18:1

 A WOMAN I HAD NOT SEEN FOR MANY YEARS came
up to me at a wedding and said, "You saved my
marriage!" She reminded me that she had once
shared with me a concern in relation to her
husband's spiritual condition, and I had said to
her, "It's not your responsibility to change your husband; that's
God's responsibility. Tell your husband what's on your heart,
then back off and let God do the rest."

For *sixteen long years* she had prayed and waited, seeing little
evidence that God was hearing or answering her. Though her
husband professed to be a Christian, there was no fruit indicating
that he had a genuine relationship with the Lord.

Then "unexplainably," she said—after all those years—the
Spirit turned on the light and brought about a dramatic change
in her husband. It was as though he had come out of a coma.
All of a sudden, he couldn't get enough of the Word. He started
keeping a notepad with him to record what he was getting out of
his Bible reading. He even talked of selling his business to devote
more time to ministry.

"In the past," the woman said, "I could hardly get him out
of bed for breakfast. Now he's going to a men's prayer meeting
at 6:30 every morning!" There is no human explanation for
what happened to change this husband, except for a faithful
God and a persevering wife who decided to pray rather than
prod and provoke.

Are you tempted to "lose heart" about a situation you've
been praying about for years? Don't stop praying! The outcome
may not be identical in your life. But the same God who sustained
this woman and intervened in her husband's life in His way and
time is able to act on your behalf and to glorify Himself in your
most "hopeless" circumstance.

 *Who in your life are you most concerned about, in terms of
their spiritual openness and interest? How serious have you
been about praying for them?*

Extreme Exposure

"I had heard of you by the hearing of the ear, but now my eye sees you; therefore I despise myself, and repent in dust and ashes."—Job 42:5–6

THE CLOSER WE GET TO GOD, the more clearly we see ourselves as we really are. As long as we compare ourselves to others, we can always find someone who makes us feel good about how well we are doing. But when we step into the light of God's holiness, our lives are brought into sharp relief. What once may have seemed clean and pure suddenly looks soiled and tarnished. The pure light of His holiness exposes the nooks and crannies, the cracks and crevices of our innermost being.

Job, for example, was a God-fearing man. His lifestyle was above reproach. His suffering was not the result of any particular sin on his part, as his friends insisted must be the case. Suffering did, however, lift the lid off his heart, exposing a deeper level of depravity than he might otherwise have seen. It also drove him to a transformational encounter with God. As a result, Job was no longer just a good man, a religious man; now he was a broken man.

The prophet Isaiah had a similar experience. Struck with a vision of the holiness of God—holiness so intense that even the pillars in the temple had the good sense to tremble—he no longer saw himself in contrast to all the depraved people around him. From then on, he operated not out of natural strength or a sense of moral superiority but out of a deep awareness of his own sinfulness and neediness. Isaiah, too, was a broken man.

To know God, to live in His presence, and to be occupied with a vision of His holiness is to know how foolish and frail we are apart from Him; it is to be broken from our preoccupation with ourselves; it is to experience the cleansing, restoring power of Christ who was broken on the cross on our behalf.

What keeps the call to repentance and brokenness from being a depressing message? How could a greater degree of brokenness open up a whole new realm of grace and fruitfulness in your life?

Weed Killers

*Put away all filthiness and rampant wickedness
and receive with meekness the implanted word,
which is able to save your souls.*—James 1:21

 SCRIPTURE DESCRIBES A twofold sanctification process that involves "putting off" our old, corrupt, sinful way of life, and "putting on" the holy life that is ours through Christ. Another word for "putting off" is *mortification*, from a Latin word meaning "to kill" or "to put to death." This involves more than getting rid of things that are inherently sinful but also cutting off influences that fuel unholy thoughts and behaviors.

There was a season, many years ago, when the television became one of those influences in my life. Even though my viewing habits would have been considered temperate by most, I began to realize that the TV was a "weed" that was choking out holiness, dulling my spiritual senses, and diminishing my love and longing for God. The Spirit tugged at my heart about this issue for (I'm ashamed to admit it) months, but I resisted doing anything differently.

One day, I finally said, *"Yes, Lord,"* and agreed to "mortify" my flesh in this area. For me, this meant making a commitment not to watch TV anytime I was alone. The result was amazing. Within a short period of time, my love for God was rekindled, my desire for holiness renewed, and my spirit began to flourish once again.

I understand this may sound extreme and legalistic to some. And I don't want to make an absolute out of a personal standard. But whenever I have made exceptions to this commitment—such as watching news coverage of a major disaster or crisis—I've discovered how easy it can be to make greater allowances and slip back into old patterns that prove to be harmful to my soul. This is one activity, for me, that needs to stay "mortified" if I am going to pursue holiness. What's yours?

 Why are we so prone to defend choices that take us right to the edge of sin, yet so reluctant to make radical choices to protect our hearts and minds?

Secret Treasure

Show me your ways, O LORD, teach me your paths.
Lead me in your truth and teach me.—Psalm 25:4–5 NKJV

 ONE OF THE GREATEST DESIRES OF MY HEART and one of my most frequent prayers over the years is that I might know the ways of God. To know His thoughts, His feelings, His heart, and even His "secrets." To have His perspective on this world, on history, on current events, on the future, on work, on ministry, relationships, my family, the church—on everything. To know what brings Him joy and what causes Him to grieve. I want to know His ways!

I don't believe He *owes* me an explanation, and there are aspects of His ways that will remain hidden to us in this present life (Deut. 29:29). But I want to know everything about Him that He is willing to reveal.

That's why, before I begin to read God's Word in the morning, I often pray the above words of David from Psalm 25. This psalm goes on to tell us the kind of man or woman to whom God will reveal His ways: the *humble*—"He leads the humble in what is right, and teaches the humble his way" (verse 9); as well as the one who *fears the Lord*—"Him will he instruct in the way that he should choose" (verse 12); "The secret of the LORD is with those who fear Him, and He will show them His covenant" (verse 14 NKJV). What an awesome thought: that the God of the universe would confide in us and trust us with aspects of His character and ways that remain hidden to those who do not fear Him.

Are you hungry to know more of the Lord? Eager to grasp His will and His purposes? God's willingness to share His secrets with His creatures is evidence of His desire to have an intimate relationship and friendship with us. Come humbly and reverently. Let Him show you His ways.

 For at least the next few days, pray the words of Psalm 25:4–5 before you begin your daily Bible reading.

Willing to Whatever?

*"Why do you call me 'Lord, Lord' and
not do what I tell you?"*—Luke 6:46

 MANY PROFESSING CHRISTIANS go through life making decisions and responding to circumstances while rarely considering, "What does *God* want me to do? What does the Scripture say about this?" But to call Him "Lord" means choosing His will, His Word, and His ways above ours. We cannot call Him "Lord" and then proceed to run our own lives.

You may say, "If I live a surrendered life like that, does it mean I'll end up serving on the mission field? Or quitting my job? Or being led to bring my parents to live in our home? Or living all alone all my life?" Maybe. Maybe not. In a sense it doesn't really matter, because by saying "Yes, Lord," you will be given the grace to do His will—whatever it is—along with joy in the doing!

Being surrendered to the will of God will not look the same for everyone. For some, it may mean being happily married for half a century. For others it may mean remaining faithful in a difficult marriage to an unbeliever. Or being widowed and left to raise young children. Or *never* marrying.

It may mean parenting many children. Or few children. Or no children. It may mean making lots of money and using it for the glory of God. Or having only your essential needs met but choosing to be content with little. It may mean owning a large, lovely home and using it to bless and serve others. Or it may mean living in a two-room efficiency in a developing country.

Regardless of the details, what matters is saying, "Yes, Lord" and then doing whatever He says to do. Total surrender to Christ as Lord simply means submitting every detail and dimension of your life to His sovereign leading and control. And there's no safer, more blessed place to be.

 *You call Him "Lord." Can you say that you are
seeking to know and follow all that you know to be
true of His will and His Word?*

A Servant's Reward

She looks well to the ways of her household and
does not eat the bread of idleness.—Proverbs 31:27

 ONE OF THE THINGS THAT STRIKES ME MOST about the "virtuous woman" of Proverbs 31 is the fact that she is so utterly selfless. She isn't focused on advancing her career, padding her bank account, or being known for her personal accomplishments. To the contrary, she seems essentially unconcerned about her own interests, choosing instead to concentrate on how she can meet the practical needs of her husband and children as well as others in her community.

One might be tempted to call her an oppressed breed, the way many homemakers have been labeled today. And yet take a fresh look at her. She is well-dressed, has plenty of food to eat, and enjoys a well-ordered, emotionally stable life. She doesn't sit around worrying about the future or fearing what might go wrong. Instead she is secure and content. Her husband is crazy about her and remains staunchly faithful to her. When he's not reminding her that she is "one in a million" or bragging about her to his friends, her children are said to be honoring and praising her. Who wouldn't be overjoyed to have the same rewards?

But how did she attain all these benefits? Not by insisting that her husband roll up his sleeves and do his fair share of the household chores (although there's certainly nothing wrong with men helping out in the home!), but by choosing the pathway of servanthood—by making the needs of her family her chief priority, second only to her relationship with God.

We are never more like Jesus than when we are serving Him and others. There is no higher calling than to be a servant.

 Do you often find yourself dwelling on the ways others are not valuing, appreciating, and helping you? If you had a true servant's heart, what might you be thinking about instead?

Restoration Project

He restores my soul.—Psalm 23:3

 I MENTIONED YESTERDAY THE MANY REWARDS OF servant-hood, and they are truly many. But it's also true that serving others day in and day out can leave us physically fatigued, falling wearily into bed at night, stressed out, and hopelessly overwhelmed. And while we may think the cure would come from resting our tired body or getting away for a vacation, we've probably all had the experience of taking time off only to come back more exhausted than when we left.

Important as physical rest and breaks may be, I'm convinced that one of the biggest reasons we struggle to handle the rigors of day-to-day responsibilities is that our *spirits* are weary, our *souls* are in need of restoration. And the remedy for that is found in spending time in God's presence.

The restoration of our souls is a ministry of the Good Shepherd. The Hebrew word translated "restore" in Psalm 23 is a word most often translated "return" in the Old Testament. It speaks of God's people returning to Him, and of God returning to His people. The word suggests "movement back to the point of departure." The implication is that He restores our souls back to their original resting place—in Him—by means of His Word and His Spirit. For "times of refreshing . . . come from the presence of the Lord" (Acts 3:19).

So if you're "running on fumes" today, operating out of your own depleted resources, finding the least little demand more than you can handle, reacting to even minor annoyances with frustration and irritation, turn your heart heavenward and ask Him to restore your soul. Let Him fill you with Himself; receive fresh stores of grace; then let Him send you back out to serve with joy—out of the overflow of His life within you.

 Have you been neglecting the essential time you need alone with God? Return to your Shepherd, and let Him restore your soul.

Marbles or Grapes?

"Unless a grain of wheat falls into the earth and dies, it remains alone; but if it dies, it bears much fruit."—John 12:24

YEARS AGO, WHEN I WAS A COLLEGE STUDENT, I heard Pastor Ray Ortlund say, "Most churches are like a bag of *marbles*—all hard and clanging up against one another. Instead, we ought to be like a bag of *grapes*—squished together so that the juice of His Spirit may flow out through us." True Christian community is something few believers ever experience because it requires that each individual let go of self and allow his life to be poured out on behalf of others.

A seed has to go into the ground and *die* in order to produce fruit. What does that kind of "death" mean for us? It means a willingness to die to our own interests, our own reputation, our own rights, our own way of doing things, our own comfort, convenience, hopes, dreams, and aspirations. To die means to lay it all down. To give it all up. To let it all go.

This may seem difficult, perhaps even unthinkable, to our self-protective, individualistic, rights-oriented minds. But as Jesus went on to tell His disciples in this passage, "Whoever loves his life loses it, and whoever hates his life in this world will keep it for eternal life" (John 12:25).

What was Jesus saying? The only way to gain your life is to give it up. The only way to win it is to lose it. We think we are giving up so much by dying. But in reality, those who refuse to die are the ones who are giving up everything that really matters. When we choose the pathway of brokenness and humility, we are choosing to receive new life—His supernatural, abundant life—flowing in us and through us.

Is there some area of your life where you are clinging to your rights? According to John 12:24–25, what is the cost of holding on to your life, and what are the rewards of laying it all down?

Light in the Darkness

The unfolding of your words gives light; it imparts understanding to the simple.—Psalm 119:130

 I AM CONTINUALLY AMAZED at the deep well of God's Word —how He touches and teaches us in new, timely, and significant ways, sometimes completely out of the blue.

Kathy Ferguson was shockingly, unexpectedly widowed in her midforties, the result of a tragic automobile accident that claimed the life of her pastor husband, Rick. The loss, of course, was more raw than words can describe, not to mention the loss of direction that soon began settling in as she dared trying to imagine what the second half of her life would entail. "The afternoon," she said, "would not look like the morning."

One day several months later, the Spirit brought to her mind this well-known phrase from the Lord's Prayer: "Your will be done, on earth as it is in heaven" (Matt. 6:10 NASB). It was as though God was telling her—in His tender, loving way, at the moment she was ready to hear it—"Rick is doing My will in heaven; you're going to do My will on earth."

God's will for her, for this time, would not look the same as it had when she and her husband had married young, when they had served together for twenty-five years as pastor and wife. But God still had a plan for her. He had not abandoned her to either loneliness or uselessness. His will "on earth" was still hers to seek, find, explore, and experience.

Such is the power of the Word of God—to minister grace at our point of greatest need, to strengthen us with truth, and to direct and sustain our hearts through life's most difficult seasons. When we hear His Word, we hear His voice. And we are given the light we need to face another day.

 Expect Him to speak as you open the Scriptures today. Highlight a line or phrase that He particularly quickens to your heart.

Blame Game

But let each one test his own work . . . for each
will have to bear his own load.—Galatians 6:4–5

 I HAVE LISTENED TO HUNDREDS OF WOMEN tell me about their broken marriages. Frequently, they describe how their ex-mate's offenses destroyed the relationship. But offhand I cannot recall more than a small handful of instances in which a woman said, "I contributed to the breakup of my marriage through my wrong attitudes and responses."

Countless others have explained to me the circumstances that "caused" things like their indebtedness, their eating disorder, their immorality, or an estranged relationship with their parents. Only rarely do I hear them take personal responsibility for their own choices that fueled these issues in their lives.

That's because when we are angry, depressed, bitter, or fearful, our natural response is to shift at least some of the responsibility onto the people or circumstances that "made" us that way.

I'll never forget the day a middle-aged woman came to the platform to give a testimony during one of our revival conferences. She introduced herself as a therapist who had been practicing for twenty-two years. Her next words were even more to the point and deeply penetrating: "I want to repent before You, my God, and before you, my sisters, for leading you astray and for telling you lies—for not saying, 'You are solely and personally responsible for your own behavior, no matter what anyone else does.' I'm sorry."

The enemy tells us that if we take full responsibility for our own choices, we will be plagued with unnecessary guilt. (We're not talking about assuming responsibility for the sins and shortcomings of *others*.) But the truth is that only by accepting responsibility for our actions and attitudes can we experience His abundant mercy and be fully free from guilt.

 Which problems and difficulties in your life do you tend to blame on others? How would accepting responsibility for and repenting of any of your own wrong actions and reactions change your perspective?

The Loving Listener

He has sent me to bind up the brokenhearted,
to proclaim liberty to the captives and the opening of
the prison to those who are bound.—Isaiah 61:1

 THROUGH NEARLY FOUR DECADES OF MINISTRY, I have encountered more pain in human hearts and relationships than I would have thought possible. From the extremes of hearing a mother tell of her adult daughter's vicious murder at the hands of a stalker, to the more common but no less hurtful kinds of circumstances that leave many dealing with betrayal, abuse, anger, and conflict, my heart—like yours—aches at the thought of such injustice and pain. We can understand the natural inclination of those who have been wronged to wish upon their offenders at least a measure of what is deserved.

But if we are going to be true instruments of mercy in each other's lives, we must deal in truth—*God's* truth. We cannot afford to coddle and empower one another in our resentment, supporting our determination to exact payment from those who have sinned against us.

Scripture is clear that the cost of unforgiveness is great. None of us can expect to live at peace with Him or to experience His blessing in our lives if we refuse to forgive our debtors. To do so is to choke out His grace and allow Satan to "get an advantage of us" (2 Cor. 2:11 KJV).

The wounds that have been inflicted on us will never be healed if they are allowed to fester. In fact, they may worsen as infection sets in. Loving sympathy can provide temporary *relief*, but nothing short of true forgiveness can produce lasting *release*, as God wrests reconciliation from the jaws of brokenness, as He restores, redeems, and (ultimately) makes all things new.

 How have you benefitted from friends who not only sympathize with your pain but who love you enough to encourage you to choose the pathway of forgiveness? Do you need to offer that kind of encouragement to a friend who has been wounded by another?

Slow It Down

He makes me lie down in green pastures.
He leads me beside still waters.—Psalm 23:2

HAVE YOU EVER NOTICED that Jesus never seemed to be in a hurry? We never see Him hustling from place to place or doubling up His schedule after running behind. We never see Him *running* anywhere, for that matter. But we do see Him walking. We see Him seated by a well in Samaria and sitting down to teach His disciples. We read of Him reclining at meals and sleeping in the hull of a storm-tossed boat.

When you think about it, hurry is simply not Christlike.

And more often than not, hurry is the enemy of spiritual intimacy. It is a pace of life that is seldom conducive to godliness, to relationships, to marriage, to anything that ultimately matters to us.

So it's not surprising—though a world apart from the harried, breathless mindset we so often exhibit—to learn that the Lord would want to lead us to "green pastures" and "still waters" (literally, "waters of rest"). For like sheep, we don't know when we need to rest. Left to ourselves, we'll just keep going until we fall down from exhaustion. And yet the more hurried our pace, the less we will truly experience our "shepherd." He knows that we can't cultivate godly character and affections when we're constantly on the run, in the red, at high RPMs. Intimacy with God (and with others) requires time, stillness, waiting, and focused attention.

So expect Him to take you to those restful places—regularly, repeatedly—not to make you less productive but to renew your perspective, remind you what really matters, refresh your soul, slow down your racing pulse, and send you out to serve Him with joy.

Even with meals to prepare, errands to run, and a job to do, there are green pastures and still waters within reach. Let Him lead you there today.

He wants to lead you to green pastures and still waters.
What could be keeping you from enjoying that place of
inner peace and rest?

Secure Connection

He humbled you, causing you to hunger and then feeding you with manna . . . to teach you that man does not live on bread alone but on every word that comes from the mouth of the LORD.—Deuteronomy 8:3 NIV

 I'M CONVINCED THAT EVERY HUMAN BEING—whether married or single, young or old, rich or poor—has unfulfilled longings. Part of the purpose behind these longings is to help us learn that ultimate satisfaction and true security can never be found in people, things, or places. In fact, when we look to anything or anyone other than Christ for fulfillment, we are setting ourselves up for sure disappointment.

During my twenties and early thirties, I spent a dozen years traveling in full-time, itinerant ministry—on the road, year-round. "Home" was wherever I slept each night. I loved what I was doing, but often longed for a more settled, "normal" lifestyle, for the ability to put down roots and have a "nest," for relationships that weren't long distance. As the years progressed, I felt these longings more keenly. Occasionally, alone at night in yet another motel room, tears of self-pity would well up in my eyes.

But time after time, that "friend who sticks closer than a brother" (Prov. 18:24) would meet me, reminding me of His love, assuring me of His presence. I would be reminded that He is my "dwelling place" (Ps. 90:1), that the one who had "nowhere to lay his head" (Luke 9:58) understood the peculiar demands of my "gypsy" lifestyle because He had been there Himself. I came to see that it is a privilege to relinquish temporal fulfillment of my desires, in order to follow Jesus and find eternal fulfillment in Him.

Jesus knows and understands the deepest needs and longings of your heart. Learn to let those unfulfilled longings press you to His heart. And realize that those longings can actually become, in the words of Amy Carmichael, "material for sacrifice"—something you can offer up to the One who gave up everything for you.

 Would you seek Him as earnestly if you didn't have some unfulfilled longings? Are you more intent on having those longings fulfilled or on seeking the only One who can truly satisfy your heart?

God in the Dock

How long, O LORD? Will you forget me forever?
How long will you hide your face from me?—Psalm 13:1

 I HAVE COME TO BELIEVE THAT ALL BITTERNESS, at some level, is ultimately directed toward God. Though it may be cloaked in anger toward a particular person or group of people who have wronged us, we seem to know intuitively that God is big enough to deal with our problems—that He could take care of them if He wanted to.

Such experiences go against everything we've been led to believe about His goodness and fairness, everything we've painted in our minds about an even-handed God who always squares things in the end. But anger or resentment toward God, I believe, comes from having a faulty view of Him.

For example, you may feel that God has hidden Himself from you, or that you are not on His radar—that He couldn't care less about what you're going through. That's when you need to counsel your heart according to the truth of His Word, regardless of what your feelings may assert.

The truth is, He is going through it *with* you and *for* you.

I love the way Isaiah so tenderly describes God's dealings with the children of Israel, even when they were reaping the consequences of their own sinful choices: "In all their affliction he was afflicted" (Isa. 63:9). And in all your suffering, He suffers too.

If you are a child of God, He has not forgotten you! He is with you, not against you. Right in the middle of your circumstances and pain. Helping you. Loving you. Hurting with you. Making you more dependent on His grace and power. Your God is fully engaged, dealing wisely with your difficulties, turning even the most agonizing circumstances into opportunities that will refine and purify you, make you more fruitful in His service, and magnify Himself through your life.

 What has God revealed about Himself—His heart, His ways, His purposes—in His Word that can steady and sustain your heart in times of adversity?

How Wonderful?

*And as he came out of the temple, one of his disciples
said to him, "Look, Teacher, what wonderful stones
and what wonderful buildings!"*—Mark 13:1

 HEROD'S TEMPLE IN JERUSALEM was still under
construction when Jesus walked past it in those final
days before His trial and crucifixion. And though
it wouldn't be completed for another thirty years,
any passerby could already tell: this temple was an
architectural wonder of the ancient world.

Oh, how impressed we can be with big buildings, big shows,
and big displays. Our hearts are too often dazzled by outer
demonstrations of success, rather than being focused on what
really matters—the condition underneath the fancy exterior.

That's why the passages and events leading up to this verse
at the beginning of Mark 13 are so instructive to us, revealing
the things that matter most to God. Jesus had just defined the
hallmarks of the law in two summary points: devoted love for
God and sacrificial love for others (12:28–31). He had rebuked
the religious leaders for wanting the "best seats in the synagogues
and the places of honor at feasts" (12:39). He had praised a poor
widow who deposited her last two coins in the collection box,
quietly outdoing the pretentious giving practices of those who
were well-to-do but bankrupt-of-spirit (12:41–44).

And yet knowing all these truths, why are we—like that
talkative disciple in verse 1 above—still so enamored with what
parades around us as "wonderful," when in reality it houses
hypocrisy and greed? And why do we work so diligently to guard
our *own* "wonderful" exteriors, often harder than we seek to
maintain purity and integrity of heart underneath?

Jesus explained to His disciple that the great temple buildings
he so admired would be destroyed and there would not be left
"one stone upon another" (13:2). A reminder to us to glory only
in that which is pure and enduring.

 *What stirs up the most wonder and amazement in you—
things that are visibly impressive, or those internal qualities
that honor and please the Lord?*

Children of the Lord

But I want you to be wise as to what is good
and innocent as to what is evil.—Romans 16:19

 BY MOST STANDARDS, I had an unusually sheltered upbringing. Believe it or not, I don't recall ever hearing a word of profanity before graduating from high school. Due to some intentional choices my parents made for our family, I knew almost nothing about the popular movies or television programs of the day.

But by God's grace and the influence of godly parents, by the time I headed off for college, I was blessed with some rare gifts: I knew the difference between right and wrong. I had been given a solid overview of the Bible. I'd hidden large portions of Scripture in my heart, had a basic understanding of the major doctrines of Christian faith, and could sing from memory all the stanzas of many theologically rich hymns.

Even more important than "knowing" all these things, I had a vital, growing relationship with the Lord Jesus—a relationship that would sustain me when I was out on my own and would motivate me to want to make God-honoring choices once I was outside the protective walls of our home. The "faith of our fathers" had become my own.

I'm not boasting about any of these things. I cannot take any credit for them at all. But I share them to remind you that children will often cultivate an appetite for what they are fed in their earliest, formative years and for that which they know claims the true affections of their parents.

Only the grace of God can cause the light to go on in the hearts of kids raised in even the most godly families. However, I'm convinced that you can't underestimate the value of children growing up in an environment where parents love God fervently and where they prize what is pure, good, and eternal.

 How are you infusing truth into your children's hearts and minds?
Are there any influences in your home that are countering that input?
If you don't have children of your own, pray for some parents you
know who want their children to love and follow Christ.

A Person of Few Words

*A fool gives full vent to his spirit, but a wise man
quietly holds it back.*—Proverbs 29:11

I REMEMBER READING ABOUT A NEW JERSEY TEEN, Brett
Banfe, who embarked on a yearlong vow of silence.
He and his friends wondered what it would be like not
to speak for an entire day, and Brett decided to extend
the experiment to an entire year. He figured out a way
to communicate sparingly with a few electronic gadgets and—
assuming the reports are true—*he made it*, breaking his silence
with a Shakespeare quote at a scheduled press conference
(followed by twenty minutes of nonstop talking)! You can be sure
it wasn't easy. In fact, after reading about Brett's feat, I decided
to take a vow of silence myself—for just forty hours. (I was alone
the whole time, though I confess to talking to myself a couple
of times!)

Reminds me of the monk who joined a monastery where he
was allowed to say only two words every ten years. At the end of
the first ten years, he exclaimed, "Bed hard!" After the second
ten years, he declared: "Food bad!" Finally, ten years later, he
blurted out, "I quit!" To which his superior responded, "I'm not
surprised. All he did for the past thirty years was complain!"

Holding our tongues is no small challenge. We so easily
say whatever comes into our heads, spewing out everything
we think or feel. We feel justified in expressing our opinions, in
venting our frustration or anger or discouragement or . . . . But
according to God's Word, spouting off whatever one thinks or
feels is a characteristic of a fool.

Proverbs 10 puts it this way: "When words are many, trans-
gression is not lacking, but whoever restrains his lips is prudent"
(verse 19). Of course, no amount of self-effort is sufficient to
restrain our words. We need the indwelling power of the Spirit
to rein in our hearts, our thoughts, and our tongues.

*Ask the Lord to put a "governor" on your tongue today, and to
enable you to speak only words that reflect the heart of Christ.
If you feel the need to "vent," tell the Lord what's on your mind,
rather than blurting it out to others.*

Blessed Beggars

*"Blessed are the poor in spirit, for theirs
is the kingdom of heaven."*—Matthew 5:3

IF WE WERE ASKED TO DESCRIBE what kind of people are "blessed," I doubt we would start at the same place Jesus did in these first words from His "Sermon on the Mount." But He came to introduce a whole new economy of blessing—a radically different way of thinking about life.

The Greek language, in which the New Testament was originally written, has two different words that Jesus could have chosen to speak of someone being "poor." The first word suggests someone who lives just below the poverty line, who is always having to scrimp and scrape to survive, who somehow makes ends meet, but just barely. *That's not the word Jesus chose.* He used another word that means a "beggar"—a person who is utterly, absolutely destitute and who has no hope of surviving unless someone reaches out a hand and pulls him up.

"Blessed" are the *beggars,* Jesus said—the broken ones, those who recognize that they are spiritually destitute and bankrupt, who know they have no chance of survival apart from God's intervening mercy and grace. In response to their desperate need, He lavishes them with the riches of His kingdom.

You and I will never meet God in revival and experience the fullness of His blessing in our lives until we first meet Him in *brokenness*, acknowledging our spiritual poverty—that we have nothing and we are nothing apart from Him. Our families will never be whole until husbands and wives, moms and dads, and young people have been broken. Our churches will never be the vibrant witness God intended them to be until their members—pastors and laypeople alike—have experienced true brokenness. Then—and only then—will come true blessing.

*When have you been most conscious of your spiritual poverty,
your utter dependence on God's grace? How can you keep that
sense, even when not in the midst of desperate circumstances?*

Help Is on the Way

Comfort, comfort my people, says your God. Speak tenderly to Jerusalem, and cry to her that her warfare is ended, that her iniquity is pardoned.—Isaiah 40:1–2

ISAIAH 40 MARKS A DISTINCT TURNING POINT in the prophet's message—from one of warning and coming judgment for the nation's sins, to one of comfort, hope, and promises of deliverance.

Seeing this shift with the advantage of hindsight and our knowledge of history, the pieces all line up. Roughly a century later, the Babylonians would swoop into Jerusalem and haul the people of Judah away as captives, where they would remain for seventy years before being released and allowed to return home. Isaiah was right.

But to those who originally heard his message, no prediction could have seemed more outlandish. The *northern* kingdom of Israel was the one in trouble, having been overtaken by the Assyrians. Judah, the southern kingdom, was fine. They were special. What could possibly happen? Yet here was God, speaking though His prophet, promising comfort to people who hadn't even been through affliction yet.

What a stunning picture this gives us of God's amazing providence—His ability to look ahead, know exactly what is coming, and make provision for us before we even get there. He is not only a God who can help us handle our current issues and pressures but One who has already prepared comfort, help, and blessing for problems that aren't even on our horizon.

Perhaps things are going pretty well for you right now. Be thankful! Be assured that whatever difficulties you may face down the road will not catch God by surprise; He has already planned ahead to provide for your needs. Through the redeeming work of Christ on the cross, He has gone where you cannot see to give you comfort you do not yet know you need.

Are you expending emotional energy, fearing the future or trying to figure out your own rescue plan? Your God has already made provision for your comfort, pardon, and ultimate deliverance—both now and in all that lies ahead.

Squeezed by Circumstances

So we do not lose heart. . . . For this slight momentary affliction is
preparing for us an eternal weight of glory beyond all comparison.
—2 Corinthians 4:16–17

 I REMEMBER TALKING YEARS AGO with a young mother who had a two-year-old child and one-year-old twins, and who said to me with a sigh, "I was never an impatient person—until I had these twins!"

She believed what most of us have believed at one time or another: the reason why we're the way we are is because someone or something has made us that way. If our circumstances were different—our upbringing, our environment, the people around us—*we* would be different. More patient, more loving, more content, easier to live with.

But if our circumstances make us what we are, then we are all victims. And that's just what the enemy wants us to believe. Because if we are victims, then we are not responsible; we can't help the way we are. God says, however, that we *are* responsible, not for the failures of others but for our own responses and our own lives.

Truth is, our circumstances do not *make* us what we are; they merely *reveal* what we are. They "squeeze" us, forcing what's on the inside to come out. As I gently shared with that exasperated mother, "The fact is, you actually *were* an impatient person before having twins. You just didn't realize how impatient you were, until God brought a set of circumstances into your life to show you what you were really like—so He could change you into someone who looks a whole lot more like Him!"

We've been deceived into thinking we would be happier if we had a different set of circumstances. But we can trust our wise, loving, sovereign God to work out His plan for our lives by using those very circumstances to show us our need and to make us desperate for His grace.

What have you been blaming on the people, problems, and
uncertainties around you? Ask God how He wants to use your
circumstances to show you your heart and to bring you to a
place of greater dependence on Him.

Healthy Proportions

I discipline my body and keep it under control, lest after preaching to others, I myself should be disqualified.—1 Corinthians 9:27

FEW PEOPLE NATURALLY LOVE THE THOUGHT of being disciplined, though we may desire the positive results that it produces. But there are no shortcuts—discipline is something we must embrace if we want to experience its sweet fruit. Christ is looking for *disciples*—those whose body, soul, and spirit are disciplined to forsake the world and follow Him.

This includes *physical discipline*, which seems relatively unimportant to some but is necessary for effective spiritual service. I have never been athletically inclined and have always disliked physical exercise. My idea of exercise is reading a book or talking on the phone—then getting up to eat! But I have found that if I am intemperate in my daily physical habits—diet, exercise, sleep—I become vulnerable in other areas of my life. If I am unwilling to be disciplined in the most basic areas of my body, what makes me think I will be disciplined on other fronts that carry even greater implications and consequences—areas such as sexual purity?

When my body is not under control, I can count on a lot of other things getting out of control—my attitudes, my tongue, how I use my time, and how I treat others. On the other hand, when I say no to my body and make it do what it doesn't want to do—such as physical exercise and moderate eating habits—I experience greater freedom to be the servant of Christ in other matters.

Catering to our flesh makes our spirits dull and insensitive to the Spirit of God. But by denying our flesh, we develop an increased appetite for God and our spirits are strengthened to become more alert, more sensitive and responsive to His Spirit.

How have you seen this connection between your physical well-being and your spiritual health? What one thing could you do to give God greater control over your body today?

Finding True Love

Above all, keep loving one another earnestly,
since love covers a multitude of sins.—1 Peter 4:8

NANCY LINCOLN WAS A YOUNG WOMAN IN "LOVE" who soon found herself pregnant—and happy for the deeper bond she was sure a baby would create between her and her Manhattan-lifestyle boyfriend. But when the news didn't strike him the same way—when he issued an ultimatum to "choose me, or choose *that*"—she did what she thought she had to do. She opted for abortion.

In the end, of course—as almost always happens—she got neither her baby *nor* her man. Only after spiraling deeper into a lifestyle of partying and substance abuse did she finally look up and see her Savior and receive His grace and forgiveness.

When marriage followed shortly thereafter to a godly man she met in ministry, she couldn't bring herself to tell him about the abortion. He knew she had made a lot of wrong choices in her young life, but she didn't want him to know about this. One night, however, after three hours of sobbing attempts to share her secret, she finally managed to get the words out. And prayed he'd understand.

She didn't have to wait long. He took her in his arms, assured her that he forgave her, and promised he would always love her. "It was the first time in my life," she told me, "that I felt unconditional love. It was as though he was Jesus in the flesh at that moment."

A hunger for love motivates many to make desperate, short-sighted choices. The willingness of God's people to demonstrate His love and grace can keep them from going there and restore them after they fall.

Perhaps *you* are that hurting person—you've confessed and repented of your sin, but are still carrying a heavy burden of shame. It may be that coming into the light with a parent, mate, or other mature believer will allow you to experience His restoring grace in a whole new way.

 How could you be a channel of His love and grace to someone in your life who lives with shame and deep regret over past sins?

Love to Worship

"Therefore I tell you, her sins, which were many, are forgiven—for she loved much. But he who is forgiven little, loves little."—Luke 7:47

 HAVE YOU EVER KNOWN SOMEONE who worshiped the Lord with great abandon, who was unusually free to express his or her love to God? Perhaps you envy this kind of freedom. Or perhaps, on the other hand, you find yourself being critical of it—questioning both the motives and appropriateness of this kind of behavior.

Why is it so hard for some of us to express our love in worship? Perhaps it's because (as one writer likens it) we still have our "roof on" and our "walls up." We are not broken toward God (vertical) and man (horizontal). Pride causes us to erect barriers between ourselves and God, as well as between ourselves and others. It makes us so concerned about what people think of us that we are imprisoned to our inhibitions.

"But that's just my personality," someone might counter. "I'm naturally shy." To which I would respond: Is it really a matter of personality, or could it actually be more a matter of pride? When our personality is surrendered to the Holy Spirit, He will express the heart of God in and through us. We will no longer be self-conscious but entirely God-conscious.

True worship begins with *brokenness* and *humility* over what God reveals to us in His Word, which leads to genuine *repentance*, which in turn leads to *forgiveness*, which produces *freedom* from guilt and bondage, which then gives us a greater capacity to *love* and *worship* God. And of course, true love and worship lead us back around to a new level of brokenness, which keeps the whole supernatural cycle continually at work and in motion.

 Ask God to fill you with love for Him that flows out of a deep awareness of how much you have been forgiven, and to enable you to express your gratitude to Him in authentic, heartfelt worship.

Company Ready

Keep your conduct among the Gentiles honorable, so that when they speak against you as evildoers, they may see your good deeds and glorify God on the day of visitation.—1 Peter 2:12

 A FAMILY I KNOW—with six children living at home—had been trying to sell their house for a year. Sometimes they would go for weeks without anyone wanting to see it. Then all of a sudden, the real estate agent would call and say, "Can we show your house in thirty minutes?" You can imagine the mad dash that ensued to get the place presentable.

In those frantic moments, my friends became adept at transforming a "lived-in" home into a showcase—in record time! The mom learned to stash laundry, dirty dishes, and other assorted household items in places that prospective buyers were unlikely to look—like the clothes dryer or the back of the family Suburban in the garage.

How would *you* feel if the doorbell rang right now, and you discovered you had a surprise visit from distant relatives? Would you have to scramble to avoid embarrassment? If you're like me, you'd probably have some closets and drawers you wouldn't want them to open. Unless you've just finished your spring-cleaning, chances are you'd be hoping your guests didn't look closely enough to see the accumulated dust, the streaked windows, or the cobwebs in the corners.

If we feel that way about our homes, what about our *hearts*? As Christians, we are called to maintain lives that can be "toured" by outsiders at any time without embarrassment, always "company ready" and open for inspection. A commitment to holiness calls us to have a life, by the grace of God, that can stand up to unannounced scrutiny—whether by God or others—even in the hidden places where outsiders might not think to look.

 Are the "closets and corners" of your life ready for "company"? What do your downtimes look like, those moments when the public persona is turned off, the doors are closed, and no one (humanly speaking) is watching?

Casting Call

*"Did I not tell you that if you believed
you would see the glory of God?"*—John 11:40

 MARTHA HEARD JESUS' PROMISE; she wanted to believe. But her brother had been dead for four days. How could God's glory possibly be seen in the midst of such huge, irreversible loss?

Sometimes the ways of God in our lives seem inconsistent with what we read in His Word. We hear that obedience to Him will cause us to "abound in prosperity" (Deut. 28:11). We hear He can turn a desert into "pools of water" (Ps. 107:35). We hear He makes a barren woman "the joyous mother of children" (Ps. 113:9). Yet the story doesn't always seem to go that way.

That's because we can't see the whole story—and, we think the story is all about us. We know what we want it to sound like and look like in *our* home, in *our* lives. But this is *God's* story He is writing and unfolding—His grand epic of redemption—and He is calling us to play a bit part, to participate in spreading His glory throughout the whole earth.

This doesn't mean pretending to be unaffected by grief, or denying the reality of unfulfilled longings. But it does mean we can press through with faith, because we know our good, wise, loving God has created the plot, and we know our role in His story is contributing to the overarching purpose of revealing His glory.

Are you willing to play the part He has written for you in His script? Are you willing to be delayed, upset, or inconvenienced for it? Because when the story has all been told, you will be able to sit back in your heavenly theater seat and see exactly how your one "simple" story line made perfect sense and contributed to the overall plot. You'll know that He had a deliberate purpose for everything. And you'll understand that God's will is exactly what we would choose if we knew what He knows.

 What circumstance are you facing that you would want to change if you were "writing the script" for your life? By faith, thank God that His script is perfect, and that in His way and His time you will see His glory revealed.

Moods and Attitudes

Now may the God of peace himself sanctify you completely,
and may your whole spirit and soul and body be kept blameless
at the coming of the Lord Jesus Christ.—1 Thessalonians 5:23

 MY RECOLLECTION OF THE YEAR I WAS TWELVE is that I cried the whole time—for no apparent reason. I remember at times being uncharacteristically reactionary and temperamental. As I look back on it, I understand better now some of the hormonal changes that were taking place as I was becoming a woman. But I have also learned that those changes were not an excuse for the moodiness and mouthiness that were part of my pattern during that year.

And it's still no excuse today.

As with other aspects of nature, God has designed our bodies to function in seasons and cycles. Certainly each season of life has its challenges. But didn't God make our bodies? Doesn't He understand how they work? Do things like menstrual cycles, hormones, pregnancy, menopause, and old age catch Him off guard?

As I get older, I keep reminding myself that it is inconceivable that the One who "formed my inward parts" and "knitted me together in my mother's womb" (Ps. 139:13) would fail to make provision for every season of life. God does not guarantee an easy or trouble-free life, but He has promised to meet all our needs and give us grace to respond to the challenges and difficulties of every season of life.

Paul's prayer at the end of 1 Thessalonians is not just for first-century believers. It is a prayer that can be claimed by any of us who face the battle to keep our bodies, emotions, moods, and conditions from justifying selfish, unloving behavior. "He who calls you is faithful; he will surely do it" (5:24).

 What fleshly, sinful responses have you been excusing,
thinking, "I just can't help it!" Thank God for the grace
and power He has provided to enable you to please Him
in every way, in every season.

Sacrifices of All Sizes

I appeal to you therefore, brothers, by the mercies of God, to present your bodies as a living sacrifice, holy and acceptable to God, which is your spiritual worship.—Romans 12:1

ONE PROMINENT PREACHER has suggested that most people think of full surrender to Christ as the equivalent of placing a $1,000 bill on the table and saying, "Here's my life, Lord, I'm giving it to You."

But the reality, he says, is more like God taking us to the bank to cash our $1,000 for quarters, then sending us out to distribute our daily sacrifices, twenty-five cents at a time.

God may be asking you simply to sacrifice the next thirty minutes to call your widowed mother-in-law who can be so negative. Or to sacrifice a Saturday afternoon to help a neighbor family pack their belongings for a move. Or to sacrifice three evenings this week to assist your child with a science project. Twenty-five cents here. Fifty cents there.

Sometimes the offerings may be more sizable—exchanging an expensive vacation or major purchase for a mission trip or church donation. And sometimes the Lord may ask for a sacrifice that makes all the others pale in comparison—quitting your job, raising a physically disabled child, releasing a son or daughter to serve Christ in an undeveloped country.

But whether these offerings fall into the category of twenty-five-cent pieces or hundred dollar bills, the sacrifices God asks of us are never pointless. Each one, whatever size, serves His higher, eternal purposes for our lives and the furthering of His kingdom. And knowing they are all for *Him* means that they are 100 percent eligible for being wrapped in His joy and purpose—none too small for meaning, none too great for giving.

What twenty-five-cent sacrifice could you make for Christ's glory in the next twenty-four hours? Is there any larger sacrifice He has been calling you to make? What could be the price of holding back?

Joined in Prayer

Now you are the body of Christ and
individually members of it.—1 Corinthians 12:27

 LOOK CAREFULLY AT THE LORD'S PRAYER (found with slightly different points of emphasis in Matt. 6 and Luke 11), and you will notice that not one singular pronoun is used—no mention of *me, my,* or *I.* Instead, you will see the words *our, us,* and *we*—collective, inclusive words that indicate this is not a self-centered prayer. That's because Jesus is not just teaching us how to pray but how to live—both in relationship with Him and with others.

Imagine you have a teenager at home who comes to you asking for something, a request that on its own is fine and appropriate. But perhaps this teen is not your only child, so you cannot be expected to act on this one isolated matter without considering how it affects the whole family.

In the same way, when we come to God, we are not merely approaching Him on our own, independent of others. We draw near to Him as one of many children, organically linked with brothers and sisters throughout the world—throughout His kingdom—with whom we share a Father. *Our* Father.

So when we pray for provision, we should be aware of needs beyond our own. When we pray for forgiveness, we should grieve over the sins of the entire church, realizing His mercy extends even to those we don't feel like forgiving ourselves. When we pray for our own spiritual protection, it is with the recognition that others are depending on us as well to bring their cause before the throne of God, where we stand as one, united in our great need of His preserving power and grace.

When we come to God in prayer, we don't come alone. That makes prayer both a great privilege and a great responsibility.

 How could this perspective affect the way you pray on a regular basis? When you pray today, rather than using mostly singular pronouns, try to remember to include the whole body, whether offering praise, confession, or petitions.

Returning Thanks

What thanksgiving can we return to God for you, for all the joy we feel for your sake before our God?—1 Thessalonians 3:9

 MY FRIENDS' GROWN SON JEFF was in a serious car accident, sustaining the kind of injuries that people don't just walk away from. Yet in response to fervent prayer by scores of family members and friends, God miraculously intervened with healing and rapid recovery.

On the long drive back from the St. Louis hospital to their home in Indiana, where his parents would be caring for him while he continued his recuperation, Jeff asked if they would tell him what happened the night of the accident and in the days immediately following. Through tears, they shared how they had rallied prayer support by phone as they drove to be near him, how his sister and two brothers had lain prostrate over his unconscious body, praying for God to spare his life, how friends had dropped everything to travel to his bedside and offer practical assistance.

Almost cutting them off in midsentence, Jeff asked his dad to pull into a Wal-Mart they were passing, then sent him in for thank-you notes, which he wrote the rest of the way home. He kept it up for days, eventually writing more than a hundred notes to those who had prayed for his physical recovery and—more importantly—his spiritual restoration.

I have found expressing gratitude to be a powerful antidote to a spirit of discouragement or entitlement. Taking time to jot a note of thanks provides a reminder of how richly blessed I've been and that I am a debtor to the Lord and to others who have extended grace to me. And on the receiving end, thank-you notes can be a wonderful means to minister grace to those who have blessed us.

We may never be able to adequately thank everyone who has played a part in our physical and/or spiritual health. But we can sure try. Starting today.

 Is the Spirit prompting you to write a thank-you note to some particular person? If possible, do it before the day is over.

Not Feeling Forgiving

Whenever our heart condemns us, God is greater than our heart, and he knows everything.—1 John 3:20

MANY PEOPLE who sincerely want to find themselves on the other side of forgiveness have bought into myths and misconceptions that have defeated their best attempts at following through. For the next few days, I'd like to help dismantle four common barriers that can easily keep us frustrated on our journey to relational freedom.

First is the assumption that *forgiveness and good feelings should always go hand in hand.* You may have genuinely trusted God to help you forgive your offender. But then the phone rings. Their birthday rolls around. A situation flares up where they handle a similar circumstance in the same insensitive way, and you feel your emotions start to heat up again.

That's when you might conclude, "I guess I haven't really forgiven because if I had, I wouldn't still feel this way." But forgiveness cannot be proven by our feelings, any more than it can be motivated or empowered by them. Forgiveness is a choice. And feelings often aren't. So it's quite possible to forgive someone the right way—God's way—and still have thoughts flash across your mind that seem to contradict the decision you made.

Forgiveness is not like planting tulip bulbs, where you never have to think about it again, and everything just naturally comes up nice and pretty in the spring. No, life goes on. Sometimes old feelings turn up when you're not expecting them, needing to be handled and replanted. But that doesn't negate what you've done. It simply gives you a new opportunity to let the Lord reign over your emotions. When you don't *feel* forgiving, that's when you just *keep* forgiving—by faith.

 What can enable you to keep forgiving when your emotions are resisting the choice?

Forgive and Forget?

In Christ God was reconciling the world to himself, not counting their trespasses against them, and entrusting to us the ministry of reconciliation.—2 Corinthians 5:19

 A SECOND MISCONCEPTION that clouds people's ability to live in forgiveness is that *forgiveness means forgetting*. But see it in terms of God's forgiveness of us. How could the One who knows everything forget anything? The Bible never says God *forgets* our sins, even though He has flung them "as far as the east is from the west" (Ps. 103:12). He simply has chosen not to "remember" them against us (Heb. 10:17), not to bring them back up again, or to accuse and condemn us with them.

Choosing not to remember isn't the same as forgetting. The fact that you have not been able to *forget* the offense doesn't necessarily mean you haven't *forgiven* it.

But why wouldn't God make this tidier? Couldn't He just purge these negative thoughts and painful memories from your mind? He could, of course. But He doesn't always choose to do so. One reason is that the memory of past hurts can provide a powerful platform for ministry to other hurting people. If you could not remember how it feels to be damaged by the blows of sin and injustice, how could you relate to the pain that people around you are experiencing?

Those memories help you realize how easy it can be for someone to give way to anger and resentment. They give you the ability to look others in the eye and say, "I've been there. I know it hurts terribly. But I also know that His grace is sufficient for you."

Thank God, of course, that He mercifully chooses to withdraw some past wounds from your memory bank. But thank Him, too, when He leaves behind enough to make you useful in ministering to others.

 Has the "forgive and forget" mindset caused you to live with any burdens that aren't yours to carry? How has God used the memory of painful experiences to make you more merciful to others?

Now and Forever

For Christ also suffered once for sins, the righteous for the unrighteous, that he might bring us to God.—1 Peter 3:18

I'VE HEARD PEOPLE SAY, "I'm moving toward forgiveness," implying their acceptance of a third subtle myth: *forgiveness is a process*. There's no question that coming to grips with what can sometimes be an awful offense (or offenses) is often a long, arduous journey. But I've watched people "working their way" toward forgiveness for years and years who simply never get there. In fact, I might go so far as to say that when forgiveness is seen as a work in progress, it seldom becomes a work in practice.

By God's grace, you can choose to forgive in a moment of time—to the level of your understanding at that point. And though additional time and hard work may be required to live out the implications of that choice, the reality of being released from the prison cell of your own unforgiveness can happen today as an established fact.

The choice for you to forgive is actually no more a slow-moving, wait-and-see process than God's forgiveness of you. Just as you were extended His grace in a moment of time, you can extend grace to others as a right-now expression of your will.

That's when the process begins. Rather than following on the tail end of a lengthy healing period, your willingness to forgive is actually the beginning point of true healing. Forgiving allows you to enter the process of restoration, not the other way around. So although you do indeed make *progress* in forgiveness over time, it is not a *process* you have to work yourself up to. Forgiveness happens, then it grows on you. You plant it, then it begins bearing fruit.

Have you been maintaining the right to hold on to unforgiveness for some offense, until you experience complete healing? How can the death of Christ for sinners motivate and enable your choice to forgive those who have wronged you?

What Do You Expect?

*"Remember the word that I said to you: 'A servant
is not greater than his master.' If they persecuted me,
they will also persecute you."*—John 15:20

 WE'VE BEEN LOOKING AT several mistruths in terms of our forgiveness of others—that it is not a *feeling*, that it is not the same as *forgetting*, and that it does not require a drawn-out *process*. One other myth regarding forgiveness is the idea that it should always *"fix"* things—or at least make them *better*.

Innate in the human heart is the expectation that life should follow an upward trend, getting richer, fuller, and more fulfilling along the way. That's why moviemakers craft stories that build in intensity and grow toward a thrilling climax. That's why people who create the rides at amusement parks build roller coasters to start slow and finish fast. That's why concerts and fireworks displays have a "grand finale."

But life generally isn't like that in our fallen world. Yes, believers in Christ know that the years we spend on earth are but a small fraction of our eternal lifetime, and that we are assured of a "forever finale" awaiting us in glory. But in the meantime, not every offender is going to repent; not every relationship is going to improve. And as surely as you have been wronged in the past, you will continue to face situations where you will again be wronged, maligned, and treated unfairly. Not even the power of forgiveness can prevent that from happening.

To expect otherwise is to set ourselves up for disappointment and to live with the foul fruit of bitterness. That's why, if we are going to live at peace with God and our fellow man, forgiveness must be an ongoing way of life.

So the next time you are faced with a hurtful, perhaps even repeat offense—in your marriage, with your children, in the workplace, at church—will you harbor resentment, or will you forgive . . . anyway?

 How would you treat others differently today if you weren't motivated by making your life easier but simply by honoring Christ through a lifestyle of humility, obedience, and love?

The Scarlet Thread

*To him who loves us and has freed us from our sins by his blood
and made us a kingdom, priests to his God and Father, to him be
glory and dominion forever and ever.*—Revelation 1:5–6

 PERHAPS A FITTING WAY to wrap up our look at some of
the misconceptions about forgiveness is to focus again
on the wonder of *God's* forgiveness. When we begin to
trace the lengths to which He has gone to make His
mercy known to us throughout recorded history—
not to mention the plans of His heart before the foundation of
the world—the breathtaking scope of His redemption story is
amazing indeed.

And the redemption of sinners is costly. In fact, it has always
required the shedding of blood.

From the coats of animal skin made to cover Adam and
Eve's nakedness, to the sacrificial ram provided for Abraham
while his son was still tied on the altar, to the blood of the
Passover lamb that spared the Israelites in Egypt, to the atoning
blood repeatedly sprinkled and poured out on the priestly altar
in the Old Testament, to Christ sharing the Passover cup in the
upper room, to the ultimate sacrifice to which all these others
pointed—Christ's death on the cross of Calvary—a "scarlet
thread" runs from one end of Scripture to the other, satisfying
the righteous wrath of God against sin and covering the shame
and guilt of sinners with the blood of an innocent substitute.

If you are still looking for motivation to forgive a spouse,
a parent, a relative—anyone who's hurt you deeply—find your
place on the scarlet thread of Scripture. See your sins attached
there in all their shame and selfishness. Try to fathom the
distance His grace has bridged between you and the wrath of
God. And with the rush of relief that floods your soul at the
sight, realize what you owe to those who deserve forgiveness as
little as you do. Follow the thread all the way home to the Father.

 *Marvel at God's love and mercy toward you, and ask Him to
make His love the source, substance, and measure of your
dealings with others.*

Loyal Opposition

The LORD is on my side; I will not fear.
What can man do to me?—Psalm 118:6

 HUMANLY SPEAKING, God's people have cause for alarm and insecurity in our day—whether on national or international fronts, or simply as families, churches, and individuals. As has always been the case, the forces of Satan and evil are arrayed against the kingdom of God and His people.

Yet God has proven that He is more than able to strengthen, sustain, and support His people, and to accomplish His eternal purposes, even in the midst of great turmoil and unrest.

I think of how He raised up Shiphrah and Puah—the Hebrew midwives whose story we find in Exodus 1. When Pharaoh issued an edict demanding all midwives to kill any son born to a Hebrew woman, these two "feared God and did not do as the king of Egypt commanded them, but let the male children live" (verse 17).

When seen against the full sweep of the Egyptian Empire, these women were utterly insignificant. And yet as Pharaoh did his dead level best to limit the growth and expansion of the Hebrews, God used two women whom we would have considered "bit players," to help further His unalterable plan. He worked through these faithful women to carry on the Jewish line by blessing the Hebrews with children. He supplied them with courage to defy cultural trends and to keep trusting in His promises.

Try as they might, no earthly edict, monarch, or efforts can hinder God from fulfilling His will. And when God wants to use someone like you to address a need or take an unpopular stance, no opposition can take you down. When you feel swallowed up and overwhelmed by the forces set against you and your family, know that a faithful, courageous minority in God's hands can still make its voice heard in heaven and can be instruments of His will being done here on earth.

 Do you ever feel helpless and frustrated, trying to live for God in this prodigal culture? How can you find strength and courage to keep pressing on?

A Mother's Legacy

She does him good, and not harm,
all the days of her life.—Proverbs 31:12

 SOON AFTER ARTHUR DEMOSS AND NANCY SOSSOMON exchanged their wedding vows, the nineteen-year-old bride became pregnant with her first child. Within their first five years of marriage, my parents had six children. (A seventh followed some years later.) Though this was not according to their original plans (they had planned to wait five years to have children!), they gladly embraced each child as a gift from God.

As I was growing up, I didn't realize that my mother's view of her calling as a wife and mother was terribly out of sync with our times. Instead of adopting the then-emerging ideal of women being liberated from husbands and home to pursue their own lives, she chose to pattern her life after the One who came to serve. Though extraordinarily gifted in her own right, my mother gladly laid down a promising career as a sacred vocalist to be a helper suitable to her husband.

In the rough-and-tumble world of business, my father was not without his detractors, but he could always count on my mother being his number-one admirer. To this day, I can never remember her speaking negatively about him to us or anyone else. It's not that he didn't have weaknesses and rough edges (though she sometimes gives that impression!), but rather that she was scarcely conscious of the negatives because of her deep, genuine admiration for him.

Her example has caused me to seek, even as a single woman, to be an encourager to the men God has placed in my life. It has helped me counsel women with difficult husbands to focus on their positive qualities and allow God to deal with their rough edges. Above all, her life has increased my desire to honor and serve the Lord Jesus and to bring forth much fruit out of intimate union with Him.

 Whether you are married or single, how can your life demonstrate the kind of relationship we as the church, the bride of Christ, are to have with our heavenly Bridegroom?

Nail the Colors

Fight the good fight of the faith. Take hold of the eternal life to which you were called.—1 Timothy 6:12

 HISTORICALLY, when navies were engaged in combat and one of the sides had reached a point of surrender, the common practice was to lower the flag (the "colors") that identified the ship. Lowering the flag was equivalent to conceding defeat.

But sometimes the ship's captain would declare he had no intention of surrendering. In order to formalize this commitment in a visible way, he would give the order to *"nail the colors to the mast."* In other words, he was taking away all options of the flag being lowered. It was instead to be hammered into the ship's very structure, impossible to be removed. The battle would be fought and won, or all on board would die in the attempt.

C. T. Studd, a British missionary in the late 1800s and early 1900s, used this word picture in urging believers to commit themselves unreservedly to the call of Christ, no matter how difficult the work or what obstacles might be encountered:

> Nail the colors to the mast! That is the right thing to do, and therefore, that is what we must do, and do it now. What colors? The colors of Christ, the work He has given us to do. Christ wants not nibblers of the possible but grabbers of the impossible, by faith in the omnipotence, fidelity, and wisdom of the Almighty Saviour.

As believers in Jesus Christ today, it is time for us to decide. Against all opposition and unpopularity, we must "nail the colors to the mast," declaring our loyalty to God and His Word, reaffirming our wholehearted commitment to live for His glory and fulfill His calling. No turning back.

 What area(s) of reservation or resistance in your life would be headed off by this kind of commitment?

A Calming Influence

"Blessed be your discretion, and blessed be you,
who have kept me this day from bloodguilt and from
avenging myself with my own hand!"—1 Samuel 25:33

 DO YOU HAVE ONE OF THOSE impossible people in your life? Maybe you work with one, or married into a family with one, or ended up on a church committee with one. And maybe you're honestly not making more of their childish, boorish behavior than is really there. Perhaps others would agree that they exhibit many of the biblical descriptors of a "fool."

How do you respond to those kinds of people? Do you sometimes end up acting as foolishly as they do, getting provoked and losing control, returning to them the same kind of ugly treatment they dish out?

Abigail was an "intelligent and beautiful" woman in the Old Testament (1 Sam. 25:3) who found herself between two men who were both acting badly—her churlish husband, Nabal, and an exasperated David. Nabal had done David wrong, and David had responded angrily with wild threats.

Then Abigail stepped between the two, calmly and resourcefully attempting to mediate their contentious dispute. As a result, this tender woman proved again that "whoever is slow to anger is better than the mighty, and he who rules his spirit than he who takes a city" (Prov. 16:32). She couldn't control Nabal. She couldn't control David. But she *could* control herself. And instead of escalating the drama or inflaming the altercation, she diffused the tensions and kept a bad situation from getting worse.

I can remember my dad telling us as kids, "You're not responsible for how others act or what they do. You're only responsible for how you respond." By God's grace we can respond to impossible people in a way that is full of grace, discernment, and wisdom.

 Is there a trying or hot-tempered person—a Nabal or a David—in your life? Even if you were to see no immediate benefit from it, what could you be sure of happening if you responded to that person with humility, kindness, and patience?

Aging Beautifully

Older women likewise are to be reverent in behavior, not slanderers or slaves to much wine. They are to teach what is good.—Titus 2:3

 WHAT DOES IT MEAN for older women to go against the flow of the world, to swim upstream into the grand and holy purposes of God for their lives? It means choosing not to spiritually retire. It means not settling for a life consumed by golf, bridge, shopping, or redecorating our homes.

There are so many younger women who need an older woman's counsel and encouragement, so many struggling sisters who could be uplifted by the love and prayers of someone who's been in their shoes. To be this kind of woman doesn't require that you have a degree in counseling or go to seminary. It merely requires a willingness to find and receive your place in God's kingdom, and to invest your life in serving Him and others.

For many years, one of my most faithful prayer partners was an older woman I knew as "Mom Johnson." I lived with her family when I was a student at the University of Southern California, and we stayed in touch over the years. I watched as Mom J continued to pursue Christ and grow in her love for Him and His Word. She aged with grace—becoming increasingly tenderhearted, prayerful, wise, and others-centered. Even into her nineties, in the sunset days of her life, she was still inviting younger women into her heart and home, encouraging and discipling them for His glory.

We need more Mom Johnsons in our world and our churches today. Unemployment rates may be high, and the options available to older people may be hard to come by. But there will never be a shortage of openings to be filled by older women who desire to live out the mandate of Titus 2.

 You may not see yourself as "older," but every woman is an "older woman" to someone! Who could you take under your wing to encourage and nurture them in their walk with of God?

A Command (and a Promise) for Life

*"Honor your father and mother" (this is the first commandment
with a promise) "that it may go well with you and that you may
live long in the land."*—Ephesians 6:2

 CONTRARY TO WHAT THE WORLD TELLS US, the command
to honor our parents has no expiration date and no
conditions attached. Whatever your age, whether you
are married or single, whether your parents are even
still living or not, God expects you to honor them.

Unlike many, I have been blessed with a heritage of godly,
devoted parents. Yet they would be the first to tell you they were
flawed. Like the rest of us, they were (are) in the process of being
conformed to the image of Jesus.

Your background may be much different from mine.
But regardless of what your growing-up years were like and
regardless of your parents' spiritual condition, you can still find
ways to honor them.

We honor our parents by speaking well of them to others
and valuing their counsel. We honor them when, instead of
drawing attention to those areas where they were not all they
could have been, we express gratitude for how God has used
them to bless and shape our lives. We honor them when we
refuse to make them a prisoner of our expectations or to hold
their failures against them. We honor them when we take time to
communicate, listen, understand, and be sensitive to their needs.
Most of all, we honor our parents when we choose to pattern
our lives after those areas where they have set a godly example.

If you want to experience God's blessing throughout the
course of your life, take this command from Scripture seriously
and personally. It's a "commandment with a promise," and it's a
commandment for life.

 *How could you honor your parents today? Rather than
focusing on their faults (real and major as they may be),
ask God to show you any ways you may have dishonored
them, for which you need to repent.*

Welcome Home

Show hospitality to one another without grumbling.—1 Peter 4:9

 "HOSPITALITY" IS NOT A SPECIAL GIFT or calling for some few believers who love throwing a party. It's not a matter of "entertaining" guests. Nor does it require having a fancy house, a big budget, or a table spread worthy of the Food Network. In fact, when you fuss too heavily over your décor, your housekeeping, your appetizers, or your fine china, you may end up fueling a spirit of pride, self-consciousness, and comparison with others.

The goal of hospitality is to humbly serve Christ by serving others, to be a channel of God's love and hospitable heart in a world of people desperately in need of finding their true Home in Him. You're not trying to impress or perform but simply to welcome friends, old and new alike, into a home where the gospel is evident in the mood, conduct, and conversation of those who live there.

Christian hospitality is a way to be actively involved in others' spiritual transformation at a practical, tangible level, participating with God in showering grace in their direction—no matter your income bracket or cooking skills. It is a mandate that flows out of being recipients of His grace and having been invited to feast and live forever in the Home Christ is preparing for us.

To invite people into your home for a simple meal, a cup of coffee, or just a bowl of popcorn, along with generous servings of conversation, prayer, and love, is to remember what your home is all about—not a place for stockpiling stuff but a God-given tool for service and ministry, for cultivating life and sharing grace.

 Even if hospitality is not your natural bent or your preferred way of serving, ask the Lord to show you one or two creative ways you can fulfill the biblical exhortation to "show hospitality to one another."

Gift List

Blessed be the God and Father of our Lord Jesus Christ,
who has blessed us in Christ with every spiritual blessing
in the heavenly places. . . .—Ephesians 1:3

 ONE OF THE OCCASIONS I make a big deal about each year is my "spiritual birthday"—May 14, 1963—the day when as a young girl I first consciously trusted the Lord Jesus to save me. Over the years, I have compiled a list of "spiritual birthday gifts"—things God has given me in Christ, gifts He has given to all of His children, according to His Word.

That list includes such treasures as peace with God, being adopted into His family, being saved from His eternal wrath, and having a purpose for living. It catalogs how He has restored my soul, given me an inheritance with the saints, empowers me to serve Him, and keeps me from stumbling before the finish line. It reminds me that He has supplied an Advocate who defends me against Satan's prosecution and accusation.

And the list goes on. I thank Him for His *nearness* through His Spirit within me, who both equips and encourages me to stay faithful in the battle. I thank Him for His *holiness*, that even when I choose to sin, He can always be counted on to be holy and faithful. I thank Him for His *mercy*, His willingness to reach down and rescue me, not only from my sins but even from my best efforts to please Him, which are nowhere near good enough apart from Christ's imputed righteousness.

Whenever you ponder what you're grateful for, be sure to look beyond the animal, vegetable, and mineral variety of God's gifts. Consider His spiritual blessings as well. Only Christian gratitude, framed and contextualized within the matchless grace of God, can help you wrap your arms around so big a package.

 What would you add to this list of spiritual blessings?
What are one or two of His gifts you haven't opened up
and enjoyed in a while?

Picture-Perfect

*"And I will manifest my holiness among you
in the sight of the nations."*—Ezekiel 20:41

THE PROBLEM WITH THE WORLD TODAY is not so much the pervasive darkness of our unbelieving culture. Apart from the light of Christ, the world will never be anything but steeped in darkness. The problem is that the children of God, who are supposed to be children of light, have taken on so many of the characteristics of the surrounding darkness. If God's people started to live like the redeemed people we are, I believe lost sinners would be falling all over themselves to repent and believe the gospel, drawn to Christ by seeing the reflection of a holy God in our conduct and character.

Shortly after my father died, our mom gave each of us kids an 8 x 10 photo of him in a beautiful silver frame. Unfortunately during a subsequent move, I stored his picture with some other belongings and didn't uncover it again until many years later. By this time, the once glistening frame had become tarnished, black, and ugly. Its soiled condition was the first thing a person would notice now when looking at the picture. Wanting to be able to display my dad's portrait again, I bought a silver polishing cloth and went to work on that discolored frame.

Rubbing it clean wasn't easy. The marks were stubborn and required no small effort to remove. But when I was finished, the frame no longer drew attention to itself; it only served to enhance and complement the picture of my father.

Others are looking to see how we respond to life, how we handle conflict, how we deal with problems, how we keep our commitments—none of which is easy to do. But when done for His glory, they draw the gaze of a darkened world to the holy One whose life and light shine through us.

What kind of shape is your "frame" in today? Which tarnished spots could use a good polishing? How does the prospect of God being glorified through your life motivate you to be a clean, polished setting in which His picture can be clearly seen?

No Holding Back

*For in a severe test of affliction, their abundance of joy
and their extreme poverty have overflowed in a wealth of
generosity on their part.*—2 Corinthians 8:2

 SHORTLY AFTER HURRICANE KATRINA struck the Gulf Coastal states, Louisiana Baptist Convention officials received an envelope containing a donation of exactly $854 in cash. As you may remember, many gifts poured in with aid for that hard-hit region. But this unusual offering came from a group of twenty men in Sumatra, Indonesia, who eight months earlier had seen their homes destroyed by a devastating tsunami. During their crisis, a Southern Baptist disaster relief team had arrived to help them, and news of the historic storm in America had triggered in these Indonesian men a desire to return the favor with a gift that represented great personal sacrifice.

While most of us have never been driven from our homes by a natural disaster, a majority of people can relate to being financially stretched at some point. At such times, our instinct may be to cut back on our giving.

Yet that may be the time to be even more intentional and sacrificial in our giving. Such gospel-motivated giving can be a means of sanctification in our lives and a means of exhibiting the generous heart of God to others.

When I was a teen, I was deeply impacted by watching my parents continue giving generously and joyfully during a devastating downturn in the business they had worked so hard to build.

"The righteous is generous and gives," God's Word says (Ps. 37:21), "and does not hold back" (Prov. 21:26). If you want to be spiritually rich, then help others be spiritually rich. At times, that may mean reducing your lifestyle and sacrificing personal comfort or convenience, in order to be able to give more. But I'm convinced that in eternity no one will ever say, "I wish I had given less." I believe most if not all of us will say, "I wish I had given more!"

 When was the last time you gave a sacrificial gift? Reflect on all God has given you in Christ, and ask Him to make His generosity the source and the measure of your giving.

Prayer + What? = Peace

Practice these things, and the God of peace will be with you.
—Philippians 4:9

 IF WE WERE SITTING ACROSS THE TABLE from each other, you could probably tell me what's stealing your peace right now without having to think too hard. You may be grieving a longtime loss that never settles far from your conscious thoughts. You may be crying yourself to sleep at night over a situation with a son or daughter who is beyond your ability to control—a failing marriage, a grandchild undergoing diagnostic tests, perhaps open rebellion against your parenting decisions. Maybe you're facing some health issues of your own, or your income just isn't meeting your monthly bills, or your church is in turmoil over some hot-button issue. (In my case, I've just hit a snag while working on this book, and am struggling to keep my emotions above water!)

You can (and should) pray about these matters, of course. But praying is not *all* you can do. "Do not be anxious about anything," the apostle Paul wrote, in a much-loved passage of Scripture, "but in everything by prayer and supplication *with thanksgiving* let your requests be made known to God" (Phil. 4:6). Then what? "The peace of God, which surpasses all understanding, will guard your hearts and your minds in Christ Jesus" (verse 7).

When prayer teams up with gratitude, when you open your eyes wide enough to look for God's mercies in the midst of your pain, He meets you with His indescribable peace. It's a promise: *prayer + thanksgiving = peace.*

Prayer is vital, yes. But to really experience His peace in the midst of problems, you must come to Him with gratitude. Costly gratitude. The kind that trusts He is working for your good even in unpleasant circumstances. The kind that garrisons your troubled heart and mind with His unexplainable peace.

 What stressful situation is weighing on you today? Have you prayed about it? Are you offering up thanksgiving along with your petitions? If so, expect your heart to be safeguarded by the peace of God that is far greater than the human mind can grasp.

Our Heart, His Garden

Let my beloved come to his garden, and eat its choicest fruits.
—Song of Solomon 4:16

 THE SONG OF SOLOMON is the story of the growing intimacy shared by a royal couple, the intertwining of two lives to become one. Much to the surprise of onlookers, the king in this story does not select his bride from the most eligible women of the city; rather, He chooses a plain, ordinary working girl, whose skin has been weathered from toiling in the family vineyard. He lavishes affection and tender words upon her, marries her, and takes her to live with him in the palace. As she responds to his initiative, she is transformed—by his grace, by his love.

The once common peasant girl becomes a queen. Once frayed from her tiresome life, she now has a purpose. Though she once resented having to work, she is now eager to serve him, increasingly centering her life around one single purpose: to bring delight and pleasure to her Beloved.

He likens his bride's heart to a garden, a trysting place where he finds great joy and satisfaction. And she responds by making her heart—her garden—a place that will always bring pleasure to him, cultivating it as a place of beauty, fragrance, and delight. The garden that was once "hers" is now his. *His.* The fragrance and fruit of the garden—all that she is, all that she has—is all for Him.

And so it is with you. The One who has chosen and redeemed you seeks refuge and delight in the garden of your heart. He wants to meet you there. He wants you to eagerly anticipate and welcome His presence. And as you commune with Him in that special place, your life will produce the sweet fragrance and fruit of His Spirit. More each season. More than the last. You will be blessed; others will be blessed.

And it is all, all for your Beloved.

 What is the condition of the "garden" of your heart? Again today, offer it to Him and ask Him for grace to make it a place fit for a King.

Joy Overflowing in Hard Places

I am filled with comfort. In all our affliction,
I am overflowing with joy.—2 Corinthians 7:4

TWO COLLEGE STUDENTS, doing summer evangelistic work in a rural community, walked up the beaten path to an old farmhouse—their presence announced by squealing kids and barking dogs. Getting no response at the screen door, they walked around to the back, where the mother was scrubbing clothes over a soapy tub with an old-fashioned washboard. Spying the unexpected guests, she brushed back her hair, wiped the perspiration from her brow and asked what they wanted.

"We'd like to tell you how to have eternal life," one of the students replied.

The tired homemaker hesitated a moment, breathed a long, exhausted sigh, and said, "I thank you, but I don't think I could stand it!"

Yes, life's demands and ordeals sometimes seem like they'll go on forever. We grow weary, at times fending off hopelessness and despair. Yet the Bible offers an alternative, based not on denial but on the reality of Christ's presence—not rescuing us out of the struggle but meeting us right in the midst of it. Knowing that we are held by a sovereign, purposeful, loving God means that joy is available in abundant supply, springing up from within, and overflowing to bless others around us.

Looking at Paul's life, we see pressures and persecutions of every type. Whips, rods, detractors, defamers. Jail time, hunger, travel, death threats. And yet thirteen times in his letter to the Philippians alone—written from a Roman prison cell—he reminded the believers to "rejoice in the Lord" (4:4).

When you don't know how much more you can take, remember where all this scrubbing and scraping is taking you. Remember what grace is doing here. Remember what joy can help you endure and who it can enable you to reflect to a joyless world.

In the midst of life's hard places, can you say with the apostle Paul: "I am filled with comfort. . . . I am overflowing with joy"? If not, what could change your perspective and release His joy in and through your life?

Where His Home Is

For thus says the One who is high and lifted up, . . . "I dwell in the high and holy place, and also with him who is of a contrite and lowly spirit, to revive the spirit of the lowly, and to revive the heart of the contrite."—Isaiah 57:15

 ACCORDING TO THIS VERSE from Isaiah's prophecy, God has two "addresses." The first one comes as no surprise: the exalted God of the universe lives in the "high and holy place." Yet He has another address that I find astounding: according to this verse, He also lives with those who are "lowly" and "contrite" in spirit.

The word *contrite* suggests something that's been crushed into small particles, ground into powder, such as a rock that's been pulverized. What is it that God wants to "pulverize" in us? Our spirit? Our personhood? No, He wants those intact—more intact, actually, than they can possibly be until we allow Him to break something else. *Our self-will.*

When we speak of a horse being "broken," we don't mean that someone physically breaks its legs; we mean that the horse's *will* has been broken, that it is now compliant and submissive to the wishes of its rider. In much the same way, we are speaking of the breaking of our self-will so that the life and Spirit of the Lord Jesus may be released through our brokenness.

Psalm 51 is a heartfelt, penitent prayer offered by King David after he committed his great sin with Bathsheba. He realized he could do nothing to earn his way back into God's favor. "For you will not delight in sacrifice," David said, "or I would give it" (verse 16). Rather, "the sacrifices of God are a broken spirit; a broken and contrite heart, O God, you will not despise" (verse 17).

Like David, we would rather *do* something to please God—pray more, read our Bibles more, memorize more Scripture, witness to more people . . . but what He really wants from us is a humble, broken spirit—stripped of all pride, self-will, and self-righteousness.

That's the heart where He makes His home.

 How "at home" do you think God is in you? What are some ways we can cultivate a lowly, contrite heart?

"I Do"

"Therefore a man shall leave his father and mother and hold fast to his wife, and the two shall become one flesh." This mystery is profound, and I am saying that it refers to Christ and the church.—Ephesians 5:31–32

 WHEN A MAN CHOOSES A WOMAN and asks her to be his wife, God intends this to be a picture of a far more significant love relationship.

If the woman is willing, they enter into a lifelong covenant, pledging their love and devotion to each other. He gives the woman his name and assumes responsibility for her well-being, taking her under the covering of his love and leadership, and committing himself to provide for her. The wife gladly takes her place under his protection, reverencing and submitting to him. Then through their union, if the Lord is willing, they give birth to children who will carry on their name and reproduce their heart.

Marriage, then, is a visible, earthly picture of a greater, spiritual reality: that Jesus has come in search of a bride and has chosen us simply because He wants to. At the price of His lifeblood, He has expressed His desire to be our "husband"—to love us, care for us, and take us as His own. When we say "I do," we enter into an eternal covenant with Him and become part of His bride, the church. He gives us His name. He takes responsibility for His bride, and we reverence Him and submit to His loving authority, with the goal of bringing forth others to bear His name and likeness.

Have you said "I do" to the Lord Jesus? Have you given up your independence in order to become one with Him? Have you come under His protection and care and taken His name as your own? If not, today could be your "wedding day"!

No relationship or pursuit in life could be more important— receive His sacrificial love for you; then spend the rest of your life celebrating and reciprocating that love and bearing spiritual fruit as you live in union and communion with Him.

 What evidence is there in your life of your oneness with Christ?

The Son of Tears

*Strive together with me in your prayers to God
on my behalf.*—Romans 15:30

AUGUSTINE WAS ONE OF THE MOST INFLUENTIAL Christian theologians of all time. His fifth-century writings in support of biblical orthodoxy and against the prevailing heresies of his day shaped Western thought for centuries to come.

He is best known to most through his *Confessions*, the personal account of his early years, filled with prideful pursuits in academia, wanton sexual promiscuity, and the persistent rejection of Christian truth. Yet in the midst of the tale of this hell-bent young man, we meet his mother, Monica—a woman who prayed fervently for her son year after year, even when there was no visible evidence that her prayers were being heard or answered.

History relates that she went to the local bishop one day, seeing if he could somehow talk some sense into her prodigal child. Looking into her eyes, he assured her that God would choose His own way of getting through to her son one day. "It is not possible," he said to her, "that the son of so many tears should perish." And so it was, that at the age of thirty-two, the son of Monica's tears stopped running from God and was powerfully converted to faith in Christ.

One of the most powerful means of grace in children's lives is the gift of praying parents. And though untold weeks and years can elapse without getting the answer they hope for, this often toilsome process is part of what He uses to sanctify believing parents, draw them closer to Him, and amaze them with the lengths He is willing to travel to rescue their children.

Are you grieving over a son or daughter (or another loved one) who is resisting God? Don't stop praying. Keep laying hold of God. The last chapter is not yet written. He is still weaving your faithful, earnest prayers into His story for their lives.

 *How could prolonged, seemingly unanswered prayer
be a means of grace in your life? In the lives of others?*

High Alert

I said, "I will confess my transgressions to the LORD,"
and you forgave the iniquity of my sin.—Psalm 32:5

 REHOBOAM INHERITED THE THRONE OF ISRAEL from his father, Solomon. But his heart was far from God, and he led the people accordingly. God raised up Egypt as an enemy to punish Rehoboam for his rebellion, and sent the prophet Shemaiah to tell him so. The Scripture tells us that in response to God's chastening hand, "the princes and the king of Israel humbled themselves" (2 Chron. 12:6). Rehoboam acknowledged that the Lord was justified in His discipline, and God spared Jerusalem from Egypt's path of destruction.

A similar challenge occurred years later during the reign of Asa, grandson of Rehoboam. Enemy threats brought fear and turmoil to the city, and Asa turned for help to the nearby Syrians—a move that displeased the Lord. So He sent the prophet Hanani to tell him so. Asa's response was far different from that of his grandfather: "[He] was angry with the seer and put him in the stocks of prison, for he was in a rage with him because of this" (16:10). Before long, Asa became mortally ill, "yet even in his disease he did not seek the LORD" (verse 12).

Both men sinned. Both were confronted with their sin. One accepted the rebuke as God's way of cleansing and renewal; the other received it as an assault on his reputation. One was restored by his humility; the other was ruined by his pride.

This same choice awaits each of us, each time the Lord in His mercy makes us aware that we have strayed from His path and wandered into danger. Will we hear and accept, or will we dodge and cover up?

 When God sends someone to point out the error of your ways—
whether a concerned friend or simply the conviction of the
indwelling Holy Spirit—how do you typically respond? With a
humble, repentant heart? Or with defensiveness and resistance?

Mercy and Truth

For all have sinned and fall short of the glory of God,
and are justified by his grace as a gift, through the redemption
that is in Christ Jesus.—Romans 3:23–24

 WILLIAM COWPER was one of the finest English writers of the nineteenth century. But he carried significant emotional baggage and turmoil into his adult years. In his early thirties, he experienced a mental breakdown, attempted suicide, and was placed in an insane asylum for eighteen months. During his confinement he came across Romans 3:25, a verse that forever changed his life:

Whom God hath set forth to be a propitiation through faith in his
blood, to declare his righteousness for the remission of sins that are
past, through the forbearance of God. (KJV)

Cowper, who had felt he was damned and beyond hope, said: "I saw the sufficiency of the atonement He had made. . . . In a moment I believed, and received the gospel." Years later, he expressed his undying wonder in a hymn that has brought hope to weary sinners for more than a hundred years: "There is a fountain filled with blood / Drawn from Immanuel's veins / And sinners plunged beneath that flood / Lose all their guilty stains."

"My sin isn't really all that bad," some may feel, shrugging off their need for God's mercy. At the other end of the spectrum, some struggle with the sense that "God can't forgive what I've done." But on a hill called Calvary, God's love for sinners established a meeting place with His holy hatred for sin.

The cross reveals the incredible price God paid to redeem us from the sins we often trivialize. Yet it also displays the love of God toward the worst of us, no matter what sins we've committed. The gospel is God's response to every denial of need and every doubt of His love.

 Has your heart grown insensitive to your need for God's forgiveness?
Are you allowing regrets to steal your joy? At the cross you will
find the mercy and truth that will both humble your heart and set
you free from the weight of your sin.

Holy and Glad

You have loved righteousness and hated wickedness.
Therefore God, your God, has anointed you with the
oil of gladness beyond your companions.—Psalm 45:7

 WHAT WORDS do you associate with holiness? Would *gladness* be one of those words? Look at it the other way around. When you think of things that make you *glad*, do you think of holiness? Or does the idea of holiness give you that feeling of being joyless, uptight, and rigid?

Why do we make holiness out to be some austere obligation or burden to be borne, when the fact is that to be holy is to be clean, to be free from the needless weight and baggage of sin? Why would we cling to our guilt-inducing pleasures any more than a leper would refuse to part with his oozing sores if given the opportunity to be cleansed of his disease?

The world tells us that the greatest thrills are to be found in indulging impurity and disdaining righteousness. But in fact, to love what is pure and to have a deep heart aversion to sin is to move toward joy—joy infinitely greater than any earthly delights can offer. To *resist* holiness, on the other hand, or to be halfhearted in its pursuit, is to forfeit true joy and settle for something far less than the God-intoxication for which we were created.

Sooner or later, sin will strip and rob you of everything that is truly beautiful and desirable. You've felt it. You know it. You've wished you hadn't, you've wished you could stop, you've wished you weren't like this. But if you are a child of God, you were redeemed to enjoy the sweet fruit of holiness—to walk in oneness with your heavenly Father, to relish His presence, to rejoice in His mercy, to experience the freedom of having clean hands, a pure heart, and a clear conscience—the promise of one day standing before Him unashamed.

Why settle for anything less? Anything less *glad*?

 Why do we sometimes choose guilt over gladness?
Contemplate the pleasures and joys to be found in
loving what He loves and hating what He hates.

No Sacrifice Too Great

*Do not neglect to do good and to share what you have,
for such sacrifices are pleasing to God.*—Hebrews 13:16

 GOD'S CALL TO LAY DOWN OUR LIVES on the altar of
sacrifice means that we give Him all that we are—
our rights, our reputation, our desires, our future
plans, everything that concerns us—first for a
lifetime, and then day by day, moment by moment,
decision by decision.

Does that seem too much to ask? Truthfully, there are
moments when—yes—I feel as if something God is asking of
me is unreasonable. It may be to provide a listening ear and a
caring heart for one more woman who wants to talk, when I'm
physically and emotionally spent at the end of a long day of
ministry. It may be to offer financial support to help a couple
provide a Christian education for their children. It may be to stay
engaged in a relationship with a difficult, demanding person. It
may be to stay positioned in my study on nights and weekends
when others are spending time with their families.

In those moments, my emotions sometimes cry out, "I've
already given so much! I just can't give any more." But that's
when I need to take a trip to Calvary and look into the eyes
of a bleeding Christ who gave everything to reconcile me to
Himself. From that viewpoint, any sacrifice of mine becomes
my *"reasonable* service" (Rom. 12:1 KJV)—"reasonable," from the
Greek word *logikos*—meaning that a full and complete sacrifice
of my life is the only *logical* response I can make.

God asks us to offer up our lives and daily circumstances as
a living sacrifice, signifying our wholehearted consecration and
surrender to the One who gave His life for us. Shall we offer to
such a Savior only our affordable gifts and free weekends, or all
that we are and have?

 *When was the last time you felt God was leading you to do
something that seemed humanly unreasonable? How does
Christ's sacrifice on the cross affect your perspective on what
He was asking of you?*

God at Work

*Oh, how abundant is your goodness, which you have
stored up for those who fear you and worked for those
who take refuge in you.*—Psalm 31:19

 IF EVER THERE WAS A SITUATION that seemed hopeless,
it was Queen Esther's. Orphaned as a girl; taken
into a Persian harem; married to a cruel, arrogant,
alcoholic husband; then faced with an edict intended to
exterminate her entire race. It was a desperate situation,
both for her and her people. Her plight seemed hopeless.

But in Esther's story, we see a powerful reminder that the
kingdom of heaven rules over every earthly kingdom. Watching
God act in her behalf, administering justice and preserving life, we
see that God can be trusted to operate within His perfect timing—
and always according to His good, sovereign, and eternal will.

When we are in the midst of our earthly dramas, we must
keep reminding ourselves of this ultimate reality. All the pushing,
shoving, badgering, manipulating, whimpering, and nagging in
the world won't solve our problems. Those tactics may help us get
our way in an immediate sense, but they are counterproductive
to His ultimate purposes. It is *God's* responsibility to orchestrate
the events and details of our lives. Our job is to wait and
cooperate with whatever He reveals to be His plan.

We tend to justify our impatient behavior, perhaps
considering it necessary in light of the desperate nature of
our situation. But when faced with a diabolical scheme that
threatened her life along with the entire Jewish race, Esther
stayed remarkably in control of her tongue and her emotions.
No hurry, no histrionics, no hysterical outbursts. Her example
provides a portrait of someone who understood that "Heaven
rules" (Dan. 4:26)—the same reason why we, too, can respond
to even our most threatening dilemmas with courage, faith, and
quiet confidence.

 *Counsel your heart with the reminder that, regardless how
complex or hopeless your situation may appear, "Heaven rules."
You can rest in the fact that God has a plan and nothing can
stop Him from fulfilling it.*

A Love Story

"I have loved you with an everlasting love; therefore I have continued my faithfulness to you."—Jeremiah 31:3

 WE ALL LOVE A LOVE STORY. That's because we were created to give and receive love. We were made for intimacy.

Yet most of us know more about the *absence* of intimacy than the reality of it. From earliest childhood we have sought to fill that vacuum, craving closeness, warmth, and affection. We long to know that we matter to someone, that someone cares, that someone who really knows us still loves us. However, even in the best of families and human relationships, the most we are able to do is somewhat dull that sense of longing. No one on this earth can completely satisfy it.

That's because the God who created this hole in our hearts is the only One who can fill it. In the Scriptures we encounter a God who moves toward us, who seeks to draw us to Himself, who knows us intimately, and who invites us to know Him in the same way.

From start to finish, the Word of God is actually one incredible love story. And wonder of wonders, it is a story that has your name and mine in it. Whether you grew up in church or in no church at all, whether your background is "respectable" or admittedly tainted, whether you're well-versed in the Bible or are just now getting acquainted with it—there is room in this love story for you.

Those who drink from the deep wells of His divine love have always found in Him the nearness their soul craves. May each day you spend in His Word and His presence slake your thirst for intimacy with the Creator-Lover—the One who fills that needy hole in our hearts with Himself.

 Have you experienced the inability of human relationships to satisfy the deepest longings of your soul? Thank God for His everlasting love, nearness, and faithfulness. Ask Him to satisfy your heart with His love.

A Difference You Can See

In that day the deaf shall hear the words of a book, and out of their gloom and darkness the eyes of the blind shall see.—Isaiah 29:18

 MOST OF US CAN'T IMAGINE what it's like not to see—not being able to describe the color yellow, or distinguish a loved one's face in the crowd, or easily navigate a street crossing. The gift of sight is an amazing blessing for which we sometimes forget to be thankful.

Yet Fanny Crosby (1820–1915), writer of more than eight thousand hymns, enough to fill fifteen complete hymnals stacked one on top of the other, enough to cause her publishers to ascribe her multiple pen names in order to make her prodigious output seem more believable, saw things another way.

She was *thankful* for the blessing of blindness.

At six weeks of age, her family physician had used hot compresses on her eyes in an attempt to cure an infection. The technique only succeeded in scarring sensitive tissue, rendering her permanently blind. However, she refused to become despondent over her inability to see. At the age of eight, she composed a bit of verse telling what a "happy child" she was, despite her physical limitation.

She later reflected in her autobiography that she never could have written all those thousands of songs if she had constantly been distracted by the sights of an interesting world. "It seemed intended by the blessed providence of God that I should be blind all my life, and I thank Him for the dispensation."

"I thank Him," she said. For blindness.

There are two kinds of people in this world: the grateful and the ungrateful. It's the difference between squandering life and sharing life, between being blinded to glory and "To God Be the Glory," between assured bitterness and "Blessed Assurance." It's a difference you can see.

 What reason for gratitude could you find in your own personal weaknesses or limitations if you chose to see them through those kind of eyes?

Healthy Living

As for you, teach what accords with sound doctrine.—Titus 2:1

 HOW MUCH ARSENIC would you be comfortable knowing was in your food or drink? Just a little? Would that bother you? The fact is, many Christians tolerate trace amounts of contaminants in their belief systems, poisoning their perspectives on everything from family issues to finances to public policy.

This is why God's Word so frequently exhorts us about holding fast to "sound doctrine." The word "sound" in the original Greek is *hugiaino*, a term closely related to our English word *hygiene*. To be sound is to be healthy, to ingest only that which is wholesome and beneficial to our lives. Insisting on sound doctrine is akin to the practice of carefully reading nutrition labels, or shopping at health food stores, or choosing organic options that are free from harmful pesticides and preservatives.

How many people do you know who go to great lengths to ensure the safety and soundness of the foods they eat? And yet how many people do you know who are just as careful to guard their hearts and minds from belief systems that can weaken their whole outlook on life and the faithful performance of their duties in the home, the workplace, and even in their local church or ministry?

Outright false doctrine isn't that hard to spot or avoid. Full bottles of poison neither tempt nor attract us. What we must be careful about is letting our spiritual intake become sprinkled with just enough error, dispensed by charismatic personalities with just enough emotional stories and funny jokes, causing us to end up believing things that slowly deaden our spiritual senses over time.

Become so familiar with God's Word and keep it so close to your heart that you'll be able to discern whether what you're hearing is truly healthy, sound teaching.

 What would you say to someone who said they don't need doctrine, that they only need Jesus? How does doctrine that is not sound impact our relationship with Christ and the way we live out our faith?

Face Time

Thus the LORD used to speak to Moses face to face,
as a man speaks to his friend.—Exodus 33:11

 WHEN SOMETHING COMES BETWEEN TWO FRIENDS, face-to-face encounters can be awkward and uncomfortable. I remember hearing a wife describe a disagreement she'd had with her husband the night before. "I lay down on our bed," she said, "and turned my face toward the wall and my back toward my husband!" It doesn't take a therapist to know there's a barrier in that relationship.

You've seen this same principle at work in your children. When one of them does something he shouldn't, where is the last place he wants to look? In your eyes. Something has come between the two of you, and the fellowship is broken.

If you have walked with God for any length of time, you know what it's like to experience a breach in your relationship with Him, to find it difficult to look Him "in the eyes" because of something you've allowed to come between you.

One of the purposes of a daily devotional time is to draw near to Him, find out what has caused the separation, and experience restored fellowship, so you can once again look into His face without shame or fear—all the sweet fruit of applying the gospel to your heart.

As you meet with God today—every day—don't forget that the ultimate purpose is not simply to gain more knowledge about Him but to *know Him* and enjoy intimate communion with Him. In fact, we can experience that fellowship in as real and rich a way as Moses did, thanks to the reconciling work of Christ on the cross and the presence of His indwelling Holy Spirit.

You may be a seasoned student of the Scripture. You may even be a Bible study leader. But if your time with Him does not lead you to know Him in a deeper way, you've missed the heart of the matter. Look again into His face today. And don't look away.

 What hindrances or distractions keep you from developing an intimate friendship with God?

Pride on Your Side?

Humble yourselves before the Lord, and he will exalt you.—James 4:10

 A MISSIONARY TO A CERTAIN REGION IN AFRICA—a man who had been greatly used by God as an instrument of revival—recalled that when he would mention (even as a passing reference) the name of another Christian to any of the national believers, they would often ask, "Is he a broken Christian?" Not, "Is he committed?" or "knowledgeable?" or "hardworking?"

"Is he broken . . . ?"

How can you tell if you're a broken Christian? One way is to consider the difference between a *broken* person and a *proud* person:

> *Proud people* desire to be known as a success. *Broken people* are motivated to be faithful and to make others successful.
>
> *Proud people* are elated by praise and deflated by criticism. *Broken people* know that any praise for their accomplishments belongs to the Lord, and that criticism can help them become more like Christ.
>
> *Proud people* keep others at arm's length. *Broken people* are willing to take the risk of getting close to others.
>
> *Proud people* are concerned about the consequences and problems caused by their sin. *Broken people* are more concerned about how their sin has grieved and dishonored a holy God.
>
> *Proud people* feel worthy of respect. *Broken people* feel a desperate need for God's mercy.

If statements like these reveal the presence of pride in your heart, don't despair; God has been merciful to show you your need. The first step of brokenness and humility is to get honest about these things, to acknowledge the true condition of your heart. Don't try to cover up, justify, rationalize, compare yourself with others, or pretend you're better off than you really are. The riches and blessings of God's grace belong to those who recognize their spiritual poverty.

 If someone were to ask your friends or family members of you, "Is she/he a broken Christian?" what would the response be?

All Accounted For

By the Holy Spirit who dwells within us, guard the
good deposit entrusted to you.—2 Timothy 1:14

As Ezra was getting ready to take a group of the exiles from Babylon back to Jerusalem, he "set apart twelve of the leading priests" (Ezra 8:24) and handed over to their keeping all the gold, silver, and precious vessels that had been donated for the temple in Jerusalem. He put these gifts into their hands and said, "The silver and the gold are a freewill offering to the LORD God of your fathers. *Watch and keep them* until you weigh them before the chief of the priests . . . in the chambers of the house of the LORD" (verses 28–29 NASB).

Along the several hundred mile journey, these men experienced opposition and struggles, including "ambushes by the way" (verse 31). But they would look back on their pilgrimage and say, "The hand of our God was on us, and he delivered us" (verse 31).

Then came the day when they reached their long-awaited destination and delivered their precious goods to the priests in the temple: "The whole was counted and weighed, and the weight of everything was recorded" (verse 34).

We are on a journey toward the heavenly Jerusalem. God has put into our hands precious treasures—the gospel of Christ, the gifts and calling He has given us, the lives of those we are called to serve; we have been charged to watch and steward them carefully. The road before us is fraught with danger and difficulties; apart from the hand of God on us on our journey, we could not make it. But the hand of our God *is* on us, and He will deliver us from every enemy along the way.

Soon we'll be at the heavenly temple in the presence of our great High Priest, and oh, the joy, when we hand Him the treasures that were entrusted to our care and say, "Lord, by Your grace it's all here; it's all accounted for."

What makes you feel unequal to your task today? Thank God that
He will give you everything required to complete it. Ask Him for
grace to be faithful in the journey and to be able to give account
with joy on that day when you finally arrive home.

Saintly Living

But sexual immorality and all impurity or covetousness must not even be named among you, as is proper among saints.—Ephesians 5:3

 WE SOMETIMES HEAR THE WORD *saint* used to describe someone who is unusually pious or virtuous. Some religious traditions venerate particular individuals who have been officially recognized as "saints." Yet when the apostle Paul wrote to the New Testament churches, he often began by addressing *all* the believers as "saints" (literally, "holy ones" or "set apart ones").

Ironically, however, many of the people to whom Paul was writing were acting like anything *but* saints. They were guilty of many of the same sins we find among believers today—divisiveness, bitterness, immorality, selfishness, a love affair with the world.

So why did Paul call these early believers "saints"? *Because that is what they were!* Their sinful hearts had been washed pure by the blood of Jesus, and Paul wanted them to see how incongruous their behavior was with their true nature. He was saying to them (and to us) in effect, "Because you *are* saints, *live* as saints!"

When a sinner becomes a child of God, he is born anew. He is set apart from Satan and the world to belong wholly to God. *He becomes a saint.* He is given a new heart, and the Holy Spirit within him begins the process of transforming him into the very likeness of Christ. He's not perfect—none of us are—but his desire is to please God. Therefore when he sins, he denies his new identity and acts contrary to the nature into which he is being transformed.

Are you a saint? If you are a child of God, the answer is *yes.* The question is: Are you living like a saint? This should be our great longing and faithful pursuit, enabled by the grace of God and the power of His indwelling Holy Spirit.

 How does knowing and embracing this truth about yourself shed light on the wasteful, enslaving qualities of your "besetting sins"?

Broken Record

"You shall not bow down to their gods nor serve them, nor do as they do, but you shall utterly overthrow them and break their pillars in pieces."—Exodus 23:24

 BONNIE'S GRANDMOTHER HAD A TERRIBLE TEMPER, one she never tamed throughout her entire life. Her (Bonnie's) mother was also an angry, caustic woman who frequently lashed out at her children. Bonnie grew up hating the ways she had been treated by her mom.

After she married and had her first child, Bonnie shocked herself one day when her little boy did something he shouldn't, and she found herself screaming at him in rage. The sound scared her, actually. Scared her to hear words she'd promised never to inflict on her own children, now coming out of her mouth with such ease and volume. She fell to her knees and begged God's forgiveness. Yet she still felt "stuck" in the patterns she had apparently inherited from previous generations.

Some months later, Bonnie heard a conference speaker challenging the audience to treat past wrongs like a "record." (Remember LP records? Before tapes, CDs, and digital downloads?) "Rather than playing those voices over and over in your mind," the speaker said, "take the record of those wrongs done to you and break it over your knee." And that's just what Bonnie did. As an act of obedience and faith, she "broke the record" of her mom's many angry outbursts toward her—the hurtful, humiliating words spoken to her as a child. She forgave her mom for ever putting those "lyrics" in her head.

As a result, a sinful pattern that had plagued at least three generations came to a decisive end because one person chose to take matters across her own knee. What ungodly, inherited traits might come crashing to a heap in your own life if you made them face a similar fate?

 Is there a "record" of wrongs done to you that needs to be broken? What patterns in your life might be brought to an end if you were to refuse to be held captive by your past and chose instead to extend forgiveness toward those who wronged you?

How Refreshing

May the Lord grant mercy to the household of Onesiphorus, for he often refreshed me and was not ashamed of my chains.—2 Timothy 1:16

 YES, PAUL WAS IN PRISON and in dire straits when he wrote these words. On death row, in fact, under tight security and extreme deprivation and duress. But still, he was the apostle Paul. So steadfast, godly, and full of faith. An ordinary man like Onesiphorus might easily have concluded that someone of Paul's spiritual stature could not possibly need comfort and assistance from someone like him. Besides, if Paul did have need of others, he must have plenty of other friends who were eager to help.

Perhaps you've had that same feeling toward certain people. Your pastor and his wife, for example, or a Bible study leader who hardly seems in need of a word of encouragement from you. More than you can know, however, those individuals may need an Onesiphorus in their life—someone who prays, expresses concern, ministers to their practical needs.

You don't really know what season another person may be going through or the challenges they may be facing. Perhaps, despite their image, they're feeling alone or disheartened. An encouraging note or a simple act of kindness may mean the world to them.

We know that Paul was in a situation where few people had stepped up to the plate to care for his needs (2 Tim. 1:15; 4:16). Some were too scared to get involved. Others maintained their own reasons for keeping their distance. But this made Paul cherish the support of Onesiphorus all the more.

How I thank the Lord for people in my life like Onesiphorus —dear friends whose encouraging words and acts have ministered much-needed grace to my heart and have helped me to stay the course and press into the battle. Thinking about those people motivates me to reach out to others around me who may be in need of refreshing and comfort from Christ.

 Name someone who's blessed your life to such an extent that you would love to thank them and encourage them in some practical way. What's stopping you? There's never a bad time to be a good refresher.

All or Nothing

"Any one of you who does not renounce all that he has cannot be my disciple."—Luke 14:33

IN THE LATTER PART OF LUKE 14, we find Jesus surrounded by a large crowd. But unlike what you or I might have been tempted to do, He never played to the audience. He wasn't concerned about His ratings. He wasn't running for office or trying to attract the biggest crowd in town. He knew full well that when some heard His message, they would lose interest in His movement. But that didn't keep Him from being straightforward.

Jesus looked at the crowd of would-be disciples and said, in effect, "If you want to follow Me, you need to understand what's involved." He didn't speak in sweeping generalities; rather, He identified specific issues that must be surrendered by those who call themselves His followers—things like our *relationships,* our *physical bodies,* our *rights,* our *possessions.* "Yes, and even [your] own life," Jesus said, because "whoever does not bear his own cross and come after me cannot be my disciple" (verses 26–27).

It's one thing to have an emotional experience at a Christian gathering where you're inspired and challenged to yield control of everything to God. It's another matter to live out that surrender once the emotion of the moment has passed—when the bus gets home from the conference, when you lose your job and the bills keep coming, when you find out you're expecting your fifth child in seven years, when your mate is diagnosed with a terminal illness.

The extent of your discipleship will be determined in the laboratory of life, through daily, moment-by-moment choices and responses that reveal how surrendered you really are to following Christ.

Do you trust Him enough to pray this prayer? "Lord, I surrender every part of my being to You afresh today. Please work out that surrender in my life every day, in every matter, from now until I bow before You in eternity."

Perfect Freedom

But now that you have been set free from sin and have become
slaves of God, the fruit you get leads to sanctification and its end,
eternal life.—Romans 6:22

THEY WERE YOUNG, FULL OF LIFE, and very much in
love. Bill promised his wife-to-be that by giving him
her hand in marriage, he would see to it that she had
everything her heart desired.

Two years later, however, while Bill was pursuing
a master's degree and running a successful, fledgling business,
the young couple found themselves gripped by the realization
that knowing and serving Christ was far more important than
any other pursuit in life. One Sunday afternoon, overwhelmed
by a sense of His right to wholly possess and use their lives for
His kingdom purposes, they fell to their knees together in the
living room of their home and asked God to claim every ounce
of their energy and resources for His glory.

Then, reaching for paper and pen, they actually wrote out
and signed a contract, relinquishing all their rights to anything
they owned or would ever own, declaring themselves at God's
complete disposal. "That Sunday afternoon," he said, "we
became voluntary slaves of Jesus."

By the time Bill Bright passed away at age eighty-one, he and
Vonette had become household names in the Christian world,
founding and leading Campus Crusade for Christ, sending out
hundreds of thousands of workers to declare the gospel around
the world. Yet in spite of his many accomplishments, Dr. Bright
often insisted that the only epitaph he wanted on his tombstone
was this simple description: "A slave of Jesus Christ." That is
how he wanted to be known and remembered.

The pursuit of prosperity, success, and significance apart
from Christ will ultimately leave you empty and grasping after
the wind. Counterintuitive as it may seem, becoming a slave
of Christ is the path to true freedom. In His service we find
privilege, purpose, and everlasting joy.

Have you ever consciously acknowledged yourself to be a
willing slave of Christ? Write a brief prayer expressing your
desire for your life to be wholly at His disposal.

Called Up

Moses said to Joshua, "Choose for us men,
and go out and fight with Amalek."—Exodus 17:9

 AS FAR AS WE CAN TELL, Joshua had no prior military training before his commission to duty. No boot camp. No practice drills. No courses in war strategy or even experience as a soldier. His very first time in battle, he was given a commander's uniform. Makes you wonder what his chances were for survival, much less victory.

I posed this question to a former army captain, who told me that a current-day officer put into such a position would have already undergone intense training and educational requirements, with at least three years' experience in the field leading a company of soldiers. My friend's assessment of Joshua's prospects for success? "It would be suicidal without divine intervention."

Perhaps you're in a situation like Joshua's. You've been thrown into a battle with no prior experience or preparation. Like Joshua, you're learning on the job, not in the classroom reading textbooks and hearing from veteran instructors but directly in the line of fire. Whether in a challenging family situation or a new ministry you've undertaken or a health crisis you never saw coming, you see no way to make it through what God has placed upon you.

Yet the Lord may have known that the only way you could really learn and grow was by being put in a position to sink or swim, where you would have to look to Him to show you how to do it—and to supernaturally intervene on your behalf as you cast yourself upon Him.

Do you want to see God work in powerful ways? Then don't run from the heat of the battle; your desperation and inadequacy provide the perfect setting to experience Him working through you and delivering you.

 What have you been thrown into lately that is way over your head? How could you handle this with grace and faith rather than panic and complaining?

A Date with Disaster

When the woman saw that the tree was good for food, and that it was a delight to the eyes, and that the tree was to be desired to make one wise, she took of its fruit and ate.—Genesis 3:6

 SATAN DECEIVED EVE by causing her to make a decision based on what she could see and on what her emotions and reason told her to be right, even when it was contrary to what God had already told her. Eve took the bite. But instead of the promised rewards, she found herself with a mouthful of worms—shame, guilt, and fear, alienated from her husband and from her God. She had been lied to. She had been deceived.

And from that moment to this, Satan has used deception to win our affections, influence our choices, and destroy our lives and relationships. In one way or another, so many of our problems are the fruit of deception—the result of believing something that simply isn't true. Satan holds out the glittering promise of a rich, rewarding life if we will just choose his way; yet he knows "its end is the way to death" (Prov. 14:12).

Regardless of the immediate source, anytime we receive input that is not consistent with the Word of God, we can be sure the enemy of our soul is trying to deceive and destroy us. What we read or hear may sound right; it may feel right; it may seem right; but if it is not in accord with the Word of God, it *isn't* right.

If only Eve had paused to consider the consequences that would certainly follow if she accepted the tempter's offer. If only she had looked beyond the allure of what was held out to her in that moment, to the far sweeter fruit of a right relationship with God, which she was about to forfeit. And if only we could see that the forbidden fruit—fruit that looks so appealing and tastes so sweet while going down the throat—will ultimately deprive us of all that is truly good and desirable.

 What is something the enemy holds out to you that appears beautiful and desirable but is contrary to God's Word? Ask God to help you choose Him—to "taste and see that the LORD is good" (Ps. 34:8).

God Is in Control

The king's heart is a stream of water in the hand of the LORD;
he turns it wherever he will.—Proverbs 21:1

 WHEN YOU TELL YOUR TWO-YEAR-OLD that he is not allowed to walk across a busy street by himself, you are not being tyrannical or cruel. You know there are "cruel" cars on that busy street, and you are acting in your child's best interests. You are using your authority to protect your child (though he may be oblivious to his need for protection).

Similarly, when we submit to God-ordained authority, we are placing ourselves under the spiritual protection and covering of God Himself. On the other hand, when we insist on having it our way and stepping out from under that covering and protection, we open ourselves up to the influence and attack of the enemy.

I have come to believe that the fundamental issue in relation to submission (whether in marriage, the workplace, or other contexts) really comes down to our willingness to trust God and to place ourselves under *His* authority. When we are willing to obey Him, it is not nearly so difficult or threatening to submit to the human authorities He has placed in our lives.

The truth is that a higher authority controls every human authority. Ultimately, *no* human being controls our lives; submission actually places us in a position of being covered and protected by our wise, loving, all-powerful heavenly Father who controls the "heart of the king."

The question is, do we really believe God is bigger than any human authority? Big enough to change that "king's" heart if necessary? Big enough to protect us and meet our needs if we take our rightful place under authority?

Placing ourselves under God-ordained authority is the greatest evidence of how big we believe God really is.

 Is there any area in which you are resisting authorities God has placed in your life? How might it change your perspective to consider this an opportunity to trust His wisdom and sovereignty?

Broken Beginnings

Search me, O God, and know my heart! Try me and know my thoughts! And see if there be any grievous way in me, and lead me in the way everlasting!—Psalm 139:23–24

Dr. C. L. Culpepper was director of a large denominational mission in the Shantung province of China in the late 1920s. Returning home from a prayer meeting one night, he felt pressed to continue seeking God into the late hours, asking "Lord, what is it in me?" He sensed a spiritual need and dryness in his life, but he couldn't put his finger on what the issue was.

The next morning, he met his fellow missionaries again for prayer and confessed his sin of spiritual pretense, which God had exposed to him during the long night before. Dr. Culpepper acknowledged that others' praise of him as a "good missionary" had caused him to be proud and to steal glory from God. He later said, "My heart was so broken, I didn't believe I could live any longer."

Out of his confession arose such widespread brokenness throughout the national Christian leadership that the entire province was soon under the sweeping avalanche of the Spirit's conviction. The resulting Shantung Revival, which burned far and wide into the 1930s, deeply impacted the spiritual landscape of China in that era.

The most dramatic revival movements in history have typically begun with a handful of humble-hearted believers. And interestingly, those men and women deemed to be the "most godly" have usually been the first to humble themselves and admit their need. Have you been waiting for your mate or children or church leaders to get right with God? He may be waiting for *you*—your brokenness—to provoke the brokenness of those around you.

When is the last time you asked God to search your heart and to show you any "grievous way"? Ask Him for a fresh work of the Spirit in your life, and for grace to respond in true brokenness and humility.

There's an Appetizer for That

So flee youthful passions and pursue righteousness, faith, love, and peace, along with those who call on the Lord from a pure heart.—2 Timothy 2:22

GODLINESS, SPIRITUAL MATURITY, AND INTIMACY with the Lord do not just happen. They are the fruit of conscious, disciplined choices and habits—disciplines that are crucial to cultivating spiritual appetites.

Some time ago I listened as a single woman in her thirties confided with me how she still misses and longs for the "intimacy" she experienced in a number of immoral relationships from her past. At the same time, she admitted that she has little desire for intimacy with God.

I shared with her that our appetites are determined and fueled by the choices we make and the input we allow into our hearts. Those who fill their minds with images from sensual movies and the like are cultivating an appetite for worldly pleasures. But those who fill their minds with Scripture, memorizing the Word and devoting themselves to prayer and worship, will experience a growing hunger for intimate relationship with God.

Recently a friend handed me a novel she recommended as a "very sweet story—worth reading." It was indeed a beautifully written, sensitive book. Several chapters into it, however, a female character was introduced who used profanity liberally and set out to seduce a male friend who lived nearby. I didn't keep the book long enough to find out how it ended. Some may consider that decision extreme, unnecessary, or even legalistic; but it was a choice borne out of a desire to fill my mind with influences that intensify my hunger for God, and to avoid those that could dull or diminish my love for Him.

Such choices are not always easy to make, but they will produce blessings and benefits in your life that will far surpass anything this world can offer.

Is there anything in your habits or intake that is fueling fleshly desires or diminishing your hunger for God? What choices would deepen your desire for God and help cultivate single-minded devotion to Christ?

Appointed to His Service

I thank him who has given me strength, Christ Jesus our Lord, because he judged me faithful, appointing me to his service.—1 Timothy 1:12

 I SUPPOSE IF THERE'S ONE COMMON COMPLAINT I hear in my dealings with others—and in my own conversations with myself—it's the strain of busyness. Weariness from the perpetual plate spinning, along with the fact that many of the tasks that fill our days seem monotonous, menial, and meaningless. The fact is, for every exhilarating responsibility I enjoy, there are ten or more tasks that take sheer discipline to perform, and for which there is no obvious or immediate reward.

That's when it's helpful to remember to be thankful for what I call "the blessing of meaningful work," and to recognize that *all* service performed at His appointing and in the strength He supplies is significant.

First Chronicles 1–9 consists mostly of lists and genealogies. It's one of those passages we're tempted to gloss over. But recently I stopped to ponder one paragraph that details the responsibilities of the Levites. Some were assigned to count the temple utensils every time they were used. Others "prepared the mixing of the spices" (9:30). And then there was Mattithiah, who was "entrusted with making the flat cakes" (verse 31).

Not exactly job descriptions most of us dream of having! But these faithful servants glorified God through embracing and fulfilling their assignment, day in and day out, one repetitive duty after another.

As meaningless as some tasks may seem, as weary as we may get, we need to be reminded that it is a privilege to be entrusted by the living God with responsibility in His kingdom. In the midst of seemingly endless duties, most of which lack glamor and will never win earthly accolades, the "burden" of our workload is lightened when we approach it as a high and holy calling, a gift to be received with gratitude.

What are some ordinary, "thankless" jobs you are expected to perform? If you cannot see anything of great value being accomplished there, how might a grateful spirit change your perspective?

Enduring Motives

Therefore I endure everything for the sake of the elect,
that they also may obtain the salvation that is in
Christ Jesus with eternal glory.—2 Timothy 2:10

 "SUFFERING," according to pastor John Piper, "is one of Christ's strategies for the success of His mission"—for the advance of His kingdom.

I saw a woman live out this principle in the midst of a heartrending situation where her husband had been unfaithful to his marriage vows, deeply wounding his family, just as their two children were nearing their teen years. Throughout the whole ordeal, she kept her eyes on Christ. She endured the painful days and torturous nights for His sake and for the sake of her kids and their fledgling faith (while still taking wise, necessary steps to confront her husband's sinful choices).

During one tender moment in the middle of this prolonged nightmare, her twelve-year-old son said to her, "Mom, since all of this happened, I've been afraid to get married some day because I'm scared I'll hurt my family the way Dad has hurt us. But you have shown him so much forgiveness and love—your example actually makes me want to get married and show that same kind of commitment to my family someday. You make me want to be a godly testimony to others, just as you are."

In time, this woman's patient endurance not only strengthened her children's faith but was also a means God used to bring her husband to repentance and to restore their marriage.

The apostle Paul was willing to endure suffering "for the sake of the elect," for the furtherance of their growth in the gospel. And we, too, even when placed in undeserved, seemingly unbearable situations, must remember who's watching and what's at stake. God may not "fix" everything as we would wish this side of eternity, but He will surely give us the grace to endure as we embrace by faith the mysterious purposes and ultimate outcome of our suffering.

How has your faith been bolstered by watching the steady,
graceful endurance of a fellow believer under pressure?
How does the perspective expressed by Paul in this passage
speak to a difficult situation you are facing?

Comprehensive Course

*[Mary] sat at the Lord's feet, and listened to
his teaching.*—Luke 10:39b

 WOULDN'T IT BE GREAT if there were a class you
could take that would teach you everything you
needed to know and provide answers for all
your problems? Maybe you've got a boss who's
impossible to please, a sinful habit you just can't
kick, a church where no one seems to be hungry for God, or a
child who's begun lying to you, and you just need some help
with how to handle it all.

Actually, there *is* such a course, and you're enrolled in it
right now—a course that addresses every issue you will ever face.
The Teacher Himself has written the textbook. And though it
doesn't claim to solve all your problems, it does have all the
resources you need to *face* your problems. Parts of the course
material can be difficult to grasp, but the Teacher is always
available—twenty-four hours a day—ready to meet with you
one-on-one so He can tailor the course to your needs and help
you better understand.

So I encourage you today to take time to sit at the feet of Jesus.
Put aside other distractions; open the ears of your heart, open His
Word, and let Him teach you. He knows just what you need, and
He is available to instruct you and guide you in His truth.

When I was studying piano performance as an undergraduate
student, the university I attended offered "master classes" in
which accomplished instructors would teach the secrets they had
acquired over many years of studying and performing. It was
a great honor and opportunity to sit under their teaching. But
nothing compares to the joy and privilege of learning at the feet
of our heavenly Master, "in whom are hidden all the treasures
of wisdom and knowledge" (Col. 2:3).

 *What could change this devotional time from a quick few minutes
into a true learning experience at the feet of Jesus?
Isn't that what you really need?*

First Mistake

Finally, brothers, whatever is true, whatever is pure, whatever is lovely, whatever is commendable, if there is any excellence, if there is anything worthy of praise, think about these things.—Philippians 4:8

 AS A RULE, people don't fall into bondage overnight. They don't just wake up one morning and discover they're addicted to food or can't control their temper. There is a progression that leads to bondage. And it begins when we start listening to and pondering things that aren't true.

That's how it all began in the garden of Eden. Eve *listened* to the lies Satan told her. I'm confident she had no idea where those lies would ultimately lead her and her family. Perhaps it didn't seem particularly dangerous just to listen to the serpent—to hear him out, to see what he had to say. Listening in itself wasn't disobedience.

But here's the key: listening to a viewpoint that was contrary to God's Word put Eve on a slippery slope that led to disobedience, which then led to physical and spiritual death. Listening with an open mind to things that are not in accord with God's Word is the first step toward bondage and destruction.

That's why it's so important to monitor the input we allow into our minds and hearts and to reject that which promotes ungodly thinking. A steady diet of worldly influences—from television, magazines, movies, music, friends, novels—will seductively shape our view of what is valuable, beautiful, and important in life.

There are no harmless lies. We cannot expose ourselves to the world's false, deceptive ways of thinking and expect to come out unscathed. Eve's first mistake was not eating the fruit; her first mistake was listening to the serpent and considering his worldview as a valid option. Mindlessly absorbing counsel or reasoning that is contrary to the truth will lead us to develop wrong beliefs that eventually place us in bondage and erect barriers in our fellowship with God.

 Can you think of something you heard recently that appealed to your interests or desires but, as you think about it, is not consistent with God's Word? Did you "listen to" it (receive it mindlessly), or did you consciously reject the lie?

Sincerely Yours

The aim of our charge is love that issues from a pure heart and a good conscience and a sincere faith.—1 Timothy 1:5

POTTERY MAKING WAS A LUCRATIVE BUSINESS in the ancient world, which meant it invited its share of shoddy craftsmen more interested in turning a profit than demanding quality. If unscrupulous artisans discovered, for example, after firing a piece of pottery that it was cracked or blemished in some way, they would often rub wax into the damaged area to cover up the offending mark. The average person couldn't detect the flaw and wouldn't know until the pot was heated that it wasn't sound and solid.

This common practice led the more respected pottery makers to post a sign over their shops that read *sin cerus*—"without wax"—indicating that their products were guaranteed to be authentic. If any cracks were detected in the hardening process, that pot was tossed out and a new one was thrown onto the wheel. Hold one of their items up to the light, and even the everyday buyer could see that it contained no hidden imperfections. It was *sin cerus.*

Sincere.

Jesus is the light of the world, in whom "is no darkness at all" (1 John 1:5). When we hold ourselves up to the scrutiny of His gaze, everything is exposed. And what does He see? A life patched over and cosmetically disguised to appear genuine and complete? Or a person who by God's grace and His empowering life within us is not afraid to be tested for cracks and character blemishes?

"If we walk in the light, as he is in the light, we have fellowship with one another, and the blood of Jesus his Son cleanses us from all sin" (1 John 1:6). No pretending, just purity. *Sincerity.*

What parts of yourself do you try to cover up in order to appear to be "good quality"? Will you let the light of Christ test your life and expose any hidden flaws or cracks? Then let His redeeming grace purify you and make you whole and sincere.

Wedding Preparations

Since we have these promises, beloved, let us cleanse ourselves from every defilement of body and spirit, bringing holiness to completion in the fear of God.—2 Corinthians 7:1

 MY GOAL IN LIFE is not that I would be free from problems or pain; it's not that I would be a best-selling author or a sought-after speaker, not that I would be secure in myself, my friends, my health, and my finances. My deepest desire is that I would glorify God by being a holy woman, and that the glory of God would be displayed through a holy church.

How I look forward to that day when you and I, along with all the other saints from all the ages, walk together down that aisle toward our beloved Bridegroom. I want to face Him with joy—radiant and unashamed—"dressed in His righteousness alone, faultless to stand before His throne," as the old hymn so beautifully expresses it.

If you are a child of God, you are part of the bride that has been betrothed to His Son. Are you anticipating and ready for this wedding? If not, what do you need to do to get ready for it? Is there a sin you need to confess and forsake? A step of obedience you need to take? A habit you need to give up—or cultivate? A relationship you need to break off—or reconcile?

Are there items in your possession you need to get rid of? Are there debts you need to pay? Are there people whose forgiveness you need to seek? Is there restitution you need to make?

Whatever it is, for Jesus' sake, for the world's sake, for His body's sake, for your family's sake, for your own sake—*do it.* In light of His wonderful promises, by His grace, and by the power of His Holy Spirit—*do it.*

Nothing could be more important. Nothing could bring Him greater glory, and nothing could bring you greater joy—both now and throughout all eternity.

 Ask God to show you what you need to do to be ready to meet your heavenly Bridegroom. Then ask Him for grace to take whatever steps and make whatever changes are needed.

Like Drinking Poison

"Blessed are the merciful, for they shall receive mercy."—Matthew 5:7

 JUST AS BASKETBALL STAR RUDY TOMJANOVICH was sprinting to break up a fight at midcourt of an NBA game in 1977, one of the participants whirled around and punched him right in the nose. Instead of simply stunning him, the sheer physics of the violent contact broke nearly every bone in his face. It almost killed him.

It happens like that sometimes, doesn't it? You can probably think of an event from your own life when things got heated, the pot began to boil over, and the next thing you knew, the damage had been done. There was no going back. The words someone said, the reactions that occurred—they forever changed your life.

But when asked if he had forgiven the opposing player for the punch that ruined his playing career, Tomjanovich responded, "Someone once told me that hating him would be like drinking poison and hoping someone else would die."

Like drinking poison and hoping someone else would die. That's a powerful word picture for what unforgiveness is like in the human heart. Though it may feel right, though it may seem justified, though it may appear to be the only option available to us, it is destructive and deadly—primarily to the one who drinks it. The very weapon we use to inflict pain on our offender becomes a sword turned inward on ourselves, doing far more damage to us and to those who love us than to those who have hurt us.

Only God's way—the way of forgiveness—holds out any hope of healing and rescue from the inevitable troubles we face in this life. And only those who walk this way will experience the reality of God's grace and mercy for their own sins.

 Have you drunk the poison of unforgiveness? What have you been hoping to accomplish by clinging to your resentment, by holding on to the right to "punish" your offender? What blessings might you be forfeiting by withholding mercy?

Consider Him

And let us run with endurance the race that is set before us, looking to Jesus, the founder and perfecter of our faith.—Hebrews 12:1–2

 WHATEVER KIND OF CRISIS OR CHALLENGE you may be facing today, your greatest need is for a fresh look at the incomparable Christ. He alone is able to save us from sin, sanctify our hearts, satisfy our souls, and sustain us when we grow weary of running and are tempted to throw in the towel.

He deserves to be the supreme object of our personal affection and attention. He must be the One on whom we steadfastly fix our eyes and our hope. Only by beholding Him can we be transformed into His likeness, becoming like Him and fulfilling the purpose for which we were created.

The writer of Hebrews goes on to exhort us, "Consider him who endured from sinners such hostility against himself, so that you may not grow weary or fainthearted" (Heb. 12:3).

Consider Him—that is the counsel most needed by our generation—and every generation. Christ is the Tonic for tired, troubled hearts. He is Wealth for impoverished souls. He is Life for those who are bored and deadened by endless entertainment and meaningless pursuits. He is Wisdom for the perplexed, Health for the wounded, Freedom for the addicted, and Grace for the guilty. He truly is more than enough!

If today finds you growing "weary or fainthearted," look to Jesus, risen from the dead, ascended, sitting at the right hand of God, victorious over all, waiting at the finish line for you and for all those He has redeemed by His grace. He is the author, the perfecter, and the finisher of your faith, and He is able to sustain you and keep you in the race.

Seek to know Him afresh today, to worship and trust Him. Don't look to lesser heroes. Look to Him. And find in Him the strength, courage, and grace you need to press on—all the way to the finish line.

 Where do you tend to look when you're struggling to keep going? What does Christ offer that cannot be found in any kind of temporal escape or diversion?

Following Where He Leads

He leads me in paths of righteousness for his name's sake.—Psalm 23:3

I'LL NEVER FORGET THE TIME I WAS FIRST CHALLENGED to consider starting a daily teaching program on the radio. From the outset, I had grave reservations about such an undertaking and was quick to list them to the Lord and others.

I knew virtually nothing about broadcasting and felt utterly inadequate and incapable of taking on such a responsibility. Beyond those practical concerns, I was in my early forties and was wishing for a more settled life than I had experienced over more than twenty years of itinerant ministry. In my mind, accepting this challenge would mean working harder than ever and relinquishing any thought of anonymity, privacy, or a "normal" life—things I selfishly wished to enjoy. I remember thinking, *This would mean having no life of my own!*

Even as a little girl, I had recognized God's ownership of my life. I had long acknowledged that I was not my own; in essence, I had signed a blank contract, giving my life wholly to God to be used for His purposes. Yet now that He was filling in some of the details, I was trying to protect and preserve part of it for myself. Finally, stepping out in faith and surrender, I said, "Yes, Lord. I am Your servant. You know my weaknesses, my fears, and my personal desires. But I will gladly embrace whatever You reveal to be Your will in this matter."

I'd be less than truthful if I said the journey since then has been easy; but His presence and grace have been with me each step of the way, and I have never regretted following Him on this path.

God's call in your life will probably look different than it does in mine—or in anyone else's. Regardless of the details, He asks simply that we bow the knee and say, *Yes, Lord.* That is the only path to joy and blessing.

Why do feelings of fear and inadequacy provide such a poor guidance system for our lives? Where is He leading you that requires faith and surrender? Ask Him for grace to step out and say, "Yes, Lord."

Hurrying God?

One thing have I asked of the LORD, that will I seek after: that I may dwell in the house of the LORD all the days of my life, to gaze upon the beauty of the LORD and to inquire in his temple.—Psalm 27:4

I HAVE COME TO BELIEVE that a rushed, hurried attitude is one of the deadliest enemies of an effective devotional life. When I once asked several hundred women to share the biggest obstacles to a meaningful quiet time practice, the issue of busyness—"not enough time"—was right at the top of their list.

Years ago, while exercising on the treadmill and listening to a recorded interview with my friend Dr. Henry Blackaby (author of *Experiencing God*), I heard something that impacted my mindset in a deep way. Dr. Blackaby told of his experiences years earlier with getting up each morning to meet with the Lord but often feeling rushed to attend to the various responsibilities of the day. He went on to share how God had convicted him that it was a grievous offense to "hurry up" the God of the universe, and how he had determined to move up his quiet time a half hour earlier so he would not feel so pressed. He did so, but found that it still made little difference. So he moved it up a half hour earlier. "And I kept moving it up until I knew," Dr. Blackaby said, "that I could meet with God as long as He wanted, without my feeling hurried."

As I heard those words from a busy man who evidences a deep, steady, fruitful walk with God, I felt a fresh sense of resolve to do whatever was necessary to secure unhurried moments where God could speak to me on a daily basis. I have failed in that resolve far too often. But I remain convinced that this is a battle worth fighting. Yes, it takes some adjustments in our schedules. But the sweet, precious fruit of lingering in His presence is worth whatever "sacrifices" may be required.

What are some of the negative consequences of always trying to meet with God "on the run"? What have been your most effective remedies to this "hurry up" feeling?

It's Beyond Me

O LORD, my heart is not lifted up; my eyes are not too high;
I do not occupy myself with things too great and too marvelous
for me.—Psalm 131:1

 THE LAST PART OF THIS VERSE has become a recurring theme for me, something I often call to mind when facing difficulties and challenges: "This is just too great for me. There is no way I can figure it out on my own. And I am not going to let my heart get all worked up over something that is so far beyond my control."

That's a good place for a child of God to be, because life brings an endless stream of unexplainable problems, unanswerable questions, unfunded opportunities, unknown speculations. Deep down, we want to be able to manage all of this, to stay in control of it, to know how all the pieces fit together. But there are puzzle pieces we will *never* have the knowledge to understand or put together without divine help. And we will stay in a continual dither of wasted time, energy, and emotion if we keep trying to sort it all out—situations we simply cannot solve before bedtime tonight—if ever.

So if you're over your head today—if perhaps the people at work or at church don't value your gifts and potential, if the people in your home won't respond as they should—this would be a good time to focus instead on calming and quieting your soul (Ps. 131:2), trusting God's wise determination of how He wants to take care of this.

Instead of seeking your own ambitions and agenda on your own timetable, trust God to place you where He wants to use you, while you concentrate on serving Him faithfully in the midst of circumstances beyond your understanding. That's one secret to a peaceful heart.

 How much of the noise in your spirit comes from being consumed
with matters beyond your comprehension or ability to control?
Stop wrestling and start resting in His wisdom and grace.

Love That Restores

My brothers, if anyone among you wanders from the truth
and someone brings him back, let him know that whoever brings
back a sinner from his wandering will save his soul from death
and will cover a multitude of sins.—James 5:19–20

THE IDEA OF TURNING SINNERS from the error of their ways is largely foreign in our day. The hue and cry of our postmodern culture is *tolerance*, which means, "You can live however you want to live, but don't try to tell me what's right for me." As deception has inundated our culture, many believers have become hesitant to stand for the truth for fear of being labeled intolerant or narrow-minded.

Many Christians not only manifest this "live and let live" attitude toward the world but also in relation to other believers who are not walking in the truth. They don't want to rock the boat or be considered judgmental. It seems easier just to let things go.

But we must remember that in Christ and His Word, we have the truth that sets people free—not because we're so smart but because God's ways are eternal and life-giving. It's essential that we understand this. The truth of God's Word is the only way for those we know and love to be delivered from darkness, deception, and death. If we truly care about them, we will prayerfully and actively seek to restore them to God's way of thinking. This is part of our gospel mandate as followers of Christ.

So let's learn the truth, believe it, live it out, and proclaim it—even when it flies in the face of our hypertolerant culture. And when you see someone you care about "wandering" in deception, ask God if He wants to use you—perhaps along with others in the body—to help bring that person back to the truth. As you seek to restore him or her, be sure to do so "in a spirit of gentleness, [keeping] watch on yourself, lest you too be tempted" (Gal. 6:1).

 Is there someone you need to confront with the wisdom of Scripture? Pray that God will grant entrance into their heart and turn them back to the way of truth.

That One Step

And make straight paths for your feet, so that what is lame
may not be put out of joint but rather be healed.—Hebrews 12:13

 "CARL" IS A FRIEND and Texas businessman who found himself under the heavy hand of God's conviction. Years earlier, he had testified as a witness in federal court, where under oath he had purposely given vague answers to direct questions, desiring to protect one of the parties involved. He hadn't told "the whole truth."

One night, unable to sleep, Carl sensed God surfacing in his heart this issue he had thought was a "closed case." He tried hard to reason it away, knowing that coming clean included the risk of going to prison for perjury. He even sought to negotiate a compromise with the Lord, confessing other sins and promising to surrender other areas of his life. But the Spirit wouldn't let him off the hook.

Finally, Carl phoned the judge's office and explained the situation to an assistant, acknowledging his fault and his change of heart. Not until twelve long months had passed did he find out for sure that neither side wanted to reopen the case.

But during a year that seemed to go on forever, his obedience in this one difficult issue opened the door for God's grace to be poured into every facet of his life. Once (by his own testimony) a proud, demanding husband and father, spiritually self-sufficient, overly concerned about his reputation, his heart was turned in a new way toward his wife and children; he began to experience a deeper level of tenderness and sensitivity toward the Lord and others. His family and friends will attest that in the more than thirty years since, he has not lost the spiritual vibrancy that resulted from that initial step of humility and obedience.

Just one step. Sometimes that's the only thing holding you back from a walk of true freedom, fullness, and fruitfulness in Christ.

 Does that "one step" come to mind as the Spirit
searches your heart today? What if new intimacy
with Him was waiting just on the other side?

Maintaining Your Distance

*For this is the will of God, your sanctification: that you
abstain from sexual immorality.*—1 Thessalonians 4:3

 THE APOSTLE PAUL wrote to New Testament believers
living in a sex-crazed world—not unlike our own—
and his bold, black-and-white words imply an across-
the-board caution: *none of us is immune from the potential
for sexual sin.* I don't care how old you are, how long
you've been married, or how settled and secure you feel today.
It happens. To people in every demographic. Both outside the
church and (sadly) inside the Christian household as well.

That's why we are admonished to "abstain"—not just once
but "more and more" (verse 1)—from every hint of sexual sin,
purposing each day to pursue purity of thought and practice.

The command to abstain from immorality is not merely
a random or capricious "thou shalt not" statement on God's
part. Sexual purity mirrors the character of God. As a faithful,
loving, covenant-keeper, He has declared us (the church) to be
the bride of His Son. The sexual relationship within marriage,
then, is a picture of His faithfulness to us and, by His grace,
our faithfulness to Him. Our holiness in every realm, including
sexual matters, is intended to reflect the holiness of the One who
has chosen and called us.

When we violate His standards of moral purity, we are
actually desecrating the biblical imagery of redemption. We are
violating the character and nature of God. We are even violating
our *own* nature since we were created in His image.

"Flee from sexual immorality," God's Word says (1 Cor.
6:18)—of every kind, in any fashion. This is not only a protection
for you and your relationships; it's a preservation of the gospel
message that your life is meant to place on permanent display.

 *Are you making any compromises in your sexual life that are
unworthy of your calling as part of the bride of Christ?
You know His will—your sanctification. Ask Him for grace
to make the choices that will display His purity.*

Why Me?

In all these things we are more than conquerors
through him who loved us.—Romans 8:37

OFTEN WHEN WE TRY TO COPE WITH DIFFICULTY and disappointment, underneath it all is a heart's cry that keeps us from experiencing God's best in our situations—those two plaintive words (spoken or not) in which we try to find solace: "Why me?"

How many times have you clung to this tart complaint, hoping to draw from it enough strength to protect your heart from further danger and damage? "Why is life so hard?" "Why did this have to happen?" "Why isn't God answering my prayers?" "Why does this problem never seem to end?" "Why am I supposed to just accept this?"

"Why me?"

We feel betrayed, left out, mistreated, and underappreciated. Like a whirlpool spinning around in never-ending circles, tugging and draining and pulling us down with every sweep of self-pity, we sink lower and lower into ourselves, into our problems, away from God, discouraged and ungrateful.

"You're telling me to trust Him and give thanks, to keep my head up. But you've never been in my shoes. If you had any idea what I've been through, you wouldn't be so quick to say that."

I promise you, if all I had to share with you were some sweet platitudes about thankfulness, I wouldn't even try to respond to real-life circumstances such as the ones you're facing. If all our faith can offer are words that only fit in a church service or a theological textbook, it would be unkind of me to extend them to someone who needs so much more than that.

But true, Christ-centered, grace-motivated gratitude fits everywhere, even in life's most desperate moments and difficult situations. Even when there are no "answers," it gives hope. Gratitude is what transforms overwhelmed strugglers into triumphant conquerors, even if their circumstances remain, for the present, unchanged.

What situation or dilemma paints the context for your most recent "Why me?" Can you think of any cause for gratitude that may lie concealed in the picture?

God Is Love

So we have come to know and to believe the love that
God has for us. God is love, and whoever abides in love
abides in God, and God abides in him.—1 John 4:16

A FRIEND in the midst of a long, hard battle with breast cancer once wrote to tell me how she had come through the experience with a deeper comprehension of the love of God, as seen through her husband's response to her double mastectomy.

"As we wept and trembled when he took off my bandages for the first time, I was so ugly, scarred, and bald. I was in intense grief that I could never be a whole wife to him again. But he held me tightly and with tears in his eyes said, 'Honey, I love you—because that is who I am.'

"I instantly recognized Christ in my husband," she continued. "As His bride, we are also eaten up with cancer—sin—and are scarred, mutilated, and ugly. But He loves us because *that is who He is.* No comeliness in us draws Christ's attention; it is only His essence that draws Him to us."

Yes, God *does* love us. Whether or not we feel loved, regardless of what we have done or where we have come from, He loves us with an infinite, incomprehensible love—not because we are lovely or lovable but because He *is* love.

If you are His child, trusting in Him for salvation, you are no longer His enemy. In spite of your rebellion and your alienation from Him, He has loved you and sent His Son to die for you. He loved you in eternity past; He will love you for all eternity future. There is nothing you can do to make Him love you less, and nothing you can do to make Him love you more. *That's just who He is.*

When does His love seem the most distant from you?
Knowing that nothing can ever separate you from His
love (Rom. 8:38–39), what are some possible reasons
for your feelings?

Audience of One

*Let the word of Christ dwell in you richly . . . singing psalms
and hymns and spiritual songs, with thankfulness in your hearts
to God.*—Colossians 3:16

LIKE THE WORLD AROUND US, many believers have
developed an addiction to being entertained. Turn
down the houselights, shine some spotlights on the
stage, and let us sit back and watch the performance.
Even at home, or in the car, we are so quick to turn
on the music and listen to others sing their songs of praise. I'm
not suggesting that it's wrong to create an atmosphere to help us
tune out distractions, or to listen to others sing songs of praise.
But have we let that become a substitute for lifting our own
voices to the Lord?

Look around the congregation during worship in the
average church and notice how many people are just standing
there, barely mouthing the words, much less singing aloud. We
are the product of a culture in which real corporate singing just
isn't done much anymore. We prefer other people to do it *for* us.
But if any group of people should love to sing, it is those of us
who've been redeemed.

I recall spending the night in the home of a friend many
years ago. A Nigerian pastor and his wife were also guests in
the same house. In the middle of the night, long after we had
all gone to bed, I was awakened by a sound unlike anything I'd
ever heard. In the bedroom next to mine, that dear couple was
singing the hymn "How Great Thou Art"—slowly, loudly, with
a heavy accent and with all their hearts. For a moment, in my
half-awake state, I wasn't sure I hadn't died and gone to heaven!

My (lack of) vocal skill is such that I'll never be asked to sing
on a platform. But why are we content to stand by as spectators
while the more polished singers and performers handle all the
worshiping duties? We are active participants in the great eternal
drama of praise, performing for a sacred audience of One.

*Have you forgotten how to use your own voice to express your
heart of praise? "Sing praises to the LORD, O you his saints,
and give thanks to his holy name" (Ps. 30:4)!*

Defy Explanation

"The Holy Spirit will come upon you, and the power of the Most High will overshadow you."—Luke 1:35

THE LATE DR. ADRIAN ROGERS once challenged a large gathering with these words: "We have no right to be believed so long as we can be explained."

Most of our lives are so very explainable, aren't they? Why? Because we generally rely on natural, human efforts and energy, abilities and plans, programs and methods. What would happen if God's people actually put their complete trust in His promises and laid hold of Him in prayer? What if we believed Him for the impossible—the reconciliation of marriages, the salvation of unbelieving friends and relatives, the spiritual transformation of wayward children, a fresh outpouring of His Spirit in genuine revival?

Don't ever forget that God-sized tasks cannot be carried out apart from His power at work in and through us. Yes, you can share the gospel of Christ with your lost friends, but you cannot give them repentance and faith. You can provide a climate that is conducive to the spiritual growth of your children, but you cannot make them have a heart for God. You and I are totally dependent on Him to produce any fruit of eternal value.

And yet God specializes in the impossible—the unexplainable —so that when the victory is won and the task is complete, we cannot take any credit. *Others* know we didn't do it, and *we* know we didn't do it.

Our calling is impossible to fulfill, apart from the power of His Holy Spirit. As soon as we think we can handle it on our own, we become useless to Him. But as we are willing to get out of the way, let God take over, and allow Him to overshadow us, we will see Him do what only He can do, and those around us will be moved to believe.

What is there about your life that is unexplainable apart from the presence and power of God? What is He asking of you that you know you can't do on your own? Thank Him for the enabling power of His Holy Spirit!

Drastic Measures

*But put on the Lord Jesus Christ, and make no provision
for the flesh, to gratify its desires.*—Romans 13:14

 I HAVE A FRIEND WHO GAVE UP NAPS because she would
inevitably become irritated with her children when they
disturbed her rest. She told me, "I decided I couldn't
take naps because I was setting myself up to sin."

A single friend in her forties told me that she can't
watch "chick flicks" because they fuel discontentment in her
heart and an excessive desire for something God has not chosen
to provide (marriage).

Another woman shared that because of her desire to be
holy, she actually had to change pediatricians. She had found
herself becoming attracted to her children's doctor and looking
forward to appointments so she could be with him.

Speaking personally, there are certain types of restaurants
it's best for me to avoid if I want to glorify God in what I eat,
unless I have some strong accountability in place.

Now we all know that naps, movies, and restaurants cannot
make us sin—we *choose* to sin. But I'm talking about being
purposeful and intentional in this battle against the flesh, being
willing to eliminate anything that fuels unholy appetites or
provides an inducement or occasion to sin.

I'm serious about this. And you need to be as well. What
kinds of triggers and situations most often lead you into selfish
indulgence? Is it alcohol? Or the Internet? Or computer games?
Or romantic movies? What did Jesus mean when He said, "If
your right hand causes you to sin, cut it off and throw it away"
(Matt. 5:30), if He wasn't talking about the willingness to take
extreme measures to avoid sinning? Continuing to fuel sin—
holding on to anything that lures you into sin—is like pouring
fertilizer on weeds and then getting frustrated because you can't
get rid of them!

 *What "fertilizer" have you been pouring on the besetting sins that
control your life? Are there any drastic measures that could render
you more free to love Christ and to walk in victory over sin?*

End Results

Love one another with brotherly affection. Outdo one another in showing honor.—Romans 12:10

IF YOU WERE ASKED TO RANK THE SEVEN QUALITIES of Christian character found in 2 Peter 1:5–7, would you place them in the same order as the apostle did? "Make every effort to supplement your faith with *virtue*, and virtue with *knowledge*, and knowledge with *self-control*, and self-control with *steadfastness*, and steadfastness with *godliness*, and godliness with *brotherly affection*, and brotherly affection with *love*."

Is that the same progression you would use? Does this track with your own goals for how you want to develop these traits in your life, building one on top of the other? I've asked myself the same question, and wondered if I might have been inclined to place "godliness" at the *end* of that list, representing the ultimate goal of living out our Christian faith.

Yet in one sense, godliness is not an end in itself. If it were, we might be led to think we could just go live in a cave somewhere and be "spiritual" the rest of our lives. But this Scripture suggests that we have not attained spiritual maturity until our godliness is being lived out horizontally, in the context of community. Godliness must ultimately find its expression in "brotherly affection" and "love"—starting within the family of God and then extending outward to others.

If we are not cultivating strong, loving relationships with other believers, if we are not exhibiting genuine love for those outside the faith, then we are spiritually deficient, no matter how diligently we're trying to live for God. Growing in Christ means growing closer and deeper with His people. Growing in Christ means growing more loving.

How would you describe your Christian friendships in terms of openness, sacrificial love, and encouragement? What about your relationships with nonbelievers in terms of your care, interest, patience, and compassion?

Dry Spells

Why are you cast down, O my soul, and why are you in
turmoil within me? Hope in God; for I shall again praise him,
my salvation and my God.—Psalm 42:11

 IF YOU HAVE BEEN A CHRISTIAN for any length of time, you have probably experienced a season of "spiritual dryness." Those dry spells can be God's way of revealing what's in our heart—whether we love Him because of the spiritual sensations He gives us, or just because He is God. They teach us to walk by faith rather than sight.

At times the dryness can be related to getting into a rut in our devotional life; perhaps we've become more focused on the mechanics than on drawing spiritual life from the Scripture and nourishing our hearts on Christ, the living Word of God. When this happens, it can be helpful to vary our routine. For example, when I feel the need for greater freshness in my time in the Word, I may take a few days or weeks out of my normal Bible reading schedule to memorize and meditate on a passage in a different part of God's Word—something that speaks to my current need or warms my heart with gospel truths.

Dry spells are also good opportunities to ask God to show us any issues that may be creating a barrier in our relationship with Him. Is there any known sin you haven't confessed or repented of? Is there unforgiveness in your heart toward a family member or an individual who has wronged you? Is there some step of obedience you know God wants you to take that you have delayed?

Psalms 42 and 43 read like the journal of a believer in the throes of a dry spell. When you find yourself in that place, follow the example of the psalmist: *look back* and remember the joys you have experienced in God's presence in the past; *look ahead* to the day when your joy will be restored; and in the meantime, determine to *look up* with expectation, knowing that "I shall again praise him, my salvation and my God."

 Have you experienced seasons of spiritual dryness in your life?
What have you learned from these times "in the valley"?

Wake-Up Call

And in every province, wherever the king's command and his decree reached, there was great mourning among the Jews, with fasting and weeping and lamenting.—Esther 4:3

 THESE JEWS IN ESTHER'S DAY were third and fourth generation expatriates living in Persia, many of them in a backslidden condition. Their ancestors had been exiled there for their sins many decades before. Some had returned with Ezra to their native Israel, but most had not. The remaining Jews had become secularized, assimilated into Persian culture. Many were Jews in name only.

But this wasn't how they were called to live or what God had in mind for them. So He used pressure and persecution to revive and purify their hearts, to help them see the depravity of the culture they'd become so accustomed to, as well as their attraction to it. He used a wicked king, a wicked decree (one that legalized their extermination), and a desperate situation to get the attention of His people.

He does the same with His people today.

In times of prosperity, when the stock market is up, when consumer confidence is high and peace is plentiful, our hearts tend to become complacent. The church becomes worldly. In His desire to turn our hearts back to Himself, God uses crises to wake us up to the fact that we've become enamored with the world around us and to make us desperate for a restored relationship with Him. He stirs up His people to seek Him in prayer and fasting, realizing that He is the only hope—both for His people and for our nation and world.

As we incline our hearts toward God, responding to crises in our nation with humility and prayer, we will begin to experience the fresh wind of His Spirit blowing through us. And He will make us what we were intended to be—"children of God without blemish in the midst of a crooked and twisted generation, among whom [we] shine as lights in the world" (Phil. 2:15).

 Pray that God will use circumstances in our nation to cause His people to "humble themselves and pray and seek [His] face and turn from their wicked ways" (2 Chron. 7:14), and that He will hear from heaven and have mercy on us and on our land.

Feeling Unforgiven?

*"So also my heavenly Father will do to every one of you,
if you do not forgive your brother from your heart."*—Matthew 18:35

 WE OFTEN QUOTE THIS PETITION from the Lord's
Prayer: "Forgive us our debts as we forgive our
debtors" (Matt. 6:12 NKJV). But the wording
of that request should lead us to ask ourselves,
"What if God only forgave me to the extent
that I've been willing to forgive those who have sinned against
me?" It's sobering to think about.

And it's something we can't ignore, for in the verses that
follow directly after the Lord's Prayer, we hear Jesus saying, "If
you forgive others their trespasses, your heavenly Father will
also forgive you, but if you do not forgive others their trespasses,
neither will your Father forgive your trespasses" (verses 14–15).

Strong words. They are so stark and direct, in fact, that we
who are saved by grace yet unforgiving in our hearts find ourselves
looking for loopholes, dodging the obvious, trying to convince
ourselves that He must have meant something less exacting.

Yet in reality, we find nowhere to hide. When we refuse to
forgive, something is blocked in our relationship with the Father.
The Scripture affirms what our own experience confirms—a
clear connection between our willingness to extend forgiveness
to others and our ability to appropriate and experience His
forgiveness for our sins.

I have met many believers who find it difficult to accept
and experience God's love and forgiveness. There can be any
number of reasons for that, of course. But one of the biggest is
a refusal to forgive others. Those who hold on to bitterness, who
refuse to forgive, cannot hope to enjoy the full, sweet taste of His
compassion and mercy.

 *Do you struggle with doubting or distrusting God's mercy toward
you? Could there be any unforgiveness in your heart that is
limiting your capacity to experience His grace and forgiveness?*

Enemy Combatants

"Because you did not serve the LORD your God with joyfulness and gladness of heart . . . therefore you shall serve your enemies whom the LORD your God will send against you."—Deuteronomy 28:47–48

 YOU DON'T WANT TO SURRENDER TO GOD'S CONTROL? Perhaps it's in your marriage, where you're bent on changing your mate, or refusing to accept him or her as God's choice for your life, or resisting your God-given responsibilities in that relationship. Perhaps it's a battle for control in another relationship—with a parent, a child, an employer, a pastor, or a friend. Perhaps you're resisting God's right to control your body—your eating, sleeping, exercise, or moral habits—or perhaps your tongue, your time, your future plans, or your finances.

Then count on it—the very points on which you refuse to surrender will become "enemies" that rule over you: lust, greed, possessions, food, sloth, immorality, anger, and other such tyrants. These will become opposing forces in a battle that none of us is capable of winning.

Whether it's our relationships, our personal disciplines, daily decisions, or recurring habit patterns—our choice either to resist or voluntarily surrender to the King comes with far-reaching implications.

When we play "king"—when we insist on establishing our own kingdom and asserting our right to rule—we set ourselves unavoidably at war with the sovereign God of the universe. Invariably we end up being ruled by oppressors. But when we bow to His kingship—when we recognize His kingdom as being supreme, when we surrender to His wise and loving control—then we can live at peace with the King, at rest in His presence. Only then will we be free from all other tyrants.

 Are there any "tyrants" in your life that could be connected with an area of spiritual resistance toward God? Consider what it would be like to be free from all "masters" except the Lord who created you, purchased you, and loves you dearly!

Join the Party

"It was fitting to celebrate and be glad, for this your brother was dead, and is alive; he was lost, and is found."—Luke 15:32

 JESUS' PARABLE OF THE PRODIGAL SON is a great story with a great ending—at least as far as the prodigal is concerned. But it is actually the story of *two* sons. And in the celebration surrounding the repentant brother's return, his elder brother's true heart was exposed.

As he approached the house after dutifully serving in the field, he heard (of all things) music and dancing. *How strange.* There hadn't been a party around that place since his rebellious kid brother left home. But rather than going to his father (could this suggest that the "model son" didn't have much of a relationship with his dad?), he found a servant and asked, "What's going on?" The servant gave him the bottom line: "Your brother has returned, and your father is throwing a party," to which the elder brother responded, not with joy and relief but with anger and a refusal to join the celebration.

I've been told that in ancient Jewish culture, when the head of the home left the party—like the father in this story, who went out to find his jealous, peeved son—the music and dancing stopped until the host returned. Isn't this a picture of what's happening in many of our churches? There's no joy, no celebrating, no partying over lost sinners being restored, because the pastor and leadership are distracted by the petty "elder brothers" who are too busy focusing on themselves and nursing their wounded pride to rejoice in the restoration of broken sinners who've returned home.

How typical of proud, unbroken people—perhaps even of ourselves—first losing sight of our own need for the gospel, then resenting God's generous display of grace, mercy, and forgiveness toward others. May the Lord guard our hearts from ever going there!

 Have you lost your excitement for gospel transformation in the lives of those around you? What does that say about the condition of your heart? What could help you rekindle a humble, tender spirit?

Which Way?

If any of you lacks wisdom, let him ask God, who gives generously to all without reproach, and it will be given him.—James 1:5

 I AM SERIOUSLY DIRECTIONALLY CHALLENGED—I have virtually no sense of direction. More than once, on leaving a hotel room, I've had to stop and ask directions from a hotel employee in the hallway—to find the elevator. Needless to say, I rely heavily on GPS or written instructions to find just about everything.

Finding God's will regarding our lives, relationships, and responsibilities can be a lot trickier than finding a hotel elevator (obviously!), a restaurant, or a doctor's office—and that's another important reason for spending time with Him on a consistent basis. No matter how good (or bad) you may be at finding your way around, you simply cannot find your way through the maze of this life on your own. You need the guidance and direction that can only be found through prayerful intake of His Word, as the Holy Spirit sheds light on the path before you.

Remember, God wants to have an intimate relationship with you. And one of the characteristics of a close friendship is the freedom to solicit counsel on issues that concern you.

I am so grateful to be able to gather ideas from various friends on subjects in which they have experience or expertise that I lack—from household repairs to insurance coverage to ministry hiring and scheduling decisions.

God wants that kind of relationship with you, one where you are quick to seek His wisdom and direction about anything and everything. So during your quiet time, bring your whole life before Him—your schedule, your questions, the challenges and decisions you are facing. Then as you read and meditate on His Word, with your heart tuned and lifted up to Him, wait prayerfully and expectantly for Him to give the direction you need.

 What matters are you facing for which you need direction? Lay them before the Lord, immerse yourself in His Word, incline your heart toward Him, and trust Him to direct your steps.

A 24/7 Calling

"But I do not account my life of any value nor as precious to myself, if only I may finish my course and the ministry that I received from the Lord Jesus."—Acts 20:24

FOR THE NEXT SEVERAL DAYS, I'd like to share ten life principles I gleaned from my dad. He's been with the Lord for decades now, and I only got to spend my first twenty-one years with him. But the things he taught me and the way of life he modeled during his brief span on earth have proved to be a rich legacy for my life. I hope you'll receive these nuggets of truth as gifts of wisdom from your heavenly Father.

The first and perhaps the most foundational is this: *Take God seriously.* My father was already an adult before Jesus captured his heart, but when He did, He got every ounce of my dad! His faith was not just a compartment or category of his life; it was the sum and substance of his existence. Jesus was *everything* to him.

I remember being on a family vacation once when we ran into a missionary couple who was staying at the same place we were. My dad struck up a conversation with them by asking (in his trademark way), "How's the 'fishing' down here?" He didn't want to know if the trout were biting; he was asking if these folks were finding the people around there open to talking about Christ. When the man answered, "I don't know, we're on vacation," my dad was blown away. He had no problem with Christians enjoying a vacation from work; but he couldn't fathom the idea of taking a vacation from serving God and sharing Christ.

Truly, the Lord did not save us for a part-time, weekends-only commitment to Him. No matter what your vocation, being His follower and servant is a 24/7 calling. Everywhere you go. Everything you are. For all of time and eternity.

Is knowing and serving Jesus what gets you up and going in the morning? Is He at the center of your thoughts and actions through the day? He deserves to be taken seriously.

In the Morning

He wakens me morning by morning, wakens my ear
to listen like one being taught.—Isaiah 50:4 NIV

 I'M GLAD TO MEET YOU EACH DAY in this *Quiet Place*, even if only for a few minutes, no matter what time of day or night you may be seeking the Lord. But I'd like to commend to you a simple practice that I believe could make a huge difference in your life. I'm referring to the habit of meeting with the Lord first thing in the morning.

Now, any time of day is a great time to seek Him. But the Scripture certainly bears out the importance and value of starting your day with Him. "I, O LORD, cry to you; *In the morning* my prayer comes to you" (Ps. 88:13); "Satisfy us *in the morning* with your steadfast love, that we may rejoice and be glad all our days" (90:14). We also know that Jesus rose early *in the morning* to be with His Father (Mark 1:35).

Start your day with God. It's something my father impressed on me from as far back as I can remember. He didn't just preach that idea—he lived it. I knew that he began every day on his knees and in the Word—regardless of what he had going on that day, how late he'd been up the night before, whatever. Before breakfast. Before reading anything else. Spending that time with the Lord was the nonnegotiable, number one priority of his day.

I know all too well the recurring temptation to dive into my day without having first met with the Lord. And it doesn't get easier—I have found that in every season of life a host of challenges conspire to keep us from enjoying a rich, consistent devotional life. You can fight back by setting aside at least a few moments of your morning to seek God in His Word. See if it doesn't turn your whole day around. Best of all, see if you don't find yourself cultivating a more intimate, love relationship with your God and Savior.

 How has God met you in special ways at the start of your day?
What happens when we make Him an afterthought and don't
turn our attention toward Him until later in the day?

Trust and Obey

Whatever the LORD pleases, he does, in heaven and on earth, in the seas and all deeps.—Psalm 135:6

MY FATHER POSSESSED (and was possessed by) a high view of God. Whereas most of us react to challenges and adversity by fretting about *our* feelings, *our* opinions, *our* plans, and *our* future, my dad was convinced that whatever he was going through was not about *him* but about *God*—about *His* eternal purposes, plans, and glory. With all his heart, he believed what Scripture affirms: that God is not only sovereign but also completely trustworthy—and not only trustworthy but also loving and good.

In other words, no matter what was happening in his life, his family, his business, his health or his reputation—and I assure you, he had his share of ups and downs—he still believed God was worthy of his trust and his obedience.

Trust and obey—so simple, yet so profoundly important.

Trust comes from *resting* in God's sovereignty, secure in the knowledge that He is Lord, that He maintains the right to do whatever He desires with His children's lives. Obedience comes from *surrendering* to God's sovereignty, not using hardship as an excuse for fretting, chafing, resisting, or resenting. Our only acceptable response is, "Yes, Lord"—even when obedience doesn't seem to be paying off with positive blessing, even when whining feels more fitting than contentment.

God's Word tells us that His will is "good and acceptable and perfect" (Rom. 12:2), not because it's always pleasing to us but because it always serves a purpose more valuable than we can see from our limited vantage point. So because the Lord does whatever He pleases, our response in every challenge of life should be, "If it pleases You, Lord, it pleases me." That's what it means to trust and obey. If He truly is God, how can we do anything less?

Is some current circumstance challenging your resolve to trust God's decisions? What would it mean to fully trust and obey Him in that situation?

Little Things Matter

Do not be deceived: God is not mocked, for whatever one sows, that will he also reap.—Galatians 6:7

 HOW MANY UNHEALTHY OR DESTRUCTIVE HABITS of ten, fifteen, twenty-five years or more have become nearly impossible for you to break? Consider the fact that at one point in life—if you could remember back clearly enough—those particularly knotty habits were a matter of one simple choice. You said yes when you should and could have said no. And now you find you can't say no.

Whether it's an eating habit, an exercise habit, a work habit, a spending habit, or any other pattern that's become ingrained in your lifestyle, those small choices from early in life now require a level of restraint you find it extremely difficult, if not impossible, to marshal. Seeds sown carelessly many years ago have produced a crop you never envisioned.

Little things matter.

That's another concept I recall my dad emphasizing as I was growing up. He cautioned us about the seemingly inconsequential choices we make each day, assuring us that what starts little will never stay little. He used to say it this way: "You are what you have been becoming." The implication is, "You *will* be what you are *now* becoming." It's an unavoidable reality. We can't help but reach a distant spot in the road if we keep walking down it the way we've been doing.

But just as little choices lead to heavyweight habits, even a baby step of repentance can set us on a different pathway, using the same spiritual logic in reverse. In acknowledging the stronghold that has been established in your life and your helplessness to change, and in relying on the power of the Holy Spirit to enable you to take each step of obedience as He directs, even the most monstrous of habits can give way to freedom and be replaced with new, godly habits—one small step at a time.

 How serious are you about taking back what your most persistent habits have caused you and cost you? What "little" step of obedience would start to change things?

Taking Responsibility

So then each of us will give an account of himself to God.
—Romans 14:12

 MY MOTHER AND I FREQUENTLY TANGLED when I was a teenager. I'm not saying that I was right and she was wrong. I see things a lot differently now than I did then. I realize that my immaturity, pride, and unwillingness to see things from her point of view often caused me to react disrespectfully when she said or did things that I felt were wrong or unreasonable.

But more than once, my dad stressed two important points to me: (1) you must honor your mother and give her due respect—period—regardless of what she does; and (2) you are not responsible for what she does—you are only responsible for how you respond to her. The issue wasn't whether my mom was right or wrong; the issue was whether my responses were right or wrong. Nothing she—or anyone else—might do could justify a sinful reaction on my part.

How many times have you blamed certain aspects of your lifestyle and makeup on shortcomings in your upbringing? How many times have you allowed your spouse's words or the actions of a friend or colleague to provoke you to respond in a sinful way?

The truth is, life will present us no shortage of people and situations that rub us the wrong way. Some offenses are merely annoying and aggravating; others are grievous injustices. In either case, we will never be held accountable for what another person says or does; we are only accountable for our own attitudes and responses.

Don't fall for the lie that says other people have the power to make you bitter, resentful, touchy, or explosive or that their wrongdoing (perceived or real) justifies ungodly responses on your part. By God's grace, you can avoid pouring fuel on the fire. With a wise, humble spirit and a "soft answer," you can overcome evil with good.

 Have you found yourself recently overreacting to others' words, actions, or disapproval? How might a keener awareness of your accountability to God help you handle things differently?

Seek Counsel

Yes, if you call out for insight and raise your voice for understanding . . . then you will understand the fear of the LORD and find the knowledge of God.—Proverbs 2:3, 5

 LISTENING TO GOOD ADVICE is a smart way to handle the decisions and turbulence that come along in life. My dad urged us to keep our ears open for wise counsel—whether in sermons, casual conversations, or elsewhere. But he went further than that. His monthly rereading of the book of Proverbs taught him (and he taught us) the importance of *proactively seeking godly input*—of taking initiative to ask for it. It's an evidence of humility—not attempting to do life on our own, or thinking ourselves beyond the need of help from others.

By heeding that bit of counsel, I can attest that God has enriched, directed, and protected my life in some amazing ways. Pastors, friends, ministry colleagues, and others have graciously offered wisdom they might never have gone out of their way to share if I had not asked them to.

That's not to say I've always wanted to hear what they have had to say—I've been told some things that were hard to receive. But God's Word assures us that "whoever heeds instruction is on the path to life" (Prov. 10:17). And even when someone's counsel is not "spot-on," or may be insensitive or lacking tact, if we receive it with a humble heart, we'll usually find it contains at least a kernel of needed truth.

I often ask for input—on a broad range of matters—from those God brings across my path. In fact, even now as a middle-aged woman, I rarely make a decision of any significance without asking a wise friend or acquaintance, "Do you have any wisdom to offer on this?" It's not because I have a hard time making up my mind; it's because I know there is protection and blessing to be found in seeking and heeding counsel.

 Where could you go for advice on a matter that's troubling or confusing you right now? Do you have a pattern of seeking out—and heeding—godly counsel?

Guard Your Heart

Above all, guard your heart, for it is the wellspring of life.—Proverbs 4:23

 CONTINUING TO SHARE ten particularly memorable things my dad taught me, I come today to a seventh principle that is so foundational, the folly of ignoring it is guaranteed to taint every aspect of your life. That's because everything you say and think, feel and do, or plan and dream is tied to a conscious decision that must be made not once but over and over again, with each new day.

Guard your heart.

Jesus told a parable that described four different kinds of soil conditions, each one representing how a person's heart responds to the Word of God, how well it allows the truth of the gospel to grow and thrive within it. Among this quartet of examples, Jesus pointed to a patch of ground overgrown with thorns and said it resembled a heart that allows other pursuits and concerns to crowd out pure, deliberate devotion to God—a heart filled with so many competing loyalties and private worries, it has little room for simple contentment with Christ.

My dad took pains to remind us that worldly stuff, distractions, riches, and pleasures—though not necessarily wrong in themselves—are normally not a friend of grace in our lives, that their tendency is to steal our affection for the Lord and to make our hearts grow cold and hard.

So be careful about what you allow to hang out in your heart—the entertainment you enjoy, the ambitions you harbor, the anxieties you refuse to relinquish into God's safe care and keeping. When you don't do the hard work of guarding your heart, you will find it occupied with things that will steal your love for Christ and sabotage your walk with God.

 Are "cares and riches and pleasures of life" (Luke 8:15) choking out the seed of God's Word and keeping it from taking root in your heart? What are these things costing you spiritually?

Invest Your Life

*So teach us to number our days that we may
get a heart of wisdom.*—Psalm 90:12

As MUCH AS I MISS MY DAD and could wish he was still here to learn from and talk to, I'm glad he didn't live to see the days of personal computers and the Internet. I don't know how he could have stood it. My dad was intentional about everything he did—work, worship, family time, even downtime and recreation—and he was especially cautious about anything that consumed large chunks of time with little to show for it on the other end. If he thought the television was a time-eater, he could not have imagined what was coming.

In a variety of ways, he exhorted us: *"Don't spend your life—invest it."*

God has given us a finite number of minutes, hours, and days. They are His, not ours, and He has entrusted them to us as stewards of that which belongs to Him. One day we will each stand before Him to give an account of what we did with the few short years He allotted to us on earth. How will we not regret all those hours we mindlessly idled away on "trivial pursuits," while giving little or no thought to how our lives could bring Him pleasure and advance His kingdom?

Perhaps you're still young and not consciously mindful of the value of each day. I assure you that the investments you make now, using your time, abilities, and opportunities to bring glory to God, will multiply throughout your lifetime and beyond.

Or perhaps you're *not* so young anymore, and you realize you've squandered too much of your life on things that will bring little return in eternity. Then start afresh today, recapturing the joy of investing yourself in worship, ministry, service, sacrifice, and renewing neglected relationships. It's not too late—or too early—to start investing your life with the long term in view.

How much of your typical day is frittered away with activities or interests that don't really matter in the long run? Offer up your minutes, hours, and days to the Lord, and ask Him how He wants them invested for His glory.

Give Liberally

*One gives freely, yet grows all the richer; another withholds
what he should give, and only suffers want.*—Proverbs 11:24

 EACH OF US KNOWS HOW IT FEELS to see the things we
don't have and wish we had them. We know how it
feels to compare our financial status with others. We
know how it feels to live in an unstable economy that
threatens every measure we take to ensure a healthy
and stable future.

But each of these common conditions has a clear, biblical
counterweight: the principle of generous giving.

No honest reading of the Scripture can lead to any other
conclusion. *God honors generosity.* "Honor the LORD with your wealth
and with the firstfruits of all your produce; then your barns will
be filled with plenty, and your vats will be bursting with wine"
(Prov. 3:9–10). That's not to say you'll become a millionaire in
exchange for being openhanded with your money, but God does
promise that all your needs will be met and you will be abundantly
blessed—in ways you cannot even begin to fathom.

I understand the temptation to hold back, to tighten up and
give less when you can't see how your income is adequate to
cover your obligations or to guarantee long-term security. We
feel more secure knowing the money is in the bank, not in the
church coffers or funding the work of a missionary or setting
food on the table for a needy family. But anytime fear or lack of
faith causes us to pull back from giving to God and others, we
actually become less, not more, secure.

"You can't outgive God," my father used to say. He
demonstrated that belief by actually giving *more* in times when
his income decreased. Our family got to witness God's amazing
faithfulness in countless ways in those seasons. Try it yourself. The
math may not make sense from an earthly perspective. But you'll
find that it's true—you really can't outgive God!

 *Have you been withholding anything from God out of fear and
uneasiness? Test Him. Experience His supernatural economy
that kicks in when we walk by faith and become channels of
His lavish grace and generous heart.*

In Eternity's Light

All flesh is grass, and all its beauty is like the flower of the field. . . . The grass withers, the flower fades, but the word of our God will stand forever.—Isaiah 40:6, 8

I CLOSE THIS TEN-DAY LOOK at my dad's legacy by describing a piece of paper I have in my files. Written in my dad's unmistakable scrawl are three short lists, written in his early fifties. The first is titled "What are my lifetime goals?" It includes several goals related to his giving, family, personal life, and business—in that order. The second, titled "Next three years," expresses his desire to get extricated from his business so he could spend more time in direct ministry. The third list, which includes three goals, has this header: "If I knew I were to die in six months . . ."

Little did he know when he made these notes, that in less than three years he would be with the Lord.

As I review these goals, it's obvious that what mattered most to him was *living in light of eternity* and in such a way as to advance the kingdom of God. That concern drove him to want to give more rather than accumulate more; it led him to care about the spiritual needs of his family; and it moved him to care deeply about the souls of those who were without Christ.

My dad knew the life-changing power of the gospel in his life, and that moved him to share Christ with anything that moved. In fact, when his longtime friend Dr. Bill Bright passed away (founder of Campus Crusade for Christ), I jested that I hoped the two men wouldn't be bored in heaven, with nobody to witness to! Lost souls mattered greatly to my dad because he knew what their rejection of Christ was costing them. He saw purpose in every person God brought his way, always alert for opportunities to share the gospel. It's because eternity mattered to him.

Does it matter to you?

Make it the supreme goal of your life to know Christ and to make Him known. There is no greater legacy.

If you knew you were to die in three years—or six months— what would you do? Ask God to shape your goals and to direct your daily decisions, in light of eternity.

Impossible?

For it is God who works in you, both to will and to work for his good pleasure.—Philippians 2:13

IN DEALING WITH HURTFUL, DIFFICULT SITUATIONS in our lives, we must ask ourselves, "Is my ability or willingness to forgive another person based on the magnitude of the offense?" In other words, is there a threshold of pain beyond which we are not required to forgive—perhaps where it is *impossible* to forgive?

The Scripture says that God has "cast all our sins into the depths of the sea" (Mic. 7:19). *Not some but all.* These include the mockery and insults of those who "despised" Him (Ps. 22:6–7), who "rejected" everything about Him (Isa. 53:3). It's one thing to be disliked; it's quite another to be *despised*—hated, scorned, spit upon, ridiculed, humiliated, betrayed, and wanted dead. Add to those our own personal sins that contributed to the guilt Jesus bore on the cross.

Yet this is the same God who "blots out your transgressions" and "remembers your sins no more" (Isa. 43:25 NIV), who found us "dead in our trespasses" and made us "alive together with Christ" because of His "great love" for us (Eph. 2:4–5).

You may not feel any natural "great love" toward the people who have brought such shipwreck into your life. No one would expect you to. But it will never be the depth of *your* love that causes you to forgive such heartless acts and attitudes. It will be— it can *only* be—the love of Christ transplanted into your believing heart and flowing through you to those who deserve it least.

When it comes to forgiveness—impossible as it may seem— our Lord would not command us to do something He would not also enable us to do. And hasn't done Himself.

Have you been sinned against in a way that seems exceedingly difficult or impossible to forgive? How does God's love and forgiveness provide the motivation and the means for you to extend forgiveness in that situation?

When We Don't Understand

And let steadfastness have its full effect, that you may be perfect and complete, lacking in nothing.—James 1:4

 HAVE YOU EVER FOUND YOURSELF wanting to intervene in the life of your mate, a child, or a friend, when it is actually God who is causing or allowing them to experience hurt? Your natural reaction is to want to spare them. To fix this. To lash out at those who are instigating it.

When Elizabeth, wife of Zechariah the priest, saw him come home from his duties unable to speak, struck dumb for failing to believe the news that these two were about to become first-time parents at their advanced age, Elizabeth had to wonder why this was happening to him.

Surely God could understand why it might take her husband a few minutes to wrap his head around the idea, shocking and surprising as it was—Elizabeth and Zechariah, soon-to-be parents of John, the forerunner of Christ—after having been unable to bear children all these years. Really? Was it fair to expect any other response from him?

Obviously we don't know exactly what God was seeking to accomplish in Zechariah's life by choosing this disciplinary measure. But neither can we always understand some of the reasons why He puts our loved ones through certain ordeals—times of being treated unjustly at work, or hammered by a string of financial setbacks, or continually wounded by a person from their past.

Yet sometimes, instead of rushing in to make things better, we must do what Elizabeth apparently did—let God be God. Let Him accomplish what He's intending to do, even through this unexplainable circumstance. Let Him have His way in the lives of those we love, knowing that He is good, praying and believing that He will get glory in the end.

 Is there something happening in the life of a loved one that seems unreasonably harsh or undeserved? Can you pray for God's will more than God's rescue?

True Multitasking

*I bless the L*ORD *who gives me counsel; in the night*
also my heart instructs me.——Psalm 16:7

 YOU MAY THINK if you spend concentrated time alone with the Lord each day, you won't have enough time to meet the needs of your family and others. On a human level, that may make sense. But in God's economy, spending quality time with Him will actually *increase* your capacity to serve others. Those who are frequently and intentionally in His presence are better able to touch others' lives in meaningful, helpful ways.

Scripture indicates that the one whose ears are open to God will have "an instructed tongue, to know the word that sustains the weary" (Isa. 50:4 NIV). Much time can be consumed struggling to come up with needed direction and encouragement for your family, friends, and others who look to you for input. But much of that frustration arises from not having God's counsel in your heart and on your tongue, fueled by regular time spent with Him in prayer, Scripture, and worship.

When those around you are emotionally or spiritually drained, do they know they can come to you, expecting to receive wise, timely words to refresh their spirits? That is exactly what can happen—if you have first been with the Lord. Even Jesus' effectiveness in ministering to the needs of others was born out of times of communion with His Father, when He would "withdraw to desolate places and pray," then rise up, knowing that "the power of the Lord was with him to heal" (Luke 5:16–17).

Do you want to be more effective in completing the many tasks and demands of your day, in meeting the needs of those around you? Then structure your day around the priority of meeting alone with the Lord, in His Word and prayer. That "quiet place" will yield increased blessings and capacity beyond what you might expect.

 Are you taking time on a consistent basis in His presence,
letting the Lord instruct you and give you what you need to
minister grace to others in need?

Judgment and Mercy

*The Lord is not slow to fulfill his promise as some count slowness,
but is patient toward you, not wishing that any should perish,
but that all should reach repentance.*—2 Peter 3:9

 SOME RESPOND TO THE BIBLICAL ACCOUNT OF NOAH by saying, "What kind of God would wipe out every living creature on earth? I could never follow a God like that." But while such happenings do reveal a holy God who exercises judgment, they also show us something else—a God of incredible mercy and patience.

Hundreds of years prior to Noah's flood, his great-grandfather Enoch warned that God was going to "execute judgment" on all people for their rampant sins and ungodliness (Jude 14–15). He even gave his son the name Methuselah, a name that many scholars believe could be interpreted, "When he is dead, it shall be sent." And sure enough, Methuselah died the same year as the flood. The building of the ark lasted around a hundred years, leaving both God's threat of judgment and His offer of mercy on full display for multiple generations.

The New Testament calls Noah a "preacher of righteousness" (2 Peter 2:5), suggesting that he warned his contemporaries of God's impending judgment and called them to repent. Even after Noah and his family were safely together inside the ark, God held back the rain for another week—seven more days of opportunity to repent. Yet God's gracious provision was persistently rejected by all but Noah's family.

In much the same way today—with the warning signs of coming judgment clear to see—most people ignore the warnings and the offer of salvation. They have other things to do and little interest in humbling themselves before God.

No one had to perish in the flood—no one could say they had not been warned and given a chance to repent. And no one has to face God's eternal wrath today. Let us tell them about a merciful, long-suffering, gracious God who still calls all people to repent, to find refuge in Christ, our ark of salvation.

 What signs of God's mercy can you recognize in your own life, family, or nation? Share one of them the next time someone accuses God of being cold and heartless.

Tale of Two Sinners

And Samuel said to [Saul], "The LORD has torn the kingdom of Israel from you this day and has given it to a neighbor of yours, who is better than you."—1 Samuel 15:28

 NEARLY A THOUSAND YEARS before the birth of Christ, two kings ruled over the nation of Israel. The first was guilty of what most would consider a few relatively minor infractions. Yet they cost him his kingdom, his family, and ultimately his life.

His successor, by comparison, was guilty of far greater offenses. In a fit of passion, for example, he committed adultery with his neighbor's wife and then plotted to have her husband killed. Yet when the story of his life was told, he was called "a man after [God's] own heart" (1 Sam. 13:14).

Why the difference?

Because when the first man, King Saul, was confronted with his sin, he reacted by justifying himself and making excuses. He was more concerned about preserving his reputation and position—about *looking* good—than about being right with God. King David, on the other hand, humbly acknowledged his failure to the Lord, took full responsibility for his grievous wrongdoing, and fully repented of his sin.

Those who are truly broken don't try to cover up their sin. They have nothing to protect and nothing to lose. Once the weight of what they've done has settled in on them, their main concern is to see that God is vindicated, that His holiness is honored and His Word is upheld.

That's why David's heart was the one God honored, just as He honors ours when we come to Him with a contrite, broken spirit. He is not as concerned about the nature and extent of our sin as He is about our attitude and response when we are confronted with it.

 How does pride keep us from coming clean before the Lord and others? In your response to the conviction of God's Spirit when you sin, are you more often like King Saul or King David?

Bundled Up

*"If men rise up to pursue you and to seek your life, the life of
my lord shall be bound in the bundle of the living in the care
of the LORD your God."*—1 Samuel 25:29

 FOUND ON MANY JEWISH TOMBSTONES, the phrase "bound
in the bundle of life" is a statement that applies to life
beyond the grave. Inspired by these words from Abigail
to David, it is a word picture that captures the idea
of taking one's valuables and prized possessions and
wrapping them up in a bundle to keep them safe and protected,
free from danger or damage.

Abigail, we know, was all too familiar with earthly problems
and hardship. Trapped in a difficult marriage with no real way to
escape her harsh, abrasive circumstances, she at least knew her
inner person was safe. No matter what anyone could do to her—
even her cruel husband, Nabal—she was confident her life was
bundled up in the life of the Lord. It was out of this secure position
that she was able to encourage David when he felt threatened.

This obviously doesn't mean that a woman in a physically
threatening situation must sit there and take anything another
person wants to dish out. (God has ordained civil and church
authorities to protect the righteous and punish wrongdoers,
and there are times when it is appropriate and wise to appeal
to them for assistance.) But it does mean that whatever unsafe
or uncomfortable conditions you find yourself living in, you
still have a sure refuge and fortress if you are a child of God.
By grace, through faith, you can take comfort in the "bundled"
mentality that describes your secure position in Christ.

In the long run, God rewards those who are faithful to Him,
while judging and ultimately destroying those who resist Him.
Not in the short-term, perhaps, but eventually. And you are in
that special place today, "bound in the bundle of life," in the
care of your eternal, ever-present Savior.

 *If eternity seems too far away to be of much hope or help to you
today, imagine if God's promises weren't there at all. Consider
and give thanks for what it means that your life—past, present,
and future—is bound securely in Christ.*

Toiling for Whom?

*There is one alone, without companion . . . . Yet there is no end to
all his labors, Nor is his eye satisfied with riches. But he never asks,
"For whom do I toil and deprive myself of good?" This also is
vanity and a grave misfortune.*—Ecclesiastes 4:8 NKJV

 WHY DO YOU DO WHAT YOU DO? You may be
busy nonstop with family and parenting. You
may work long hours, constantly dealing
with other people. But is it possible that your
primary goal each day is just to get things done
or earn a paycheck? To clip through your agenda? To check
items off your "to-do" list? Is it possible that you view *people* in
your life—your children, coworkers, friends, or clients—as props
to help you succeed at your goals, rather than genuinely loving,
serving, and blessing them, investing in their lives, and helping
them become all God created them to be?

I can think of seasons in my own life when this has been
true—when being focused on my own agenda and objectives
has kept me from nurturing relationships with those around
me. If we maintain that mindset long enough, we may end up
being cut off and utterly alone, with nothing but our personal
benchmarks and ambitions to keep us company.

The person described in Ecclesiastes 4:8 is someone who—
perhaps unintentionally—has been laboring for his own benefit,
driving at his own pace, and likely running over others in the
process. One day he wakes up and asks, "Who am I doing all this
for? For me? So I can sit here all alone to enjoy my achievements?"
He finally realizes (too late?) that "two are better than one . . . for
if they fall, one will lift up his fellow" (verses 9–10).

So yes, work hard. But be sure that your hard work and
sacrifice are not wasted on yourself. For if you aren't doing what
you do from a heart of love, deepening your relationships with
others, you will only gain things that are not worth having, while
having no one with whom to share them. Living *for* yourself
eventually means living *by* yourself.

 *Is your to-do list squeezing out time for meaningful engagement
with other people? Ask God to make you sensitive and responsive
to the people He puts in your path today.*

Faulty Vision

I have set the LORD always before me; because he is
at my right hand, I shall not be shaken.—Psalm 16:8

I HAD STARTED TO NOTICE that one of my eyes was becoming extremely irritated, and I was having trouble wearing my hard contact lens. At first I assumed I was having some sort of allergic reaction, which I attempted to treat with antihistamines. But the problem persisted—becoming so bothersome, in fact, that I had to remove the lens for a few days until I could get an appointment with my eye doctor.

After examining the aggravated eye, he explained that I was not having a problem with allergies. Nor was there anything wrong with the eye itself. The problem was with my contact lens. It had somehow become misshapen and was rubbing against my eye. If I wanted to restore my vision, I needed to replace the damaged lens with a new one.

In much the same way, a damaged view of God can affect the way we view everything around us—including the way we view ourselves. For example, if we've constructed in our minds a god who is weak, impotent, and not in control of every detail in the universe, we will also see ourselves as being helpless. We'll be overwhelmed by the storms we face.

What we *won't* see is that what is causing the irritation and turmoil within our souls is not the people or circumstances we think are annoying us. The problem is that we are looking through a damaged lens.

That's why it is so important that we keep our vision aligned with truth, believing who God says He is, rather than the distortions and lies we so easily accept about Him. Having a right view of Him keeps our whole world in sharper focus.

Ask God to show you if any of your current distresses in life
are the result of attitudes and beliefs about Him that may
seem to square with your experience but are not consistent with
biblical truth.

Preparation Matters

A voice cries: "In the wilderness prepare the way of the LORD;
make straight in the desert a highway for our God."—Isaiah 40:3

IF YOU KNOW YOU HAVE AN IMPORTANT MEETING with the owner of your company first thing tomorrow morning, when do you begin preparing for it? Do you put off thinking about it until after you've gotten up, exercised, showered, dressed, and eaten? Do you then suddenly look at your watch, grab some crumpled clothes out of the dirty laundry, race to the car, arrive thirty minutes late, find a seat around the table where the others are already assembled, and hastily start scribbling out notes for your presentation? Not if you care about your job, you don't.

Preparation is essential, whether you're making plans for a critical meeting, a family vacation, a musical performance at church, or a weekend cookout with friends at home. So why should preparation be any less crucial in meeting with God? Cultivating a deep, ongoing relationship with Him through His Word requires some planning ahead.

In fact, I would say that one of the greatest hindrances to a meaningful quiet time is the failure to have a prepared heart, whether from mindlessly surfing the Internet for hours the night before, or going to bed anxious and worried, or waking up not knowing where you laid your Bible the last time you had it.

Hour after hour throughout each day, our eyes and ears are lured by the world around us. The sights, sounds, and demands of our surroundings have a way of capturing our minds and hearts. It's no wonder, then, that we so often find ourselves distracted and hurried, trying to have a quiet time when our hearts are far from quiet. A little bit of preparation can make a big difference.

Does a lack of preparation affect your times with God?
How could you more effectively prepare to meet with Him?

Resurrecting Love

Put on then, as God's chosen ones, holy and beloved, compassionate hearts, kindness, humility, meekness, and patience, bearing with one another and, if one has a complaint against another, forgiving each other. . . .—Colossians 3:12–13

 JEANNIE AND HER HUSBAND were five or six years into marriage, and whatever feelings had once been there were long gone. *Hate* was not too strong a word to describe what raced through her heart whenever she was particularly angry with him. In a desperate attempt to salvage what little was left of their relationship, they planned a Valentine's getaway and hoped something might spark.

It didn't.

Yet while forcing their way through a strained, disappointing weekend, with no storybook romance to come to their rescue, they did exercise the self-control and presence of mind to make one new promise together: they would stop speaking harshly to each other. It just wasn't worth the effort and emotion anymore. Nor would they confide and complain to friends, "Do you know what he did? Do you know what she said?" Surely they could do that much.

Sometimes the big things really do come down to size when we start doing the little things—like not talking cruelly to each other, not unleashing our little put-downs, not giving unkind reports behind their back. At least that's what happened in Jeannie's situation. Six months down the line, they looked up from their once decaying marriage and found that God had indeed resurrected what was dead and dying. Twenty years later, their lives have become a picture of committed, joyful love.

No, not every bad situation is sure to get better like this. But it will *never* happen unless someone is willing to surrender their rights even in simple, basic ways. Simple, daily acts of humility and kindness, energized by the Spirit and love of Christ, may be just what it takes to get (and keep) God's grace and power flowing through your most difficult relationship.

 In whatever relationship this most applies to you, what are one or two small, sacrificial steps you could take for the sake of peace and restoration?

From Trying to Triumph

But thanks be to God, that you who were once slaves of sin have become obedient from the heart to the standard of teaching to which you were committed, and, having been set free from sin, have become slaves of righteousness.—Romans 6:17–18

 CHRIST DIED TO OVERCOME SIN and set us free from its dominion. But when we choose to sin rather than obey God, we are giving back to sin the right to rule in our lives, choosing to live as "slaves of sin." And when we make those choices repeatedly, we establish habit patterns that can be extremely difficult to break. Trying to do right, then failing—trying and failing, trying and failing. I'm sure you know what I'm talking about.

That's when the devil begins to convince us that our lives can never be any different, that we will always be enslaved to these sinful habits of ours. We think, *What's the use? I'm just going to blow it again anyway! This thing is going to defeat me the rest of my life.* So we give up. We concede defeat. Satan has succeeded in making us believe we cannot walk in consistent victory over temptation and sin.

And that's a lie.

Remember this: what we *believe* determines the way we live. If we believe we are going to sin, then we will. If we believe we have no choice but to live in bondage, we will. If we believe we can't live victorious lives, we won't. But even though it's true that you and I are powerless to change ourselves, we can experience real, everyday victory over sin through Christ's finished work on the cross. Satan is no longer our master, and we are no longer helpless slaves to sin.

So if you are in Christ, "the Spirit of life has set you free in Christ Jesus from the law of sin and death" (Rom. 8:2). That's the gospel truth.

 Where are you feeling the most defeated and spiritually demoralized? One single hour lived in truth can become a day, a week, a month, a year, a lifetime. Christ has conquered. Live in His victory.

God Has Promised

This is my comfort in my affliction,
that your promise gives me life.—Psalm 119:50

THE HEBREW PATRIARCH ABRAHAM surrendered himself to the purposes and plans of God with no tangible guarantee that his obedience would ever "pay off." But even when he could not see the outcome of his faith, he believed God. He staked his life, his security, his future—everything—on the fact that God was real and would keep His promises. That was the foundation on which his faith rested. That's what motivated his repeated acts of surrender. *God's promises.*

It was faith in the character and promises of God that enabled Abraham and his wife, Sarah, to embrace an itinerant lifestyle for more than twenty-five years, despite the disappointment of infertility and other unfulfilled longings.

It was faith in the promises of God that motivated him to surrender the best land option to his nephew Lot, trusting that God would provide a suitable inheritance for him. It's also what gave him courage (at the age of seventy-five!) to take on the massive military machine of the allied kings of the East in order to rescue his errant nephew. Then when he was tempted to fear reprisals from the defeated kings, God bolstered his faith with a rehearsal of His promises: "Fear not, Abram, I am your shield; your reward shall be very great" (Gen. 15:1).

At times, the call of God on our lives may require us to relinquish things or people we can't imagine living without—material possessions, a job or promotion, a mate, a child, the respect and understanding of our closest friends. But the promises of God provide a powerful antidote to all our fears. They free us to step out in faith and surrender.

What hardship or challenge are you facing that seems particularly daunting? How could God's promises carry you beyond your fears into a place of trust and surrender to His will?

Casting Down or Lifting Up?

Do not let your heart turn aside to her ways, do not stray into her paths;
For she has cast down many wounded, and all who were slain by her
were strong men.—Proverbs 7:25–26 NKJV

FEMINISTS HISTORICALLY HAVE PORTRAYED WOMEN as oppressed victims—and it's true that far too often in this sinful, fallen world, women have been grievously mistreated. Where possible, we can and should seek to see injustice remedied. These situations, however—no matter how serious—do not relieve women of responsibility for any ways that we ourselves may be not only victims but also perpetrators. No failure on the part of men can strip us of accountability for our behavior and our influence on them.

We know that women can be instrumental in the moral downfall of men. But there are other ways we can bring down the men around us. I have noticed, for example, that some of the most "spiritual," biblically knowledgeable women in the church are also the most intimidating. I have heard men say in effect, "I can't lead my wife [or, the women in my church]. They know too much." Some of these men feel as though they need advanced theological degrees in order to be the spiritual leaders Christian women claim to want. The problem, of course, isn't how much these women know—but their lack of a humble, teachable spirit.

As I ponder Proverbs 7, I find myself wondering how many men I've cast down and wounded—perhaps not morally but spiritually. How many have I discouraged or intimidated? In how many settings have I had a controlling spirit and subtly emasculated the men around me?

I want to lift up the hands of the men He has placed in my life, to pray for them and be their cheerleader. For sure, they have weaknesses, as we all do. But we can be mighty instruments of grace in their lives as we encourage them and trust God to make them mighty men in His service.

From cutting digs and comments to other forms of intimidation, control, and discouragement, ask God to show you any ways that you may be "casting down" one or more men in your life.

Morning Drive

I rise before dawn and cry for help;
I hope in your words.—Psalm 119:147

 THE ESSENCE OF SATAN'S DECEPTION is that we can live our lives independently of God. He doesn't care if we believe in God or fill our schedules with a lot of spiritual activities—as long as he can get us to run on our own steam rather than living in conscious dependence on the power of the Holy Spirit.

Six times in the Old Testament, we read that David "inquired of the LORD" (1 Sam. 23:2, 4; 30:8; 2 Sam. 2:1; 5:19, 23). David knew he was nothing apart from God, that he could not make it on his own. In fact, the first thing he did each morning—before turning to the business of the day—was to turn his heart toward the Lord in prayer. "In the morning you hear my voice" (Ps. 5:3).

Too often I find myself turning my attention to the details and tasks of the day without first taking time to "inquire of the LORD." What I'm really saying (though I'd never actually *say* it) is that I can handle this day on my own. I can do my work, keep my home, handle my relationships, and deal with my circumstances just fine, all by myself. I don't *really* need Him.

Sometimes I sense He may be saying to us, "You want to manage this day yourself? Go ahead!" Then, even though we can create a lot of dust and activity, we ultimately end up having nothing of real value to show after a day spent making our own decisions and operating in our own strength.

Only by humbling ourselves and acknowledging that we cannot make it without Him—that we *need* Him—can we count on His divine enabling to carry us through the day.

 How does your morning typically start? What does your routine say about whether your confidence is in the Lord, or in yourself and your ability to manage things?

Holy Heartbreak

"You have not obeyed my voice. What is this you have done?"—Judges 2:2

 SOME TIME AGO, I found myself with a deeply distraught friend who had recently learned that her husband had been unfaithful to her. At one point she collapsed on the floor next to my feet and began to sob uncontrollably. As I knelt down and began to weep with her, she said with raw, painful emotion, "I never imagined I could hurt so deeply or feel so rejected!"

For perhaps twenty minutes, she cried and cried, devastated, grieving over this breach in the intimate, exclusive relationship she had once shared with her husband. Holding her there in my arms, I remember feeling a whole new sense of what our sin and unfaithfulness does to God. I hope never to forget that picture.

Somehow we have managed to redefine sin; we have come to view it as normal, acceptable behavior—something perhaps to be tamed or controlled but not to be eradicated and put to death. We have sunk to such lows that we can not only sin thoughtlessly, we can even laugh at sin and be entertained by it. I have heard virtually every conceivable kind of sin rationalized by professing Christians, including some in full-time Christian service.

I wonder if we would be so cavalier about sin if we had any comprehension of how the Lord views it. Our sin breaks the heart of our Lover-God who created and redeemed us for Himself. To say yes to sin is to fall into the embrace of a paramour. It introduces a rival into this sacred love relationship. It is to treat His grace as if it were cheap and something to be lightly regarded.

 What makes it so hard for us to see our sin for the grievous offense it really is? When was the last time you truly remembered this fact, and how did it change you?

When Prayer Weeps

When he drew near and saw the city,
he wept over it.—Luke 19:41

OUR SAVIOR was "a man of sorrows, and acquainted with grief" (Isa. 53:3), an Intercessor who "offered up prayers and supplications, with loud cries and tears" (Heb. 5:7). Jesus prayed with intensity and fervor. Prayer wasn't a matter of reciting meaningless or dispassionate words. Prayer was how He poured out His heart on behalf of those He came to save. Prayer hurt.

And so when He looked out over Jerusalem, the city where within a week He would spill His atoning blood, He saw things most people do not see. He didn't only see buildings and crowds engaged in the daily hubbub of activity. He saw the hearts of men and women—people who had rejected God's right to rule over their lives.

And the sight elicited holy, compassionate, hot-hearted tears—not just water beading in His eyes, with a few drops escaping to trail down His face. The word "wept" used in Luke 19 to describe His response on the outskirts of Jerusalem speaks of sobbing, bawling, wailing aloud, the kind of anguish usually reserved for mourning a death.

Most of us don't often weep over the spiritual needs of others. Perhaps that's because we don't see people the way Jesus sees them. And we don't see the broken heart of a holy God whose mercy and grace have been rejected. For when we do, our hearts will break with His.

How great is our burden for those who suffer around us, not only in hospital waiting rooms and funeral homes but in the unseen dungeons of their own sin? To have the heart of Christ is to grieve over their rejection of their King and to join our Savior in His intercession.

Ask God to help you see the people around you through Jesus' eyes.
Ask Him to give you His heart for those in your city who do not
know and have not received Him.

When God Comes Near

Clothe yourselves, all of you, with humility
toward one another, for "God opposes the proud
but gives grace to the humble."—1 Peter 5:5

IT'S A THEME THAT RUNS ALL THROUGH SCRIPTURE: God *resists* the proud (see Prov. 3:34; James 4:6). The concept in these verses is that God sets Himself in "battle array" against the proud; He stiff-arms them; He keeps them at a distance. God repels those who feel they are self-sufficient, who take unholy pride in their own accomplishments.

On the other hand, the parallel theme—equally clear—is that God pours grace on the humble. As an ambulance races to the scene in response to a call for help, so God races toward His children when they humble themselves and acknowledge their need.

As Charles Spurgeon reminds us, "He that humbles himself under the hand of God shall not fail to be enriched, uplifted, sustained, and comforted by the ever-gracious One. It is a habit of Jehovah to cast down the proud and lift up the lowly."

Do you wonder why God sometimes seems so far away? Could it be that He is withdrawing and resisting you because of unseen roots of pride in your heart? Could one of the reasons behind this feeling of distance be an unspoken sense that you can manage pretty well without Him? "For though the LORD is high, he regards the lowly, but the haughty he knows from afar" (Ps. 138:6).

Do you long to be closer to God? Do you miss the sense of His nearness you once knew? Even as the father of the prodigal son drew his broken, repentant boy to his chest, embracing and restoring him, so our heavenly Father draws near to and lavishes His grace on those who come to Him with humble, broken hearts.

Ask God to show you any places where pride may be lurking in your heart and causing Him to resist you. Let Him know that you want every vestige of pride to be removed, that you want to be clothed in humility.

When God Says No

*He who teaches man knowledge—the L*ORD*—knows the thoughts of man, that they are but a breath.*—Psalm 94:10–11

ONE OF MY HEROES IN THE FAITH is Gladys Aylward, the revered missionary to China who worked tirelessly for the cause of the orphaned and oppressed. She once recalled how as a young girl in London, she had dealt with two great sorrows: the shortness of her stature and the color of her hair. All her friends, it seemed, were taller than she, and each had beautiful golden hair, while hers was "boring" black. She often prayed that God would reverse these undesirable traits in her physical appearance, making her look more like the girl she wished to be.

Years later, however, standing on a wharf in the teeming, Asian country where God had sent her to share His gospel mercies, she looked around and saw people everywhere who were as short as she was—and each had jet black hair. In that moment she realized that God had known what He was doing all along. By saying no to her youthful prayer, He had answered her perfectly—beyond her wildest imagining.

Each of us can recall times when we wanted something from God that He seemed unwilling to grant. Yet the passing years may have already revealed to you that His answer was far wiser and better than yours would have been. You didn't need *that*; you needed *this*. And God has used your life to reveal His glory more clearly because of it.

Then let this same heart and mind inform your praying today, even when it seems as if no other answer of His could possibly substitute for the one that seems best to you. Let Him be God. Trust His answers.

 Can you live with "no" being an answer? If not, then what has prayer actually become for you? What does God want prayer to be?

Searching for Gold

I rejoice at your word like one who finds great spoil.—Psalm 119:162

ONE OF THE SKILLS my dad encouraged us to acquire as teens was speed-reading—a way to cover large amounts of material in a short amount of time. He was quick to suggest two things, however, that should never be read for speed: *love letters* and the *Bible*.

No one receiving a love letter would dream of hastily skimming through it. Instead, the recipient pores over its contents, reading and rereading it, searching between the lines for every nuance of meaning.

The Bible is a "love letter" of sorts, revealing God's heart to us. And the more carefully, frequently, and thoughtfully we read it, the more we will be able to grasp His loving heart and intentions toward us.

The psalmist described God's Word as being "more precious than gold, than much pure gold" (Ps. 19:10). No one walks down the street and stumbles onto vast stores of gold, any more than a person who hastily or casually reads the Word can expect to mine its deepest riches. Searching for and extracting gold from the earth requires enormous effort, time, and perseverance.

According to King Solomon, searching for biblical wisdom and insight is like looking for "hidden treasures" (Prov. 2:4). So when reading your Bible, pause frequently to meditate on its meaning, asking God to reveal the stores of treasure it contains. Absorb the Scripture into your system by pondering it, dwelling on it, going over it again and again in your mind, considering it from many different angles—until it becomes a part of you. Until you've seen "gold" shimmering there.

What do your reading, study, and meditation practices suggest about the value you place on God's Word? Do you think of it as a love letter to be cherished, as gold worth searching and digging for?

Come, See a Man

*So the woman left her water jar and went away into town
and said to the people, "Come, see a man who told me
all that I ever did. Can this be the Christ?"*—John 4:28–29

"COME, SEE A MAN."

How many times had her Samaritan neighbors heard this woman tell them to "come, see [yet another] man" to whom she had given her affections?

We know from her encounter with Jesus at the well in Sychar, she'd been married five times, and the man with whom she was presently involved wasn't her husband at all. So this new man must be the seventh. What's one more?

Understandably, then, her statement would have been just another reason for the townspeople to roll their eyes at her, except that this Man—this Jesus—had looked into her soul and seen everything she'd ever done. And though meeting someone who possessed that kind of knowledge should have been a terrifying experience to a woman with her kind of past, this Man had proven to be a source of abounding grace.

In spite of what He knew about her, He had received her. And He promised if she would bring all her needs, desires, and past failings to Him, He would satisfy her with "living water" that would never stop replenishing her thirsty, repentant spirit.

That's what draws *me* to this Man—to this Jesus. He knows everything about me and yet still loves me. He has seen into recesses of my heart that I keep hidden even from myself, yet when I come to Him and am willing to bring those places into the light, He offers boundless stores of fresh grace.

Why should anyone believe us when we tell them to "come, see a man" who has changed our lives forever? Not because of who *we* are but because of who *He* is.

*Does anything about yourself or your story make you
shy away from telling others about Christ? If He has
saved you, then your story is worth telling.*

Here Indefinitely?

O LORD, make me know my end and what is the measure of my days; let me know how fleeting I am!—Psalm 39:4

 ARTHUR MILLER, famed playwright of *Death of a Salesman* and other well-known twentieth-century works, died of heart failure on February 10, 2005, at eighty-nine years of age. I happened to hear of his passing on the news that evening. My ears perked up when the CBS anchor said that Miller had once been asked what epitaph he had composed for his tombstone, to which he replied that he hadn't given it much thought: "I expect to be here indefinitely."

The fact is, none of us is going to be here "indefinitely." We are not invincible. We will not always be able to bounce back from every physical challenge, like every time before. And although we may be reluctant to dwell on the inevitability of our own deaths—"the pain, blood, and guts of it all," as my pastor friend Ray Ortlund said—the perspective and wisdom that come from living within this reality help to frame what really matters to us today. It keeps us worshiping God for His eternal mercies and promises, knowing they will infinitely outlast our present trials, and are indescribably more glorious than all our earthly enjoyments.

The story has been told that Francis of Assisi was tending his garden one day when some women approached and asked what he would do if he knew he was going to die before sunset that day. His answer was simple: "Well, I hope that I could finish this row."

When we come to terms with the reality of our limited life span on earth, we can calibrate our goals and ambitions with greater wisdom and can live unsurprised and unterrified by the prospect of our physical death. We can be our most spiritually healthy. We can experience His peace. We can know what we're really living for.

 Have you reflected recently on the brevity of life? How might doing so make a difference in your current activities, attitudes, and relationships?

Just Because He Says So

*Let us continually offer up a sacrifice of praise to God,
that is, the fruit of lips that acknowledge his name.*—Hebrews 13:15

 OH, HOW I WISH it was enough for you and me to do things *just because God has told us to*—no other reason required. Not because it would give us whiter teeth and fresh breath, or improve our debt-to-income ratio, or soften a strained relationship. No—just because He says so.

Like being thankful, for instance.

"Offer to God a sacrifice of thanksgiving," His Word says, "and perform your vows to the Most High" (Ps. 50:14). "Give thanks to the LORD; call upon his name; make known his deeds among the peoples" (105:1). The Psalms alone are filled with exhortations to "thank the LORD for his steadfast love, for his wondrous works to the children of men" (107:8).

Later, in the few pages of his Colossian letter, the apostle Paul challenges believers to be "always" thankful (Col. 1:3), "abounding" in gratitude" (2:7), devoting ourselves to prayer, "being watchful in it in thanksgiving" (4:2). The "attitude of gratitude" is a clear command and expectation of God. Even when we don't feel so inclined or are more mindful of our problems than our blessings, we are told to give glory and gratitude to Him.

So if you're sitting down to dinner, be thankful.

If you're getting ready for bed, be thankful.

If you're coming out from under a two-week cold and cough, if you're paying bills, if you're cleaning up after overnight company, if you're driving to work, if you're changing a lightbulb, if you're worshiping in church, if you're visiting a friend in the hospital, if you're picking up the kids from school or practice . . .

Be thankful. If for no other reason than that God has commanded it.

 This day, "let us continually offer up a sacrifice of praise to God"!

Ever-Present Help

But David strengthened himself in the LORD his God.——1 Samuel 30:6

 IF YOU'VE EVER REACTED TO LOSS AND ADVERSITY by falling to pieces, bemoaning your fate, perhaps seething in anger at the people who are easiest to lash out at, you can relate to David's ragtag bunch of fugitive fighters who had returned from the battlefield, their services unwanted, only to see smoke rising from their city in the distance. Amalekite raiders had struck while they were away, burning their homes, stealing all their belongings, even kidnapping their wives and children.

The Bible says they "wept until they had no more strength to weep" (1 Sam. 30:4). Then, not finding ample solace in their shared grief, they starting looking for things to throw and people to blame——even David, whom they threatened to stone for taking them off on a failed mission, leaving their families exposed to danger.

But although he was no less distraught than any of the others and had suffered as great a loss as all the rest, the Scripture records that "David strengthened [*encouraged*, KJV] himself in the LORD his God." Instead of reacting in anger, self-pity, bitterness, or revenge, he turned instead to his sole, trustworthy source of aid, realizing no one and nothing else could give him comfort.

He went to God. That's all he had.

We don't like being in situations where we have no one to turn to——no one to understand or help us solve our problems. In a crisis, your spouse and children may prove to be unhelpful or unavailable. Friends and counselors may not be accessible when you need them. That's when you will discover that God can encourage you more effectively than anyone else could anyway——*if* you turn to Him.

When everything is crashing around you and no one is there to help, strengthen yourself in the Lord your God.

Where do you tend to turn for counsel and support when you are in distress? What might it look like for you to "strengthen [yourself] in the LORD"?

His Strength for Our Weakness

He gives power to the faint, and to him who has no might he increases strength.—Isaiah 40:29

 DO YOU HAVE A LITTLE VERSE OR PHRASE that's become a sort of theme in your life, a quick reminder you repeat to yourself when you're heading into an important meeting, or pushing through a long day, or coaxing yourself out of bed in the morning? I do. On first hearing, it's not particularly deep or complex. It's just a simple lyric adapted from a children's song that many of us learned long before we could begin to fathom its meaning:

"We are weak, but He is strong."

Over the years, this little phrase (along with its melody, from the chorus of "Jesus Loves Me") has often been my first, conscious waking thought. And oh, how I need this truth reinforced in my thinking day after day. Because beneath its nursery school exterior lies a profound truth about an incredible exchange God offers us. We give Him our weakness; He gives us His strength.

When we go forth into battle each day, we are no match for sin and temptation. No match for the challenges facing our families, our friendships, our futures. But our enemy, no matter how fierce—and his encroaching world system, no matter how thick and oppressive—is no match for our Lord. Yes, "we are weak." But even more true, "He is strong!"

If we were writing the script for our lives, we probably wouldn't assign ourselves the same tasks God has given us. We'd play it safe. We'd choose parts we could more easily manage. But by placing us into situations beyond our ability to handle, God allows us to experience something greater than our own feeble capabilities. We get the opportunity to "be strong in the Lord and in the strength of his might" (Eph. 6:10).

 What obstacle or issue is proving more than you can handle today? Once you come to the end of your own strength, once you acknowledge your utter weakness, you will be in a place to enter into His endless, limitless strength.

Changed Identity

He said to him, "What is your name?"
And he said, "Jacob."—Genesis 32:27

 A RECURRING THEME OF SCRIPTURE is that God uses things and people that are broken. The patriarch Jacob, for example, had received a promise of blessing as a young man, but he had never been able to embrace it because he was always trying to control and manage life on his own terms. Not until he found himself in an impossible situation at the river Jabbok, wrestling with the angel of God, a day away from facing the approaching army of his estranged brother Esau, did he experience the blessing that had so long eluded him.

I wonder, during his hard, hopeless struggle, if Jacob experienced a flashback to that moment many years earlier, when his blind, elderly father, Isaac, had said to him, "Who are you, my son?" (Gen. 27:18). "I am *Esau*," Jacob had responded deceitfully, trying to wrest a blessing from his father by raw self-will and effort. This time, however, dominated by One infinitely stronger, he responded to a similar question with an answer that reflected a heart and will that had finally been subdued by grace.

"What is your name?"

"Jacob."

This time, there was no pretending, no posturing, no conniving, no self-justifying. Just the bare, naked truth: "I am *Jacob*, the schemer, the deceiver, the manipulator. That's who I really am." And once he admitted the truth, God gave him a new name—*Israel*—meaning "prince with God," representative of a new character. In conceding defeat, Jacob won his ultimate victory. With his natural strength broken down (and with the reminder of a limp that was always with him from that day forward), God could now clothe him with spiritual power.

Do you want to be a usable instrument in God's hands? His blessing and power flow through those who have been truly broken before Him.

 Are you trying to maintain control, to manipulate God to fulfill your purposes, rather than surrendering yourself to His purposes? How might God be trying to bring you to the end of yourself?

One Visitation, Two Purposes

. . . when the Lord Jesus is revealed from heaven with his mighty angels in flaming fire, inflicting vengeance on those who do not know God and on those who do not obey the gospel of our Lord Jesus.—2 Thessalonians 1:7–8

I WAS SURE I HEARD STRANGE NOISES coming from my garage. The longer it went on, the more concerned I became. Had someone broken in? Was I in danger from a prowler lying in wait, ready to burst into the house?

Giving in to my fears, I finally called the police. I breathed a sigh of relief when two kind, burly officers arrived at my door. They quickly allayed my fears by asking questions and assuring me they'd deal with the situation. But when they stormed into my garage, one hand on their pistols, shouting at the top of their lungs, "Police!" they paid quite a different kind of visit on my phantom intruder.

Fortunately, there wasn't anyone actually in there. False alarm. (Turned out a friend with a spare garage opener had returned some items without letting me know, so as not to disturb my study!)

When Jesus returns to earth a second time, He, too, will be paying two very different types of visits on mankind.

One will be to rescue those who have believed in Christ, to deliver them from death and consummate the salvation of their souls. But His other purpose will be to bring judgment and punishment on the wicked, to call the unredeemed to account. One visitation but two distinct purposes.

Our world wants to believe that everyone will be saved in the end, that God's justice will ultimately be waived in favor of a sweeping, free pass. But sin has its "wages" (Rom. 6:23), and those who reject His salvation will not escape eternal judgment. As we look forward to His appearing, celebrating our coming redemption, may we also be faithful to share His gospel of grace with those in danger of experiencing God's righteous wrath.

How seriously do you take God's judgment of sin—that those who will not bow to Him as Lord cannot hope for Him as Savior? Based on your relationship with Christ, do you have reason to eagerly anticipate or anxiously dread His return?

Change of Mind

"He answered, 'I will not,' but afterward he
changed his mind and went."—Matthew 21:29

 FOLLOWING HER FRESHMAN YEAR IN COLLEGE, Shannon Etter spent the summer in Papua, New Guinea, where she began to question what she had previously sensed to be God's call on her life to serve full-time on the mission field. Living under mosquito nets in bamboo huts suspended high off the ground, eating whatever could be caught in the river, and having to use an outhouse took all the shine off this childhood dream. She could stomach the idea of doing it short-term but not permanently. Not as a lifestyle. *Better get yourself another girl.*

It wasn't until several years later, while sharing offhand with a friend how she had once entertained the idea of becoming a missionary, that God challenged her to rethink her reluctance. "All the reasons you've told me for changing your mind are not godly reasons," this friend boldly exhorted. "You need to get down on your knees and ask Him what He wants to do with your life. And whatever He tells you, you need to trust Him for the strength to be obedient."

God's plans for your life may be different than what you would have chosen if you were writing the script, but obedience will always lead to true joy, fulfillment, and fruitfulness.

Perhaps you've pushed aside a calling from God—whatever that calling might have been—out of fear of inconvenience or a desire to go a different direction. Though the original opportunity may have passed you by, remember that God's will is not so much tied to a place or a position as to the condition of your heart. God cannot bless the fearful or willful choices of your past, but He can—and He will—bless a repentant heart, a heart that now says "Yes, Lord."

 Are there any areas where you have been ignoring or resisting
God's leading in your life? Follow the advice of Shannon's friend.
Get down on your knees and ask Him what He wants to do with
your life . . . then trust Him for the strength to be obedient.

Thanks Where Thanks Is Due

John answered, "A person cannot receive even one thing unless it is given him from heaven."—John 3:27

 CERTAINLY, THERE IS EVERYTHING RIGHT about striving to maintain a positive outlook on life—being grateful for one's health, or for a chance visit with a friend in the grocery store aisle, or for a flower reaching full bloom in the garden, surprising you one morning as you step out the door on an otherwise gloomy day. How wonderful when our hearts awaken to the fact that we have so much to be thankful for!

But thankful to whom?

The problem with Christless gratitude is that, nice as it is, it's out of context. It's a gratitude that generically tosses its thanksgivings into the air, not sure if they should be directed toward good breaks, good genes, good fortune, or the good Lord. And we as believers simply cannot be content to consider this sufficient—not when there's a level of gratitude that offers us so much more than merely feeling good about how things are going.

How can it ever be appropriate to thank our "lucky stars" for even a single blessing that comes our way, when in reality it has come from the One who thought up stars in the first place—the One who wants us to know that He has engraved us on the palms of His hands (Isa. 49:16), who loves us "from everlasting to everlasting" (Ps. 103:17). Why would we want to miss that?

It is only by recognizing that our blessings have a single Source—a real, personal, living, and loving Giver—that gratitude becomes authentic, Christian gratitude: recognizing and expressing appreciation for the benefits we have received from God and others.

 Why is it important for us to acknowledge God as the source of the countless gifts we receive from His hand? Is there any gratitude in your heart that you need to turn Godward?

At His Pleasure

*Whatever you do, work heartily, as for the Lord and not for men,
knowing that from the Lord you will receive the inheritance as your
reward. You are serving the Lord Christ.*—Colossians 3:23–24

 YOU MAY HAVE HEARD IT SAID OF A CEO that he or she
"serves at the pleasure of the board." That means the
exec is not the ultimate authority; they are accountable
to their board and their mission is to fulfill the wishes
and priorities of the ones who hired them.

We have a motto in our ministry that we try to keep in mind
as an undergirding principle for how we perform our work:

"I serve at the pleasure of my Lord and Savior Jesus Christ."

This helps us remember who's boss. We don't work to
please ourselves or our friends. We don't even ultimately work
to please our constituents and listeners, doing whatever they say,
letting their wishes drive our mission and calling. Our staff, our
leadership, myself included—we serve only at the pleasure of
Jesus. That means He can send me wherever He wants and tell
me to do whatever He desires. He is my Master, and I am His
willing servant.

As you read the New Testament epistles, notice how many
times the authors of these letters identify themselves in this
manner. Paul called himself "a servant of Christ Jesus" (Rom.
1:1); Peter—"a servant and apostle of Jesus Christ" (2 Peter 1:1);
Jude also—"a servant of Jesus Christ" (Jude 1). Even James, who
was actually the half-brother of the Lord Jesus and might have
felt inclined to include this family connection in his credentials,
chose instead to introduce himself as "a servant of God and of
the Lord Jesus Christ" (James 1:1). This was their claim to fame;
it was the way they wanted to be known.

We're not always inclined to see it this way, but the fact is that
it is a great privilege, an honor, to be the bond servant of Christ.

You might even say . . . a pleasure.

 *What would be different about the day ahead if you
entered it saying, "I serve at the pleasure of my Lord
and Savior Jesus Christ"?*

The Final Word

He sent out his word and healed them, and delivered them from their destruction.—Psalm 107:20

 All of us at one time or another have been on the receiving end of harsh, hurtful words. And when those words land on a tender, sensitive heart—or if they were spoken to you at a young, impressionable age—the enemy knows just how to bring those ugly statements to mind out of nowhere, causing you to feel wounded, inferior, and rejected all over again. You almost can't help it.

But that doesn't mean you're without help in responding back with confidence and strength. You see, Christ, the living Word of God, became flesh and lived among us (John 1:14). While on this earth, He endured slander, scoffing, and scorn that spewed out of hateful, angry hearts. When He went to the cross, He took upon Himself the weight and consequences of all those sinful words. In so doing, He stripped the power of every evil word spoken over you to defeat and devastate you.

That doesn't mean you will forget every haunting, upsetting thing that has ever been said to you. In God's wisdom and love, He may use the memory of those words to keep your heart tender before Him and to make you more tenderhearted and merciful toward others. But it does mean that you don't need to live in bondage to those verbal darts.

By His grace and the power of His Spirit, not only can you shield yourself from their harm, you can also keep from using your own words to harm others, breaking the cycle of reviling and retaliation.

So when you feel condemned or controlled by what others have said to you, run back to the cross, where Christ, the living Word of God, died to heal the wounds caused by sin (yours and others') and to deliver you from the destruction of cruel words.

 What damaging words would you lay at His wounded feet today, believing that His Word can heal and restore your heart?

Love Me Not?

No one ever hated his own flesh, but nourishes and cherishes it,
just as Christ does the church.—Ephesians 5:29

 LOW SELF-ESTEEM is one of the most common diagnoses of our era. This is why learning to "love ourselves" has become such a popular mantra of pop psychology—the world's prescription for a culture plagued with a sense of worthlessness.

But we cannot bestow worth on ourselves, nor do we experience the fullness of God's love by telling ourselves how lovable we are. Scripture says that we were created in His image, that He loves us, and that we are precious to Him. Our need is not to love ourselves more but to receive His incredible love for us and to rejoice in His design and purpose for our lives.

According to Scripture, the truth is that we already love ourselves—immensely. We naturally look out for our best interests and are deeply sensitive to our own feelings and needs, acutely conscious of how things and people affect us. The reason some of us get hurt so easily, in fact, is not because we hate ourselves but because we love ourselves! We want to be accepted, cherished, and treated well. If we didn't care so much, we wouldn't be so concerned about being rejected, neglected, or mistreated.

So the fact is, we do not hate ourselves, nor do we need to learn to love ourselves more. We do need to learn how to *deny* ourselves so we can do something which does *not* come naturally—to truly love God and others.

Our problem isn't so much a "poor self-image" as it is a "poor God-image." Our real need isn't for a higher view of ourselves but for a higher view of God. When we see and esteem Him rightly, then we will esteem ourselves rightly—as objects of His immense love, whom He has chosen to rescue and redeem from our sin by His grace. It doesn't get any better than that!

 What does it mean to you to be loved by God?
What difference could that make in how you view yourself?

A Passion for Holiness

"And the nations will know that I am the LORD,"
declares the Lord GOD, "when through you I vindicate
my holiness before their eyes."—Ezekiel 36:23

DESPITE CHURNING OUT A LOT OF RELIGIOUS ACTIVITY, many people who call themselves believers today have rewritten the law of God, prostituting His grace, turning it into a license to sin. Lust, greed, materialism, anger, selfishness, pride, sensuality, divorce, deceit, ungodly entertainment, worldly philosophies—little by little, we've let down our guard, cultivated a relationship with these sworn enemies of holiness, and in many cases, welcomed them into our churches and given them a home there.

Where are the men and women who love God supremely, who fear nothing and no one but Him? Where are the saints who live like saints, whose lives are above reproach in their homes, their work, their speech, their habits, their attitudes, their finances, their relationships?

Where are the children of God whose eyes are filled with tears, whose knees are sore from pleading with God to grant the gift of repentance, whose hearts ache when they see an unholy church entertaining herself to death?

Where are the Christian leaders with the compassion and courage to call the church to be clean before God? Where are the moms and dads and young people willing to deal thoroughly and decisively with any and every unholy thing in their hearts and their homes?

The church has been waiting for the world to get right with God. When will we realize that the world is waiting for the *church* to get right with God? It is time for us to repent, to pursue holiness by His grace and for His glory. We can scarcely imagine the impact that will be felt in our world when the holiness of Christ is seen in and through His people.

Has the Spirit identified anything unholy in your heart, home, habits, or relationships? What is keeping you from dealing with it? What difference might it make if our world could see a reflection of a holy God in those of us who are called by His name?

What Are You Waiting For?

From of old no one has heard or perceived by the ear, no eye has seen a God besides you, who acts for those who wait for him.—Isaiah 64:4

 WHAT KIND OF PERSON does God respond to? Who is the most likely candidate for revival? Who will be the next to see the usual order of things turned upside down in a mighty season of divine refreshing and empowering, as the mountains tremble at His presence (Isa. 64:1)?

According to the prophet Isaiah, God moves powerfully on behalf of those who "wait for him."

When we use that word—"wait"—we typically mean it in a *passive* sense. We say we're waiting for summer to get here, or the school year to end, or a package to arrive. It's not something we're thinking about all the time. Only when something jogs our memory do we focus on it.

But the Hebrew word for "wait" used in Isaiah 64:4 is an *active* word. It means to tarry, to long, to cling or adhere to. It has the sense of something that is uppermost on a person's mind.

The psalmist expressed this sense of earnest longing when he said, "My soul waits for the Lord more than watchmen for the morning" (Ps. 130:6). If you've ever worked a night shift—or sat up through the night with a fussy infant—you know how eagerly you "wait" for the morning to come!

God promises to "meet" (Isa. 64:5) with those who wait for Him in this way, those who attentively, expectantly incline their hearts toward Him—standing on tiptoe as it were to get a glimpse of His glory.

And that's what revival is, really—an encounter with God. That meeting may take place on a personal level or as a family. It may be an unusual visitation of God's Spirit that engages your entire church or community—or even engulfs an entire nation. But it begins when God responds to those who want nothing other than Him, who have little else on their minds but desiring Him, whose hearts are truly *waiting* for Him.

 What causes us to "wait" with such intensity for things that are much less important than our need for God's intervention? What would "waiting for God" look like in your life?

Help for the Weary

Is anyone among you sick? Let him call for the elders of the church, and let them pray over him, anointing him with oil in the name of the Lord.—James 5:14

MANY COMMENTATORS believe that the "sickness" referred to in this passage is not limited to physical illness but includes those who are "weak" or "weary" from various types of suffering. Unfortunately, we have developed a mindset that only "professionals" are qualified to help people who suffer with emotional or mental ailments.

Now I'm not suggesting there's no place for people who've been trained in these fields, provided their counsel is rooted in the Word and ways of God. Let's not forget, however, that God has placed within His body the resources we need—His Word and His Spirit—to minister to hurting people. The church should be able to take the ointment of Scripture and apply it to each other's needs.

So when you're hurting, when your soul is sick, let the body of Christ minister grace to you in the name of Jesus. After you have first prayed yourself, take the initiative to share your needs with others in the body—particularly your spiritual leaders who have been given responsibility to care for your soul. Ask them to pray for you. Confess any sin that may be causing emotional weakness or sickness in your life, and be willing to stay accountable through the process of healing and restoration.

You may or may not "feel" immediately better, but you will know you're being counseled by the sure Word of God, that you're surrendered to His sovereignty and looking to Him for the care and direction you need.

As long as we are in these bodies, we will experience varying degrees of pain, distress, and difficult emotions. And while healing may indeed come, the focus of our lives should be on the glory of God and His redemptive purposes in this world. Everything else is expendable. True joy comes from abandoning ourselves to that end.

 Do you need to humble yourself and seek prayer and assistance from the body of believers in which He has placed you?

He Speaks

And God said, "Let there be light," and there was light.—Genesis 1:3

 HAVE YOU EVER THOUGHT ABOUT what life would be like if God had never spoken? What if He had never communicated with man? What if He had never given us His written Word? Try to imagine a world in which no one had ever heard the voice of God, a world in which there was no Bible.

Yes, we would know there *is* a God because "the heavens declare the glory of God" (Ps. 19:1). But how would we know what He is like? We were created to bring Him "pleasure" (Rev. 4:11 KJV), but how would we know what pleases Him?

Had God not chosen to speak, to reveal Himself, we would have no standard of right and wrong. We would not know how we are to live. And though we might experience some vague sense of guilt when we sinned, we wouldn't know why—nor would we know what to do about it. We wouldn't have any way of communicating with our Creator. Our lives would be pointless and frustrating. Imagine having to go through life without knowing anything of the promises of God, the commands of God, the love and mercy of God, the will of God, or the ways of God.

Thankfully, we do not have to exist in such a spiritual vacuum. God *has* spoken. He *has* revealed Himself to us. Of all the natural wonders on our planet, and all the manufactured wonders that have been designed, engineered, and produced by the skillful endeavors of man, none comes close to equaling the wonder of these three small words found in the first chapter of Genesis: *"And God said . . ."*

 Think of the last time God spoke to you through His Word, through a sermon, through biblical counsel from a friend or family member. Don't take His voice for granted.

Immediately

And immediately the flow of blood dried up, and she felt in her body that she was healed of her disease.—Mark 5:29

I LOVE THAT WORD—"IMMEDIATELY." This woman who had suffered with a dreadful blood disease for twelve years, who had exhausted every other form of relief, who had spent all her money trying to find a cure for her condition, reached out to Jesus, and was healed "immediately."

No, not all of our problems will go away "immediately," even when we come close enough to touch the hem of His garment. There is often a long, daily process of sanctification involved in fully experiencing the healing and wholeness He brings to our spirits.

But be reminded today that He does have the ability and power—in a moment of time—to do what everyone else says will take a lifetime. I have known people who have spent a small fortune on therapists and counselors, with little if any apparent relief for their addictions, emotional pain, or dysfunctional relationships—only to find that when they reached out to Christ, His Word, and His truth, they were set free in a relatively short period of time from issues that had plagued them for years.

That's because Jesus knows how to get to the heart of the problem, down where much of our pain originates. That sin. That bitterness. That hatred or resentment. That lie we have believed.

As with the woman suffering from the discharge of blood, Jesus wants to go to the source—the dark spring that's causing many of our chronic difficulties. When we invite Him to go there, He can do what all the world's Band-Aids can never accomplish.

The healing touch of Christ is not a substitute for a lifetime process of growth in grace and striving against sin. But when He chooses, He is able to deliver chronic sufferers who come to Him in faith and earnestly appeal for that which only He can do.

Are you placing your hope in human or divine means of help for the issues that plague you? Do you believe that Jesus really could heal you and set you free?

Storm Shelter

The name of the LORD is a strong tower; the righteous man
runs into it and is safe.—Proverbs 18:10

I REMEMBER HEARING OF A FAMILY IN OKLAHOMA CITY whose home was in the path of a devastating tornado. With the power out and the winds howling, they rushed for shelter inside the tiny confines of a hall closet, just as the sounds of splintering wood and shattering glass began echoing above them, all around them. When the storm had finally passed and they emerged from hiding, the grim reality set in. Their house had been completely destroyed. Only one thing remained standing—their hall closet—their one chosen place of refuge. And therefore, *they* remained standing too.

When we are in the midst of real crisis—when the storm is intense and threatening to tear us apart—we will usually go anywhere we can to escape the danger. All we know is what we're running from, even if we're not so particular about what we're running to.

But our ultimate safe place, our one, unfailing "strong tower," is the "name of the LORD"—not just God in general but those wonderful attributes of His that make Him sufficient for every storm. We run to His character of faithfulness and goodness. We run to His heart of love and compassion. We run to His ways of wisdom and refining. "In the shadow of your wings," David cried, "I will take refuge, till the storms of destruction pass by" (Ps. 57:1).

Isaiah wrote about a man who would be "like a hiding place from the wind, a shelter from the storm" (Isa. 32:2). That Man is none other than our Lord Jesus Christ, the only sure place in times of danger.

Know where you're running. And know you are safe.

Is there a storm beating down on you today? In your home?
Your marriage? Your personal integrity? Where are you turning
to find relief and safety?

Costly Gratitude

*And he took a cup, and when he had given thanks
he gave it to them, saying, "Drink of it, all of you,
for this is my blood of the covenant, which is poured out
for many for the forgiveness of sins."*—Matthew 26:27–28

 WITHIN HOURS OF HIS ARREST, HIS TRIAL, and ultimately His crucifixion—on a night when Jesus, from a human perspective, had every reason for giving in to self-pity, resentment, and murmuring —the Son instead spoke words of *thanks* to His heavenly Father, words that flowed from a thankful heart.

This was not just an obligatory blessing offered up before a meal. He understood that these emblems in His hands represented His own body and blood, soon to be broken and poured out in horrific fashion for the salvation of sinful man. And yet when you harmonize the gospel accounts, it appears that Jesus paused at least three times during the Passover observance to *give thanks*—to say in effect, "Father, I gladly surrender Myself to Your calling for My life, whatever the cost."

He gave Himself to God and to the world not under coercion but with abandon—even with gratitude—thankful for the privilege of obeying His Father and fulfilling the mission He had been sent to earth to complete.

My own heart is convicted as I write these words, thinking how often my service for the Lord and others is tinged with shades of reservation or clouded with resentment over the price to be paid. Perhaps you feel the same inner conviction of His Spirit. Then, oh, may the thankful Spirit of Christ overflow our hearts, motivated by His example and enabled by His power. May He forgive us for our thankless self-absorption and help us to live lives—like His—of costly gratitude.

 For what circumstances or aspects of your calling are you the least inclined to be thankful at this moment? Can you— will you—lift your "cup" up to the Lord and give thanks?

Drawn to Danger

But each person is tempted when he is lured
and enticed by his own desire.—James 1:14

 IT ALL STARTED WHEN SOME FRIENDS CAME OVER to make grape juice in my kitchen—150 quarts of grape juice! And while the project went smoothly enough, all those bushels of freshly picked grapes and the large pots that caught their sugary nectar drew a swarm of fruit flies that eventually wafted upstairs into my study, multiplying by the hour and causing no small annoyance. I had no idea how to get rid of them!

But my friends did. Putting a chunk of banana in the bottom of a drinking glass, then inverting a paper cone over the top and sealing it with tape, they set the homemade contraption on my desk while I waited for the tiny pests to be lured in by the scent. It didn't take long. Soon, one after another, those invading insects began descending through the tiny hole and into the glass, only to find themselves hopelessly trapped inside. The plan worked! I could hardly believe it.

While watching the capture and demise of the unwanted flies, I couldn't help thinking of Eve—eyeing that luscious fruit, imagining how much pleasure it held for her, only to find that what she thought would bring her fulfillment actually paved the way to her coffin. I also couldn't help thinking of myself, and how often I too have allowed myself to be drawn in to things I thought would make me happy but proved to be a snare.

What a vivid reminder of how easily we become trapped by what we think we want, and conversely, how much pain we can avoid by applying God's grace in saying no to sin and yes to Christ. If we are in Him, we don't have to be in bondage—we can be free. Rather than being drawn by our fleshly desires toward death, let us remember what (who) saves us and choose life.

 Is your heart being lured into some enticing trap? What perceived benefits make the temptation seem irresistible? What resources has God made available to help you resist the temptation?

Balanced Diet

All Scripture is breathed out by God and profitable
for teaching, for reproof, for correction, and for
training in righteousness.—2 Timothy 3:16

 IMAGINE GOING TO THE REFRIGERATOR, closing your eyes, and grabbing whatever items your hands happened upon, to make a snack for yourself. Instead of a ham and cheese sandwich, you might end up with a plate of olives, mustard, and sour cream—not especially appetizing or nourishing.

Yet this describes the way many people approach the Word of God. They blindly "grab" whatever passage they first come to, in no particular sequence or order, not realizing that by separating Scripture from its larger context, they are missing a sense of how what they are reading fits into the whole scheme of things—not to speak of the fact that true meanings can easily be misunderstood, making them vulnerable to embrace error.

It's true that not all parts of the Bible are equally easy to digest. "Meals" from Chronicles or Ezekiel may not seem as succulent as the Psalms, the gospel of Luke, or John's epistles. Yet as one nineteenth century author put it, "The Bible resembles an extensive and highly cultivated garden, where there is a vast variety and profusion of fruits and flowers: some of which are more essential or more splendid than others; but there is not a blade suffered to grow in it which has not its use and beauty in the system."

From beginning to end, the Bible is one grand epic of redemption—the story of a God who created man for fellowship with Himself, watched as man rejected His overtures, and then stooped down to restore man to Himself through the cross. If you want to see the story in its full panorama, if you want to enjoy a more balanced spiritual diet, make sure you're not skipping over certain portions of the Word.

 Are there portions of Scripture you find yourself reading most
often, to the neglect of other parts of the Word? Take time
soon to visit a less familiar section of the "garden," and see
what fresh beauty God may reveal to you there.

Trust Me

For God alone, O my soul, wait in silence, for my hope
is from him. He only is my rock and my salvation, my fortress;
I shall not be shaken.—Psalm 62:5–6

 ANN BLOCHER WAS TOLD SHE HAD BREAST CANCER when her five children were all young adults. After battling to control her condition with chemotherapy and diet, including a brief season of blessed remission, she finally went home to be with the Lord, roughly ten years after her initial diagnosis.

As she walked through that tempestuous, uncertain decade, she faced numerous fears about her future and her family. In particular she struggled with a desire to be part of her children's lives, knowing cancer threatened to deprive her of the privilege. But she discovered that what God was asking of her really came down to trust. Three years before her home going, she expressed that thought in a bit of poetry:

> Can you trust Me, child?
> Not only for ultimate eternity, of which you know next to nothing, and so are not tempted to meddle—
> But for the little span of your life between the Now and Then, where you envision decline and
> separations and failures, impairments, pain, bereavements, disappointments—
> Do you find Me qualified to be Lord of your last days?

Isn't this the real issue for every child of God? *Can you trust Me?* The truth is, whatever your fears, unknowns, or challenges, He has promised to provide for you, share His pleasures with you, protect you, and give you His enduring presence.

God gives no guarantees of where He will lead you, no certain knowledge of difficulties you will encounter on the journey. Yet we know the character of the One in whom we have placed our trust. And we know His promises will more than offset whatever risks, dangers, or losses He may allow into our lives.

 "Can you trust Me, child?" What might God be asking you to trust Him with or for in this season and for the foreseeable future?

Point of Entry

For what partnership has righteousness with lawlessness?
Or what fellowship has light with darkness?—2 Corinthians 6:14

 EVER SINCE I WAS BORN AGAIN AS A YOUNG GIRL, I have longed to experience a more intimate relationship with God and enjoy the reality of His presence. The psalmist expressed this same desire when he asked (and answered), "Who shall ascend the hill of the LORD? And who shall stand in his holy place? He who has clean hands and a pure heart" (Ps. 24:3–4). His words remind us that only those who are holy can draw near to a holy God.

We know that those who are in Christ have been declared holy—in right standing with God, positionally. However, as redeemed sinners, we cannot cling to our impatience, gluttony, slothfulness, and moodiness, and expect to enjoy intimate fellowship with God—any more than a teenager who willfully violates his parents' instructions can look confidently into their eyes when he returns home, any more than a wife who lies to her husband about exceeding their credit card limit can expect to enjoy marital intimacy when the lights are turned out at night.

We can sing praise choruses loudly enough to be heard in the next county. We can join sellout crowds in cheering for God at concerts and conferences. We can applaud speakers who stir our emotions. We can have mystical spiritual experiences. But none of these will draw us one iota closer to God if we are ignoring or cherishing sin in our hearts. "Blessed are the pure in heart, for they shall see God" (Matt. 5:8).

"Who among us can dwell with the consuming fire?" the prophet asked. "He who walks righteously and speaks uprightly" (Isa. 33:14–15). "For the LORD is righteous; he loves righteous deeds; the upright shall behold his face" (Ps. 11:7). Intimacy with our holy God is reserved for those who love and choose the path of holiness.

 Are you enjoying close fellowship with God, or is there some breach between you and Him? Is there any distance-causing sin that you are clinging to, unwilling to repent of?

Speck Work

"Or how can you say to your brother, 'Let me take the speck out of your eye,' when there is the log in your own eye? You hypocrite, first take the log out of your own eye, and then you will see clearly to take the speck out of your brother's eye."—Matthew 7:4–5

OFTEN, AFTER ENDURING THE UNDESERVED PAIN of another's sin against us, we (the *offended*) become the *offender* in the way we respond to the original or ongoing injustice. So even though we may have done little or nothing to provoke what first happened, we have now added our own sin into the mix. And it is our own sin that we must deal with first.

In this familiar passage from the Sermon on the Mount, Jesus emphasized the importance of dealing with our own sin before trying to deal with others' failures. This isn't to minimize what our "brother" may have done but rather to affirm that it's hard to be objective about *his* sin when we've got a beam in our own eye. It's hard to help him deal with his issue—not to mention hypocritical on our part—if we haven't confessed our own sin, even if it was a reaction to his sin in the first place.

So be honest: Has someone else's sin begotten sin in your own life? Then confess it—to them, if possible and appropriate. Not in a way that excuses you, not in a way that blames them for pushing you to it, not in a way that leads you into even more sin by stirring up your anger against them. Take full responsibility for your own sin.

"But I'm only 5 percent responsible for this whole thing!" Then assume 100 percent responsibility for your 5 percent. Humble yourself. Clear your conscience. Seek forgiveness. Then let God use you to minister grace to your brother in need.

Do you have a fractured relationship with another person? Is it possible that you have been overlooking your share of the blame—just as you feel the other person has done? What might an honest evaluation expose in your own heart?

Path of Least Insistence

"I will leave within you the meek and humble,
who trust in the name of the Lord."—Zephaniah 3:12 NIV

IF YOU LIVE IN AN AREA WHERE TORNADOS have occasion to strike, you know the immense destruction they can cause. You've seen the downed limbs, the garbage and building debris strewn about. You know what a mess they can leave behind to be picked up later.

But don't we do the same thing ourselves sometimes, "touching down" with destructive force in our families and workplaces and in our interactions with others? Through curt email responses, critical words, and short-tempered reactions, we can ravage our relationships. By being mouthy, controlling, and negative, we leave a swath of emotional and relational debris and expect others to clean up the mess.

But while the world esteems those who are assertive and stand up for their rights, who speak their mind and get results, God esteems those whose emotions and responses are under His control. Though the world looks at meek people and says they're weak, God looks at the meek and says they remind Him of Jesus.

Meekness does not come naturally to any of us. It is a work of grace—something we cannot expect to obtain without His aid. It is the sweet fruit of trusting in the Lord and allowing Him to live His life and cultivate His humble, meek spirit in and through us.

And though meekness may require the relinquishing of our rights, Scripture assures us that it also results in "abundant peace" (Ps. 37:11), "fresh joy" (Isa. 29:19), and the opportunity to "inherit the earth" (Matt. 5:5)—having all that really matters in life, even if it means not having all we really want at the moment.

How would others describe the kind of wake you leave behind?
What would your spouse say? Your children? Your coworkers?
What kind of impact do you want to have?

True Hope

For the LORD is good; his steadfast love endures forever,
and his faithfulness to all generations.—Psalm 100:5

 SEPTEMBER 1, 1979, IS PERMANENTLY ETCHED in my memory. I had spent the weekend of my twenty-first birthday visiting my family near Philadelphia. On that Saturday afternoon, my parents took me to the airport to catch a flight to Virginia, where I was serving on the staff of a local church.

When I landed in Lynchburg, I received a call from my mother, telling me that my father had suffered a heart attack and instantly had gone to be with the Lord. There was no warning. No time to say final goodbyes. My forty-year-old mother was left with seven children, ages eight to twenty-one.

The tears flowed freely in the days, weeks, and months that followed. But in that moment when I first learned of my dad's home going, the Lord did something especially gracious for me—He reminded me of the truth. Before there was any other conscious thought, before the flood of tears was released, He brought to mind a verse I had read not many days earlier. Paraphrased, it said: "God is good, and everything He does is good" (Ps. 119:68).

My dad had spent the first twenty-one years of my life teaching me this truth. And now, at that crucial moment, the truth proved to be a fortress for my heart. I missed my dad terribly—I still miss him, these many years later. I never had a chance to know him as an adult daughter. There are so many things I wish we could have talked about.

But I knew then, and I am even more sure now, that *God is good, and everything He does is good*. When sight, sense, and emotions scream to the contrary, this is the bedrock truth that will always prove to be an unshakable foundation for our hearts.

 Once we dismiss, discount, or doubt the goodness of God,
where can that lead us? How can you cultivate deeper trust
in the goodness of God?

Never without Hope

"He shall be to you a restorer of life and a nourisher of your old age."—Ruth 4:15

ONE OF THE THINGS I LOVE about the heart and ways of God is that no sooner do we fail or step out of His will, than He begins to unfold His plan (already in place) to redeem our situation and restore us back to Himself. We see this in the life of Naomi and her family after they had fled from Bethlehem to Moab during a time of famine, intending to stay for just a brief time in that godless land but eventually settling there.

Over the course of years, Naomi's husband died, as well as her two sons, leaving her destitute and lonely with only her widowed daughters-in-law for company. She was far away from home with little to give her life meaning. Hope had ebbed away, and her conversation belied her disappointment with God.

But in seasons of adversity, pressure, and problems, the important question is not so much "Why is this happening to me?" as "What is God doing in this situation, and how can He use it to bring glory to Himself?"

The well-known account of Naomi's return to Bethlehem with her daughter-in-law Ruth and their redemption through the kindness of Boaz demonstrates that God can take a family reeling from serious failures and missteps and restore them back to a life of purpose—one that redirects their family line—and future generations—to Christ.

You may find yourself at a point where you cannot see a good ending to your situation, having chosen your own or followed another's straying path away from God's plan. Yes, there may be more pain to endure, more consequences to encounter. But God can be trusted to work through even the most twisted circumstances of life to fit you for even greater service, to accomplish His kingdom purposes, and to give you a bright and hopeful future.

Are you more focused on your failure or those of others, or on the redemptive plan and purposes of God? Do you believe that God can redeem and restore what may seem to you to be a hopelessly tangled mess, and bring glory to Himself in the process?

Something Old, Something New

We all, with unveiled face, beholding the glory of the Lord,
are being transformed into the same image from one degree
of glory to another.—2 Corinthians 3:18

NO SOONER HAD I TURNED FORTY than I started receiving catalogs promoting products guaranteed to combat the effects of aging. They promised me clearer skin, fewer wrinkles, more energy, prettier nails and hair. The implication was that as I get older, what matters most is looking and feeling younger.

The fact is, however, I *am* getting older. And in our fallen world, this means my body is slowly deteriorating. I look in the mirror and see lines that weren't there a dozen years ago, along with a full head of gray hair. I've had to start using a larger print Bible. And even with regular exercise and watching what I eat, I just don't have the physical stamina I had at twenty.

But I refuse to buy into the lie that those things are ultimate tragedies or that my biological clock can somehow be reversed. Naturally I'm not trying to *hasten* my physical decline, but neither am I consumed with fighting off the inevitable. As I get older, I want to focus on those things that God says matter most—things like letting His Spirit cultivate in me a gracious, wise, kind, and loving heart.

I know there is a process taking place in my physical body that will not be reversed this side of eternity. But I also know that "the path of the righteous is like the light of dawn, which shines brighter and brighter until full day" (Prov. 4:18). By God's grace, our spirits can continue to grow richer, fuller, and stronger, even as our outer bodies are going the way of all flesh.

How do you try to balance accepting the unavoidable challenges
of aging with the desire to be a good steward of your body?
What can you do to cultivate and strengthen your inner life and
spirit, even while your physical body is declining?

Gratitude and the Will of God

Give thanks in all circumstances; for this is the will of God in Christ Jesus for you. —1 Thessalonians 5:18

 As TRUE BELIEVERS, we want to know God's will for our lives, especially when it comes to major, life-ordering decisions. But interestingly, when we go to the Scripture for insight on discerning His will, we don't find a lot about things to do, places to go, or people to meet. That's because God's will is not so much a place, a job, or a specific mate as it is a heart and a lifestyle.

And according to the verse above, one fundamental aspect of that lifestyle is an attitude of gratitude.

Sure, details matter to God. And He can give us the wisdom to make decisions about those details as we seek Him and walk in line with the principles of His Word. But live long enough, and you find that the choices only change by year, degree, and color. A decision that's huge today is soon replaced by yet another batch of issues and options for the next season of life.

That's when you discover that the will of God is a whole lot bigger and broader than fine-print details and exact measurements. Instead it's characterized by a handful of simple constants that overshadow your specific questions and your appeals for direction. In other words, you may find yourself a lot closer to hearing God's heart on a certain matter, not by making pro- and con- lists or anguishing between multiple options but simply by doing what you already *know* to be His will.

So when faced with perplexing circumstances, when you don't know what to do or which way to go, *give thanks*—and you'll likely find Him giving the discernment you need to make wise, God-honoring decisions.

 Are you seeking to discern God's will for a particular decision or area of your life? Are you obeying the parts of His will that you already know? How about the matter of "giving thanks in all circumstances"?

In His Time

Wait for the LORD; be strong, and let your heart take courage;
wait for the LORD!—Psalm 27:14

 SARAH IS HAILED IN SCRIPTURE as a woman who reverenced and obeyed her husband. On at least one occasion, however, when God did not act as quickly as she felt He should, she decided to try handling matters on her own.

You most likely know the story. God had promised her husband, Abraham, that he would have many descendants and would be the father of a great nation. But Sarah was now *seventy-six* years old and still childless. Impatient with waiting, she decided someone had to do something, so she put pressure on her husband to take action, employing a common practice of the day by which a barren woman could produce a child through one of her servants.

At first, her plan seemed to work splendidly. But it didn't take long for the situation to turn sour. The relationship between the childless wife and the expectant servant became unbearable, leading Sarah to go back to Abraham and say, "You are responsible for the wrong I am suffering" (Gen. 16:5 NIV). (Can't help but feel for Abraham!) And although God supernaturally intervened some thirteen years later to give Abraham and his wife a child of their own, the son born of Abraham and Hagar's union became a source of great conflict and grief to them (not to speak of untold generations to come).

How many times must Sarah have looked back in regret and said to herself, "Why couldn't I have waited on the Lord? Why did I have to manipulate that situation?"

Yes, we can take the reins and try to solve our problems in our way and on our timetable—and we may even be able to achieve some immediate results. But remember: *God always acts on behalf of those who wait for Him.* Far better to trust His wise plan than to reap the painful consequences of charging ahead and taking matters in your own hands.

 Is there a matter where you are manipulating to get your longings fulfilled or to see your circumstances changed, rather than waiting on God to act in His time and His way?

For Their Sake

*"And for their sake I consecrate myself, that they also
may be sanctified in truth."*—John 17:19

THIS VERSE HAS OFTEN BEEN a source of motivation
and challenge to me as I have wrestled with issues
of surrender and obedience. When I am tempted
to secretly indulge my flesh, to be slack in my work,
to be harsh with my words, or yield to self-centered
emotions, the example of Christ who consecrated His life to
God for our sake helps me stop and think about the influence
my lifestyle has on those around me.

It's bad enough for us to make choices that hurt our own
relationship with God. Yet how much more serious to be the
cause of someone else deciding to sin. So as we consecrate our
lives to God and let Him sanctify us by His truth, we do so not
only for our own sake and for Christ's sake but also for the sake
of others.

I once heard someone say about a ministry leader, "If I
was ever to decide not to be a Christian—and I almost did—it
would be because of that man." The truth is, other believers
are affected by our choices. And to a significant degree, the lost
world determines its view of God based on the lives of those
who profess to know Him. I wonder how many people have been
dissuaded from believing in Christ because of something they've
seen or experienced from those of us who bear His name.

Why must you be willing to say no to your flesh and yes to
God, day in and day out? Because of the price Jesus paid to
make you holy. Because the world desperately needs to see what
God is like. Because this is your created purpose and destiny.
Because your consecrated life may inspire someone who's
watching you to turn from sin, look to Christ, and choose the
pathway of holiness.

*Have you considered how your choice to cling to sin or to
live a holy, set apart life affects your family, your children,
your friends, your legacy? Does your life motivate the people
around you to live a holy life?*

Jesus, the Word of God

In the beginning was the Word, and the Word was with God, and the Word was God.—John 1:1

THERE ARE MANY HELPFUL PLANS and methods you can use for reading the Bible. Personally, I like to vary my approach from time to time. But whatever plan you choose, don't let yourself become a slave to the method. Remember that the goal is not just getting through the Bible but getting the Word into *you* and getting you to *Jesus*—cultivating a growing relationship with the living Word of God.

One of the most sobering passages of the Bible addresses this matter. The Pharisees of Jesus' day were renowned for their vast knowledge of the Old Testament Scriptures. Yet one day Jesus looked them squarely in the eye and said, "[God's] voice you have never heard, his form you have never seen, and you do not have his word abiding in you" (John 5:37–38).

I can just imagine those indignant, bedecked scholars turning red in the face, sputtering under their breath, "What does He mean? Who does He think He is? He's just a blue-collar worker! He's never even been to seminary! And He's telling us that we've never heard God speak and His Word doesn't dwell in us? Why, we've spent our whole lives mastering the Bible! If we haven't heard God's voice, who has?"

But Jesus wasn't finished. "You search the Scriptures because you think that in them you have eternal life; and it is they that bear witness of me, yet you refuse to come to me that you may have life" (verses 39–40). They were missing the whole point of their study.

If we master the content of the Bible but don't end up knowing, loving, worshiping, serving and being mastered by Jesus, we too miss the whole point, and set ourselves up to become twenty-first century Pharisees. So, yes, get into the Word; study it diligently, but as you do, don't miss Jesus!

 In your reading and study of God's Word, are you getting to know Christ in a more personal and real way? Ask Him to reveal Himself to you through His Word and to give you faith to keep coming to Him to find life.

Jesus among the Lampstands

To the angel of the church in Ephesus write: "The words of him who holds the seven stars in his right hand, who walks among the seven golden lampstands."—Revelation 2:1

 A LOT OF PEOPLE ARE FED UP with the church today, many of whom have been in it for most if not all their lives. The drift away from local church fellowship, worship, and community represents a troubling trend, fueled by everything from fatigue and disillusionment to practical convenience. Many no longer see the church as a relevant, necessary part of their lives. And they're leaving.

But lest we think we can just walk away from the church or discard it as an unnecessary option, be reminded that Christ is attached to His church. You cannot separate the "head" from the "body" (Eph. 5:23). To walk away from the church is to walk away from Christ and what He is doing in the world today.

No, the church in general is not perfect, nor is yours in particular. The first-century church itself struggled with all sort of issues, as evidenced throughout the New Testament writings. And yet, where do we see Jesus when He reveals His message to the apostle John? He is walking among the "lampstands," the visual image of local *churches*. He holds their leaders, their people, and their entire identities in His hand. He will not—cannot—forsake His own body and bride. He loves her, cares for her, and dwells within her.

So weep for the church. Intercede for her. Plead with God to restore her to righteousness, unity, and great usefulness in our time. But do not walk away from the church. Even knowing what He knows about the faults and foibles of the churches, Christ still walks in and among them. He laid down His life for the church; He is committed to protecting, preserving, and purifying her. How can we not love the church, bear with it, and join Him in seeking its revival and restoration?

 What is your current relationship with your church? How might the things that distress you about the church become your reason to draw nearer rather than distance yourself?

King over All

In him we live and move and have our being.—Acts 17:28

THE CONCEPT OF A SOVEREIGN KING who exercises absolute control over His subjects is one that our egalitarian, Western minds find difficult to embrace. We want to have a say in the matter, to vote for the leader of our choice. We don't want to bow before an all-powerful monarch. What we really want is to *be* the king, or at least to have a representative form of government.

Our fallen bent finds the thought of someone exercising control over us insufferable and demeaning. But whether we buy into it or not, the sovereign rule of God and the lordship of Christ is a nonnegotiable reality. *He is God, and we are not.* In recognizing and coming to accept this unalterable, eternal truth lies the key to great freedom and peace.

No one would consider a mother of young children to be unreasonable for insisting on being in control of the minivan she's driving her family in. That's because she knows how to drive and her children don't. She's the only one in the vehicle who is capable of keeping everyone secure and protected. The fact that she doesn't share the driving with her preschoolers doesn't make her a control freak but rather a loving, responsible authority, appropriately asserting her rule over her children.

The God revealed to us in Scripture is King—*the* King over *all* kings—which includes the sometimes petulant would-be king we see when we look in the mirror, the one who so persistently tries to occupy the throne of our hearts. Oh, that we could grasp that it is entirely fitting that the King of all—the One who created and holds together every molecule of the universe—should exercise unquestioned control over our lives. And oh, that we could realize the safety and security afforded us in yielding to that control.

Do you relish or resist the thought of relinquishing control of every area of your life to God? What makes His control so reasonable and right?

He Is Enough

But he said to me, "My grace is sufficient for you, for my power is made perfect in weakness." Therefore I will boast all the more gladly of my weaknesses, so that the power of Christ may rest upon me.—2 Corinthians 12:9

 AS A CHILD OF GOD, you will never face a circumstance that exceeds His grace. Where sin abounds, His grace will always much more abound. When you are weak, He is strong. When you are empty, He is full. When you have no resources left of your own, His divine resources have not even begun to be depleted. When you can't, He still can.

The truth is, whatever you're going through right now, His "grace is sufficient for you." And whatever you'll go through tomorrow, or next year, or fifty years from now, His grace will be sufficient for you then too.

His grace is sufficient to deal with the memories, wounds, and failures of the most scarred or sordid past. His grace is sufficient for a lifetime of singleness or a half-century of marriage to a spouse with no interest in spiritual matters. His grace is sufficient for a single mother trying to raise four children or a divorced dad trying to salvage a relationship with his kids around unreasonably restrictive custody arrangements.

His grace is sufficient for the parents of three toddlers— or three teenagers. His grace is sufficient for the person who's tending to the care of elderly parents, for the empty nester, for the woman going through the change of life, for the widow living on Social Security, and for the invalid in a nursing home.

We need to keep speaking this truth to ourselves and reminding those around us of its eternal reality. In every season, in every circumstance, His grace is sufficient. For you. And for me.

 What situation in your life feels beyond the reach of God's grace? Counsel your heart with this truth: "His grace is sufficient for me!"

God Our Refuge

The LORD of hosts is with us; the God of Jacob is our refuge.
—Psalm 46:11 NKJV

 PSALM 46, LIKE SO MANY OTHERS, speaks of seasons and situations that could just as easily be pulled from our present-day headlines or personal journals. I mean, we've all experienced times in life when it seemed as though major regions of our world were literally "giving way" (see verse 2). We've seen natural disasters either up close or on television, watching the furious "roar and foam" of the earth's destructive waters (verse 3). And each day's news provides us visual evidence of the "nations" boiling over in violent "rage" (verse 6).

In eleven short verses, the psalmist uses this kind of language we can relate to, to paint for us the very real fears and feelings of helplessness that can overwhelm us. And yet even with so many graphic ways of describing grave troubles, the *centrality of God* is at the heart of this song—the psalmist refers to Him specifically by name no fewer than eleven times in these same eleven verses.

Five times he speaks of Him as *Elohim*—the powerfully transcendent One, supreme above every storm and struggle. Another time he identifies Him as *Elyon*, the Most High. He is *Yahweh*, a name reflecting God's covenant with His people. He is *Jehovah Sabaoth*, the commanding Lord of hosts. He is the God of Jacob, true to His Word and His promises.

He is *God*—"our refuge and strength, a very present help in trouble" (verse 1)—sure and steady even when our world is at its most topsy-turvy. Therefore, we need not be dismayed or overcome by the tumults of life, because God truly is "in the midst" of each moment, and we "shall not be moved" (verse 5). Everywhere we turn, in everything we face, we find our God already there; we find Him to be our sure hiding place.

 Have you lost sight of God in the midst of your current circumstances? He has not lost sight of you. Run to Him and find a refuge for your soul.

Gratitude-Laced Prayer

Pray without ceasing.—1 Thessalonians 5:17

 THERE'S NOTHING WRONG WITH BEING totally honest with God, coming before Him with our hurts and pains and intercessions, imploring Him to help and heal. But prayer is more than asking; it is also a vehicle for worship and gratitude. And until we allow our interaction with Him to involve more than our list of woes and needs, we will miss much of what our relationship with Him is meant to entail.

Think about the overall makeup of your prayers. Are they out of balance in favor of asking and seeking? Are they top-heavy with complaints about your current condition or circumstances? What if, even in those times when you're in desperate need of God's intervention, you were careful to lace your prayers with expressions of gratitude—not as a (futile, of course) way to try manipulating His favor but simply acknowledging that because of His love and grace, you are still experiencing grace and blessings in the midst of your ordeal?

These are important questions to ask ourselves, not to discourage honesty or deny reality but to help train our hearts to view our challenges and concerns within the context of God's goodness. We are so prone to allow our problems to eclipse our recognition of His benefits. Even before His answer is in sight, we can still thank Him for countless reasons—for being here, for listening to us, for working all things according to His will. As surely as our "supplications" and "intercessions" are specific, heartfelt, and weighty, so should our "thanksgivings" be (1 Tim. 2:1)

If you've always wanted prayer to be as natural as breathing, then try paving the way with gratitude. And see if prayer "without ceasing" doesn't become your experience instead of your exception.

 Remember, prayer flows from a heart convinced of its need for God and His desire to bless His people out of His vast storehouse of grace. Ask Him to keep growing that kind of heart in you today.

Humble vs. Haughty

Charge them not to be haughty, nor to set their hopes on the uncertainty of riches, but on God, who richly provides us with everything to enjoy.—1 Timothy 6:17

 WE LOOKED YESTERDAY at how gratitude should be a leading element of our prayer lives, a major contributor to how we relate with God the Father. But this will only happen as we allow gratitude to become a part of who we are, the way we think, our reflexive response to life. Over the next several days, I'd like to highlight a number of differences between grateful and ungrateful people, so we can tune our hearts to more earnestly and faithfully sing God's praise.

First, grateful people are humble, while ungrateful people are proud. Gratitude is a revealer of the heart, not just a reporter of facts, events, and details. And among the things revealed most clearly in those who express gratitude as a way of life is a heart of humility.

I can still hear my dad answering the everyday question "How are you?" by saying, "Better than I deserve." What prompted this kind of response from him, as opposed to the usual, "Oh, just fine"? It's because Art DeMoss never got over the fact that God had saved him—and that if he'd really gotten what was rightly coming to him, he would have been over his head in heartache.

Every hint of ingratitude is an indicator of pride in our hearts, the idea that we deserve more than we're getting, that we're inherently worthy of being treated more generously by God or others. Oh, we think we deserve so much. But how thankful we should be that God has *not* given us what we deserve, choosing instead to extend mercy and grace. Pride is the father of ingratitude and the silent killer of a grateful heart.

 Is there any resentment or frustration lurking in your heart over something that God hasn't provided, fixed, or performed? How would a humble heart view that situation differently?

Full vs. Empty

"Then take care lest you forget the LORD, who brought you out of the land of Egypt, out of the house of slavery."—Deuteronomy 6:12

IN CONTRAST TO OUR TENDENCY to become despondent, discouraged, and disgruntled when facing adverse circumstances, I think of the apostle Paul who, from the bowels of a Roman dungeon, deprived of all but the most basic necessities of life, wrote in a thankful note, "I have all, and abound; I am full" (Phil. 4:18 KJV). His friends had largely abandoned him; his enemies were numerous and relentless. Whatever creature comforts he had enjoyed at one time were now far away and probably destroyed. From a human perspective, he was stripped bare of everything but mere existence, and yet . . . he considered himself to be *full*.

A grateful heart is a full heart, whereas an unthankful heart is an empty one. The difference between being full and empty is not usually the difference between rich or poor, at home or away, cupboards bursting or thinly lined with soup cans and Ramen noodles. The difference, almost always, is gratitude.

Steve Dale, a syndicated columnist who answers people's questions about their pets, received an email from a reader seeking advice regarding her twelve-year-old boxer that was at risk of losing one leg to a cancerous tumor. Dale responded that three-legged dogs actually adjust fairly quickly after surgery and are soon getting around nearly as well as before. "The psychological trauma of being expected to feel sad because they've lost a limb just doesn't seem to occur. Instead, quite the reverse, they act overjoyed to be alive."

Oh, to be more like Paul—and a three-legged dog. To have a full heart even when deprived of wants and pleasures, rather than an empty heart despite being surrounded by God's abundant blessings. Gratitude is often the difference between pervasive sadness and pure satisfaction.

Have you been feeling empty or deprived? Make a mental (or written) "gratitude list" of what God has provided, and see if you don't begin to feel that you are really full in the things that matter most.

Contented vs. Complaining

Sing praises to the LORD, O you his saints,
and give thanks to his holy name.—Psalm 30:4

 TRUE STORY. A church group from New Bern, North Carolina, had traveled to the Caribbean on a mission trip. As part of the week's experience, their host took them to a leper colony on the island of Tobago— proof that cruise ships and exotic getaways see only a small part of what life is really like in these tropical "paradises."

While there, they held a worship service in the campus chapel. As you can imagine, the sight of emaciated lepers filing into their seats on the bare pews bore deeply into the mind and heart of each visitor to this unfamiliar scene.

But no memory left its mark like this one: when the visiting pastor asked if anyone in the crowd had a favorite hymn they'd like to sing, a lone patient seated awkwardly on the back row, facing away from the front, turned her body slowly and with great effort in the pastor's direction.

"Body" would perhaps be a generous description of what remained of hers. Her face had no nose, no lips. Just bare teeth, askew within a chalky skull. And yet raising her bony nub of an arm to see if she might be called on to make a request, she appealed with croaky voice, "Could we sing 'Count Your Many Blessings'?"

Leave it to a grotesquely deformed leper to remind us that *grateful people are characterized by thankful words, while ungrateful people are given to murmuring and complaining.* Some grumble at why God puts thorns on roses. Others notice, with awe and wonder, that God has put roses among thorns. May we still sing our old familiar songs even when overwhelmed by ever-present difficulties.

 In a typical day, do you speak more words of complaint or of thankfulness? What does your response reflect about your heart?

Life-Givers vs. Life-Takers

As they go through the Valley of Baca they make it a place
of springs; the early rain also covers it with pools.—Psalm 84:6

IN CLOSING THESE DAYS on the distinguishing marks of gratitude, I must acknowledge that my natural bent is to react to difficult people and circumstances in a negative way. When asked how I'm doing, the first thing that pops into my head is often a burden I'm carrying, a challenge I'm facing, or a deadline I'm working under. Perhaps the same is true of you.

But what are we telling people by being so quick to verbalize these concerns? How are we reflecting on the God to whom we claim to belong? And is it any wonder if people aren't lining up at our door to ask how they can know Him?

Thankful people are refreshing, life-giving springs, while unthankful people are life-takers and joy-robbers. Not that there aren't appropriate times and settings to share our troubles with a caring friend. Not that "I'm fine" should always be the automatic, canned answer whenever people speak to us. But ingratitude is toxic. It poisons the atmosphere in our homes and workplaces. It contaminates hearts and relationships. We may be obsessive about spritzing away bacteria from our tables and countertops, but nothing is more contagious to those around us than an ungrateful spirit.

Well, maybe one thing is.

Gratitude can be as contagious as its evil twin. So if you're tired of living in an atmosphere where all the joy and beauty have been sucked out through negative, unappreciative words and attitudes, you can make a change. You can become the type of person you've always wanted to be around—the kind of person who makes Jesus and His gospel winsome to all who come within reach.

Two kinds of people: grateful and ungrateful, worshipers and whiners. Which kind of person are you? Which kind of person do you truly want to be? Talk to the Lord about it.

Help Me

*Then the people of Israel cried out to the L*ORD *for help.* —Judges 4:3

I DON'T KNOW if there is any sweeter sound in God's ears than when His people cry out to Him, *"Help, Lord!"* Of all the things He's trying to teach us, of all the places He's trying to take us, the loving goal of His long-suffering discipline in our lives is to bring us to the point of recognizing our desperate need of Him.

The book of Judges illustrates this truth through a series of oft-repeated cycles in Israel's history. Over and over, Israel's descent into *disobedience* was followed by God's *discipline*, which was eventually followed by the people's *desperation*, then finally their *deliverance*. The intervening period between disobedience and desperation lasted as long as seven years (Judges 6:1), eight years (3:8), eighteen years (3:14), twenty years (4:3), even forty years (13:1).

During those lengthy stretches of time, Israel's sin resulted in their experiencing great misery, generally at the hands of pagan, neighboring nations. They likely did everything they could imagine to get these Canaanite enemies off their backs and out of their lives, and they probably cried about it a lot with each other.

But when they finally cried out to God, they found Him to be merciful—He responded to their humility by coming to their rescue and restoring them to a place of blessing and rest.

The Lord knows exactly what it takes—and how long it takes—to get our attention when our hearts stray from Him, wandering pridefully away from His presence and provision. And when we reach the end of ourselves and cry out to Him for mercy, we realize that His discipline actually demonstrates the depth of His love and commitment to us. His severe mercies bring us home.

Are you experiencing God's discipline for some area of disobedience? Have you come to the point of desperation yet, or are you still clinging to your own ways of thinking or certain sins? Humble yourself and cry out to Him. He will hear your cry and deliver you.

Surrendered and Satisfied

These all look to you, to give them their food in due season.
When you give it to them, they gather it up; when you open
your hand, they are filled with good things.—Psalm 104:27–28

 IN THE FIRST RECORDED ACT IN TIME AND SPACE, God spoke with authority and power, bringing light, life, and order to the darkness, emptiness, and chaos of the universe. All creation, including—initially—the first man and woman, lived in glad, wholehearted surrender to His sovereign control and will.

This surrender did not strip the creation of dignity or freedom. To the contrary, surrender was—and still is—the source and means of true freedom and fullness. The sovereign Creator God ruled over His creation with tender love, inviting His creatures to engage with Him in a divine dance of sorts, in which He led and they followed. In turn, their needs were abundantly met, they fulfilled their created purpose, and they existed in harmony with God and each other.

Psalm 104 describes this original, ideal state. We see a definite, unquestioned hierarchy in which God acts, initiates, directs, sets boundaries, and lovingly rules over His creation. In response, the creation looks to Him, waits for Him, bows before Him, surrenders to His control, and simply does as He directs.

As a result, "the earth is satisfied" and "filled with good things" (Ps. 104:13, 28). To surrender to the Creator's control is not onerous or burdensome. To the contrary, that is the place where stress, struggle, and strain give way to blessing, abundance, and peace. When we are not vying with our Creator for control, life is what the old-time hymn writer describes as "perfect submission, perfect delight."

 Are you experiencing the inner rest, peace, and simplicity of living in full surrender to God? Are there any areas of your life where you are vying for the control that rightly belongs to Him?

Keeping Our Bearings

You keep him in perfect peace whose mind is stayed on you,
because he trusts in you.—Isaiah 26:3

HAVE YOU EVER BEEN PERPLEXED or even (truth be told) peeved with God? Perhaps it started with a promotion that went to someone else; perhaps a financial setback that's forced you to live far below the standard you'd envisioned for yourself or had grown accustomed to. Perhaps you're single in a married world. Perhaps you've been trying to have children without success.

Why would God taunt us, we ask, at such raw, vulnerable places? And yet we must learn how to accept what we receive (or don't receive) from Him. We must be willing to bow to His sovereignty. This is the hard work of Isaiah 26:3—the submissive discipline of keeping our minds "stayed" on the Lord, trusting Him in ways we cannot see or understand, in places where we must learn to be content with mystery.

Airline pilots learn how to trust their instruments. When they fly into a storm or whiteout conditions, they can easily become disoriented. Their sense of direction can get turned around, altering their ability to make sound decisions. In situations like these, they must make a conscious choice to believe the instruments rather than what their eyes and instincts are telling them. Otherwise, they put their lives and those of their passengers in danger.

For believers, God's Word is our instrument panel. When our feelings betray us and contradict His truth, insisting that God doesn't care or that He's made a mistake, we dare not rely on what we think we know, allowing confusion or disappointment to dissolve into frustrated anger. We must trust that what the Instrument says is true. We must let God employ the great teachers of trouble and time to enlarge our hearts and expand our vision of Him.

What are your feelings and emotions telling you today?
How do they compare with what your "instruments"
are telling you? Which are you going to believe?

The Whole of Our Lives

I say this for your own benefit, not to lay any restraint upon you,
but to promote good order and to secure your undivided devotion
to the Lord.—1 Corinthians 7:35

I RECALL ONE OF MY FORMER PASTORS challenging us as members of his congregation to "go for broke with God." I like that. Tireless, wholehearted abandon to the will and work of the Lord ought to characterize our lives.

But does it?

Many years ago, Communist leader Vladimir Lenin issued a similar challenge, though regarding a much different aim and objective, when he declared, "We must train men and women who will devote to the revolution not merely their spare evenings but the whole of their lives." If the Communist revolution could call its followers to that kind of 24/7 devotion to its cause, what does it say when we as Christians model the idea of measured, "part-time Christian service," while being careful to protect plenty of time to fulfill our own pursuits? Is Jesus not worthy of the "whole of our lives"?

This doesn't mean, of course, that a man or woman devoted to Christ can never relax or take a vacation without feeling guilty about it. But the older I get, the more I find myself evaluating my activities, my hobbies, and my leisure time in light of the price they will bring in eternity. From time to time, I sense the Lord directing me to cut back on, or even eliminate altogether, certain legitimate activities that are robbing me of time to pursue Him, things that are keeping me from making an eternal investment in the lives of people.

To be devoted to doing what pleases God, to live in the light of eternity, to be His willing bond servants—this is to fulfill the purpose for which we were created and to know the greatest possible joy in this life and the next.

Are you giving God merely your "spare evenings,"
or the whole of your life?

Alternate Plans

And God is able to make all grace abound to you,
so that having all sufficiency in all things at all times,
you may abound in every good work.—2 Corinthians 9:8

 I'VE HEARD A LOT OF TALK IN RECENT YEARS—you probably have too—about people preparing for disaster laying up stores of water and food in their homes, bracing for impending doom by gathering all the provisions and nonperishables they can put away. They're known as "preppers." In case the worst happens, they want to be sure they've got sufficient goods stored away to be able to survive.

While the Scriptures certainly instruct us to be prudent in preparing for the future, planning ahead to care for the needs of our families, it strikes me that we don't hear as many people talking about how they can meet the needs of others in times of crisis. Frequently, the concern seems to be more about *self-*preservation.

By contrast, the Macedonian churches of Paul's day, though faced with severe challenges to their personal safety and financial prospects, begged earnestly for the "favor" of helping other believers who were struggling to make ends meet (2 Cor. 8:4). In giving sacrificially out of their own need, they were laying up "treasures in heaven" (Matt. 6:20) and manifesting the generous, giving heart of Christ.

A downturn in the economy can cause people to wring their hands and get in a dither over how dire the outlook appears. Yet as followers of Christ—confident in His ample promises and providence—we should view such difficult times as opportunities to showcase to the world the goodness and grace of our God. And few things make this statement more profoundly than when we are generous givers, especially when seen against the backdrop of conditions that make self-preservation such a natural reflex.

So, plan, prepare for the future. But in all your preparations, don't forget to be mindful of the needs of others.

 What are some practical ways you could express the generous heart of God to others during these trying days?

Little Monsters

Therefore let anyone who thinks that he stands take heed lest he fall.
—1 Corinthians 10:12

MOST OF US have become so familiar with our sin that we no longer see it for the deadly monster it truly is—more dangerous than wild bears, more destructive than blazing forest fires. Ask Nebuchadnezzar, who lost his mind because he refused to deal with his pride. Ask Samson, who was reduced to a pathetic shred of a man because he never gained control over the lusts of his flesh. Ask Achan, Ananias, and Sapphira, who each lost their lives over "small," secret sins.

You may never crawl into bed with someone else's mate, but your heart for God can be just as easily destroyed by allowing jealousy, anger, self-pity, worry, or gluttony to go unchecked in your life.

Nineteenth-century Anglican bishop J. C. Ryle cautioned against being naïve toward sin's influence and potential: "I fear we do not sufficiently realize the extreme subtlety of our soul's disease. We are too apt to forget that temptation to sin will rarely present itself to us in its true colours, saying, 'I am your deadly enemy and I want to ruin you forever in hell.' Oh, no! Sin comes to us, like Judas, with a kiss, and like Joab, with an outstretched hand and flattering words."

Are you content to maintain a "certain level of sin" in your life, keeping yourself convinced that you can tame and manage it? Mark it down: *there is no such thing as a small sin.* Every unconfessed sin is a seed that will inevitably produce a multiplied harvest. As Charles Spurgeon warned, "Those who tolerate sin in what they think to be little things will soon indulge it in greater matters." Run to the cross; confess any sin the Holy Spirit has convicted you of, and trust Christ to root it out of your life—before the monster begins to outweigh you.

 Please, O Lord, may I never bring reproach to Your name by failing to take sin seriously, by clinging to even a single one.

Getting into Practice

But solid food is for the mature, for those who have their powers of discernment trained by constant practice to distinguish good from evil.—Hebrews 5:14

I ONCE HAD THE PRIVILEGE of interviewing Joni Eareckson Tada, a dear friend who has lived her entire adult life as a quadriplegic, the result of a teenage diving accident. During the course of our conversation, I asked her, "Joni, how do you maintain such a joyful spirit with all the challenges you deal with on a daily basis?" I admit I was seeking her counsel as much for my own heart as for our radio listeners.

After only the slightest pause, she said, "You know, Nancy, I think I've just disciplined myself for so many years to 'give thanks in all things,' it's now simply become my reflex reaction."

Oh, how that statement penetrated my heart that day! I realized that for years, my own "reflex reaction" to difficult circumstances had been to whine rather than give thanks to God from the outset. Fretting, giving in to discouragement, expressing negative thoughts about pressures and problems—these had too often become my default setting. Perhaps you'd have to admit the same thing. And perhaps that's why a joyful spirit continues to elude us.

The grateful heart that springs forth in joy is not acquired in a moment; it is the fruit of a thousand choices. It is a godly habit that over time becomes a strong muscle in our spiritual makeup. And though it can do nothing to make us more loved and accepted by God, our gratitude does become a reliable measure for where our hearts truly stand with Him. It shows how well we're growing in grace.

Look for opportunities today to give thanks when your default would be to murmur or complain. Ask the Lord for grace to keep giving thanks until gratitude becomes your reflex reaction to all of life.

The King and I

"I did not believe the reports until I came and my own eyes had seen it. And behold, the half was not told me."—1 Kings 10:7

 THREE THOUSAND YEARS AGO, an Arabian queen learned of a foreign king whose achievements and wisdom were legendary. Determined to see for herself, she gathered together a large caravan, loaded down her entourage with rare and expensive gifts, and then traveled the twelve hundred miles to meet this amazing monarch.

Upon her arrival, she was warmly greeted by the king. He listened as she told him all that was on her mind, including many difficult questions she had been waiting to ask him. But her questions were no match for his knowledge and perception. He answered them all, willingly and easily. The things she had heard about him, the reputation that had been ascribed to him—it was all true. She had now seen it with her "own eyes."

When the time finally came to return to her homeland, she did not go away empty-handed, for "King Solomon gave to the queen of Sheba all she desired and asked for; he gave her more than she had brought to him" (2 Chron. 9:12 NIV).

Each day offers us another opportunity to see firsthand the vast stores of wealth our King Jesus claims as His own, to ask Him our hard questions, to share all that is on our hearts, to listen intently as He reveals to us the secrets of His kingdom. And when we go back to our place—to our daily tasks and duties—we will not go empty-handed. We will return with more than our hearts can contain, for He will give us far more than we could ever have brought to Him.

 Have you been relying on secondhand reports about the greatness of God? Why not "taste [for yourself] and see that the LORD is good" (Ps. 34:8)!

Cleansing Properties

"Already you are clean because of the word
that I have spoken to you."—John 15:3

DO YOU SOMETIMES FEEL like all you ever do is clean? That's because things tend to get dirty—clothes, children's hands, kitchen floors, bathrooms, vinyl siding, entryways, even our own bodies. Dealing with the dust, crumbs, and grime that accumulate in life is a necessary, never-ending process.

In the Old Testament tabernacle, we find a striking picture of this need for washing. Before entering the Holy Place to represent the people before God, the priest would first stop at the bronze altar where an innocent animal would be offered as a sacrifice for his own sin and for the sin of the people. Then he would move to a bronze basin—the laver—where he would wash his hands, returning to that laver throughout the day as he performed his sacred duties.

What can we learn from this cleansing ritual? Obviously, you and I do not always live up to our holy position and prospect. We live in a corrupt world; we inhabit a contaminated flesh; we have a way of getting our spiritual feet, hands, and clothes soiled from the temptations and rigors of the day. So we, too, when we come into God's presence—though our sin has been blotted out by the blood of Christ—must come to the "laver" to wash our hands and feet of whatever may have defiled us, being purified by the pure "water" of His Word.

That is why, as I open His Word and begin to read, I often pray: "Lord, wash me with Your Word."

So let us frequently ask the Holy Spirit—before and after reading the Scripture, and throughout the day—to apply His Word to our hearts, cleansing and purifying us of all sin. "Sanctify [us] in the truth; your word is truth" (John 17:17).

What has His Word revealed in your heart recently?
Be quick to agree with Him, humbly confess any sin,
appropriate His cleansing grace, and rise up to serve
Him in the freedom and joy of a pure heart.

Unseen Forces

*Therefore take up the whole armor of God, that you may
be able to withstand in the evil day.*—Ephesians 6:13

 IN A SCENE that bears the characteristic staccato pace of
Mark's gospel, we find Jesus teaching in the synagogue
one day (Mark 1:21–27) when suddenly a demon-
possessed man unexpectedly upset the proceedings,
raising his voice and challenging Jesus' authority.
Without blinking an eye, Jesus sternly rebuked the unclean spirit
within the man. A moment's convulsion and the shriek of a loud
voice followed, and then it was all over. Jesus had faced evil's
intentions head-on. And won.

Fast-forward to today: by the time you get up in the
morning, an unseen battle has already been raging for hours in
the heavenlies. Within the mystery of God's sovereignty, He has
given the forces of hell the temporary right to contend with Him
and His own. And you as His child start each day in the crossfire
of this cosmic duel.

On the face of things, it may only seem like a lack of desire
to spend time alone with the Lord in prayer and His Word. It
may feel like the press of the day's upcoming schedule, disturbing
your thoughts before your feet hit the floor. It may sound like the
typical morning review of ongoing issues with your marriage,
your children, your job, your general life situation.

What it may *not* seem like is what it actually is: the
presence, activity, and involvement of Satan's forces, drawing
you away from God, wrestling you back down into fear, doubt,
discouragement, and sinful reactions.

So stand to your feet. Recognize the real enemy. Invite your
victorious Lord into this challenge. And win the first battle of
the day by knowing where the true battlefield is. Consciously
take your place within the ranks of the One before whom even
hell's most defiant warriors must ultimately concede defeat.

 *What would change in your approach if you remembered that the
real enemy is not the people, things, and circumstances in your life?*

Above and Beyond

"So do not fear; I will provide for you and your little ones."
Thus he comforted them and spoke kindly to them.—Genesis 50:21

I'M ALWAYS AMAZED when I read how Joseph responded to his brothers who had injured him so deeply, who had put him in a position to be wronged over and over again in Egypt—providing him with years' worth of fodder for a lifetime of bitterness. Yet because forgiveness had already become the choice of his heart, Joseph set out to bless the very brothers who had gotten him into this mess in the first place. Not only did he refuse to return evil for evil, not only did he restrain himself from retaliating, but he actively, intentionally reached out to minister to their needs.

That is supernatural! And what a picture it is of Christ's redeeming, restoring heart that reached out to us when we deserved God's wrath, lavishing upon us His grace instead. It's the theme behind Paul's instruction to the Corinthians regarding a church member who had grievously sinned and was now in need of restoration: "forgive and comfort him," Paul exhorted, and "reaffirm your love for him" (2 Cor. 2:7–8). *Go above and beyond.*

Does that sound too hard in your case? It should. It is *much* too hard. It is something only God can do through you. But remember, it doesn't have to be anything spectacular—just a simple act of grace and kindness. Start there. See what happens. Then be willing to watch where God directs you to go next, until you actually begin finding joy—*His* joy—in blessing the one(s) who have treated you so badly.

This is the gospel at work. This is street-level obedience. This is how wounded people like us "overcome evil with good" (Rom. 12:21), and in so doing, we, like Joseph, become a picture of Christ's redeeming, restoring mercy and grace.

How could you show kindness to someone who has brought pain into your life? Even if your gesture doesn't affect them, how might it affect you?

Let's Make a Deal

Having begun by the Spirit, are you now being perfected by the flesh?—Galatians 3:3

WE CAN BE A LEGALISTIC LOT. Put the option of daily devotions on the table most mornings, and too often the factor that finally tips us in the direction of prayer and Bible reading is the one that says, "God will be disappointed in me if I don't." So we approach Him, fearing that our day is likely to turn disastrous otherwise. We think He'll treat us better if we just do this one little thing for Him. We treat our devotions like a good luck charm, hoping to buy ourselves smooth passage through the hours ahead.

Oh, dear friend, when will we stop thinking we make points with God by carving out a few reluctant moments to spend in His presence? When will we understand He has already shined His favor on us because of what Christ has done to please and satisfy Him, not because of anything we do to attract His notice?

Even on those days when our hearts burn to worship Him, when we eagerly sit at His feet and delight in His personal fellowship, His love for us is no greater than on those other days when we perfunctorily press through the religious paces or ignore Him altogether.

What we miss by neglecting Him is not the chance to impress Him with our sacrifice; what we miss is the experience of meeting with Him, of learning from Him, of being refreshed, steadied, and reoriented by drawing near to Him through His Word and His Spirit.

Having a "quiet time" is not a means of earning God's favor; it is the privilege of a child of God who is grateful to be the recipient of His lavish grace and who desires to enter into an ever more intimate relationship with his heavenly Father.

In what other ways do you perform "spiritual acts" or good works, in hopes of "purchasing" God's approval or blessing? Let your devotion and service flow out of a glad and grateful heart that has already received His grace.

Victory in Jesus

*But whatever gain I had, I counted as loss for the sake of Christ.
Indeed I count everything as loss because of the surpassing worth
of knowing Christ Jesus my Lord.*—Philippians 3:7–8

 YOU LIKELY KNOW THE STORY OF ERIC LIDDELL, the Scottish athlete whose faith and courage during the 1924 Paris Olympics were vividly portrayed in the award-winning film *Chariots of Fire*. You recall his principled decision not to participate in his primary event—the hundred-yard dash—because the qualifying heats were to be held on a Sunday, and how he then went on to win the gold medal in a race for which he'd never trained, setting a world record in the process.

The choice Eric made as a young athlete to honor God was characteristic of choices made throughout his life. In 1925, he returned to North China to serve as a missionary, as his parents had during his childhood. After years of faithful ministry, he was interned in a Japanese concentration camp where he joyfully and generously ministered to his fellow prisoners. During his detainment, he developed a brain tumor that impaired his bodily functions, leaving him partially paralyzed. Dying.

On February 21, 1945, Eric lay in a hospital bed, struggling to breathe, drifting in and out of consciousness. Suddenly his body erupted into a violent convulsion. Shocked, the nurse tending to his care scooped him up into her arms, trying to calm his trembling body. Then, in those fleeting seconds before he slipped into a coma, she heard him speak these final words in a barely audible voice, no doubt reflecting on the span of his life's choices: "Annie," he said, "it's complete surrender."

Complete surrender.

Whatever the issue or battle before you today, however trivial or daunting, whatever the cost, whatever your fears, wherever it may lead you . . . when this life is all said and done, may that be the tale of your life and mine: "It's complete surrender."

 The choices Liddell made as a young man set the trajectory for his life and carried him all the way to the finish line. Is there anything about the way you are living today that you may wish had been different when you come to the end of your life?

Grace under Fire

A thorn was given me in the flesh, a messenger of Satan to harass me, to keep me from becoming conceited.—2 Corinthians 12:7

HAVE YOU EVER WONDERED what life would be like if you weren't burdened with that one temptation, that one particular weakness? We've all heard of people who wrestled with terrible addictions for years but who one day found the taste completely removed from their mouths, delivered not only from its angry hold but from its very attraction. Oh, what we wouldn't give for the Lord to deliver *us* so decisively and dramatically from our besetting sins!

While God certainly could operate that way, and sometimes does, in most of our lives, I'm not sure that approach would be as much of a blessing as we might think. Consider what might happen if God were to give us instantaneous, permanent freedom from our recurring struggles with certain sins. Would we be prone to be more self-sufficient, less dependent on Him for daily, overcoming grace? Would we somehow think we'd finally figured out this problem ourselves through sheer effort and willpower? Would we proudly credit ourselves for conquering something that had put up such a daunting fight with us for as long as we could remember?

So, this side of heaven, I wonder if we're not better off having to deal with these Achilles heels, these persistent tendencies God could obviously deliver us from and yet in His wisdom—and, yes, in His grace—He leaves behind for us to require His help in overcoming.

I think Christ often grows larger in our eyes by continuing to be our rescuer and deliverer, rather than by making each test an easy *A*. These repetitive opportunities to run to Him and His Word, to humble ourselves and cast ourselves on His mercy—we can't call this a lack of His attentiveness or help; it's really a canvas for the display of His grace and power.

When have you experienced God's grace to enable you to say no to sin and yes to Christ? May the new day be your next opportunity to see it again.

A Pastor's Heart

*Respect those who labor among you and are over you in the Lord
and admonish you, and . . . esteem them very highly in love
because of their work.*—1 Thessalonians 5:12–13

 How I thank the Lord for the many godly pastors and spiritual leaders He has placed in my life over the years. I think of Pastor Earl Connors, for example, who baptized me when I was five years old. He's with the Lord now, but I still have fond memories of him.

His pastoral prayers from the pulpit each Sunday morning made a lasting impression on me. As a little girl, it sometimes seemed as if those prayers went on forever—especially on hot, muggy, summer Sundays in a building with no air-conditioning. But today I'm thankful for a childhood pastor who prayed faithfully for his people.

I recall, too, Communion services, and how he would distribute the elements to the deacons one by one, after they had served the congregation. As he worked his way across that front pew where the men were seated, he would quote memorized Scripture about the atoning death and sacrifice of Christ. Hearing him wash our congregation in the Word comforted and blessed me. It drew my heart to love the Lord Jesus.

I could name numerous other pastors and teachers who have made a significant investment in my life. You no doubt could name some as well. But do the spiritual leaders in your church and your life—those who serve you currently as well as those who've been part of your Christian heritage—do they know how much you appreciate and respect them? Have you taken the opportunity to tell them?

If not, make this a priority in the days ahead. Write a note. Send a card. Give them a call or tell them in person. You might even give them a check to take their mate out for dinner. Esteem them highly in love for their work's sake. They need your encouragement more than you know. And you need to express your gratitude more than you know.

 In addition to offering positive affirmation directly to your pastor and church leaders, pray for them often and look for opportunities to speak well of them to others.

Taste Test

I want you to be wise as to what is good and
innocent as to what is evil.—Romans 16:19

 SATAN USES SOME OF THE SAME TACTICS with today's parents that he used with Eve. Remember how he convinced her that by eating the forbidden fruit she would learn something she needed to know? "When you eat of it your eyes will be opened . . . knowing good and evil" (Gen. 3:5). And he was right. When Eve ate, her eyes *were* opened. She *did* learn something she hadn't known before: the experience of evil.

But see how clearly the Bible tells us whose goal this was? Not God's. He never intended that we should know evil by experiencing it for ourselves. Satan, on the other hand—even this many years later—has never stopped employing this tried-and-untrue approach. He still says to us, "Here, you need to taste this." And he says to parents, "Your children need to taste for themselves too. If you shelter them from the 'real world,' they'll never be able to fit in and survive."

Is that a parent's calling, though? To rear children who can "fit in"? The longing of every Christian parent should be to bring up children who love God with all their heart, soul, mind, and strength—children who have a vibrant, personal relationship with the Lord Jesus—children who stand out as bright and shining lights, penetrating the darkness around them.

Believing moms and dads should be seeking to raise up not just "good kids" but children who enthusiastically embrace the truth, who love righteousness and hate evil, who will be used by God to *change* the world, not just survive within it.

Of course, parents cannot control the hearts and choices of their children; but should not we plead with the Lord to give to the next generation (and their parents) this kind of heart?

 What firsthand "knowledge of evil" do you wish you'd never tasted? How can you aspire to be "innocent as to what is evil," while still living and serving in this world that loves and promotes evil?

Sneaky Sin

But each person is tempted when he is lured and enticed by his own desire. Then desire when it has conceived gives birth to sin, and sin when it is fully grown brings forth death.—James 1:14–15

WHEN THE ROMEROS first got Sally as a pet, she was only about a foot long—mildly frightening to some, but apparently harmless. The family was more than comfortable having her in their home. Eight years later, however, Sally had grown to more than eleven feet in length, tipping the scales at nearly eighty pounds. One day without warning, she became unpredictably violent with their fifteen-year-old son and ended up strangling him to death.

That's what Burmese pythons are capable of doing.

In one fatal moment, the creature that had seemed so docile and harmless was exposed as a deadly beast. The "pet" the unsuspecting family had brought into their home, cared for and nurtured, turned on them and proved to be a destroyer. In a sense, no one should have been surprised at the turn of events, for in the end, the python merely did what was its nature to do.

So it is with sin. Though it may entertain us, play with us, sleep with us, and amuse us, its nature never changes. Inevitably, it will always rise up to bite and devour those who befriend it.

If we comprehended the true nature of sin, would we not want to do everything in our power to stay away from it? But because Satan is so effective at disguising the sinfulness of sin, we don't always recognize it for the evil it is.

We must keep reminding ourselves that sin—even our favorite, most familiar sin—is dangerous. Pretending it's harmless doesn't make it any less so, and growing accustomed to having it around doesn't cancel out its intentions. Don't think you're different, that you'll be able to handle it. Sin—all of it—has the ability to destroy you. Get rid of it before it becomes impossible to live with.

Do you have any "pet" sins? Do you think you can play with them and not get hurt?

Redeemed and Loved

How precious to me are your thoughts, O God! How vast is the sum of them! If I would count them, they are more than the sand. I awake, and I am still with you.—Psalm 139:17–18

MANY BELIEVERS carry around a nagging sense of worthlessness. I think the enemy of our souls must relish and fuel such thoughts. In contrast, the Scripture reveals the great value God places upon us: we were on His mind in eternity past; from the point of our creation, He has lavished upon us His extravagant love, making us the object of His affection and attention. His truth counteracts the lies that so easily steal our joy.

God's heart for His chosen people is seen in a poignant picture in Ezekiel 16—a picture of His finding them naked like a helpless baby at a time when "no eye pitied you, to do any of these things to you out of compassion for you." Yet He reached down to them in their pitiful condition and "spread the corner of my garment over you and covered your nakedness; I made my vow to you and entered into a covenant with you, declares the Lord God, and you became mine. Then I bathed you with water and washed off your blood from you. . . . I clothed you . . . I adorned you with ornaments . . . You ate fine flour and honey and oil. . . . And your renown went forth among the nations because of your beauty, for it was perfect through the splendor that I had bestowed on you" (verses 5, 8–11, 13–14).

What does all this say about the worth God places on His chosen ones? Should we conclude that we are an afterthought to Him, an object of His disapproving scorn? No, He saw us in our miserable, wretched condition and sent His beloved Son to this earth, to die on the cross to purchase our redemption. He has rescued us and poured out His favor on us. So when tempted to feel belittled or insignificant, bask in the Father's great love for you and worship Him for His amazing grace.

 Will you choose to believe what you (or others) feel about yourself or what God says about you?

Let It Go

This was to show God's righteousness, because in his divine forbearance he had passed over former sins.—Romans 3:25

 "FORBEARANCE" isn't a word we hear much today, but if we learn to practice it on a daily basis, it can become one of our greatest weapons in staving off bitterness, contention, and unforgiveness. To *forbear* means to show restraint, to be patient in the face of provocation, to be long-suffering, willing to put up with people's actions and inactions—to let things go.

Forbearance is actually a by-product of love, the kind of love, as Paul put it so eloquently in 1 Corinthians 13, that "is not provoked . . . does not take into account a wrong suffered . . . bears all things, believes all things, hopes all things, endures all things" (verses 5–7 NASB).

Yes, some offenses need to be confronted and dealt with. But many others—most, in fact—just need to be overlooked and put away. (Our problem is, we tend to confront the sins we should overlook, and overlook the sins we should confront!)

A lack of forbearance in our homes and everyday circumstances causes us to exaggerate offenses until, as Charles Spurgeon said, "a [fly's] egg becomes as huge as ever was laid by an ostrich." It magnifies tension and intensifies conflict. It erects walls in relationships, makes us petty and peevish, and severs us from our friends. I'm convinced that many divorces could be averted if one or both partners would practice the grace of forbearance. Many tensions and misunderstandings in the workplace would vanish if we would be more forbearing with one another.

Bigger issues are sure to arise, requiring a great measure of forgiveness. Learning to forbear today is valuable practice for being able to forgive later.

 Name something in recent memory that you should have let go instead of allowing it to slow bake. What might be different now if you had?

Disappointment with God

*Why do you hide your face? Why do you forget our
affliction and oppression?*—Psalm 44:24

 HAVE YOU EVER FOUND YOURSELF resenting God for
allowing a person to manipulate or mistreat you, for
not stepping in and helping you avoid disaster, for
not sparing you the consequences of what seemed
like an innocent mistake? Undoubtedly, you have
faced circumstances where you found God's ways inexplicable
at best or even disturbing. There are those who would suggest
that part of the healing involved in moving beyond these hurtful
events is to *forgive God* for the part He played in this.

But think about that. *Us? Forgive God?* As though He had
wronged us and needed pardon. To think we possess this kind of
power over the righteous, sovereign God is to demean Him and
to inflate our importance.

No, God doesn't need forgiveness from us. He is never
guilty of making mistakes. In fact, the thing you may consider a
cruel injustice on His part may actually turn out to be the best
thing that ever happened to you. It can—by the Father's all-wise
grace—be transformed for your good, for His glory, and for the
advance of His eternal kingdom.

So I ask you to look again into the heart of God, seeing
someone who has a deeper, more loving plan for your life than
you could ever figure out on your own, even if you find yourself
in the midst of deep pain. He will use this disappointment, this
heartbreak, this unspeakable circumstance to teach you, train
you, and fulfill His holy, eternal purposes for your life. The
alternative—bitterness or anger against God—can do nothing
but make things worse and further delay your healing.

 *How can you tell when legitimate, transparent honesty before
God has morphed into sinful anger and "demandingness"
toward God? Are you anywhere near that line?*

Reflections

But as he who called you is holy, you also must be holy
in all your conduct, since it is written, "You shall be holy,
for I am holy."—1 Peter 1:15–16

MY HOUSE sits on a hill overlooking a river. This morning, as the sun shone brightly through the trees on the opposite bank, their likeness was magnificently reflected on the still waters below. This lovely mirror image caused me to pray, "Lord, may others see Your likeness reflected in me; may my life reveal to them just how lovely and pure You are!"

Our lives are meant to make God believable to our world. As others see His image in us, they should be drawn to worship and "give glory" to Him (Matt. 5:16).

Do your attitudes, words, and behavior give others an accurate picture of Him? Do you sometimes profane His holiness by a complaining or controlling spirit, by harsh or coarse conversation, by sexually impure choices or morally compromised relationships?

It saddens me to think how often I have given others a distorted perception of God through my ungodlike choices and responses.

God is holy, and therefore we must be holy. And because God is holy, we *can* be holy. Through the sacrificial death of Christ on our behalf, His obedient life has been credited to the account of all who place their trust in Him. If you are a child of God, the Holy Spirit lives in you. He is not only the *standard* but also the *source* of your holiness, purifying your unholy heart so that the world will know what God is like.

To be holy as He is holy—what an awesome responsibility. But more than that, what an astounding privilege that the Holy One should choose us—fallen and flawed as we were apart from Him—that He should redeem us from our sin, and then reflect through us the splendor of His holiness in this dark world.

Will you allow God to reflect His holy character through you today?

When Repenters Repent

*"Those whom I love, I reprove and discipline,
so be zealous and repent."*—Revelation 3:19

 FOR OVER TWENTY YEARS, the people of Romania suffered under the iron-fisted, Communist rule of Nicolae Ceauşescu. Christians were especially targeted by the regime and were subjected to intense intimidation and relentless harassment. They were ridiculed and were referred to in derision as "repenters."

In the early 1970s—in the midst of such adversity—a pastor in the town of Oradea began to preach an unusual message. Burdened that many Christians had become conformed to the culture rather than to Christ, he insisted that "the repenters must repent." He was straightforward in pointing out specific sins that he felt were hindering the church from experiencing true revival.

Many in the congregation responded to his call—the repenters repented. They began to take holiness seriously; they turned from everything they believed was displeasing to God.

When they did, God visited that congregation in revival. Lives were transformed, lost people began to come to faith in Christ, and the church exploded in growth.

The revival could not be contained within a single church. It spread to other churches in the surrounding area and ultimately its impact was felt throughout the entire nation. The revived believers were infused with courage and began to stand up for their convictions. Many believe that this movement of the Spirit was one of the factors that ultimately led to the overthrow of the Ceausescu regime some fifteen years later.

The first message of Jesus' earthly ministry was "Repent, for the kingdom of heaven is at hand" (Matt. 4:17). His last message to the church recorded in the pages of Scripture was "be zealous and repent." Imagine what might happen in our day if the "repenters" were truly to repent.

 Are you living and walking as a "repenter"? What evidence of true repentance has there been in your life in recent months?

Worshipful Response

*Mary therefore took a pound of expensive ointment
made from pure nard, and anointed the feet of Jesus
and wiped his feet with her hair.*—John 12:3

 MARY OF BETHANY was the one who "sat at the Lord's feet and listened to his teaching" (Luke 10:39). But she was not satisfied merely *receiving* from Jesus. As she listened to His heart, she longed to *respond*—to give back to Him as He had given to her. Three of the Gospels, in fact, record her poignant display of devotion at a dinner prepared in His honor.

So it is always the case that worship flows out of hearts that have experienced the inflow of His grace. In Exodus 14, we read the dramatic account of God parting the waters of the Red Sea, delivering His people from the advancing Egyptian army. And what was the response of the Israelites to this grand display of His redemptive power? They stopped and sang and exalted the Lord.

When the crippled beggar outside the temple saw the power of God revealed on His behalf, he responded by "walking and leaping and praising God" (Acts 3:8). When Jesus bestowed healing on ten desperate lepers, "one of them, when he saw that he was healed, turned back, praising God with a loud voice" (Luke 17:15). The fact that nine of the ten failed to give thanks did not go unnoticed. Jesus asked, "Was no one found to return and give praise to God except this foreigner?" (verse 18).

Our loving, heavenly Father delights in making Himself known to us and lavishing His grace upon us. But such astounding gifts call for a response on our part. When He reveals Himself through His Word, He is worthy of our worship. When He encourages our hearts by His grace, we owe Him worship. And when the conviction of His Spirit leads us to confession and repentance, should our hearts not respond in heartfelt worship?

 Do you tend to hurry past or overlook God's presence and acts in your life? Don't forget to return to Christ the worship due Him for His manifold grace on your behalf.

Why Are You Crying?

"I cry to you for help, and you do not answer me."—Job 30:20

 DO YOU KNOW WHAT IT IS to cry out to God for help and relief, only to feel that He is turning a deaf ear to you? At those times, we may rightly counsel our hearts that His seeming refusal to answer our plea is grounded in His all-wise awareness of what we truly need. We can remind ourselves that His delay may be part of His divine design to sanctify us or to create a more suitable backdrop for His glory. But at times there may be even more behind His silence.

For instance, sometimes our crying and wailing is motivated solely by a drive to see our situation resolved, to be extricated from the pressure, and to have a more comfortable life. We grieve the loss of our "grain and wine" (Hos. 7:14), while our hearts remain in quiet rebellion against Him, unwilling to be changed and conformed to His will.

At other times we groan over our unknowns while simultaneously withholding obedience to Him in matters we *do* know about, issues where we're being "faithless" (Mal. 2:13–14), even while claiming to be faithful followers of Christ.

Or His lack of visible aid may at times be due to this biblical principle: "Whoever closes his ear to the cry of the poor will himself call out and not be answered" (Prov. 21:13). Refusal to respond compassionately to the needs of others can result in God's refusing to respond to our needs as well.

The ordeals He allows into our lives are sometimes intended to force us to face up to areas where we're keeping Him at arms' length, even while crying out to Him to draw near to us. Be honest about *these*, and the situations that cause your loudest cries will become sure opportunities for Him to meet your deepest needs.

 Are any of these prayer inhibitors present in your heart, even as you plead with the Lord about the hard places you're enduring?

Ear Piercing

But if the slave plainly says, "I love my master, my wife, and my children; I will not go out free" . . . *his master shall bore his ear through with an awl, and he shall be his slave forever.*—Exodus 21:5–6

NOWHERE IN THE SCRIPTURE or in ancient historical records do we find a single instance in which a servant made the choice referred to in Exodus 21. So why did God even suggest such a scenario? Why even mention the option of a slave developing such a strong, loving relationship with his master (and with the wife and children he'd acquired during his years of service) that he did not wish to be rightfully, legally released from his obligations?

Like so many other Old Testament pictures, I believe this one was intended to point us to Christ—and to depict our relationship with Him.

When the Lord Jesus came to earth, He took "the form of a servant" (Phil. 2:7). In obedience to His Father's will and out of love for Him—and for the bride and family His Father had given Him—He offered Himself as a bond slave so He could deliver those who were in bondage to sin (Heb. 2:10–18). Speaking prophetically of the atoning death of Christ, the psalmist David wrote, "Sacrifice and offering you did not desire, but *my ears you have pierced.* . . . I desire to do your will, O my God" (Ps. 40:6, 8 NIV).

Through the example of Christ, we see what no one before Him had ever chosen to do—to bear willingly the marks of His submission, becoming the bond slave who symbolically fulfilled the literal exchange described in Old Testament law.

Following in the steps of their Master, the apostles and New Testament writers saw themselves as bond slaves of Jesus Christ, choosing to be bound to Him by ties of love and devotion and to give their lives in His service.

Will we choose to be so marked as the willing slaves of Christ?

Thank Him for coming to earth and taking the place of a bond slave for your sake. Have you ever consciously acknowledged to the Lord Jesus that you have made the choice (having first been chosen by Him) to be His devoted slave . . . forever?

Unpacking for Paradise

*But nothing unclean will ever enter it, nor anyone who
does what is detestable or false.*—Revelation 21:27

IF YOU WERE TRAVELING OR MOVING to another part of the
world, you'd give careful thought to how you packed.
You wouldn't want to be burdened, for example, with
snowsuits, mittens, and winter boots if you were headed
for a tropical climate. Even if you were only relocating
from one part of town to another, you'd likely do a good bit of
sorting and eliminating, throwing out certain pieces of worn-out
furniture and outdated décor—anything that wouldn't fit well in
your new surroundings.

The fact is, you and I *are* preparing for a move. A real one.
The ultimate one. We're packing for a relocation adventure to
our eternal home. And that means giving thought and attention
to what life in this new place is going to be like and what we need
to be doing to get ready for it.

What we need to keep. And what we need to get rid of.

Three times in the last two chapters of the Bible, our
heavenly home is referred to as the "holy city" (Rev. 21:2, 10;
22:19). It's holy because it's where God lives and rules. A place
of indescribable joy and beauty. A place free of sickness and
sadness. *A place without sin.* "New heavens and a new earth in
which righteousness dwells" (2 Peter 3:13). And since no sin is
allowed in this holy destination, why would we want to hold on
to it now?

"Therefore, beloved, since you are waiting for these, be
diligent to be found by him without spot or blemish" (verse 14).
This world is just a staging area for eternity. Start packing (and
unpacking) for your trip today.

*Ask God to show you any "household sins" or unnecessary
"clutter" in your heart that you need to part with to be ready
for your move to heaven.*

Blessing of Obedience

"Therefore you shall keep his statutes and his commandments, which I command you today, that it may go well with you and with your children after you."—Deuteronomy 4:40

 IF YOU'VE EVER SEEN *THE MIRACLE WORKER*, the story of Helen Keller and her teacher, Anne Sullivan, you well remember the dining room scene. Helen had long been allowed at mealtime to paw through the serving dishes, steal from others' plates, and eat with her fingers. But what her family saw as unavoidable, her tutor saw as an opportunity to begin changing her new pupil's life for the better.

The situation got ugly before it got any better. During what Miss Sullivan described as an hour and a half of warfare, utensils were thrown, things were broken, chairs were knocked over. And though it was only a first step—and hardly a tidy one at that—the ordeal resulted in Helen at least technically eating her breakfast with a spoon and folding her napkin. A new course had been set to move her from a life of chaos and confusion to one of order, self-control, and amazing discovery.

"I suppose I shall have many such battles with the little woman," Miss Sullivan wrote in recalling the moment, "before she learns the only two essential things I can teach her: obedience and love."

When God speaks to us about obedience—which He does more than five hundred times in the Old Testament alone—His desire is not to take from us but to give to us. Contrary to what the enemy may suggest, His commands are not limitations on our joy or freedom. Obedience—Spirit-motivated, grace-enabled, Christ-exalting obedience—is the path to blessing. And when we find ourselves wanting the blessing without the obedience part, we must remember that there is no more satisfying, joyful place to be than trusting, loving, and obeying our heavenly Father.

 What are some of the blessings you have experienced as a result of choosing to obey God? What consequences have you experienced as a result of going your own way? Why would you not choose the former?

Elder Care

Do not receive an accusation against an elder except from two or three witnesses.—1 Timothy 5:19 NKJV

UNLESS YOU'RE MARRIED TO A PASTOR or grew up in a pastor's home, few of us have a good understanding of what life as a pastor is really like. The difficult people. The unexpected phone calls. The level of expectation that far exceeds one man's ability to meet it. Such ingredients are a recipe for people to say and think all kinds of things that are not exactly true or would be understood much differently if they had a more accurate frame of reference. Everyone has their own perception, and unfortunately, many are far too free to share theirs when it comes to critiquing the performance of their pastors and spiritual leaders.

So what do you do when you hear a critical word about your pastor? The Scripture gives instruction for dealing with leaders who fall into sin or fail to discharge their duties. However, our default response should be not to "receive an accusation" against them. Many of the criticisms that are voiced have little if anything to do with a man's biblical qualifications for leadership but rather are someone's personal judgment of his character and style.

Don't let your home or heart become a breeding ground for careless charges about your church leaders. Doing so can be toxic and extremely damaging in a body of believers. Don't go around repeating things you may have heard. God has provided a process for dealing with allegations involving violations of biblical mandates, but apart from such abdication of spiritual responsibility, your pastor needs your love, understanding, and support. Be quick to show appreciation, slow to entertain negative reports, and determined not to sin by spreading gossip.

How do you handle conversations that put your spiritual leaders in a negative light? What are the dangers to you and to others of fueling or being a party to those discussions?

Pliable in His Hands

I lift up my eyes to the hills. From where does my help come?
My help comes from the LORD, who made heaven and earth.
—Psalm 121:1–2

 SPIRITUAL BROKENNESS in a believer is meant to be an ongoing way of life, not just an occasional, crisis experience.

Yes, true brokenness is a lifestyle. Moment by moment. Agreeing with God about the true condition of your heart—not as everyone else sees you or thinks you to be but as *He* knows you to be. Helpless. Unable. Poor and needy. Totally dependent upon His grace working in you and through you.

Further, brokenness is not primarily a feeling or emotion that we wait for to overwhelm us. While our emotions will be involved, true brokenness involves a choice, an act of the will. It is our response of humility and obedience to the authority of His Word and the conviction of His Spirit.

Brokenness means saying "Yes, Lord," responding to Him in complete surrender, yielding to His desires without chafing, stubbornness, or complaint. It means allowing God to soften the soil of your heart, breaking up any clods of resistance that keep the seed of His Word from penetrating and taking root. It means being soft and pliable in the Artist's hands, like wax or clay, not hardening yourself against whatever tools or circumstances He chooses to shape and refine you. It means the shattering of your self-will so the life of Christ can be released through you.

This is brokenness. This is living out the heart of Christ who was broken for you. And this may be what is standing between you and a life that looks more like Christ's steadfast ability and less like your stumbling inability. In choosing the pathway of humility and brokenness, by His divine grace, He will lift you up and the pieces of your life will come together in one God-glorifying whole.

 Are there aspects of your will that keep rearing up and pushing back against His will? Choose the pathway of brokenness, for that is the (only) place of true blessedness.

Wisdom from Above

And [Jesus] said to them, "Let us go on to the next towns,
that I may preach there also."—Mark 1:38

How did Jesus know what priorities to tackle, what needs to respond to on a given day, as He saw before Him a whole world that needed to be redeemed? How did He know when to teach the crowds and when to leave them behind so He could spend time with His disciples? How did He know what one person He should pull aside and minister to? How did He know how to handle each individual situation—whether to touch the blind man's eyes or simply speak healing over him, or to make mud and rub it on his eyelids? How did He know He was supposed to rebuke one group for their unbelief yet encourage another man who admitted to struggling with doubts?

How, in fact, when Peter reported to Him that "everyone is looking for you" (Mark 1:37), did He know it was time to "go on to the next towns," especially when His disciples might reasonably have been asking, "But why? We could stay booked here for at least another month! There are so many people who need You. Why move on?"

I think verse 35 gives us the key: "Very early in the morning, while it was still dark, Jesus got up, left the house and went off to a solitary place, where he prayed." Jesus knew what was on His Father's to-do list for His day, because He had been quiet enough, long enough, to listen to His Father's heart.

Some of us have no clue what God wants us to do with the rest of our week, much less the rest of our lives. We can't figure out how to solve the conflict in our homes, how to meet the needs of those closest to us, or how to make even the simplest of decisions. Could the reason be that we haven't sat still long enough (as Jesus did) to ask God for direction? Might our answer be waiting there?

What distractions have been crowding out your time with the Lord? Purpose to make that time the number one priority of your day, as Jesus did, and trust Him to direct and order your steps.

Deeper Issues

"And the gospel must first be proclaimed to all nations."—Mark 13:10

 EVERY CRISIS THAT ARISES IN OUR WORLD is actually an opportunity—an opportunity for us as God's people to put the gospel on display. It's easy to become exercised over how this situation may affect us personally, to get caught up in the facts and figures and nonstop news coverage. But what if all this is really a chance to shine a spotlight on His grace and glory, to make Him known, even as He orchestrates circumstances to make people realize their fallenness and to make them desperate for His redemption and provision through Christ?

I think that's part of what Jesus was saying to His disciples in Mark 13 as they discussed coming world events. These distressing days would put them in dangerous settings. They would be tempted to cower in fear. People they cared about would be mistreated and suffer. But the important thing was to "bear witness" of who God is and what His Word says is true (verse 9). Seizing the opportunity to proclaim the gospel and proclaim His kingdom was what mattered most.

You may not see yourself as being up to such a challenge, not smart enough or well-spoken enough to communicate God's Word effectively, not bold enough to share Christ's love and mercy with others. But think about the disciples Jesus was addressing. They were not well-educated. Not well-connected. For the most part, they were common, ordinary laborers. And yet God chose them, filled them with His Spirit, and sent them out into the world so powerfully armed with the truth that not even the titanic Roman Empire could prevail over them.

So regardless of how much influence you think you have or don't have, know that God has a purpose for you in these trying days: to live out and talk about the gospel of Christ.

 Ask God to make you sensitive, alert, and prepared to use every possible opportunity to point people to Christ.

Flood of Gratitude

[Be] abounding in thanksgiving—Colossians 2:7

 PAUL'S EXHORTATION TO THE COLOSSIAN CHURCH has the idea of a river overflowing its banks during flood season, leaving no section of nearby ground untouched by the surging waters. Except *this* flood— far from being a torrent of destruction—flows forth as a steady stream of blessing. A flood of gratitude.

I frequently see this "gracious flood" among my coworkers in the ministry where I serve. Most of them are required to raise all or a portion of their monthly financial support— as missionaries. Many of them live on an income considered inadequate by today's standards. And yet I can attest that these *grateful* servants of God, rather than holding tightly to their relatively meager supply, excel in the grace of *giving*, meeting each other's needs for everything from clothing and household items to fresh vegetables and auto repairs.

It's gratitude at work.

How might it work in your own life? Imagine your gratitude for God's grace causing you to reach out in practical ways to the people you know and care about, being sensitive to needs in the lives of those in your church and family. Imagine the impact in a world characterized by isolation, selfishness, and fractured relationships if we were to adorn the gospel we profess by living it out through mutual care, concern, generosity, and sacrifice. The truth we proclaim would become believable. God would be glorified.

That's what can happen every day of the week when God's grace becomes real in our lives, when we return thanks for all we've received through Christ, when our first response to any situation is to be grateful both to God and others. Gratitude has a way of abounding and overflowing—not only being received and deposited but daily withdrawn and multiplied.

 What are some practical ways your gratitude flows out in generosity to others? Ask the Lord to make you a person who truly "abounds [overflows] in thanksgiving."

Lot of Trouble

Abram settled in the land of Canaan, while Lot settled among the cities of the valley and moved his tent as far as Sodom.—Genesis 13:12

 FROM THE STORIES WE READ OF LOT as a contemporary of his uncle Abraham, we basically walk away with a negative impression—leaving us to wonder why the New Testament references him as a "righteous man." But to his credit, Lot did not personally participate in the outright wickedness of Sodom. In fact, he found himself "tormenting his righteous soul over their lawless deeds" (2 Peter 2:8).

So indeed, Lot was righteous—the only way any of us are—by the gracious gift of God working through his faith, weak as that faith may have been. And yet we're not mistaken to observe inconsistencies in Lot's walk. Because even as a follower of God, Lot did not diligently guard his heart. He fueled a thirst and appetite for the things of earth. He tried living with one foot in the kingdom of God and the other inside his corrupting culture, and thereby led his family into a love affair with the world.

It comes as no surprise, then, that his daughters married men who disdained Lot's spiritual beliefs and rejected his pleas for them to escape the coming judgment. It follows their perverse history that after fleeing Sodom, his daughters would scheme to get their father drunk, then take turns sleeping with him so they wouldn't be childless.

Lot's worldly values had led him to move his family to a city characterized by arrogance, immorality, and perversion. And though the price he paid for his temporal values seems high, it is a reminder that the law of sowing and reaping holds true. "Righteous men" (and women) must continually choose to say no to sin and yes to righteousness. We cannot have it both ways. "Friendship with the world is enmity with God" (James 4:4).

 The Scripture warns us to hate "even the garment stained by the flesh" (Jude 23). What elements of worldly life remain too attractive to you?

Written Remembrance

And the LORD said to Moses, "Write these words,
for in accordance with these words I have made a
covenant with you and with Israel."—Exodus 34:27

PRIOR TO THE INVENTION OF THE PRINTING PRESS, people didn't have their own copies of the Word of God. The Bible was painstakingly copied out by hand and passed down from one generation to the next. While we should be immensely grateful for the wide availability of the Scriptures today, I believe something precious has been lost to us who can so easily purchase a printed version of the Bible.

We miss the value of taking time to copy out portions of Scripture.

Do you remember when your elementary school teacher would instruct the class to copy a list from the chalkboard or a page out of a textbook? It seemed like meaningless busywork at the time. But she knew if you wrote out the material for yourself, you were more likely to grasp and remember the concepts.

And that's why God instructed Moses to write out the words of the Law by hand, instructed the people to "write them on the doorposts of your house and on your gates" (Deut. 6:9), and instructed the elders to write "all the words of this law very plainly" on the stones of the altar (27:8). He even laid down a command for any future king of Israel, telling him to "write for himself in a book a copy of this law" so he might "read in it all the days of his life" and "learn to fear the LORD his God by keeping all the words of this law and these statutes, and doing them" (17:18–19).

Writing out the Scripture can help us remember it. Help us keep it. Help us live it.

Consider taking time to write out selected passages of Scripture
that particularly speak to you. See if they don't go from your
hand to your heart.

Words of Life

When the cares of my heart are many,
your consolations cheer my soul.—Psalm 94:19

 MY FRIEND NANCY EPPERSON shares how when her children were little, she would use a special marker to write Bible verses on her kitchen countertops. Each week, a different verse, to be quoted and re-quoted until she and her children could recite it from memory. By the end of the week, after the ink had faded a bit, she would scrub the counter clean to make room for a new verse, etching the words of Scripture into each heart in her home.

One rainy day she was in the kitchen quoting a verse that had once been inscribed on her countertop, when her eighteen-month-old son toddled in behind her. Speaking into the gloom of the morning, Nancy began saying, "This is the day which the LORD hath made . . ." to which her tiny son completed in his childish voice, ". . . I will rejoice and be glad in it" (Ps. 118:24 KJV).

What a need there is to counsel our hearts according to the truths of God's Word, to "teach them diligently" to our children (Deut. 6:7), and to "write them" into our lives (Heb. 8:10). Both we and the generations coming behind us must endure a world that is often dark and distressing. We are confronted by challenges that seem to leave no other option than worry and panic. But His Word is our sanity. It is what keeps us from losing our equilibrium when all around us appears to be spinning out of control. It tethers us to truth, mentally and emotionally, protecting our minds, and reorienting our perspectives.

Store up God's Word in your heart. Memorize it; meditate on it; allow the Spirit of God to personalize it to your life. And be continually renewed as God uses it to transform you into the likeness of Christ.

 If you're not already in the habit of memorizing Scripture, select one verse to memorize and meditate on this week. Watch how God brings it to bear on your current circumstances.

Debt Collection

As the Lord has forgiven you, so you also must forgive.—Colossians 3:13

THERE ARE TWO BASIC WAYS of responding to life's hurts and unfair experiences. The first and most natural response is to become a *debt collector*, one who sets out to make the offender pay for what he's done. Until we get a satisfactory apology, until we determine that an adequate penalty has been paid, we reserve the right to keep him in prison, to punish him for what he has done.

Think Esau and Jacob. A birthright deceptively stolen. Then, by a trick, a family conspiracy—Esau was stripped of the rightful expectation of a father's blessing and a life of prosperity.

"So Esau bore a grudge against Jacob . . . [and] said to himself, 'The days of mourning for my father are near; then I will kill my brother Jacob'" (Gen. 27:41 NASB). He was storing up his resentment, biding his time, waiting to exact his revenge.

But who actually ends up paying the higher cost in these kinds of transactions? Who carries most if not all the residual pain left over from the original offense? Beyond that, what about the resentment and anger that invariably accrue to the debt collector, leaving him or her in perpetual bondage to past offenses? Maddening loops of endless analysis and reliving the circumstances in which the now festering wounds were inflicted. It's all part of the cost of being a debt collector.

Thankfully, God offers us another way—a better way—calling us to the pure, powerful choice of *forgiveness*, pursuing wherever possible the pathway of reconciliation. No, it's not the natural way, but neither is it a take-or-leave option that only some super-Christians can be expected to take. Our fellowship with God requires and depends on it. And life-giving freedom is the sweet fruit that grows from it.

Are you trying to exact payment for an outstanding debt? What price are you paying for doing so? Why not let it go? Turn your offender over to His courtroom and be set free.

Delusions of the Discontented

*And you murmured in your tents and said, "Because the L*ORD *hated us he has brought us out of the land of Egypt, to give us into the hand of the Amorites, to destroy us."*—Deuteronomy 1:27

 IN CASE YOU SKIPPED IT, take a moment to reread that verse. What accusation did the Israelites hurl at the God who had redeemed them from four hundred years of slavery? Do you find it inconceivable that such words could come from the Israelites' mouths? "The LORD *hated* us"? "He brought us out of . . . Egypt . . . to *destroy* us"? How could a rational person possibly come to such a conclusion?

Ten paralyzing plagues against the hostile Egyptians, followed by the sight of these lifelong enemies frantically tossing gold and silver into their knapsacks—*anything* to make these slaves hurry up and leave town. Miraculous deliverance at the Red Sea. Daily manna appearing fresh and freely available on the ground each morning. Pure water gushing from a flinty rock, slaking the ravenous thirst of both man and beast. How could these merciful acts be construed as even a cold lack of concern, much less a deliberate intent to kill?

But this is what comes of forgetting. This is what comes of keeping our attention focused on the perceived shortages of today rather than on God's many faithful proofs from the past and His glorious promises for the future. This is what comes of allowing discontentment to become a default mindset and lifestyle.

This is how a person—any person—starts believing things that aren't true.

So be diligent to guard your heart from discontentment's grand deceptions. Otherwise, these same shocking statements and attitudes of the Israelites may well, over time, become the ones you start believing as well.

 Have you ever felt that God was uncaring or even hostile toward you? Take time to reflect on how He has shown mercy, grace, and love to you.

A Holy Purpose

Even as he chose us in him before the foundation of the world, that we should be holy and blameless before him.—Ephesians 1:4

YOUR HOLINESS is not secondary to whatever other goals you may have for your life. It is God's supreme purpose for your life—something He desired, planned, and made provision to accomplish in you before He even created the world. We're talking about both *positional* holiness—the righteousness of Christ that has been imputed to every believer—as well as the *practical* holiness He is working out in us, which will one day finally be *perfected* holiness.

As an earthly groom eagerly anticipates the moment when his bride walks down the aisle to meet him, beautifully arrayed in a spotless wedding dress, so the Lord Jesus anticipates the day when we—His church—will appear before Him, free from all defilement, clothed in His righteousness, to be His holy bride forever.

And as an engaged woman eagerly, lovingly prepares for her wedding, desirous to be her most beautiful for her groom, so the thought of being wedded to our holy Groom should motivate us to spend our lives on earth in pursuit of this goal, knowing that holiness is our ultimate end and Christ's great desire for us.

God's goal in saving you was not just to make your few years on earth more enjoyable. He had an eternal end in view. His intent was to make you holy, as He is holy, that you might perfectly glorify Him, bring Him pleasure, and enjoy intimate fellowship with Him for all eternity. That is why He chose you—nothing less!

So from the moment you set your feet on the floor each morning, till the moment you lay your head on the pillow at night, don't lose sight of this grand purpose of the ages. You have a reason for living this day; you have an eternal destiny. With both eyes set on pleasing Christ, let Him sanctify you by His grace.

Have you consciously embraced the fact that God has chosen you to be "holy and blameless before him"? How could considering your ultimate end and calling affect the way you live today?

When It Hurts to Pray

O Lord, how long shall I cry for help, and you will not hear?
Or cry to you "Violence!" and you will not save? Why do you make me
see iniquity, and why do you idly look at wrong?—Habakkuk 1:2–3

 I HAD BEEN PRAYING with a number of close friends for a long time about a particularly desperate situation. Finally it became apparent that the door we so earnestly wanted to see Him open had been completely, permanently closed. After all our believing and agreeing, God had delivered an outcome that was totally contrary to what we had been pleading with Him to do.

For months afterward, I could hardly read my Bible; every time I came to those promises about how God hears and answers prayer, I felt confused and mocked. Sure, I knew the truth in my head and in my theology. But why did God put those promises in His Word if they're not always true?

If you've been a Christian any length of time, you have probably felt the same way at some point. Maybe you're feeling that way right now. What's the use of praying? Is it even worth laboring and wrestling with God over a child who's making wrong choices, or an elderly parent who's struggling to survive, or a family crisis that seems unrelenting? Things just keep getting worse, and God doesn't seem to be listening or answering at all—in fact, things seem to be getting worse!

The prophet Habakkuk knew those feelings all too well. He prayed long-term for the pain of his people to be healed. But he came to understand—as we all must—that God's ways are right, and that prayer is as much (or more) about listening than about talking. If we will quiet our accusatory thoughts and words against God, He will recalibrate our hearts and will reveal to us the answers and perspective we need to face our situation, even without knowing all the whys.

 Try making your prayer, particularly over this difficult situation, more of a listening exercise. Trust His Word more than your feelings. Trust His heart more than your own understanding.

He's Perfect

"My beloved is dazzling and ruddy, outstanding among ten thousand."
—Song of Solomon 5:10 NASB

THE FIFTH CHAPTER of the Song of Solomon opens with the bridegroom knocking at the chamber door of his bride. He wants to be with her, to spend time with her. But she's tired and ready for bed. She just doesn't feel like it. Yet after making her excuses, she finally gives in to his persistence and gets up to open the door—only to find him gone! Distressed, she runs out into the city, asking people, "Have you seen him? Do you know where he is?"

Verse 9 describes the young women of the town responding to her, in effect, "What's so special about this man that you miss him so much? Certainly there are others like him—or even better. Can't he be replaced?" In pondering their question, she starts reminding herself (reminding them as well) what makes her beloved so special. No, he is unique—there is no one else like him. He is "chief among ten thousand" (NKJV).

In this exchange, emanating from this portrait of human love and marriage, I believe we see a glimpse of our heavenly Bridegroom, the Lord Jesus. He is not only our Savior; He is our priceless treasure. He is not just good enough; He is lovely; He is perfect. Nothing and no one on earth is more desirable than He.

Only when we realize what we have in Jesus will we stop spending our lives in pursuit of things and people that can never fully satisfy. To realize that perfection is found only in Him is to come to the end of our striving, to stop trying to manufacture perfection in ourselves or using others to create a more perfect life for us. Perfection is already here. His name is Jesus. "I am my beloved's and my beloved is mine" (Song 6:3).

Have you been disappointed lately in others or in yourself? Express to the Lord what it is about Him that stands out above all others; affirm that there is no one else like Him and that no one can meet and satisfy your soul's deepest longings apart from Him.

Until the Noise Stops

When the house was built, it was with stone prepared at the quarry, so that neither hammer nor axe nor any tool of iron was heard in the house. —1 Kings 6:7

 IF YOU'VE EVER BEEN NEAR A CONSTRUCTION SITE, you know how noisy such places can be. The drilling, sawing, welding, excavating. But when Israel's temple was being built during Solomon's reign, it was constructed of stones that had been hewn, shaped, and cut to size at an off-site quarry. By the time those stones reached the building area, no construction noise was necessary; they were already prepared and could now be arranged and fit together to make an edifice where God's glory could be displayed.

I believe there's a spiritual analogy in this Old Testament picture. Right now, you and I are in the quarry. We're feeling the rumble of life's heavy machinery, the blunt edge of the shaping tools. The pounding blows are slowly separating us from our deep, rock-hard attachments to this world. But like "living stones" (1 Peter 2:5), we are being shaped and sized for placement in a faraway temple fit for the glory of God. This pain has a purpose. All this hammering and chiseling is taking us somewhere. Somewhere heavenly and eternal.

If you're feeling disappointment today, perhaps it's because you're demanding that life—here and now—be free from pain and suffering. But that's simply not life here in the quarry; that's the life held in reserve for us at a later time, in another place. We will never know the pain-free, sorrow-free, trouble-free existence of heaven until we have been fashioned and fitted for our eternal Home by our wise, heavenly Builder who is forming us into "a spiritual house" (verse 5), a dwelling place for His holy presence. So till that day, let Him do His Hammering, chiseling work in your life. One day the work will be complete, and God will be forever at Home in His holy temple.

 How can this analogy help you persevere while you are still in the "quarry," being shaped and fit for your future as part of His temple?

Can't Help It?

We know that our old self was crucified with him in order that the body of sin might be brought to nothing, so that we would no longer be enslaved to sin.—Romans 6:6

WE SEE THINGS ABOUT OURSELVES we wish were different, things we know are not pleasing to the Lord. But rather than accept personal responsibility for them, we all too easily blame other factors, circumstances, or people—we blame our hormones, our upbringing, our family situation, our stressful schedule. We imply that *others* have made us the way we are, that we are primarily victims reacting to wounds or conditions inflicted on us by outside sources.

It's not really our fault. We can't help the way we are.

And that's exactly what the enemy wants us to believe. Think back to the original sin committed in the garden of Eden. No parents, spouse, or children accounted for Eve's decision. She certainly couldn't blame her environment, seeing that it was pristine and perfect in every way. She had no financial struggles, no troubles at work, no weeds to pull, no unpleasant neighbors, and no in-law problems! She simply made a personal choice—likely the same choice you or I would have made, either earlier or eventually.

So it's not others. It's us. Like Eve, our problem begins inside, in our own hearts. Now that may sound defeatist and depressing. But the liberating implication of this truth is that we *do* have a choice. By God's grace, we *can* help it. We are *not* forced to go on living in bondage to our circumstances, incapable of choosing more redemptive reactions. To believe otherwise is to think we are doomed to fail, that we must remain perpetually unhappy and frustrated. No, we can be changed by the indwelling power of the Holy Spirit—changed into someone who takes responsibility . . . and experiences the liberating power of the truth.

What are the most common circumstances you blame for your unkind, impatient reactions? How could accepting personal responsibility for your own actions set you free from bondage to people and circumstances beyond your control?

Distractions, Distractions

But Martha was distracted with much serving.—Luke 10:40

I DON'T KNOW ABOUT YOU, but when it comes to my own quiet time, many of the distractions that make it difficult for me to concentrate on the Lord are not external but come from my own mind. Frequently, no sooner do I sit down to enter God's presence than I begin thinking of a whole variety of things I need to do—calls to be made, emails to be responded to, projects to be followed up on . . . . I sometimes even get a sudden, new burden for housecleaning!—*anything*, it seems, to keep from quieting my heart before the Lord and letting Him speak to me.

The seventeenth-century English poet John Donne expressed this tendency well, describing what is all too familiar to anyone who's ever desired to set his heart on things above: "A memory of yesterday's pleasures, a fear of tomorrow's dangers, a straw under my knee, a noise in my ear, a light in mine eye, an anything, a nothing, a fancy, a chimera in my brain troubles me in my prayer."

How true.

While I cannot claim to have succeeded at overcoming such scattered, wandering thoughts, I've learned that I can minimize the effect of these distractions by taking a proactive approach. Rather than stopping to attend to unrelated thoughts and tasks as they come to mind, try simply jotting them down on a notepad for later. In fact, rather than fighting them, let the fact that they've intruded into your quiet time become a prompt to pray about them—right now! As you seek the Lord for wisdom on these matters, He'll help you prioritize your day around His will.

Most likely, the battle with distractions isn't going to go away. But we can ask the Lord for grace not to let those distractions keep us from experiencing focused, meaningful time in His presence.

How could you apply these or similar tactics to combat the barrage of stray thoughts and other interruptions that encroach on your time with the Lord?

Fill in the Blanks

*A word fitly spoken is like apples of gold
in a setting of silver.*—Proverbs 25:11

 SOMETIMES THE BIBLE is most intriguing by what it doesn't say—like when it reports on Mary's visit to her older relative Elizabeth, soon after the angel's stunning appearance, merely by saying that she "remained with her about three months and returned to her home" (Luke 1:56).

I wonder what these two talked about in their extended time together? In addition to the obvious, wonder-filled conversations surrounding their surprise pregnancies, I can imagine the picture of an older woman counseling and mentoring a younger woman, sharing with her how to love her husband and family well, how to be "self-controlled, pure, working at home" (Titus 2:5)—all those things designed to occur in woman-to-woman discipleship.

We do know that upon first sight, Elizabeth had spoken words of blessing and encouragement to Mary, inspiring a response of praise, thanksgiving, and worship (Luke 1:43–55). So I'd be surprised if those next months weren't taken up with even more opportunities for the two women to edify each other with words of wisdom and grace, encouraging each other with God's promises, and rejoicing in the unfolding of His great redemptive plan. Wouldn't you think?

All of which leads me to ask: How alert are you to seize the chance to speak words of significance, love, and challenge to those around you? We waste so many of our words. We throw them away on weather observations, movie reviews, and idle gossip. What would happen if you committed to speak of more important things when interacting with your family, friends, and coworkers, even going so far as to seek out those who need a caring mentor in their lives? Don't leave your best words unspoken when they could accomplish so much in those around you.

 Who has God placed in your life (younger or older) who could benefit from spending time with you, and from hearing wise words from your heart? Ask the Holy Spirit to direct and use you in those one-on-one encounters and opportunities.

False Hoods

And we all, with unveiled face, beholding the glory of the Lord, are being transformed into the same image from one degree of glory to another.—2 Corinthians 3:18

 THE CHILDREN who ring your doorbell on Halloween, masquerading as clowns and pirates, are not *really* clowns and pirates, of course. They're only pretending to be. They're wearing a mask or costume that makes them appear to be something much different from the person underneath.

But don't we do the same thing ourselves? Far too often? We go around masquerading as "good Christians" when the truth is, inwardly we are not like Christ at all but rather are lazy, selfish, bitter, angry. We put on our smiles and spiritualized talk, hoping everybody sees us as the person we present ourselves to be.

If what we really want, however, is not just to masquerade as a godly person but to truly *be* like Christ, then we must start at the only place this transformation can occur—face-to-face with Jesus, gazing upon Him, exposing ourselves to the unfiltered light of His truth, the authority of His voice, and the power of His Word. Keeping our eyes steadily upon Him, enabled by the power of His indwelling Spirit, we soon begin to think as He thinks, to love as He loves, to obey as He Himself obeyed the will of His Father. *To be like Him.* Inside and out.

Do you want to be a gracious, kind, and loving person? Do you want to be more authentic, less prone to deception and compromise, confident in times of uncertainty and change? You *can* be, but not by taking shortcuts and not by fixing your attention on earthly things. You *will* be (1 John 3:2), but not without letting "the face of Jesus Christ" burn His image into your innermost being.

 Are there areas of your life where you are masquerading as a godly person, masking what's really inside? How could you more consciously and consistently fix your eyes on Christ, and how would that gaze change you into His likeness?

Thanks Anyway

I will bless the LORD at all times; his praise shall continually be in my mouth.—Psalm 34:1

THE CHOICE BEFORE YOU AND ME TODAY is this: Do we only give God glory for the parts of our lives that are going the way we want? Or do we worship Him, trust Him, and give Him thanks just because He is God, regardless of the dark, painful, incomprehensible places we encounter along our journey?

Look, it's a sacrifice either way. If we go on without gratitude, choosing to be bitter, bemoaning our fate, we force ourselves to live in these already unhappy conditions with the added drag of our gloomy disposition. We sacrifice peace; we sacrifice contentment; we sacrifice freedom and grace and joy. But what if we could maintain all these things—and even increase them beyond anything we've ever experienced—by making just *one* sacrifice: the sacrifice of thanksgiving?

If you must go through what you're facing now anyway (should God choose not to lift it from you miraculously, which He can always do and for which you may certainly pray), why make it even worse by withdrawing from His grace and fellowship, enduring life on the raw edge without relying on Him for help? Be it disappointment, be it physical suffering, be it mental or relational anguish, why not see what could happen if you let your pain drive you closer to His side?

Yes, to give thanks in all things may require a sacrifice. And no, it may not change your situation, perhaps not even a little. But it will put you in the only position possible for experiencing everything God desires for you throughout this hard stretch of life. That's the promise of gratitude.

It may feel a bit insincere to give thanks under certain circumstances, perhaps even manipulative. But we counsel and train our hearts by such steps of obedience. Offer the sacrifice of thanks, and let God's truth lift and sustain your spirit.

The Way Back

*Seek the Lord, all you humble of the land, who do his
just commands; seek righteousness; seek humility.*—Zephaniah 2:3

 GOD WANTS TO REVEAL HIS PRESENCE AND GLORY to His people today. He wants to fill our hearts, homes, churches, and ministries with His love and His Spirit. He wants to pour out His grace on the dry, thirsty ground of our lives. He wants to restore our "first love" for Jesus, rekindle the fire of devotion that once burned brightly in our hearts, reconcile broken relationships, and rebuild the parts of our lives that are in a state of disrepair.

In short, He wants to revive our hearts.

And it all begins with brokenness and humility. No exceptions, shortcuts, or substitutes.

Brokenness is God's prescription for nearly every condition that ails human hearts and lives, because *pride* in one form or another is almost always at the root of our most difficult issues—fear, sinful bondages, fragmented relationships, communication barriers, generation gaps, unresolved conflicts, guilt, shame, self-absorption, addictions, hypocrisy, even insecurities and excessive shyness. You may have resigned yourself to one or more of these realities; you may be hiding behind their high, thick walls, not wanting to relinquish control or admit weakness. But every one of those walls can crumble through genuine brokenness and humility.

Do you need a fresh infusion of God's grace today? Do you long to experience abundant life, to live in the realm of the supernatural, to enjoy the free flow of His Spirit? Do you want to be set free from those selfish, sinful patterns that plague your walk and poison your relationships? Do you want to find fullness of joy?

Then I challenge you to a radically new way of thinking and living, in which the way up is down, in which death brings life. Brokenness and humility are truly the pathway to your wholeness.

 What might happen if you abandoned your pride and relinquished your hold on your rights? What do you really stand to lose? What do you stand to gain?

That God May Be All

"Truly, I say to you, he will dress himself for service and have them recline at table, and he will come and serve them."—Luke 12:37

 THIS VERSE NEVER FAILS TO MOVE ME. The speaker is Jesus Himself, describing what He will do on that day when He returns for us. Read it again. Can you fathom it? The King of the universe, donning a servant's uniform and coming to wait on us. To *serve us*. It takes my breath away.

And yet there's more. In the prophetic consummation of that cosmic battle that's been intensifying ever since Lucifer first asserted his will against God, we hear "loud voices in heaven, saying, 'The kingdom of the world has become the kingdom of our Lord and of his Christ, and he shall reign forever and ever'" (Rev. 11:15). The Son joins His Father on the highest throne in heaven and earth, to rule forever as the Sovereign Lord.

But in keeping with the character and heart of our Servant-King, His very last action occurs not with loud, crashing cymbals of majestic conquest but with the lush, sweeping sounds of . . . *surrender*: "Then comes the end, when he delivers the kingdom to God the Father after destroying every rule and every authority and power. . . . When all things are subjected to him, *then the Son himself will also be subjected to him who put all things in subjection under him, that God may be all in all*" (1 Cor. 15:24, 28).

Yes, when everything is said and done, the conquering King will turn over to His Father all the kingdoms He has overcome, all the spoils of war. As time gives way to eternity, the Son of God will bow His head in one final, magnificent act of surrender. Watch and worship.

 "Your attitude should be the same as that of Christ Jesus" (Phil. 2:5 NIV). How does your attitude reflect the heart of the Lord Jesus? How is it different than His?

Three Questions

"Run now to meet her, and say to her, 'Is it well with you? Is it well with your husband? Is it well with the child?'"—2 Kings 4:26 NKJV

WHEN THIS DISTRAUGHT MOTHER came to meet Elisha, he asked a series of penetrating questions, with the intent of finding out how she was (really) doing and what he could do to help.

We would do well to ask those we care about these same three simple questions periodically—and not to settle for superficial answers.

Is it well with you? Are you doing all right? How is it with your soul?

How about with your marriage? Are you walking in love, putting each other first, staying morally pure?

How about with your children? Do they have a heart and hunger for God? How can I pray for them or encourage them in their faith?

The point of probing in this way is not to be nosy, overbearing, or suspicious. It's just that these are some of the first things people stop wanting to talk about in any depth or detail when things are starting to slip off center, when priorities are being compromised, when pride is blocking access to the sensitive areas of their hearts.

These areas are also some of Satan's prime targets—the places where many people are particularly vulnerable. By inviting them to open up about issues involving their homes and hearts, you're becoming part of their protective cover. And by being available to pray and provide needed support and encouragement, you're truly helping.

So be willing to bring up these core subjects in others' lives. Be patient, listening to what they're really saying. Be the kind of friend who loves them in ways most others are too busy to do. And don't forget to point them to Jesus at their greatest points of need.

When's the last time you talked heart to heart with one of your close friends or family members? Pray about making your next conversation a significant one. And, be willing to open your life up to be asked these kinds of questions by others.

Do It Right

Set the believers an example in speech, in conduct,
in love, in faith, in purity.—1 Timothy 4:12

 I'LL NEVER FORGET THE DAY, during the early days of *Revive Our Hearts* radio, when I was recording a teaching series on the book of Ruth in front of a studio audience. Bob Lepine, cohost of *FamilyLife Today*, was sitting in on the recording as he was coaching me and serving as an advisor to our ministry. After one particular session, he stood up and said, "I'd like for you to do that again. Your main point was a bit confusing and could be more clear."

Well, that was *not* what I wanted to hear. I knew it would be difficult to collect my thoughts on the spot and start again. But I also felt I needed to heed his counsel. So I immediately began rearranging my notes while one of the women in the audience led the others in praying for me. We retaped the broadcast (which happened to be on women having a responsive spirit to godly male leadership!), and Bob was right. It did turn out better.

But what made the day particularly memorable for me was when a woman came up afterward and said, "Nancy, the thing that impacted me the most today was watching how you responded to Bob's direction when he asked you to do a retake of that program. That had to be hard for you, but you modeled what you were teaching, and that really spoke to me."

I wish my reactions under pressure always impacted people in such a positive way! But the fact is, our unguarded reactions and responses teach a lot more than we realize; in many cases, they speak louder than what we *tell* others is right.

That's why it's so important to develop a lifestyle of Spirit-controlled responses—godly patterns that kick into gear when we're under pressure. A humble, godly lifestyle will make your message believable and help others get what you're talking about.

 What evidence of Christian character have your friends, family, and coworkers seen in you lately? If those around you followed your example in every area of life, what would their lives be like?

Well Received

The steadfast love of the LORD never ceases; his mercies never come to an end; they are new every morning; great is your faithfulness.—Lamentations 3:22–23

 OH, HOW BLIND WE CAN BECOME to God's grace. How quickly we forget that His "new every morning" mercies are not gifts we deserve; they are graces given by His loving hand to fallen creatures—those who have no right to expect such "steadfast" care and attention from One so pure and holy.

When we subconsciously consider God obligated to give us each day's bounty of blessings, we shut our eyes to His true loveliness and glory; we cheapen the grace that not only sustains us through life's battles but also keeps joy flowing into and out of our hearts; we experience the gradual loss of humility, contentment, enjoyment, healthy relationships, and the sweet walk with Christ that provides our only access to abundant life.

So the apostle Paul had good reason to list ingratitude right in the middle of such evil companions as abusiveness, heartlessness, brutishness, treachery (2 Tim. 3:1–5)—because that's where it belongs. Ingratitude is no less heinous a sin. It leaves us equally empty and hard inside.

And yet so powerful is the influence exerted by ingratitude that when we displace it with its bright opposite—when we turn our hearts to God in sincere thankfulness—a number of other sins are sure to be dislodged from our lives as well. As Paul said, "Let there be no filthiness nor foolish talk nor crude joking, which are out of place, but instead let there be thanksgiving" (Eph. 5:4). Because when gratefulness returns, it carries with it the attending blessings and beauty of holiness.

 Take a few moments to focus on and enumerate the mercies you have received from His hand since waking up this morning.

Household Holiness

For your obedience is known to all,
so that I rejoice over you.—Romans 16:19

 I REMEMBER HEARING FROM A FRIEND whose ninety- and ninety-two-year-old parents had recently moved out of the house where they had lived for fifty years. As part of this massive relocation project, my friend had spent an entire month sorting through a lifetime of their accumulated "stuff"—correspondence, financial data, clippings, photos. Taken together, these various artifacts amounted to a fairly complete record of their lives. Each image and expression told a part of their story, captured in random, simple snippets of everyday activity.

After poring through this leftover collection of memorabilia and paperwork, my friend observed with a sense of wonder, "There was not one single thing in my parents' belongings that was inconsistent with the profession of their faith in Christ." Their private lives were as clean, pure, and authentic as their public image.

How would you fare if someone were to sift through all your possessions, your checkbook registers and credit card receipts, your tax returns, your daily planners, your phone bills, your past emails and text messages, a complete record of your Internet activity, the music on your iPod, your collection of DVDs and video games? What would people find? What conclusions might they draw? And what would it mean if they could say, as this grateful son said of his parents, that they found your life exemplary through and through?

It would be among the highest compliments anyone could pay. It would remind us that a lifestyle of purity and integrity—over the course of a lifetime—is not a recipe for a cold, rigid, cheerless existence. In the end, it is everything we want. And more.

 Do you have any possessions or places in your life that you'd be embarrassed to have others scrutinize? Do you need to do some "housecleaning" yourself, before others do it for you?

How Are You Feeling?

*Set your mind on things that are above, not on things
that are on earth. For you have died, and your life is
hidden with Christ in God.*—Colossians 3:2–3

I DON'T KNOW HOW YOU'RE FEELING TODAY. Maybe not the best. Tired? Stressed? Hurt or angry? Perhaps bored or lonely. Or sad or forgotten. It could be one or more of many different emotions, each of which knows its well-worn, familiar way to your heart. And every time this feeling shows up, it wants to dictate how you orient your day, how you react to other people and situations that arise, how you perceive God's nature and character. Everything.

But here's one thing I do know. If left to roam wild, those feelings and emotions will likely lead you to think and do things that are inconsistent with God's plan for your life. They will persuade you to believe things about Him, about yourself, and about your circumstances that run counter to the truth. If you let them, those emotions will seek to distort your view of God and keep you from seeing Him as the faithful, loving, actively engaged God He reveals Himself to be. That's why feelings, as fickle and unreliable as they are, cannot be allowed just to come in and take over. They must be disciplined, managed, and controlled.

And this job calls for Scripture. Lots and lots of Scripture. Not limited exposure through once-a-week-or-less church services but a daily, lifelong commitment to immerse yourself in its truth. In fact, your soul needs megadoses of the Word—much as you pump vitamin C and echinacea into your system when you have a cold—to help build up your spiritual immunities and reserves, blocking the chances for wrong ways of thinking to infect your heart and put you out of commission.

So stop nursing those feelings. Get your nose in the Bible, and see things for how they really are. See Him for who He really is.

*Are you getting sufficient intake of the Word into your system?
How might you keep it with you throughout the day for additional
doses as needed?*

Have a Good Day

Whoever desires to love life and see good days,
let him keep his tongue from evil and his lips
from speaking deceit.—1 Peter 3:10

 I LIKE TO THINK OF PETER having a particular person in mind when he wrote these words (actually lifting them from Ps. 34, as those who make a habit of living in the Scriptures are able to do). I can almost imagine someone having complained to the great apostle about a situation in his or her life—some cruel injustice, some harsh circumstance, some difficult relationship. "How am I supposed to handle this?" the man or woman may have asked Peter, hoping he could offer some wise counsel to help alleviate the problem—or at least fix the person who was causing it!

But instead, Peter shifted the perspective away from the place we often like to keep it—on the troubling issue itself, as well as on its chief offenders—and put it back on the opportunity embedded within the problem. This ordeal is a place to "do good," an opening for the offended to "seek peace" in the midst of strife (verse 11).

Yes, the situation may hurt, and yes, the whole thing may be grossly unfair. But fixing the problem is God's business, whose "face is against those who do evil" (verse 12). Demonstrating His character so that He gets ultimate glory—that's *our* business.

We are so driven to avoid being hurt, to dull the pain, to take the aspirin. But we need a theology like Peter's that goes beyond the aspirin—a life that doesn't run from the cross but is actually *all about* the cross. Some of our worst headaches may not go away this side of eternity, but each one holds potential for a "good" and godly response from us.

 Is your energy focused on trying to stamp out your problems or on seeking to handle them with grace, humility, and faith?

The Anti-Blessing

*Do not speak evil against one another, brothers. The one who
speaks against a brother or judges his brother, speaks evil against
the law and judges the law.*—James 4:11

 CURSING IS SOMETHING I JUST DON'T DO. Never have.
Or so I thought until the Lord used verses like the
one above to show me that four-letter words are
hardly the full scope of the curser's vocabulary.

The Greek word used translated "cursing" in
James 3:10, as well as the similar word used here in 4:11, both
carry the same general idea. To curse means to "speak evil
against," to say thoughtless words either to or about someone,
to give what amounts to an "anti-blessing." It's much more than
profanity; it's wounding others with our tongues.

And the Bible says, "Don't do it."

This kind of talk can cause irreparable harm to people's
hearts and spirits; it tears them down in both our and others'
estimation. Such cursing is also one of the key descriptors of
an unbelieving lifestyle. That's what 1 Peter 2 says, referring to
this kind of language as typical conduct for the pagan Gentiles
(verse 12). First Peter 3 says so as well, contrasting a Christian's
behavior with those who "repay evil for evil or reviling for
reviling" (verse 9). For a believer to "curse" others by speaking
evil of them is to behave like a practical atheist.

So let's purpose in our hearts to stop acting in ways indicative
of non-Christian beliefs and conduct—starting with the way we
speak to and about others. Not even in jest will we say hurtful
things that belittle one's value as a bearer of His image. Cursing
in any and every form is a lie about whose we are.

 *Do you owe anyone an apology for speaking evil against them?
Ask God to speak blessing through you as you talk to and about
others today.*

Root Issues

See to it that no one fails to obtain the grace of God;
that no root of bitterness springs up and causes trouble,
and by it many become defiled.—Hebrews 12:15

A "ROOT OF BITTERNESS" may seem the least of your concerns today. In fact, given the type of situations you've dealt with in life—the injuries you've received unjustly, through the actions or inactions of others—bitterness can seem like a birthright. Your safety zone. You may actually feel incapable of any other response.

But be sure of this: bitterness is a fallback position doomed to failure. If left unacknowledged and unaddressed, God's Word says its poison will infect both you and others beyond anything you ever imagined possible. Ask around, and you'll hear the unpleasant proof. Not only is it sin, it is senseless.

But it is not incurable, because God's grace is tailor-made for just such situations. Jesus is a compassionate Savior who was perfected "through suffering" (Heb. 2:10). As a result, not only has He gained our eternal salvation, but He also knows how it feels to be treated harshly, to be taken advantage of, to be misunderstood. And He knows exactly where to apply His healing grace in your hurting, wounded heart.

That root of bitterness will infest every inch of ground in your life if you let it. But God invites you—*urges* you—to reach out and receive His grace, to come to His throne "with confidence," knowing you will receive His all-sufficient help (4:16).

In so doing, your heart will be set free from the vise of unforgiveness. You'll be released to love and serve both Him and others. No longer will that root of bitterness trouble you and adversely affect those around you. Instead, God's grace will flow through you to others, blessing everything and everyone you touch.

 Imagine life without the chronic, low-grade fever of bitterness dulling your senses, consuming your waking and sleeping thoughts. Will you cry out for His grace to remove every vestige of bitterness?

Throne and Cross

Then Jesus told his disciples, "If anyone would come after me, let him deny himself and take up his cross and follow me."—Matthew 16:24

 WILLIAM BORDEN grew up in a socially prominent home in Chicago as heir to the Borden dairy estate. His family was so affluent, in fact, that his parents gave him a cruise around the world as a high school graduation gift. But what stood out to young Bill Borden while sailing from one continent to another were not the exotic sights and sounds of each port of call but rather the deep spiritual needs of people all over the globe. His pampered heart was breaking. God was calling him to devote his life to full-time Christian missions.

He would later write in his journal while attending Yale University, "Yes, Lord, that's what I'm willing to do." But what amounted to the crux of the issue was defined by this simple word picture that he committed to paper and etched into his mind: "In every man's heart, there is a throne and a cross. If Christ is on the throne, self is on the cross; and if self, even a little bit, is on the throne, then Jesus is on the cross in that man's heart."

A throne. A cross. On which one have you placed yourself, your hopes, your things, your desires?

To deny ourselves and take up our cross, so that Christ may be given His rightful place as Lord. That is the surrender we are called to make as believers, day in and day out. To say yes to God. To bow the knee. To receive the wisdom and warnings of His Word as our marching orders.

So make sure the furniture that occupies your heart is occupied appropriately. There can only be one throne. Make it His own.

 What might it mean for you to take up your cross and for Christ to be on the throne in your heart today?

A Deeper Shade of Forgiveness

"Pray for those who persecute you, so that you may be sons of your heavenly Father who is in heaven."—Matthew 5:44–45

DEPENDING ON THE NATURE AND CIRCUMSTANCES of your relationship with a particular person who has wronged you—especially in one of the more tragic and scarring of ways—it may not be appropriate for you to reconnect face-to-face or reestablish ongoing contact with them. You may need to ask a pastor or a mature, godly friend to help you navigate this sensitive area safely and biblically.

But no matter who it is or what they've done, you can at least do this: you can pray for them.

No, you are *commanded by Christ* to pray for them.

You may sigh and say, "I don't think I can ever pray for God's blessing on that man or that woman. I don't even *want* God to bless them!" But I assure you, as you begin to do it anyway out of simple obedience to the Word of God, you'll discover what I've found to be true in my own life: you cannot long hate someone you're praying for, someone you're asking God to bless and restore to a right relationship with Him.

Our main goal for our offenders should be their reconciliation—first and foremost with God and then, if possible and appropriate, with us and with others who may have been affected. We may not be able to bring about this ultimate objective, but we can build bridges of love and blessing across the divide so that the way is at least available. How they respond is up to them. But how can we keep the walls up, refusing to seek their blessing and restoration, and expect to experience free-flowing fellowship with God ourselves?

Is there someone who has wronged you so deeply that it seems impossible to pray for them? The same Savior who prayed for forgiveness for His enemies as He suffered on a cross can enable you to pray that God will redeem and restore your enemy.

Safe beneath His Wings

Keep me as the apple of your eye; hide me in the shadow
of your wings, from the wicked who do me violence,
my deadly enemies who surround me.—Psalm 17:8–9

 WE ARE ALL TOO FAMILIAR with the enemies we face in life—enemies from our past, enemies of our nation, enemies who seek to take personal advantage of us. We sometimes even encounter enemies in our homes and churches.

But the most threatening, persistent enemies we have to deal with are often those that hide out in our own hearts. False perceptions, temptations, destructive ways of thinking—these internal enemies can launch their attack against our hearts and minds, seeking to derail our faith, draw us into sin, or drown us in despair. Sinful tendencies, seething anger, and self-loathing thoughts are hard to know how to guard against.

Yet certainly these enemies are among those from which God promises to "hide" us in the shadow of His wings. When we draw near and look up to Him, trusting ourselves to His watchful, powerful care, we find Him able to help us resist even our most determined, entrenched internal adversaries.

Within that still, safe place, we can stop our striving and find protection as He covers us with the soft feathers of His grace and love. In that place, we are free to humble ourselves and admit our need. In that place, we don't have to pretend we are strong or try to impress others with the image that we have got it together. In that place, we can rest while God works—while He Himself becomes our defender and champion against the lies and habit patterns that have worn us weary with their ceaseless badgering.

Run into His arms. Be gathered beneath His wings. No enemy can touch you there.

 Which of your unseen enemies feels the most ferocious to you today? Don't try to ward them off on your own. Let the Lord do your fighting for you.

Blessed Brokenness

Come, let us return to the LORD; for he has torn us, that he may heal us;
he has struck us down, and he will bind us up.—Hosea 6:1

 BRIAN AND MELANIE ADAMS had a good marriage. They were both believers, committed to each other, trying to lead their eight children to follow Christ. After nineteen years of marriage, however, the intimacy they had once experienced had gradually eroded. "The dinner table had grown larger and larger between us with the addition of each child," Melanie said, "and I had almost come to accept that we would never experience the closeness we both longed for and needed."

They decided to attend a marriage retreat, and as they sat through a message on the second day, Melanie found herself preparing in her mind a lecture for Brian on the need for change in his life. But instead, she recalls, "God began to peel back the layers of my own heart, and what He revealed was not pretty: bitterness, hardness, rebellion, worst of all a dependence on my own righteousness and an underlying pride that corrupted it all."

Soon she began to cry. Then weep. When they were finally able to get away privately by themselves, she sobbed uncontrollably as confession came pouring forth like infection being drained from a lanced wound.

Why would anyone choose to be broken like this? Well, why would a person check into the hospital for invasive surgery? Because they love pain? No, it's because they know the only way to get rid of the disease and experience healing and restoration is to go through this painful process.

We choose the pathway to brokenness because it ultimately brings blessedness. The very thing we dread and are tempted to resist can actually become the means of God's greatest blessings in our lives.

 Are there spiritual toxins—infected attitudes or ways of thinking—that need to be lanced from your heart? Let God do His work, painful as it may be, and trust Him to restore you to a place of spiritual health and blessing.

For Crying Out Loud

Evening and morning and at noon I utter my complaint
and moan, and he hears my voice.—Psalm 55:17

 YOU MAY FEEL KIND OF PITIFUL, as I do at times, when you're crying out to the Lord all by yourself with no one around. Just you. Just Him. No one else to talk to. Nowhere else to turn. But even in the midst of what our enemy might call a foolish display of emotions or a pure waste of time—even when you know you're just a tiny voice among millions doing the same thing in other places—you can be sure God hears your cry. Your personal cry.

Any mother will tell you she can pick out her baby's cry from a cacophony of bawling children in the nursery. Just because they're all screaming at once doesn't keep her child's voice from rising above the din—not to *her* ears.

So don't hold back from seeking God's presence and His loving attention amid whatever troubling situation may surround you today. Perhaps you're reeling from the painful revelation that your spouse has been unfaithful to your marriage—in desire if not in deed. Perhaps you've been given reason to believe your son-in-law is being angry and abusive toward your daughter and grandchildren. Perhaps your job is on shaky ground and the next month will determine whether the company can afford to keep you or not. Perhaps you're torn between what appear to be equally reasonable choices in a difficult major decision, and you don't have clear direction which way to go.

Then whether "evening" or "morning" or "at noon"—or an all-day combination of all three—don't be ashamed to raise your cry to the heavens. He will hear. He will deliver. And He will be glorified.

 If you're uncomfortable crying out to the Lord
as His Word invites, what might account for
your hesitancy to take your deep concerns to Him?

Speak Up

I thank my God in all my remembrance of you.—Philippians 1:3

 GRATITUDE IS NOT THE QUIET GAME. It begs to be expressed, both to God and to others. "Silent gratitude," Gladys Berthe Stern said, "isn't much good to anyone."

So if a certain cashier has been consistently pleasant at the grocery store, why not stop by to tell the manager what a delight you've found his employee to be and how thankful you are for her attitude. He'll be glad to pass along the compliment, and she'll go home encouraged and freshly motivated about her work.

If a neighbor's flower bed catches your eye every time you pull into the driveway, try walking over and telling her how much you admire her for the hard work she puts into tending her yard and how it just seems to get more beautiful year after year.

If your pastor's messages encourage your heart and deepen your walk with God, don't assume he just automatically knows this or gets tired of hearing how his ministry is impacting people's lives. Look him in the eye and thank him for his faithfulness to bring you the Word, or jot him a note with a few specifics of how something he said really spoke to you.

And, of course, when you're captivated by a glorious sunset, or comforted in sorrow, or uplifted by some sweet reminder of the hope God gives in the midst of life's many problems and challenges, make your praise not only ring in your head but roll off your tongue. Spoken words of praise and thanks have the power to dissipate the spirit of heaviness that can cling to you like a wet blanket.

Tired of feeling lifeless and weighed down? Then speak up!

 What are some things that can keep us from noticing and expressing appreciation for the blessings we receive from God and others? Ask God to give you eyes to see those blessings today and purpose to take the time to give thanks.

In Good Standing

*And let us consider how to stir up one another
to love and good works.*—Hebrews 10:24

 YOU WOULD THINK the giant redwoods in the California forests—some of which tower 350 feet into the air and are more than 2,500 years old—must possess an enormous root system extending hundreds of feet into the ground underneath. But actually, the roots on a redwood are extremely shallow—no deeper than six to ten feet. So how do these massive trees stand a chance of staying upright for even ten seconds, much less thousands of years?

The secret is not in the depth of the roots but in their interconnected nature. Since the trees grow close together, their root systems become intertwined around each other. So when the storms come and the winds blow—as they definitely do in that part of the country—the redwoods stand strong because they're not standing alone. Each of them supports and protects the other.

What a great picture this gives us of our need for one another in the body of Christ. We were designed to grow in community together as believers, not in isolation but having our root systems intertwined with each other, providing mutual nourishment, protection, and support.

God's design is that the lives of believers—particularly within the local church—should be characterized by this kind of interdependence, not merely present in body but actively involved in sharing and giving and serving and learning—together. We need accountability and encouragement from each other if we expect to keep ourselves vertical. It's not an option; it's a matter of survival.

 Do you experience that kind of interconnectedness in your relationships with other believers? If not, you're missing something you need. And others are missing something you can give.

Yield Signs

Then the LORD *said, "Is it right for you to be angry?"*—Jonah 4:4 NKJV

 SUCCESSFUL, HEALTHY RELATIONSHIPS and cultures are not built on the *claiming* of rights but on the *yielding* of rights. Even our traffic laws reflect this principle. You'll never see signs that say, "You have the right of way." Instead they instruct us to "Yield" to oncoming cars, to "Slow" for the safety of work crews, to "Stop" from driving into a contested intersection. This is how traffic flows best.

It's also how *life* flows best.

The Old Testament prophet Jonah vividly illustrates the natural, human tendency to claim rights and then become angry when those "rights" are violated. Jonah felt he had a right, for example, to dislike the pagan Ninevites. He had a right to minister where he wanted to minister. He had a right to control his own environment, to have things go the way he wanted them to go—to see those nasty Ninevites judged by God! And when the Lord acted differently from how Jonah thought He should, "it displeased Jonah exceedingly, and he was angry" (Jonah 4:1).

But God didn't sympathize with Jonah's wounded feelings, any more than He sympathizes with ours when we complain about the long lines, the wrong number, those perceived violations of our dignity that leave us moody and uptight at best—angry and estranged from God at worst—when our mindset becomes one of being easily offended by anything that slows us down, ties us up, or interferes with our plans.

The only way to get off this spiritual and emotional roller coaster is to yield what we claim as *our* rights to the One who ultimately holds *all* rights. The alternative is not a place we really want to go.

 Have you found yourself being upset lately because of claiming rights rather than yielding your rights to God? Let God ask you the question He asked Jonah: "Is it right for you to be angry?"

Daily Delighting

"Then I was beside him, like a master workman, and I was daily his delight, rejoicing before him always, rejoicing in his inhabited world and delighting in the children of man."—Proverbs 8:30–31

PROVERBS 8 uses a literary device known as *personification*, treating wisdom as though it's an actual being. But many commentators believe this passage is also reflective of Christ, the Wisdom of God. Read it yourself, and see if much of this chapter doesn't bring to mind things you know and love about the Lord Jesus.

By the time you near the end, however, you may find something that surprises you—a characteristic of Christ that is lost on those who see Him as stern, heavy-handed, and impossible to please. In verses 30–31 above, we see Him standing beside the Father in eternity past, actively engaged in the details of creation, and delightedly enjoying not only His relationship within the Godhead but His relationship with humanity.

Yes, before time began, Jesus the Christ was "delighting"—*in us!*

Because of our sin, of course, we often find ourselves on the receiving end of His discipline and correction. Loving though it is, His sanctifying work in our lives can make us feel like He's demanding more of us than anyone should expect. But stand again and gaze on this scene from the earliest moments of creation, and see your Savior rejoicing in His inhabited world—in you.

Then take it a step further. See Him desiring to share with you the same kind of close, joyful relationship that He Himself has enjoyed with the Father for all of eternity. Amazing.

"These things I have spoken to you," He would later tell His disciples, "that my joy may be in you, and that your joy may be full" (John 15:11). That's what God wants for us—fullness of joy that flows out of being in union with Christ and having Christ alive in us. Thanks to the redeeming work of Christ on the cross, that relationship, that joy, can be ours today.

What does it mean to you that Christ delights in His relationship with His Father and with you? Are you taking time to rejoice in His love and in your relationship with Him?

Seeking His Pleasure

Thou art worthy, O Lord, to receive glory and honour and power: for thou hast created all things, and for thy pleasure they are and were created.—Revelation 4:11 KJV

YOU AND I EXIST FOR ONE REASON ALONE: to bring God glory. We were created for His pleasure. Only in fulfilling this grand purpose for our lives do we discover true significance and meaning. This is life in a nutshell. And there could be no higher, more magnificent, calling.

So of all the things you think about each morning when you get out of bed, and again each night before going to sleep, remember who God is, and remember why you are here. Then throughout the day, as you evaluate everything that's happening to you, as you make decisions, as you respond to unanticipated or unwelcome circumstances, filter it all through this primary grid, not asking, "Does this bring *me* pleasure?" but "Does this bring *God* pleasure?" Not asking, "Does this make *me* look good?" but "Does this make *God* look good?"

If the glory of God is your supreme passion, this one desire will define your goals and objectives, your interests and activities. The longing for Him to be glorified will define *you*.

Recently, while experiencing a circumstance that was shaking my world, feeling myself becoming reactionary and resentful, I discovered again the importance of counseling and recalibrating my heart according to God's Word. As He brought my thinking back into alignment with His truth, I reflected in my journal, "If I fixate on how all of this affects *me*—my comforts, my desires, my fulfillment, my security, my need—then I have made 'myself' an idol. But this is not about *me*. It is about denying self and crowning Christ as Lord, seeking His glory and pleasure above all else."

Amen. Pleasing Him is truly life's greatest pleasure.

Have God's desires and yours been in conflict lately? Would you trust and honor Him enough to tell Him you want His way, His pleasure, above your own?

Debt of Gratitude

I must perform my vows to you, O God;
I will render thank offerings to you.——Psalm 56:12

 NUMEROUS TIMES IN THE PSALMS, we read verses about paying "vows" to the Lord. Most often these references come from people saying to God that when He's answered their prayers for deliverance, they promise to bring Him a thank offering in grateful response for His aid and comfort.

This is certainly the case in the verse above from Psalm 56. Looking at the context, David appears to be in one of those frequent situations in his life when he was endangered—this time by the cruel and ever-threatening Philistines. He had been seized, commentators believe, by these bitter enemies of God's people and now found himself in a full-blown crisis situation.

You undoubtedly know "full-blown" and "crisis" by their first names.

And just as you've likely done on such occasions, David reacted to his grim circumstances by earnestly appealing to the Lord for help, promising to fulfill his vows of gratitude in return.

All of this reminds me that thanksgiving is a debt. It is something we owe. When we bring our thanks before God, we are recognizing Him as the source of every blessing, every protection, every heartbeat, every rescue from every trial—even when His chosen form of deliverance just means supplying us the perseverance we need to see it through. We have no life, no hope, no health, no grace, no strength, no peace, no holiness, no *anything* apart from what He has given and continues to give us.

So if you're holding an outstanding debt of gratitude today, fulfill your obligation to deliver your thanks to Him. He deserves it all.

 What deliverances and provisions has God made for you, for which you've not yet given thanks? Now would be a good time!

Now Thank We All Our God

Then Job arose and tore his robe and shaved his head and fell on the ground and worshiped.—Job 1:20

 MARTIN RINKART was a seventeenth-century Lutheran pastor serving in his hometown of Eilenberg during the height of the Thirty Years' War. A walled city, Eilenberg soon found itself overrun with refugees and injured troops, bringing on not only fear and overcrowding but a deadly wave of disease, pestilence, hunger, and want.

The Rinkart home became a makeshift refuge of sorts for many of the sick and stranded. And though limited with hardly enough food and supplies to care for his own family, Martin ministered tirelessly to the needs of those around him. When other pastors fled for safety, he stayed on, eventually conducting more than *4,500* funeral services that year.

One of those was for his wife.

And yet at some point amid these dire events, Martin composed a family grace to be said by his children before meals—a hymn still sung today all across Germany at state occasions and national days of remembrance: "Now thank we all our God, / With hearts and hands and voices, / Who wondrous things hath done, / In whom His world rejoices; / Who from our mother's arms / Hath blessed us on our way / With countless gifts of love, / And still is ours today."

When we sing these words in the comfortable surroundings of a Thanksgiving service at church, we smell turkey in the oven, warm bread on the table. We hear the voices of relatives, enjoying reconnecting and conversing with one another.

But make no mistake: this joy-filled refrain wasn't birthed in the settled quiet of a country cottage. It was forged in pain and suffering and grief and death. True Thanksgiving comes at a cost. And no circumstances are so dire that they can't produce hymns of joy and thanks on the lips of those who know their God.

 Are you facing circumstances that make it difficult for you to praise God? Ask Him to help you offer up in this very place a sacrifice of thanksgiving.

Come Closer

I will praise the name of God with a song;
I will magnify him with thanksgiving.—Psalm 69:30

Do you long for a greater sense of God's nearness? The Scripture says He inhabits the praises of His people (Ps. 22:3 KJV). If we want to be where He is, we need to go to His address—the place where He lives.

In the Old Testament, the tabernacle was the first place God set apart to meet with His people. In front of the entrance to the Holy of Holies—the sacred seat of God's manifest presence—stood the altar of incense, where every morning and every evening, the priest would offer up the sweet aromas representing the prayers and thanksgiving of God's people.

But those ancient rituals were only types and symbols of a relationship that we as New Testament believers can enjoy with Him anytime, anyplace. Through Christ's sacrifice on the cross, we have been granted permanent access to the Father, whose gates we can enter at any moment "with thanksgiving, and his courts with praise" (100:4). If we desire His presence, worship and gratitude can always take us there.

So see what happens when you open your heart afresh to the Lord, lifting up your eyes and voice to "magnify him with thanksgiving." Yes, see if expressing your gratitude doesn't actually "magnify" Him in your eyes, increasing your sense of wonder toward this One who knows your name, counts the hairs on your head, and manifests His love for you with one blessing after another. See if the practice of praise and thanksgiving doesn't transport you nearer to Him—not just where your faith can believe Him but where your heart can sense Him.

Praise puts you inside God's living room. It paves the way to His presence.

A heart of thanksgiving will draw you not only closer to God but also to others, as they are attracted to your grateful spirit. A thankful life is an antidote for loneliness.

The Anatomy of a Big Heart

. . . bearing with one another and, if one has a complaint against another, forgiving each other; as the Lord has forgiven you, so you also must forgive.—Colossians 3:13

 WHEN WE HEAR OR READ the stunning accounts of forgiveness in the lives of ordinary people— those who have been thrust into extraordinarily stressful circumstances and still been able to emerge with grace and generosity—it's doubtful they just suddenly developed this huge capacity to forgive. More likely, they had been practicing forgiveness and forbearance all along, in the everyday, spilled-milk situations of their lives.

Take the woman who forgave the man who raped her, leaving her not only pregnant with his child but HIV-infected, yet who still says, "Every time we feel the pain, we need to forgive again"—

Take the man who watched his father shot dead over a few dollars in his wallet, but who one day shook that same attacker's hand, saying, "I forgive you, and it's over"—

Take the mother who was struck head-on by a speeding, unlicensed driver, killing her two children and leaving herself in critical condition, but whose first words to her husband upon waking from a drug-induced coma were, "Did you forgive him?"—

Such heroics don't just happen. They are almost always borne out in people who knew what it was like to forgive long before the stakes became truly life changing.

And you can be one of those people too—when your mother-in-law says something that hurts your feelings, when a motorist talking on his cell phone nearly runs you off the road, when someone walks right by you at church without speaking, when your adult children don't call you as often as you'd like, when your spouse fails to notice something special you did for him.

That's where big, grace-filled hearts are born.

 Are there certain things you can't imagine being willing to forgive if they were one day thrust upon you? Let God enlarge your heart and your capacity for grace, by choosing to forbear and forgive those "little, everyday offenses" that come your way.

To Higher Ground

*It is the glory of God to conceal things, but the glory of
kings is to search things out.*—Proverbs 25:2

 ONE OF MY FAVORITE VACATION SPOTS is in western
Wyoming, near the Teton mountains. I recall being
there many years ago, and setting out on a walk one
morning through thick, early fog that had caused
the entire mountain range to disappear from sight.
For me, it was a moderately difficult climb. (My idea of fun is
usually more along the lines of working jigsaw puzzles!) As I
gradually worked my way up from the valley floor, starting at
6,500 feet above sea level, my heart started beating fast; I began
to perspire; my legs felt wooden. It took enormous effort to keep
pressing on.

Then all of a sudden, my ascent took me above the mist and
fog, and my efforts were rewarded with an incredible view of the
towering Tetons that hadn't been visible from lower elevations.
No longer was I aware of my racing pulse and tired legs. It was
as if those magnificent, snow-covered mountains had burst forth
that morning from the earth. The view from the top made it
worth it all.

"It is the glory of God to conceal things," to show Himself
beyond our reach and understanding. This is what makes Him
God and us human. Yet at the same time, because of His
gracious desire to make Himself known to the children of men,
our glory is found in devoting ourselves to searching out His
ways, believing that one day our search will be rewarded.

For those who press on to know Him, we have His promise
that one day we will step out of the fog into clear, dazzling
sunlight, beholding a view more magnificent and spectacular
than any we've ever seen before—the sight of our Savior's face—
making all the work and all the waiting far more than worth it.

 *Do you feel fogged in today, unable to see above the clouds of your
circumstances? Know that your climb is taking you to a place
where you can see Him and His glory more clearly.*

A Fresh Glimpse

For I know my transgressions, and my sin is ever before me.—Psalm 51:3

 I'M GUESSING you're probably not in the midst of an affair or involved in some blatant act of spiritual rebellion. But if you've grown up in church, lived a basically moral life, and been surrounded most often by Christian family and friends, one of your greatest personal struggles—like mine, at times—may come from not seeing yourself for the sinner you are, not thinking of your own sins as being truly wicked.

When we cease to sense the seriousness of our sin, however, we also cease to be moved by the wonder of Christ's atoning sacrifice on the cross. Our hearts become dry and crusty. *We've heard that. We know that. We get that. So what?* I know all too well what it's like to hear one more sermon, sing one more song, sit through one more Communion service, observe one more Passion Play, yet be strangely unstirred by the whole thing.

That's why I am so thankful for those moments—painful and gut-wrenching though they may be—when God has struck me with the hard knowledge that my sin equates to spiritual adultery against Him, when I have been overcome by what it cost Him to forgive sins I so casually commit. In the light of His holy presence, sins I had minimized or thought I could "manage" seem depraved and monstrous instead. Shameful. Horrifying.

I'm not suggesting that God intends for His children to live under the weight of transgressions we've already confessed. Thanks to Christ, "where sin abounded, grace abounded much more" (Rom. 5:20 NKJV). But I am convinced that periodically, every believer needs to be given a fresh glimpse of the corruption of indwelling sin, apart from which the cross of Christ ceases to be precious in our eyes.

When was the last time God opened your eyes to see the grievousness of your sin? If it's been awhile, ask God to help you see your sin from His perspective. Then look with fresh wonder at the price Christ paid for that sin on the cross.

Precious Pages

Your statutes have been my songs in the house
of my sojourning.—Psalm 119:54

 MARGARET NIKOL was exiled to the United States from Bulgaria in her midthirties, arriving with only two possessions—her concert violin and a single page from the Bible.

Yes, just one page.

When the Communists had seized power in her home country years earlier, they had ransacked homes and churches, confiscating hymnals and Scriptures—sometimes right out of the hands of those who owned and treasured them. When the authorities burst into the home of one woman in Margaret's church looking for Bibles, she sat on her cherished copy, to keep it from being spotted. After the police left, she went to the church and tore out one page after another, to share with other believers, rather than risking the whole thing being consumed in the fires of hatred.

One of those pages went to Margaret who was only twelve at the time—parts of Genesis 16–17, the promise of God to give Abraham and Sarah a son. She read it over and over and over again.

Imagine her emotions, then, when she found herself in a Christian bookstore ten days after reaching America, walking past shelf after shelf of Bibles—black ones, blue ones, green ones, red ones, little ones, big ones. For twenty-five years she had prayed, "Lord, I so want to have Your Word!" Now, here she stood in the middle of the shop, clutching a Bible to her chest, weeping with the sheer joy of holding in her hands for the first time an entire copy of God's Word.

Margaret's story makes me want to pick up my Bible, just hold it in my hands, and thank God for this precious Book, a privilege that many believers worldwide (and throughout history) cannot fathom. Even more, it makes me want to read it—every page—and cherish it as the treasure it truly is.

 Thank God for the privilege of having such free and easy access to His Word, and ask Him to deepen your love for it.

The Fragrance of Devotion

And when the disciples saw it, they were indignant,
saying, "Why this waste?"—Matthew 26:8

 A NUMBER OF PEOPLE were present the day Mary of Bethany, oblivious to the curious stares and mumblings of those around her, poured out her love to the Lord in a memorable, costly act of worship. And none of those people walked away unaffected.

To the men who wondered, "Why this waste?" her display seemed foolishly extravagant. They did not have eyes or hearts to recognize the infinite worth of worship. They considered all this effort and expense better directed somewhere else, preferably toward a more practical demonstration of devotion.

Jesus, on the other hand, was greatly pleased by the "beautiful thing" she had done for Him (verse 10), while Mary herself experienced the unintentional effect of becoming fragrant with the precious ointment used to anoint His feet, and even more so, as she wiped those feet clean with her hair.

The impact of our worship is much the same. Those who do not understand the nature of an intimate relationship with God may think we're being "wasteful" by spending so much extended time alone in His presence, pouring out our love and gratitude before Him in such unrestrained ways. Think of all the more useful, sensible activities we could invest our time and resources in!

Yet regardless of the reactions of those who misjudge and disapprove of our actions, true worship cannot help but make our own lives more fragrant, perfuming the environment around us, just as it did Mary's. Our homes, our churches, even our places of work and business will bear the sweet scent of our devotion. Most important, of course, the Lord Jesus will be pleased, which ultimately is all that really matters. Worship, offered in its purest form, is guaranteed to make a difference in all directions.

 What are some of the most noticeable marks of those who are intentional worshipers of Jesus? What kind of fragrance exudes from their lives?

The Gift of the Spirit

The earth was without form and void, and darkness was over the face of the deep. And the Spirit of God was hovering over the face of the waters.—Genesis 1:2

 WHAT A PICTURE this verse in the creation account paints of our lives prior to God's intervention. Formless, empty, and dark—utterly incapable of transforming ourselves into something whole or useful. And yet the Spirit was "hovering"—alive and active. And through His initiative, chaos gave way to order, emptiness to fullness, darkness to light.

But that life-giving, redeeming work of God was not just for our initial salvation. Throughout our lives, we remain dependent on Him for everything related to life and godliness. None of us can live—even for a moment—without this ministry of the Spirit, filling up the empty spaces, shining supernatural light into the darkness. Were it not for Him, no aspect of our lives could boast a shred of goodness or a single reason for hope. Yet by His transforming grace and power, He is able to speak life and light into the most dire situation.

A picturesque passage in Isaiah 32 captures His work well, describing a season among God's people that gave all indications of hopelessness. "For the palace is forsaken, the populous city deserted; the hill and the watchtower will become dens forever, a joy of wild donkeys, a pasture of flocks; *until the Spirit is poured upon us from on high;* and the wilderness becomes a fruitful field, and the fruitful field is deemed a forest" (verses 14–15).

Your world may seem dark, confusing, and murky at the moment, whether due to circumstances within or outside of you. But God's Spirit is present; He is actively at work, breathing life into places void of life, making barren places thrive, doing the impossible, filling, energizing, transforming, interceding, revealing Christ. Oh, what cause for hope and joy the blessed Spirit of God gives us!

 How conscious are you of the gift and the role of the Holy Spirit in your life? Are there dark or needy areas of your life you feel helpless to change? How does Genesis 1:2 give you hope?

He Cleaned My Shoes

As each has received a gift, use it to serve one another,
as good stewards of God's varied grace.—1 Peter 4:10

IN THE EARLY 1930s, Dawson Trotman began what became the Navigators ministry, an organization that currently fields thousands of staff members on college campuses and other missionary settings around the world. Among his contributions to the kingdom was being asked by young evangelist Billy Graham in the 1950s to develop a tool for following up with and discipling the masses who were responding to Christ at his large crusades. Dawson Trotman was a great man, known and admired by many great people.

The true greatness of this servant of the Lord is seen in a story told of a visit he once made to Taiwan, in which he hiked with a national pastor back into a mountain village to meet with believers who lived and worshiped there. As the two men walked for miles through the dense trails and heavy underbrush, their shoes became caked with mud. And though the Taiwanese pastor must have had dozens of memories to share of the time he spent one-on-one with this noted American leader, when asked what he remembered most about Dawson Trotman, he said, "The thing I remember most? He cleaned my shoes."

Imagine what that obscure pastor must have thought when he woke up in the morning and realized Dawson Trotman had gotten up before him to wash the mud off his shoes before they resumed their hike. And imagine what others would think about the Lord Jesus if we, His followers, were to be more sensitive and responsive to their practical needs, manifesting the grace and servant heart of Christ—"in order that in everything God may be glorified" (1 Peter 4:11).

What are people most likely to remember about you?
That you cleaned their shoes? Got your hands dirty?
Served them in Jesus' name? You can. And they will.

Your Quiet Place

*I would hurry to find a shelter from the
raging wind and tempest.*—Psalm 55:8

DO YOU KNOW WHAT IT IS TO HAVE *DEVOTIONS* without having *devotion?* I do.

We carry out the routine of reading our Bibles and saying our prayers without truly cultivating a love relationship with Christ. We're busy with a multitude of spiritual activities, yet we've lost perspective of whom we're serving—and why.

We're "devotionless."

I have observed that one of the most telling indicators of this condition is to be found in our response to pressure. Everywhere I go, I meet people who are stressed and strained by life. I see it in their eyes; I hear it in their voices. Too often I see the telltale signs looking back at me in the mirror. I know what it's like to respond to situations out of weariness, speaking from an impatient, demanding spirit. I know what it's like to contend inwardly with God Himself, feeling the tears of frustration fill my eyes, angry at what's happening (or what's not happening).

I know of only one place where this stressed-out, angry, reactionary self can be changed—through a conscious, deliberate, daily choice to sit at Jesus' feet, listen to His Word, receive His love, and invite His transformation. To have devotion.

When we get into His presence, the whole world looks different. When we draw close to His heart, we find mercy where we deserve only judgment; we find forgiveness for all our petty, selfish ways; we find grace for our inadequacies, peace for our troubled hearts, perspective for our distorted views, and mercy that's fresh, though it's been there all along.

In that quiet place, the storm raging around us may not immediately subside. But in Him, we find an eye in the midst of the storm. The storm *within* us is made calm.

*How long has it been since you experienced true devotion
in His presence? What keeps you from entering that quiet
place more often?*

The Name

"Pray then like this: 'Our Father in heaven,
hallowed be your name.'"—Matthew 6:9

 IN OLD TESTAMENT DAYS, Jews sometimes referred to God as "the Name." So greatly did they revere His personal name, *Jehovah*, that they would not even dare to utter it. Just "the Name." That's because God's name carries the weight of His entire character and attributes. Just as our names stand for who we are, God's name stands for who He is.

And supreme among our goals in life is that we would "hallow" that name. Glorify it. Esteem it. Draw others' attention to it. Stand amazed at it and at all it represents. God is jealous for His name—He considers it a serious offense for us to cheapen it or allow anything to dim His glory. That's why one of His first commandments to His people was: "You shall not take the name of the LORD your God in vain" (Ex. 20:7). The opposite of hallowing His name is to profane it, to treat it as something common; to use His name with a lack of respect or to live in such a way as to reflect negatively on His character.

In placing this petition at the beginning of His model prayer, Jesus declared that no other item on our prayer list—no health concern, no relational breakdown, no financial shortfall—nothing should rank higher than this single request. In fact, in praying for our specific needs and concerns, our chief desire should be that His answers would provide an opportunity to shine a spotlight on His magnificent name.

As God's children, how concerned are we about upholding the reputation of our Father's name? And if we who have been given His family name do not treat it with reverence, how can we expect His name to be reverenced in the world? What a tragedy to have it said that "the name of God is blasphemed among the Gentiles because of you" (Rom. 2:24). May His holy name be magnified this day in and through our lives.

 What would it look like for God's name to be hallowed in our world? In our churches? In your home? In your heart?

God Hears

And they said, "Has the LORD indeed spoken only through Moses?
Has he not spoken through us also?" And the LORD heard it.
—Numbers 12:2

 HAVE YOU EVER HAD A GRIPE with someone in a position of spiritual leadership? It may have been your pastor or some other church leader. It may have been a leader in a ministry where you serve. It may have been your husband. Maybe they weren't leading the way you thought they should. Or perhaps you felt your gifts were being overlooked. Whatever the reason, you felt justified in verbalizing your criticism.

Maybe you're nursing one of those "gripes" today.

Then learn a lesson from the life of Miriam, who had become jealous of her little brother Moses, the one God had raised up to lead His people. It seems she was tired of being stuck in the background. Unhappy about her perceived lack of influence. As a result, she grew increasingly critical of Moses, pointing out things that bothered her about him or tweaked her sense of fairness.

And "the LORD heard it"—not just when the words finally came out of her mouth but long before then, when her heart began beating to the drum of discontentment, dissatisfied with the role God had entrusted to her.

God not only heard Miriam; He hears us. He hears our grumblings, whether expressed outwardly or merely nursed inwardly. He knows our resentment, our competitive spirits, our proud comparisons, and our bent to make ourselves look better by putting others down. He knows when our hearts are wanting more (or different) than what He has given.

So let this be a day of awakening and repentance for us—a time to come clean from our proud self-seeking ways, being grateful instead for every opportunity the Lord gives us to serve and for what He is accomplishing through others, lifting up rather than tearing down God's appointed leaders.

May He hear the sound of a humble heart at rest.

 Ask God to show you what is at the heart of any dislike,
resentment, or jealousy you may have displayed toward a leader.

A Charge to Keep

*Blessed is the one who reads aloud the words of this prophecy,
and blessed are those who hear, and who keep what is written in it,
for the time is near.*—Revelation 1:3

YOU'RE PROBABLY familiar with this verse from the prologue to John's Revelation. People tend to have one of two reactions to this intriguing book of the Bible: they either avoid it because of its mystery and imponderable imagery, or they consume themselves in it, trying to piece together the sequences and timetables of future events. Truly, there is much in Revelation that is beyond the understanding of the most astute Bible scholars. Yet the Apocalypse contains many things we can be absolutely sure of—such as the "blessing" of this verse.

And yet even here lies more mystery than immediately meets the eye. I can understand the blessing that comes from *reading* the book of Revelation, as well as from *hearing* it. But *keeping*—how does one "keep" this book with all its cryptic symbols and perplexing plotlines?

What this suggests to me is that the main point of this prophetic book is not a puzzle to be put together: it is a revelation of Jesus Christ, the One we are to *obey*. All the blessings promised in Revelation—from the "marriage supper of the Lamb" (19:9) to the "first resurrection" (20:6) to the washed robes and access to the "tree of life" (22:14)—flow out of God's blessing on those who read, hear, and *keep* His Word. Jesus Himself spoke of the blessings that come to "everyone . . . who hears these words of mine *and does them*" (Matt. 7:24).

Herein, too, lies the key to greater understanding of the mysteries of God's Word: we are given grace to grasp more of His heart and His eternal plans as we *keep* those parts of His Word that we already have come to know and understand.

 There is much in Scripture that is difficult to understand. How faithfully are you obeying the passages you do understand?

Known in High Places

God chose what is foolish in the world to shame the wise; God chose what is weak in the world to shame the strong.—1 Corinthians 1:27

ONE OF MY FAVORITE BIBLICAL ROLE MODELS is Mary of Nazareth. Her life illustrates many characteristics of those God uses to fulfill His redemptive purposes in our world.

In spite of all the attention historically accorded to Mary, the fact is, her background was pretty unspectacular. She was not from a wealthy or notable family. When the angel appeared to her, she was just a young teenage girl engaged to be married, doubtless doing what engaged girls do—dreaming of being married, of the home she and Joseph would live in, of the family and future they would have. I don't think she was expecting her life to be used in any exceptional way.

The significance of this woman who played such a significant role in God's redemptive story was not based on any of the things our world values so highly—background, physical beauty, intelligence, education, natural gifts and abilities. *What gave her life significance was her relationship to Jesus.* We would not be aware of her existence at all if not for the fact that she was related to Him. That is what made all the difference in her life—and it is what makes all the difference in our lives as well.

Don't assume you have to be extraordinary to be used by God. You don't have to have exceptional gifts, talents, abilities, or connections. God specializes in using ordinary people whose limitations and weaknesses make them ideal showcases for His greatness and glory.

Your true identity is not found in a job, a mate, or a child, in a position or a possession. What gives your life value and significance is the indwelling life of Christ. Your relationship with Him and your responsiveness to His calling in your life are what make you usable for His kingdom purposes.

Do you sometimes feel inferior to others who serve Christ so visibly and remarkably? Thank God that there is no limit to how He can use anyone who knows and is available to Him.

First Love

*"But I have this against you, that you have abandoned
the love you had at first."*—Revelation 2:4

 IF SOMEONE were to stop by your home unannounced
today, would you scurry to close off certain rooms so
your guest couldn't see what's inside? We all know the
feeling of hoping we remembered to pull the door shut
on some of those living areas that we aren't exactly
eager for anyone to see.

The same motivation that causes us to partition certain parts
of our home from visitors' eyes can also make us want to board
up certain sections of our lives from God. Yet no barrier can
keep Him from seeing inside the innermost parts of our hearts,
just as He saw into the inner recesses of a hardworking, long-
suffering church in the ancient city of Ephesus and observed
a compartment they undoubtedly hoped would avoid scrutiny.

For even with their enduring and industrious reputation,
even with their great patience and courage in standing up to
the high risks of Christian faith in their pagan culture, they had
neglected one important area that couldn't help but affect their
whole house.

Yes, they *served* God, but they were no longer doing so out of
true *love* for God or others.

Could the same be said of us? We may make a good
impression when it comes to doctrinal soundness and dutiful
service. People may say nice things about what we've done,
about the nice "decorating choices" we've made. Yet our house
stands in a "fallen" condition unless we "repent," take time to
"remember" how it used to be (verse 5)—back when we loved
Him with all our heart—and rekindle our "first love" for Christ.

Of all the rooms you keep spruced up, make sure your love
for Christ never grows cluttered. And remember that the interior
rooms of your heart—your motives and passions—are never out
of view of the all-seeing, all-knowing eyes of Christ.

 *Ask God to show you what He sees as He examines your heart.
Is your service motivated by pure, devoted love for Jesus?*

Fear Not

"Do not fear what you are about to suffer."—Revelation 2:10

LIVE LONG ENOUGH, and you'll know—life is a seedbed of suffering. "Man is born to trouble as the sparks fly upward" (Job 5:7). There's no getting around it.

But don't run past the counsel of Christ to the first-century church in Smyrna, a group that would later produce such notable martyrs as Polycarp, burned at the stake for his allegiance to Christ. Christ's words are reassuring to those of any era who are called to lay down their lives for the faith. But they also speak to each of us as we face painful losses, harrowing challenges, and unsettling threats to our norms and preferences.

"Do not fear," Jesus says, "what you are about to suffer."

Our hearts are so prone to fear. We fear what we *don't* know. We fear what we *do* know. We fear things that are happening now, things that might happen in the future, and even a host of things that will never happen at all. The word for "fear" in this verse is one from which we derive our word *phobia*, originally meaning "to be put to flight." The specter or presence of trouble makes us want to run and hide.

But as followers of Christ, we do not have to live on the run. For if we appropriately fear God, we have no need to fear the threats of man, the valley of suffering, or the shadow of death. Wherever we go, whatever we do, our God is there with us. He "know[s] our tribulation" (Rev. 2:9), and His promises will prove to be stronger than whatever pressures or losses may lie ahead.

"When I am afraid, I put my trust in you" (Ps. 56:3). Say it: "I will not fear."

What anticipated troubles and concerns give you the most reason for fear today? You can confidently choose not to fear whatever may lie ahead, for your life and your future are safely in His hands.

Jealous Anger

"And to the angel of the church in Pergamum write: 'The words of him who has the sharp two-edged sword.'"—Revelation 2:12

 YOU MAY HAVE NOTICED we've been touring some of the cities of the ancient world the past few days, hearing again Christ's messages from Revelation to those believers who called these places home. One of those was the capitol city of Pergamum, home to wealth and fashion, learning and the arts, as well as a center of pagan and imperial worship.

To the Christians in this thriving city, Jesus presented Himself as One possessing the "sharp two-edged sword" of God's truth, willing to use this sword even against His own people (verse 16) if they continued to dabble in or tolerate the false teachings and sinful practices of the day.

To hear Jesus present Himself so "sharply" to His people may not seem to square with the tender, loving nature we've come to expect from Him. But in His Word, God declares Himself a "jealous" God (Ex. 20:5). He abides no rivals. Therefore, whenever we operate by the misguided thinking of our culture, making lifestyle choices that defy God's covenant authority over us, He is offended by our spiritual adultery. He is wounded by our heart attachments to other lovers. So His anger is a righteous, even welcome anger, designed not to destroy us but to separate us from all that prevents us from enjoying the full blessings of loyalty and faithfulness to Him.

We should be thankful, then, that our God loves us enough to pursue our affections so violently, restoring us to right relationship with Him, realigning us with His truth, returning us to spiritual health. Rather than being disillusioned or confused by that purifying, refining process, we should find safety and security inside His fiery, jealous love.

 How have you experienced the sword of truth cutting into your divided loyalties? Thank Him for His willingness to use it when needed.

Hang in There

"The one who conquers and who keeps my works until the end, to him I will give authority over the nations."—Revelation 2:26

 DO YOU EVER GET TIRED OF FEELING that you're constantly going against the flow? This is especially true when you're swimming upstream not only against the world but at times even against the culture within the church—the people we ought to be able to feel the most comfortable with. Yet with so much unwise, unbalanced teaching being proclaimed and accepted these days, with so many troubling practices and lifestyles masquerading as normal Christian living, the tension is always there. And from what my mailbox and in-box tell me, I'm not the only one who feels the strain.

It would be so much easier just to live and let live, to avoid running the risk of appearing cantankerous, contentious, or narrow. But as tiring as it may be to continually have to defend truth from error and to uphold standards of holiness in a permissive culture, and as much as we may wish we weren't considered strange for not going along with the flow, we are called by God to "hold fast" the truth He has revealed to us in Scripture (Rev. 2:25). Though the path of least resistance is seductive and promises a more relaxed journey, we are meant to be on the watch for that which can lead us and others astray. That's part of our calling.

But thankfully, as Jesus reminded His followers in the industrial city of Thyatira, the perseverance that comes from true, saving faith—God's empowerment to go against the grain over the long haul—comes with promises that make it well worth the effort. Those who learn to rule their passions in this age, those who care about His kingdom coming and His will being done on earth as it is in heaven, will one day rule with Christ in the age to come. Then the weariness and resistance will be forever over.

 In what settings and over what issues do you find yourself feeling this kind of battle fatigue? What can keep you going when you want to throw in the towel?

The Smell Test

"I know your works. You have the reputation of being alive, but you are dead."—Revelation 3:1

 SITTING ON THE PIANO LID in my living room is a lovely arrangement of flowers, attractively arranged inside a clear glass vase. Their fresh appearance makes you want to lean your face near and take in the fragrance—which some people actually do. One person even commented on how great they smelled. But these flowers, as you've likely guessed, are not real. While they give every outward indication of being authentic, they are no more alive than the dust they collect.

And neither are some of us.

Sadly, this is true of too many of our churches. True of too many of our families. True of what happens inside the four walls in too many of our homes—lives that are not the same in private as they are by reputation. Artificial.

Jesus' words to the church in Sardis expressed this very concern. Many of those first-century church members were apparently like an alarming number of people who line the seat cushions of our churches today—people who are nice enough, who look and sound Christian, but have never truly bowed the knee and surrendered their lives to the Savior.

Others, though perhaps redeemed, had allowed apathy and complacency to wear down the sharp edges on their gratitude for God's favor, the awareness of their need for His grace. They may still be active, but deep down where it really counts, they are passionless. Busy about everything except cultivating closeness to Christ.

Could the same be said of your life? Please don't move beyond the conviction of the Holy Spirit, not if He is speaking to you about areas of your life where spiritual vibrancy has given way to private indifference and coldness. Artificiality can sometimes be hard to spot. But Christ is not deceived by our outward appearance. He knows.

 Have you stopped to rehearse the life-giving power of the gospel recently? What evidence is there that you are spiritually alive?

Open Door Policy

"Behold, I have set before you an open door,
which no one is able to shut."—Revelation 3:8

 THE ANCIENT CITY OF PHILADELPHIA, built along a key trade route that emptied into the eastern reaches of the world, was basically a "missionary" outpost, designed to transport Greek culture to a new, rugged continent. But for the church that worshiped there, Christ said He had much more to accomplish than the city fathers envisioned. He intended to give them an "open door" of service and kingdom influence, the opportunity to advance the gospel through whatever avenues He chose to unlock.

He promises to do the same through His people in our day.

Yet you may feel limited from pursuing the type of ministry you wish to have. You may feel hemmed in by responsibilities and obstacles that are shutting down what you sense to be His will for you, the direction you believe He means to take you. The doors may be open for some people, it seems, but not for you.

Then wait patiently for Him to turn the key—when the time is right, when you're fully prepared, when the climate for fruitful ministry is most conducive. And be faithful and content with the doors He has opened to you already—doors that may not exactly be the ones you were looking for, but if turned by the keys of His wisdom and power, are places He can use you effectively today.

Those doors we try to force open will carry the marks and nicks of our own selfish ambition and shortsightedness. But when we wait for Christ to open a door of service for us, we can be sure He will grant all the grace we need to handle every challenge that lies on the other side.

 Which doors of ministry has Christ opened to you in this season?
Had you perhaps lost sight of these by looking for others?

You're Being Pursued

"Behold, I stand at the door and knock. If anyone hears my voice and opens the door, I will come in to him and eat with him, and he with me."—Revelation 3:20

 THE QUESTION IS OFTEN ASKED, given the context of this familiar verse from Christ's message to the Laodicean church, whether He was speaking to backslidden believers or (as is more popularly preached and understood) to the unregenerate in need of a Savior. I think the answer is probably both. Any person in either of these conditions has pushed Christ to the outside walls of his or her life; Jesus' rule is unheeded and His presence unwanted in their heart.

Has that scenario ever defined *you*—even in recent days?

And yet where do we find Him in this picture—this One we've sought to distance ourselves from, this grace-filled God we've spurned through our sins, idolatry, and rebellion? He is knocking. Approaching. Pursuing. Seeking to reprove and discipline, yes. Calling us to zealous repentance, yes. But all because He loves us and desires fellowship with us (verse 19). He draws near that we might reciprocate His active, attentive love, experiencing new life and intimacy with Him.

The fact is, if He did not pursue us, we would never pursue Him. Man's fallen condition is such that we would rather starve on our own empty calories than dine on the Bread of Life. We'd rather die of thirst than admit our need for Living Water. And die we would—if not for a God who comes to our doorstep, stands outside our living space, and humbles Himself to knock for admittance from those of us who should be on our knees begging Him to enter in.

This is love. The amazing grace of our long-suffering Savior, who patiently waits for us to let Him fill our lives with Himself.

 Is Christ knocking at your heart's door today?
How will you respond?

Can't To-Do It All?

"I glorified you on earth, having accomplished the work that you gave me to do."—John 17:4

 RARELY CAN I SAY AT THE END OF THE DAY that I have completed the work I set out to do that day. To the contrary, I frequently drop into bed at night with a long, mental list of the unfinished tasks I had hoped to take care of that day. All of which makes me wonder: How was it possible for Jesus to finish His life's work—the entire plan of redemption—in such a short period of time, only a few years? Talk about a to-do list!

We find a clue in Jesus' own words—a powerful truth that sets us free from the bondage of stress and frustration about all the things we have to do. Notice what work Jesus completed: "the work that *you* [His Father] gave me to do." *That is the secret.* Jesus didn't finish everything His disciples wanted Him to do, or everything the multitudes wanted Him to do. But He did finish the work that *God* gave Him to do.

There will seldom be enough time in a twenty-four-hour day for you to do everything that is on your to-do list. For sure, there will never be enough time for everything that is on everyone else's list for your life! You can't spend time with every person who wants to talk, read all the books you'd like, and tackle every project you're interested in, all while keeping every room in your home presentable for guests who might drop by.

But what a relief to realize you don't have to. All you have to do is the work God assigns to you. And believe it or not, there is always time (and grace) to do everything that is on *His* to-do list for you.

 Ask God to give you wisdom to know what is on His agenda for you to do today, and to give you the ability to say no to "good things" that He has not assigned to you at this time.

Peace in Our Lifetime?

The government shall be upon his shoulder, and his name shall be called Wonderful Counselor, Mighty God, Everlasting Father, Prince of Peace.—Isaiah 9:6

 BACK IN THE EARLY 1970S, there were some who thought Secretary of State Henry Kissinger was going to usher in world peace through his far-reaching diplomatic efforts. Then, in 1977, media mogul Ted Turner announced his intentions to give a billion dollars to promote the work of world peace through the United Nations. And perhaps you remember the day in March 2004 when the Reverend Sun Myung Moon and his wife were crowned the King and Queen of Peace in the Dirksen Senate Office Building in Washington, DC, surrounded by more than a dozen members of Congress, religious leaders, and other distinguished guests.

Obviously, the desire for peace is universal—even if the only true source of peace isn't universally sought or understood.

For if people really knew this Prince of Peace—this *Sar Shalom*, the true governor or ruler of peace—they would already be experiencing a restored relationship with God, the only cure for our sin-sick hearts and souls. They would even now possess the ability to infuse forgiveness into their broken relationships, providing the key ingredient that can break the pattern of estrangement. And they would be fully assured, by God's redeeming grace, of being privileged and present when peace finally does come again to earth, when Christ is enthroned as the King He already is and will one day be revealed to be.

Imagine that. It's really coming. Peace in our (eternal) lifetime. But only through the Prince of Peace.

 How can our lives display a foretaste of this lasting peace, even in times when true peace seems so elusive?

Merciful and Mighty

*"To the L*ORD *your God belong heaven and the heaven*
*of heavens . . . yet the L*ORD *set his heart in love on*
your fathers."—Deuteronomy 10:14–15

 Many people and religions in the world today would tell you otherwise, but the God of the Bible is the one true God, the omnipotent God—the "Mighty God" of Isaiah 9:6. The Hebrew term for this title is *El Gibbor*, a name that speaks of His strength, His power, His valor. God's authority is untouchable, beyond all challenge.

Ask the children of Israel at the base of Mount Sinai if this description of Him is true. After the incident with the golden calf, when more than three thousand fell in judgment, the people realized God was an unrivaled champion. The substitute idol they had constructed to replace Him ended up being burned to a fine powder and poured into a mountain brook. No wonder Moses found an agreeable audience afterward when he declared God "the great, the mighty," the awesome "God of gods" (Deut. 10:17).

But perhaps even more astounding is that this "God in three persons," as the reverential hymn proclaims, is both "merciful and mighty." The same God who saw His tablets of Law shattered in Moses' holy disgust chose to provide a second set so His people wouldn't have to live without them. He who lashed out in retribution never broke covenant with His chosen remnant.

We, too, will continue to find that we cannot separate these two glorious aspects of God's nature. He is as fierce as He is loyal. He is as mighty as He is merciful. And that mighty, merciful God is the One who humbled Himself, took on our humanity, and came to this earth to save us—lawbreakers all—from our sin.

Let us remember that the baby in the manger is the mighty God. And let us worship and adore.

 Why do we need a God who is both mighty and merciful? How have you experienced both His might and His mercy in your life?

Eternally His

"When he established the heavens, I was there."—Proverbs 8:27

ETERNITY is a concept we have no way to process or get our minds around. God always was. He always will be. Past tense, future tense—both are basically irrelevant to a God who is ever-present.

When I think of Christ being everlasting, I think of the Old Testament character Melchizedek, described for us through his encounter with Abraham in Genesis 14 and interpreted further in several chapters of Hebrews. We're told that he was a priest, the king of Salem, but more importantly that he represented a type of Christ, "without father or mother or genealogy, having neither beginning of days nor end of life, but resembling the Son of God," continuing as a "priest forever" (Heb. 7:3).

Eternal. Everlasting.

No, we may not exactly understand the idea, but by God's grace we can certainly enjoy it—relationship with a Priest and King who has always existed, who will never die, and who can never be replaced. "Of the increase of his government," the Scripture declares, "there will be no end" (Isa. 9:7). He is eternal in His person, in His attributes, and—thankfully—in His continual ministry to us.

That's why Paul could say with such confidence that "he who began a good work in you will bring it to completion" (Phil. 1:6), because our God will still be living and active to the "day of Jesus Christ" and beyond. That's why when you and I fall—which we often do—we forever have a "great priest over the house of God" who "always lives to make intercession" for us (Heb. 10:21; 7:25).

We are blessedly, eternally His.

 Spend some time today celebrating the fact that in a world where nothing lasts forever, your God does. Your God is!

Divine Visitation

*And they glorified God, saying, "A great prophet has risen among us!"
and "God has visited his people!"*—Luke 7:16

 THE THEME OF DIVINE VISITATION runs throughout both
Old and New Testaments. We notice it near the end
of Genesis when Joseph, seeing ahead into the slavery
his descendants would one day endure in Egypt, said
to his sons and brothers, "I am about to die, but God
will *visit* you and bring you up out of this land to the land that he
swore to Abraham, to Isaac, and to Jacob" (50:24).

In God's sovereign timing, deliverance from Egyptian
bondage would not take place until some four hundred years
later. But when He did arrive, it was with awesome power
and tender compassion; He declared that He had "seen the
affliction" of His people and had "heard their cry" for relief
(Ex. 3:7). This wasn't a social call; it was the history-changing,
redemptive act of almighty God, concerned about His children
and coming to their rescue.

By the time of Luke 1, four hundred years had again passed
since the voice of the prophets had fallen silent in Israel, a season
of long, spiritual famine in the land—"not a famine of bread,
nor a thirst for water, but of hearing the words of the LORD"
(Amos 8:11).

Yet in the fullness of time, at the end of this darkened
passage, God once again strode into time and space, sending
word to a priest named Zechariah that his soon-to-arrive son
would herald the coming of the Son of God. "Blessed be the
Lord God of Israel," Zechariah would later say, "for he has
visited and redeemed his people and has raised up a horn of
salvation for us" (Luke 1:68–69).

Seen against this historical backdrop, Christmas takes on
a whole new meaning. Not a nice holiday for cookies and get-
togethers. But a divine visitation, necessary to deliver us from
our spiritual captivity and meet our desperate need.

 *How might this biblical perspective alter the way
you celebrate Christmas this year?*

Christmas Songs

*Serve the LORD with gladness! Come into his presence
with singing!*—Psalm 100:2

 SINGING HAS ALWAYS BEEN an important part of biblical faith and practice, a frequent expression of worship and praise. But it's interesting, of all the songs captured in Scripture, how many of them are clustered at the beginning of Luke's gospel.

They're not just songs; they're Christmas songs.

No, they're not the familiar carols we sing at church during the Sundays of December. And they're definitely not the "Let It Snow" variety that may touch us in sentimental ways but can do nothing to move our souls with true wonder. These jubilant songs from the pages of God's Word seek to scale the vast reaches of His greatness, glory, and goodness. They celebrate His redemptive purposes and plans. They resound with awe and majesty at the coming of our Lord in a Bethlehem manger.

They . . . sing!

Elizabeth's song—sometimes called the *Beatitude* (Luke 1:42–45). Mary's song—the *Magnificat* (verses 46–55). Zechariah's song—*Benedictus* (verses 68–79). The angel's announcement to the shepherds (2:10–12), followed by the *Gloria* of the angel chorus (2:14). And then there's Simeon's song of worship to the child Jesus in the temple (verses 29–32)—known as the *Nunc Dimittis*, from the Latin of the hymn's opening phrase, "Now you let depart." Six in all.

So even if this year's holiday season feels unusually labored and exhausting—perhaps tinged with feelings of sadness or loss, with difficult circumstances that cast a shadow over what was once an exuberant season of celebration—maybe the best way to find your joy rekindled is to settle back into those first two chapters of Luke again, take your place in the gathering choir, and join the rousing offering of worship going forth in praise of our Immanuel.

Christmas is for singing.

 Why do you think singing is so important to God and to His people? Do you habitually sing to the Lord—not just at Christmastime but throughout the year?

The God Who Stoops

Who is like the Lord our God, the One who sits enthroned on high, who stoops down to look on the heavens and the earth?—Psalm 113:5–6 NIV

 FATHER DAMIEN was a Belgian priest in the 1800s who left his comfortable home to live in a quarantined village of lepers on the Hawaiian island of Molokai. For sixteen years he served these outcasts of society, learning their language, building homes for them, organizing schools and choirs. Rather than being careful to keep his distance, he willingly drew himself into their lives, bandaging their wounds, sharing the same serving dishes at mealtime, touching the untouchable.

Then one day he rose before his congregation, a group of the terminally diseased whose lives had been so deeply impacted by his love and compassion, and began his sermon by referring to *"we lepers"*—not just those who sat before him listening but also the man who stood preaching. No longer was he merely living among them; he now shared their fatal diagnosis. He would live as they lived and die as they died.

Touching as it is, this story is only a faint glimpse of what our Lord Jesus has done for us—humbling Himself to come and live among us in this sin-infected world, condescending to our pitiful condition, taking on a frail human body, becoming as one of us, reaching out to and serving the most hopeless and needy, and ultimately going to the cross, taking our sin upon Himself, and dying our death.

This One so majestic that He must "stoop" even to gaze on the glories of heaven traveled all the way down into our meager existence, seeking our welfare at the expense of His own.

How unthinkable, then, that we should ever exalt ourselves, defend our rights, or resist His right to order our lives. We have been saved only because He saw fit to lower Himself so that we might be set on high with Him.

 Lord, we cannot fathom the gap You stepped across to reconcile us to the Father. Give us a fresh sense of wonder at what this means.

When He Comes

*Behold, he is coming with the clouds, and every eye will see him,
even those who pierced him.*—Revelation 1:7

 CHRIST CAME THE FIRST TIME as an infant, born in time and space, small and weak. He will return as the everlasting King, great in strength and glory.

When He came the first time, His glory was shrouded and concealed from human view; when He comes the second time, His glory will shine brightly. His first coming was obscure, witnessed by a few poor shepherds and the like. Few recognized who He was. At His second coming, every eye will see Him, and all will know who He is.

He came the first time as the Lamb of God; when He returns, it will be as the Lion of the tribe of Judah. At His first coming, He was judged and condemned to die by sinful men; when He returns, it will be as the Judge, to execute justice and judgment on all who have refused to repent of their sins.

When He came the first time, only a few bowed to pay Him homage; when He returns, every knee will bow and every tongue confess that Jesus Christ is Lord. The first time, He washed the feet of His disciples; when He returns, all His enemies will be under His feet.

The first time He came, He wore a crown of thorns; when He returns, He will be crowned with many crowns, the King upon His throne. He came the first time to make peace between God and man; when He returns, it will be to make war on those who have rebelled against Him.

He came the first time as our suffering Savior; He will return as our sovereign, reigning Lord.

Hallelujah! Come quickly, Lord Jesus!

 How near does His victorious return seem to you today? What change of focus does this soon-and-very-soon reality bring to your current situation? How clearly does this glorious hope characterize your life?

Priority Seating

*For the LORD gives wisdom; from his mouth come knowledge
and understanding.*—Proverbs 2:6

 AS WE PREPARE TO CLOSE OUR TIME TOGETHER, having met with God each day in this *Quiet Place*, I'm thoughtful of what we'll need as we launch out into another year of serving Him, serving others, and bringing glory to His name. Truth is, we will fill our time in the coming year with *something*, just as in all the years before. We'll live out the true priorities that exist at the core of who we are, despite whatever priorities we profess. But will they be the *right* priorities? Will they help us stay purposeful, intentional, and focused on God's plan for us?

They can—if we keep first things first.

So for these final ten days, I'd like to take that one word—P-R-I-O-R-I-T-I-E-S—and help you build a biblical platform for starting into the new year on a strong, spiritual footing.

I'm letting "P" stand for *prayer.* Now you may have been hoping for something a little more practical; but prayer is actually the starting point for learning how to handle both the expected and the unexpected, the highs and the lows, the erratic rhythm of everyday life.

In prayer, we ask God for several things: for wisdom; for clear direction; for help in being faithful, disciplined, and obedient in the way we use our time. As we seek Him in prayer, I believe He will give us our marching orders for this season of life, ordering our steps in accordance with His unique plans for us.

What is birthed in our hearts through prayer will flow into the hours and days that eventually add up to our lifetime. Prayer makes sure we live with a humble acknowledgment of our need for His grace, knowing He is our only hope for staying on course and fulfilling our created purpose.

 If you're not already doing so, begin asking God regularly to show you His agenda and priorities, to order your schedule and your steps, and to fulfill His kingdom purposes in and through your life.

Steady Diet

I have treasured the words of His mouth more than my necessary food.—Job 23:12 NASB

NOT UNTIL ABOUT A HUNDRED YEARS AGO did the word *priorities* (plural) even exist. *Priority* was simply a singular word, from the Latin *prior*, meaning "first." And only one thing can be first. Right? Leave it to our own harried generations to turn "priority" into a dozen competing alternatives vying for our attention.

That's why, to avoid becoming fractured and distracted, it's so important to *review God's priorities for our lives*—the first "R" of P-R-I-O-R-I-T-I-E-S. And the number one priority for every child of God—married, single, young, old, male, female, in every season of life—is our walk with God. Everything else flows out of that. When that is in order, our other priorities will become clear. If we're too busy to nurture our relationship with God, then we're too busy.

So don't try navigating even a single day without spending time in the Scripture, listening to Him speak, getting to know His heart, and letting His Spirit illuminate and personalize His Word to you. No exceptions.

The practice of centering our lives and days around seeking Him was first impressed on me by my dad who took this so seriously that his practice was: "No Bible reading, no breakfast." Even if the typical demands of your morning preclude you from opening the Word first thing, be sure to set aside some moments each day—morning, noon, or night—to reorient your life around the Lord.

As you do, ask yourself if knowing and glorifying God is the chief reason you draw breath into your body. Based on the way you spend your time (including your "free time"), is He your true priority? The more consistently you spend time in His Word and on your knees before Him, the more your answer to that question will bring joy to His heart. And yours.

 What pulls you away most often from getting into God's Word? Do you really believe these competing attractions are worth the price you've paying?

Good Measure

*Examine me, O LORD, and try me; test my mind
and my heart.*—Psalm 26:2 NASB

TO THE FIRST OF THREE "I'S" in the word P-R-I-O-R-I-T-I-E-S, I've assigned the task of taking *inventory*, determining in practical, measurable terms whether our lives truly bear out the chief purposes God has given us to pursue. How easily we lose sight of His bigger picture while buried in our daily minutiae and details, then wonder why we don't feel like we're getting anywhere, no matter how hard we push and pedal.

One eye-opening way to gauge where you stand is to keep a time log of a full week's activities in fifteen- or thirty-minute increments, then looking back and evaluating how much of your time you're actually spending on the things you're meant to be doing. Which of these activities are contributing to fulfilling the priorities God has established for you in this particular season of life? (If you have children at home, you may want to go through the same exercise in relation to their activities and those of your family.)

You may find, depending on the patterns that show up from doing this exercise, that you're just letting life happen, and that you need to be more intentional about your choices. Or you may discover that your life is being shaped more by others' expectations than by God's priorities—that some of the things you're doing are based on guilt, or a desire for approval, or a need to make a good impression.

What you're seeking in the end is the freedom to be who God is calling you to be—not just in theory but in practice. For when your activities have a reason—God's reason—you can be less affected by the opinions of those who may not understand. You can experience the pleasure of God by knowing you're trusting Him to direct your steps and to use your life as He sees fit.

As we head into a new year, consider taking a week sometime soon to keep a log of how you're using your time. Ask the Lord if there are any activities you are involved in that may not be on His agenda for this season of your life.

First Order of the Day

Direct my footsteps according to your word.—Psalm 119:133 NIV

 UNLESS YOUR SITUATION IS UNUSUAL THIS YEAR or for some reason you're doing your gift-giving exchanges at another time, this day likely orbits around one central event and objective—celebrating Christmas. And you wouldn't dream of letting anything interfere with that.

But why isn't every day so carefully prioritized? Why, when we know we're capable of letting something like Christmas completely arrange the choices we make, do we not diligently endeavor to keep the rest of our lives so similarly focused—to *order* our schedule according to God's priorities for our lives (borrowing the "O" from our acrostic of P-R-I-O-R-I-T-I-E-S)?

I'm reminded of the old teaching illustration you've perhaps seen demonstrated yourself, where a conference speaker begins filling an empty jar with various pea-sized marbles or pieces of gravel, which eventually take up most all the space inside the container, leaving no room for the bigger balls—the bigger rocks—that need to be placed inside somehow.

But if the big rocks go in first—if the most important priorities are in place before adding anything else—a lot of the smaller items will still fit into the jar as well, managing to work their way into a spot around the two or three main ingredients. And if for some reason the "jar" of your day simply cannot accommodate these minor incidentals, then you've only missed out on something of small consequence, not the much larger loss of seeing a key priority left out for yet another day.

You've likely carefully planned the activities of this Christmas Day. May you allow His Word and His Spirit to order *every* day around His kingdom priorities.

 Do you often find yourself frittering away your life with nonessentials, rather than ordering your days around those things that matter most?

Tyranny of the Urgent

"I am doing a great work and cannot come down."—Nehemiah 6:3

As THE LEADER OF THE EFFORT TO REBUILD the walls of Jerusalem after the ransacking of Nebuchadnezzar's armies and the Jewish exile in Babylon, Nehemiah faced many distractions to his work. Perhaps the hardest to resist were the urgent demands by his enemies to come down and meet with them, to engage in a discussion about what in the world he was doing.

Though realizing their intentions were to cause him harm, I suspect Nehemiah might have welcomed the chance to stand eye to eye with those who had repeatedly opposed his efforts and attacked his motives. But he had spoken with them once before (Neh. 2:19–20), and realized that any further talking was a waste of both his time and breath. So despite their repeated appeals to draw him away from his central focus, he resisted the interruption.

Resist. That's another of the key principles—the second "R" in the word P-R-I-O-R-I-T-I-E-S—that we must master if we hope to fulfill what God has placed us here to do.

Jesus Himself demonstrated this principle when, upon hearing that His good friend Lazarus had fallen deathly ill, He chose to resist what everyone was surely expecting of Him—to drop whatever He was doing and rush to the dying man's bedside. But Jesus knew what everyone else would soon discover—that He had something much more important to accomplish (raising Lazarus from the dead!) than would be possible if he jumped up to fulfill the urgent demand (keeping his friend from dying). He knew the difference between being driven by others' insistence and steadfastly following the will of His Father.

If we desire to fulfill His kingdom agenda for our lives, we must resist the tyranny of the urgent, choosing to slay dragons rather than merely kill houseflies.

Is your day commonly redirected by interruptions that seem more pressing than the matter at hand? How can you discern whether God is using those interruptions to redirect your schedule or whether they are distracting you from focusing on His priorities for your day?

Please Advise

Where there is no guidance, a people falls, but in an
abundance of counselors there is safety.—Proverbs 11:14

QUICK REVIEW TODAY before moving on to the second half of our ten-day consideration of how to live by wise, godly P-R-I-O-R-I-T-I-E-S. We've looked at the importance of *prayer* and the need to *review* God's priorities for our lives, followed by taking *inventory* of how we're using our time, the deliberate *ordering* of each day, and the need to *resist* seemingly urgent demands that threaten to derail us from what is truly important.

A sixth and vital instrument to add to this toolbox is the practice of seeking *input* from others in helping us determine God's priorities for various seasons of our lives. Seeking (and heeding) godly counsel is a mark of humility. And God pours out His grace on the humble.

If you are married, the counsel of your mate can be an invaluable source of up-close perspective and help in evaluating and ordering your priorities. The protection of leaning on each other, learning from one another, is part of the blessing God provides through marriage.

Whether married or not, God has likely placed around you an array of people who have much to offer by way of life experience, insight, and helpful counsel—wisdom you may never tap into if you don't ask for it. I can't count the number of times I've solicited input from others about my priorities— ranging from my schedule to my personal giving—asking questions, listening, and being led by God's Spirit as He uses them to speak into my life.

As followers of Christ, we're part of a family. And we need each other's help. Don't try to make it alone. Never think of yourself as too smart nor your situation too complicated to seek and receive wise counsel and put it into practice.

 Who in your life could help you think through specific matters related to your priorities in this season? Why don't you ask them?

Time Management

Look carefully then how you walk, not as unwise but as wise, making the best use of the time, because the days are evil.—Ephesians 5:15–16

THE BIBLE frequently describes contrasting viewpoints —obedience and disobedience, faith and fear, trust and doubt. The passage above compares the mindset of the wise with that of the foolish.

Whereas a fool lives for the moment, without thought for the future implications of his choices, wise people make their decisions against the backdrop of eternity, considering how their choices will make a difference in the long run. *Will this matter a hundred years from now? Five years from now?* That's how a wise person thinks.

Fools live for themselves, don't care to be reflective, and are often careless and undisciplined in the way they handle their time. The wise, by comparison, live for the glory of God, aren't afraid to examine themselves closely, and are thoughtful and intentional in how they steward the resources that have been entrusted to them.

You might say—picking up the "T" from P-R-I-O-R-I-T-I-E-S —they *take advantage of the time* God gives them.

This may mean catching up on a thank-you note or two in the ten minutes while you're waiting on a child at school or soccer practice. It may mean, rather than leafing through the months-old magazines lying around in a doctor's office waiting room, you bring along your own reading material instead— the book or correspondence you can never seem to get around to. It may also mean spending a half hour coloring with your preschooler or listening when a friend wants to talk, realizing that those moments are not wasted time but are opportunities for nurturing life and relationship.

Does this mean we can't ever take time off or just "have fun"? Of course not. But it is a call to be wise, to redeem the time and make the most of every opportunity, always keeping eternity in view.

Does your overall use of time suggest that you are a wise or foolish person? How wise and intentional are you about the use of those "spare moments" that arise in the course of your day?

Hounding Your Foxes

"Catch the foxes for us, the little foxes that spoil the vineyards,
for our vineyards are in blossom."—Song of Solomon 2:15

 LIKE ME, you probably have certain spaces in your house where things just tend to collect and pile up. "Junk drawers," we call them. Some people even have "junk rooms" that never seem to get unpacked, a landing place for the cast-offs that don't have anywhere else to go.

If we're not careful, however, our whole *lives* can become inundated with unnecessary stuff and time stealers. Some of these things may have been useful at one time, but now they're just taking up room we can't really afford to spare. Like the "little foxes" mentioned in Scripture, they can steal us blind until we get serious about catching and dealing with them.

The "foxes" that steal precious time from your life may be the obvious ones—TV, movies, social media. But some may be more subtle things, like certain relationships that consume lots of time and focus but are unfruitful or worse. Or perhaps it's your children's nonstop schedules—activities intended to keep them well-rounded but that only end up burning you—and them—out.

Other "foxes" that can snatch away bits and pieces of life are the toxic attitudes we allow to hang around in our hearts—the moodiness, complaining, and ingratitude that sap our energy while multiplying the time it takes to get everything done.

Look around. You'll spot even more.

If you'll do this—if you'll *identify the "little foxes"* that rob you of time, margin, and spiritual vitality and if you'll purpose to eliminate those things that are unnecessarily "cluttering" your life—you won't have to climb over so much junk to stay flexible to God's agenda. When He calls, you'll be ready.

 Name some of those foxes in your life. How might you be more
fruitful if they were eliminated? What steps could you take as
this year draws to a close to begin dealing with them?

Get Here

I know that nothing is better for them than to rejoice, and to do good in their lives, and also that every man should eat and drink and enjoy the good of all his labor—it is the gift of God.—Ecclesiastes 3:12–13 NKJV

 WE COME TODAY TO THE NEXT TO LAST LETTER in the word P-R-I-O-R-I-T-I-E-S, and to a spiritual discipline that's become nearly extinct in our whiz-bang world of at-your-fingertips technology. With the possibility of another incoming message being only moments away at any point of the day or night, with our pockets abuzz from cell phone gadgets drawing our attention away from the flesh-and-blood people right in front of us, it has become almost impossible to just sit down and enjoy life.

But that's where the "E" comes in—the challenge to *experience* each moment and season to its absolute fullest. To be "all there," wherever you are.

I dare you to try it.

"For everything there is a season, and a time for every matter under heaven" (Eccl. 3:1). So whatever it's time for you to be doing right now, do it with all your heart and for His glory. If it's time to work, then get busy and put in a full day's labor. If it's time to take a break, then live this moment in prayerful gratitude to God or in attentive interaction with the people around you. If it's time to rejoice, let yourself go in celebrating the goodness and blessings of the Lord. And if it's time to weep, then weep hard. Pour out to Him the pain you're enduring, the repentance His conviction is calling for, or throw your arms around a dear friend or family member who's hurting today and needs you close and undistracted. If you're married, cherish your mate; if you have children, enjoy them—don't squander the present, wishing for a different season.

Don't fixate on past failures or memories, and don't relocate into future dreams and anxieties that are currently in reserve for another time. You're here right now. Live like it—"it is the gift of God."

 Ask God to help you fully experience and enter into the season and circumstances in which He has placed you—the relationships, responsibilities, opportunities, and even challenges—for His glory.

May He Rejoice Over You

My times are in your hand.—Psalm 31:15

MY CLOSING PRAYER FOR YOU is that you wake up tomorrow with the concepts we've considered in relation to P-R-I-O-R-I-T-I-E-S, leading you nearer to the heart of God, more in love than ever before with this One who is said to "rejoice over you with gladness" and "exult over you with loud singing" (Zeph. 3:17).

If His heart were hard or disapproving toward us, we might be justified in running to other sorts of priorities, blazing our own trail through life. But our God is the One who controls the times and seasons. He is Lord over all, and (by His grace and the gift of saving faith) He has come near to us through Christ Jesus with love in His heart and "healing in His wings" (Mal. 4:2 NKJV). He is never in a hurry, yet He is never late and is always on time. He is God and He is ours.

So we can trust Him, seeking always to *stay sensitive and fully surrendered to Him*. We can ask Him at the start of each new day (and yes, the start of each new year) to direct our path, to order our steps, to show us when an interruption is really an opportunity, and to protect us when the enemy seeks to destroy.

Let us pray, then, with the psalmist David, "Make me to know your ways, O LORD; teach me your paths. Lead me in your truth and teach me, for you are the God of my salvation; for you I wait all the day long" (Ps. 25:4–5). Then at the end of our lives, along with the Lord Jesus, we will be able to say to our Father, "I glorified you on the earth, having accomplished the work that you gave me to do" (John 17:4).

Then He will take us from this *Quiet Place* into heavenly places.

Gracious Father, on the eve of this new year, we ask that You would make our hearts ever more sensitive and surrendered to Your Spirit. May we know You, follow You, and glorify You every day that You give us on this earth and then for all eternity in Your presence. Through Christ our Lord, Amen.

O Lord,

I launch my bark on the unknown waters of this year,
  with thee, O Father as my harbour,
      thee, O Son, at my helm,
      thee, O Holy Spirit, filling my sails.
Give me thy grace to sanctify me,
      thy comforts to cheer,
      thy wisdom to teach,
      thy right hand to guide,
      thy counsel to instruct,
      thy law to judge,
      thy presence to stabilize.
May thy fear be my awe,
      thy triumphs my joy.
Length of days does not profit me
      except the days are passed in thy presence,
      in thy service, to thy glory.
Give me a grace that precedes, follows, guides, sustains,
      sanctifies, aids every hour,
  that I may not be one moment apart from thee,
  but may rely on thy Spirit
      to supply every thought,
      speak in every word,
      direct every step,
      prosper every work,
      build up every mote of faith,
      and give me a desire
         to show forth thy praise;
         testify thy love,
         advance thy kingdom.

Amen.

The Valley of Vision, adapted

NOTES

January 21   Rubel Shelly, "Great Themes of the Bible (#28—Our Tongues)," http://www.rubelshelly.com/content. asp?CID=10371. Accessed February 7, 2011.

Cary Leider Vogrin, "Barton Could Face Arson Charges in 2 Jurisdictions," *The Gazette*, Colorado Springs, June 18, 2002. http://findarticles.com/p/articles/mi_qn4191/ is_20020618/ai_n10004016. Accessed February 7, 2011.

January 28   William Gurnall. *Leanings from William Gurnall*, comp. Hamilton Smith (Morgan, PA: Soli Deo Gloria, 1996), 104.

February 10   Henry Drummond, *Natural Law in the Spiritual World*, #1908: The Chance World, *Encyclopedia of 7700 Illustrations*, Paul Lee Tan (Rockville, MD: Assurance Publishers, 1979), 487.

February 25   Charles H. Spurgeon, *Evening by Evening* (Alachua, FL: Bridge-Logos, 2005), December 1.

March 14   Gracia Burnham with Dean Merrill, *To Fly Again* (Wheaton, IL: Tyndale House, 2005), 54–55.

April 9   *The Complete Word Study Old Testament* (Chattanooga: AMG, 1974), 2372.

April 19   "Student to Start Yearlong Vow of Silence," http:// abcnews.go.com/US/story?id=95952&page=1. Accessed April 9, 2011.

April 25   Norman Grubb, *Continuous Revival* (Fort Washington, PA: Christian Literature Crusade, 1997), 15.

April 29   From a message at a pastoral leadership conference in 1983, given by Dr. Fred Craddock.

May 8   Reading adapted from *A Mother's Legacy: Wisdom from Mothers to Daughters* by Barbara Rainey and Ashley Rainey Escue (Nashville: Thomas Nelson, 2000), 105.

May 9   Norman Grubb, *C. T. Studd: Cricketer and Pioneer* (Fort Washington, PA: Christian Literature Crusade, 2008), 144.

June 7   From an acceptance speech by Dr. William R. Bright, receiving the 1996 Templeton Prize for Progress in Religion, delivered in Rome, Italy, at The Church of St. Maria in Trastevere, May 9, 1996.

June 19   John Feinstein, *The Punch: One Night, Two Lives, and the Fight That Changed Basketball* (Boston: Little, Brown, and Co., 2002), introduction.

August 4   Charles H. Spurgeon, *Cheque Book of Bank of Faith: Daily Readings* (Scotland; Great Britain: Christian Focus Publications, 1996), 210.

August 27   Richard Cecil, *The Remains of the Rev. Richard Cecil*, from the 11th London edition; ed., Josiah Pratt (New York: Robert Carter; Philadelphia: Thomas Carter, 1843), 159.

August 28   Permission for use granted by Betty and Clarence Blocher.

September 14   Steve Dale, "My Pet World," *The Tennessean,* June 29, 2007.

September 15   Cited by Dr. Joe McKeever in "Doing the Right Thing Regardless," August 21, 2006. http://joemckeever.com/mt/archives/000358.html.

September 20   Cited in *The Whole of Their Lives*, epigraph, from *Lenin on Organization*, 44, par. 7, Daily Worker Publishing Co., 1926. Lenin first wrote these words in the Social Democratic newspaper *Iskra,* No. 1, in 1900.

September 22   J. C. Ryle, *Holiness: Its Nature, Hindrances, Difficulties, and Roots* (Welwyn, Hertfordshire, England: Evangelical Press, 1985, reprint), 7.

     Charles H. Spurgeon, *1000 Devotional Thoughts* (Grand Rapids, MI: Baker, 1976), nos. 404, 204.

October 5   C. H. Spurgeon sermon, "Forgiveness Made Easy." http://www.spurgeon.org/sermons/1448.html.

October 13   Helen Keller, *The Story of My Life* (New York: Dell Publishing, 1961), 265.

October 29   From a sermon preached at the funeral of Sir William Cokayne, cited in *The English Spirit*, 79.

SCRIPTURE INDEX

PROVERBS

Source Index

 CONTENT FOR *THE QUIET PLACE* has been adapted from the following books by Nancy DeMoss Wolgemuth, as well as transcripts of her radio programs:

- *A Place of Quiet Rest: Finding Intimacy with God Through a Daily Devotional Life*

- *A 30-Day Walk With God in the Psalms*

- *Becoming God's True Woman* (editor)

- *Brokenness: The Heart God Revives*

- *Choosing Gratitude: Your Journey to Joy*

- *Choosing Forgiveness: Your Journey to Freedom*

- *Holiness: The Heart God Purifies*

- *Lies Women Believe: And the Truth that Sets Them Free & Companion Guide*

- *Lies Young Women Believe: And the Truth that Sets Them Free & Companion Guide* (coauthored with Dannah Gresh)

- *Seeking Him: Experiencing the Joy of Personal Revival* (coauthored with Tim Grissom)

- *Surrender: The Heart God Controls*

- *Voices of the True Woman Movement: A Call to the Counter-Revolution* (editor)

To find these and other resources by Nancy, visit ReviveOur Hearts.com/transcripts and ReviveOurHearts.com/store.

About Nancy

**NANCY DEMOSS
WOLGEMUTH** grew up in a
family deeply committed to
Christ and to the cause of world
evangelization. At an early age, she
surrendered her life to Christ and sensed His call
to invest the rest of her life in His service.

Nancy graduated from the University of Southern
California with a degree in piano performance. Since
1979, she has served on the staff of Life Action Ministries,
a revival ministry based in Buchanan, Michigan.

Today, Nancy speaks into the lives of women through *Revive
Our Hearts* (an outreach of Life Action Ministries) and the
True Woman movement, calling them to freedom, fullness,
and fruitfulness in Christ. Her love for the Word and the
Lord Jesus is infectious and permeates her online outreaches,
conference messages, books, and two daily nationally
syndicated radio programs—*Revive Our Hearts* and *Seeking
Him with Nancy DeMoss Wolgemuth.*

She has authored sixteen books, including *Lies Women Believe,
A Place of Quiet Rest*, and *Choosing Gratitude*. Her books have
sold more than 2,000,000 copies, have been translated into
twenty languages, and are helping women around the world
discover, embrace, and delight in Christ and His mission for
their lives.

Nancy likes to think of herself as a "wedding coordinator"—
helping the Bride get ready for the Wedding to our heavenly
Bridegroom!

About *Revive Our Hearts*

 THROUGH ITS VARIOUS OUTREACHES and the teaching ministry of Nancy DeMoss Wolgemuth, *Revive Our Hearts* is calling women around the world to freedom, fullness, and fruitfulness in Christ. We offer sound, biblical teaching and encouragement through:

- **Resources**—Nancy's books, True Woman imprint books, and a wide range of audio/video resources

- **Broadcasting**—two daily, nationally syndicated broadcasts reaching nearly one million listeners a week

- **Conferences**—including events designed to equip women's ministry leaders and pastors' wives

- **Websites**—ReviveOurHearts.com, TrueWoman.com, and LiesYoungWomenBelieve.com offer daily blogs and a large, searchable collection of electronic resources for women in every season of life

We are believing God for a grassroots movement of authentic revival and biblical womanhood, as we encourage women to:

- Discover and embrace God's design and mission for their lives,

- Reflect the beauty and heart of Jesus Christ to their world,

- Intentionally pass on the baton of Truth to the next generation, and

- Pray earnestly for an outpouring of God's Spirit in their families, churches, nation, and world.

For more information and to sign up for The Daily Connection email with a daily dose of quotes and resources from Nancy's radio teaching, visit us at www.ReviveOurHearts.com. We'd like to hear from you!

Acknowledgments

ONCE AGAIN, OUR FRIENDS AT *MOODY PUBLISHERS* have proved themselves to be able and servant-hearted partners. *Holly Kisly* championed this book from the outset and tirelessly invested her heart and considerable gifts at every stage of the birthing process. *Pam Pugh*'s input and eye for details made this a better book, and *Greg Thornton*'s leadership, engagement, and encouragement continue to bless and enhance our publishing efforts.

This book would not have happened without *Lawrence Kimbrough*'s herculean, unflagging efforts, over the course of many months, to mine and shape content from more than a dozen books and a decade of radio transcripts. Lawrence, I can't thank the Lord enough for you!

Every undertaking that has my name attached to it is supported and improved by the devoted, capable, mostly unsung team of men and women who serve with me at *Revive Our Hearts*. During those extended seasons when I am sequestered working on a book, *Mike Neises* (Director of Publishing), *Martin Jones* (Managing Director), and *Sandy Bixel* (Executive Assistant) bear more of the load with me than anyone else will ever know. The Lord sees, He knows, and He will reward all those sacrificial labors!

And only the Lord knows the extent to which I have been strengthened and sustained in this journey, through the intercession of many faithful *Praying Friends*. *Thank you* for being channels of His enabling grace to this undeserving, grateful servant.